Finlay Dun

American farming and food

Finlay Dun

American farming and food

ISBN/EAN: 9783337201289

Printed in Europe, USA, Canada, Australia, Japan

Cover: Foto ©Andreas Hilbeck / pixelio.de

More available books at **www.hansebooks.com**

AMERICAN FARMING

AND FOOD

BY

FINLAY DUN

AUTHOR OF 'LANDLORDS AND TENANTS IN IRELAND' 'VETERINARY
MEDICINES, THEIR ACTIONS AND USES' ETC.

LONDON
LONGMANS, GREEN, AND CO.
1881

All rights reserved

PREFACE.

THE PRESENT VOLUME is the result of a visit to the United States in the autumn of 1879. I then travelled through the wheat regions of the Red River, Manitoba, and the great Mississippi basin, examined crops and farming in Illinois, Minnesota, Dakota, Iowa and Kansas, and inspected some of the valuable herds and studs of Kentucky and other states.

Wherever I went I found everyone courteous, and ready to furnish information regarding the country and its wonderful and varied resources.

Amongst many things new and notable to a stranger, I was particularly impressed with the sobriety, assiduity, adaptability, and energy of the people; their appreciation of the advantages of education; their ingenious application of labour-saving machinery; and their progress in almost every department of industry.

Farming in America does not, however, as yet, invariably receive the liberal and skilful attention it deserves. It is frequently conducted in a rapid, nay even in a rude manner; small labour and cost are expended in the production alike of grain crops and live stock; but a great deal of the land is deep, fertile, and easily worked, and even with indifferent management yields remunerative returns.

The great grain crops and rapidly increasing herds and flocks more than suffice for home requirements, and the United States now export annually about eighteen million quarters of wheat or one-third of their production, more than one-half of their hog products valued at 17,500,000*l.*, about one-tenth of their beef and mutton representing 7,000,000*l.*, besides butter and cheese estimated at 4,000,000*l.* Nor have these surplus supplies reached their maximum, either in the States or in Canada. They will necessarily be largely augmented as settlement extends West and South, and capital and labour are more widely employed in agricultural development. Improved transport facilities will compensate for the longer distances over which agricultural produce will be carried. The preservation and refrigeration of perishable products, so generally and successfully adopted in America, notably economise and cheapen food, and are destined largely to add to the quantity and variety of edible produce forwarded from the New World to the Old.

The greater part of these observations on American farming and food were communicated in 1879 and 1880 in a series of letters to 'The Times.' By permission of the proprietor they have been revised, added to, and reproduced in book form.

ESTATE OFFICES,
2 PORTLAND PLACE, LONDON, W.

CONTENTS.

CHAPTER		PAGE
I.	Introductory	1
II.	Statistics of American Farming	11
III.	Land, Land Laws, and Taxation	25
IV.	Landowners, Farmers, and Labourers	38
V.	The Cheap Movement of Grain	52
VI.	New York Meat Supplies	61
VII.	Fruit and Vegetable Culture	74
VIII.	Farming in the New England States	85
IX.	Pennsylvania Farming	105
X.	Agriculture in Ohio	127
XI.	An Agricultural Exhibition in Michigan	145
XII.	Chicago Grain and Cattle Trades	160
XIII.	The Red River	197
XIV.	Manitoba	222
XV.	St. Paul, Minnesota	236
XVI.	The Minneapolis Flour Trade	255
XVII.	Lumbering and Prison Life	268

CHAPTER		PAGE
XVIII.	South-Western Minnesota	279
XIX.	Prairie Farming in Minnesota	294
XX.	Land and Crops in Southern Dakota	322
XXI.	Land and Prospects in Iowa	332
XXII.	Farming in Kansas	351
XXIII.	Missouri Farming and St. Louis Trade	378
XXIV.	Kentucky Agricultural Resources	397
XXV.	American Competition in Wheat and Meat	421
	Index	471

AMERICAN FARMING AND FOOD.

CHAPTER I.

INTRODUCTORY.

THE United States of America, including lakes and rivers, have an area of nearly four million square miles. They occupy fully thirty times the extent of the British Islands. They extend 1,300 miles from the 30th to the 49th degrees of north latitude. The sun occupies four hours in rising over the 3,000 miles of continent. The vast extent, diversified aspect, varied climate, and wide distribution of good, easily worked, level land, confer great capabilities for growing food for man and beast. The physical geography of this continent has made admirable provision for agricultural and other industries. The great mountain ranges consisting mainly of granitic rocks, the early upheavals of the western world, are chiefly situated several hundred miles from the eastern and western seaboards; and, unlike those of the Old World, mostly run north and south. This configuration widely distributes the watery treasures distilled from the Atlantic and Pacific oceans. The great lakes and rivers, scattered throughout many regions, continually contribute their quota of moisture. In the moister localities between the oceans and the great mountains, fringing both sides of the continent, forests occur, equalising the distribution of rain and proving a ready source of wealth. On the prairies, plains, and plateaux a drier climate prevails, proving less favourable for the growth of trees.

The mountain chains enclose vast basins, the site of ancient inland seas. The Green and Adirondack mountains, extending from the Canadian dominions running through New York State, and at a lower elevation sweeping westward over New Jersey and Pennsylvania, approach the Alleghanies and enclose a basin which forty years ago comprised the chief cultivated portion of the United States. The great central or Mississippi basin is bounded on the north for nearly two thousand miles by the Laurentine mountains of Canada; on the east by the Appalachians, which include the Alleghanies and other ranges which proceed from the Dominion boundary, southwest, towards the Gulf of Mexico; on the west by the Rocky Mountains which run from Alaska south to Mexico. This triangular basin, fifteen times larger than Great Britain and Ireland, once a huge inland sea dotted with islands which are now undulating hills and subordinate watersheds, is watered by the Mississippi, the Missouri, and other tributaries which wind their slow and tortuous way into the Mexican Gulf.

Gradual denudation of these old mountain ranges, the spread of their *débris* over plain and valley, frequent upheavals of later stratified rocks, and the operation of ice-floats have secured the wide distribution and intermixture of minerals, and produced great varieties of soil. No country is so abundantly and almost ubiquitously furnished with mineral wealth. From New York to the centre of Alabama, in scattered valleys amongst the foot hills of the Alleghanies, are anthracite deposits conveniently situated for the supply of New York, Baltimore, and eastern cities. On the western slopes of the Alleghanies are great fields of bituminous coal, often close to the surface and cheaply worked. Coal is found also in Ohio, Iowa, Missouri, and Kentucky; indeed, M. Jules Marcou, in the text of his map of the United States, declares that the coal measures occur with short intervals, from the Atlantic to the Pacific. Iron ores are tolerably plentiful; deposits hitherto unknown are constantly being discovered. Preparations are in active progress for the extensive working of valuable ores in the eastern part of Kentucky. Building stones and clay for bricks are widely distributed. Colorado and New Mexico are rich in lead and silver. In minerals, as well as in the precious metals, the United States is very independent of other countries.

American soils, the *débris* of varied geological formations, are most diverse. North of New York, throughout most of the New England States, granite, porphyry, and greenstone afford by their disintegration valuable plant food; but along the coast the soil is thin and poor, and cultivation is impeded by quantities of stones and large boulders. South from New York along the Atlantic shores as far as the confines of Florida, tertiary and quaternary deposits overlie for the most part cretaceous rocks. Often there is superimposed a deep friable diluvium, admirably adapted, as in New Jersey State and Delaware, for vegetable and fruit growing. In Kentucky, where the carboniferous measures and the blue limestone are in juxtaposition, the famous feeding Bluegrass specially flourishes. The prairies of the Mississippi basin, a generation ago known as the Great Central American Desert, the home of the wild herbivora and the Red Indians, are now fittingly styled the 'land of promise' and of 'plenty.' Their northern zones are occupied with wheat, their southern with Indian corn. They largely consist of a friable loam reposing on beds of sand, gravel, or clay. They are generally fertile, unencumbered with trees or stones, easily turned over with a six-inch furrow, by a pair of light horses, are often two to four feet deep, are adapted for the growth of almost any description of crops, and without manure for ten or twelve years consecutively grow fair crops of wheat.

Diversified physical conditions necessarily affect the climate. The mountain ranges gather for several hundred miles the ocean-begotten clouds, are the scenes of violent, often sudden, tempests, and have a rainfall many times greater than the plains below. These great plains and prairies stretch far beyond the visible horizon, often have a slope of only two feet to the mile ; their flat monotony at long intervals is diversified by river, lake, or ravine, and occasionally by belts of plantation. The weather on these vast levels usually maintains a somewhat unvarying uniformity. Bountiful rains, which in a land of hill and dale continually drop fatness, are scarce. Mist and fog are almost unknown. During winter intense cold continues steadily for weeks or months, according to latitude or situation. The thermometer in Minnesota, Northern Dakota, and Nebraska often stands as low as $-20°$. But the atmosphere is dry, the sun shines, and although all agricultural labour is arrested, the winter is described as pleasant and healthful. Stormy weather often occurs about the spring and autumn equinoxes. Thunderstorms sometimes disturb the even equilibrium of the season. Blinding blizzards of drifting snow sometimes darken the atmosphere for days, and render it dangerous to go even a few yards from home. The summer heat, once begun, is tolerably continuous and intense. Days from July and March are not alternated, as they are apt to be in our more fickle climate. In Missouri and other Southern States, after a short winter, spring begins in February ; before May the temperature in the shade will reach $80°$; a few weeks later it will mark $100°$. Even as far north as Winnipeg, sunstroke is not uncommon. Under the blaze of the burning sun the fresh greenery of early spring soon becomes dry and brown ; the bright verdure of English grass is sadly wanting.

Tables published by Mr. E. A. Schott thus record the temperature at various stations :—At West Point,

Dairying is extensively pursued, especially in the Eastern States. In New York and Pennsylvania States alone are 2,374,600 milch cows, being rather more than the number returned in Great Britain. But, like other descriptions of farming, the dairy business is travelling west. Everywhere milk is more freely and frequently used than in England. Adults as well as children drink it at every meal. The best butter in New York is stated to be brought from Iowa. Creameries and cheese factories, first established in 1851, extend throughout Illinois, Iowa, and Minnesota, and butter is thence sent regularly 1,200 miles to New York and other eastern markets. It is collected by the great transportation companies, who send their refrigerating cars to the western producer, furnish ice and all necessary attendance, and forward butter, as well as fruit and meat, in admirable condition to New York and other eastern markets at 50 to 80 cents. per cwt. for a transport of upwards of 1,000 miles. Nowhere are long distances made so light of, time economised, remote producers and consumers brought together, and the bountiful fruits of the earth so widely and cheaply distributed.

Farmers in the Eastern States, like their brethren in Great Britain, for some years have suffered from Western competition. On cheap, easily tilled, virgin soils, wheat, live stock, and dairy produce are economically raised and are conveyed eastward at low rates by railroad, lake, and river. The eastern farmer, with reason, complains that his western competitor has his produce forwarded 600 or 800 miles to market for about the same cost that he pays for delivery over 100 miles. Stimulated by abundance of cheap land and cheap transport, grain-growing, stock-raising, and feeding are all pushing west, where more scope, opportunity for individual enterprise, and profit are looked for.

During long years there must still be room and to spare for all comers. Little more than one-tenth of the available food-producing area of the continent is yet occupied, and made the best of; of many fertile regions not one-twentieth is yet made profitable use of; a great deal of what is cultivated is still worked very imperfectly. The wastes are, however, being peopled. Mechanics and men of science are year by year aiding to increase agricultural production, to render it more certain and cheap, to convert it into more convenient portable forms. Reduction or removal of the high duties at present imposed upon the necessaries and comforts of life must occur during the next few years, and will greatly aid the American farmer. Americans have got thoroughly imbued with, and are profitably acting upon, Adam Smith's admirable precepts :—'Wealth arising from the solid improvements of agriculture is most durable. No equal capital puts in motion a greater quantity of productive labour than that of the farmer. Not only his servants, but his cattle become producers. Nature, too, labours along with man. Her work remains as a gain after deducting everything which can be regarded as the work of man.'

Agriculture occupies nearly half the population of the States. No other American industry compares with it in extent of operations, rapidity of development, and increment to the national wealth. She feeds liberally about 48,000,000 of people at home; she contributes fully four-fifths to the 165,000,000*l.* annual exports. She averts famine and high prices of food amongst the nations of the Old World. She has earned the ready money which especially during the last two years has become plentiful in America, which has given an impetus to all other industries, which has been the chief agent in maintaining exchanges in favour of the States, and in rapidly reducing their great national debt.

CHAPTER II.

STATISTICS OF AMERICAN FARMING.

THE statistics of American farming published annually by the Department of Agriculture at Washington strikingly demonstrate the food-producing capabilities of the Western world. They point to rapidly increasing production far exceeding the needs of her own people. They testify to surplus supplies of grain and meat available for several generations of the more thickly peopled countries of Europe. Diversity of climate and situation, as already stated, secure great diversity of production. Rice grows on the swampy river banks in Carolina and Georgia, on the old sugar lands of Louisiana, and yields annually about 90,000,000 lbs. Cane sugar, chiefly produced in Louisiana, on the Mississippi, beginning some 200 miles above and extending 60 miles below New Orleans, although not such an important industry as formerly, occupies 150,000 acres and produces annually about 208,570 hogsheads of sugar, being 13 per cent. of the total requirements of the States; and 13,524,000 gallons of molasses, together worth nearly three million pounds sterling. The growth of Sorghum Saccharatum or amber cane sugar, which does not require the swampy situation or tropical heat necessary for the growth of cane sugar, is profitably extending in Minnesota, Iowa, and Missouri, and promises to become a very important industry. Throughout the Southern States 12,500,000 acres are devoted to cotton, yielding a return of 40,000,000*l.* sterling, producing besides a valuable crop of cotton-seed, which is tenaciously held by a Mississippi clique who decorticate and grind it, export a large amount of the oil especially to France, whilst a still larger proportion of the useful residual feeding cake comes to Great Britain. Half a million acres produce tobacco; the cultivation is extending, and the yield annually exceeds 4,600,000*l*. Five million acres are occupied in fruit-growing, and probably half as much in the production of vegetables; the fruit and vegetables together in a favourable season reach to half the value of the wheat.

Of still greater dietetic and national importance are the grain crops and potatoes, which occupy about 105,000,000 acres. Wheat covers one-third the total area of the grain crops; it represents three-fifths the acreage devoted to Indian corn: it exceeds by ten times the area of the wheat crops of the United Kingdom; it is grown at an average cost of 40*s.* an acre; one-third of the produce is now exported. Indian corn is the most extensively cultivated crop, is grown at 36*s.* an acre, is largely converted into

Acreage of Wheat and Maize.

beef and bacon, and used for the making of whisky; but only 7 per cent. of it is exported.

Oats occupy 37 per cent. of the area of the British corn crops, but are only about 8 per cent. of those of the States; in northerly regions, where live stock are much kept, they are more extensively grown; 32 lbs. per bushel is the standard weight; not one-hundredth part of the quantity grown is exported. Barley constitutes about one-fourth of British corn crops, but in the States it does not reach one-sixtieth part; one-third of the production is in California; the samples generally are thin and shrivelled; 48 lbs. is the usual standard weight per bushel, 50 lbs. is the weight in California; for many purposes its place is taken by the more cheaply grown and productive Indian corn. Rye, most largely grown in New York and Pennsylvania, as at home, is occasionally cultivated as a spring fodder crop. It occupies 1,622,700 acres, or nearly the same area as barley or potatoes, affords 16 to 20 bushels an acre, and where well manured, besides produces about two tons of straw, which is now in good demand for paper making, sometimes realising 3*l*. per ton of 2,000 lb.

Potatoes are produced at one third of the cost bestowed upon them in this country. I have seen a tolerable crop grown where the prairie sod is raised with a stocking axe, the potato set dropped in, and the turf turned down by the foot. The quality is generally excellent. Owing to summer drought, the crop of 1879 generally was light; the average of the previous nine years is 88 bushels; the heaviest yield recorded is 110 bushels in 1875. The supply varies from 2·5 to 3·8 bushels for each unit of the population: 1,776,800 acres are devoted to its cultivation; fully one-seventh of the produce is grown in New York State; taking a series of years the average price is 2*s*. 5*d*. per bushel. The value of the potatoes annually exported exceeds 100,000*l*. Swedes, mangels, and other green crops, demanding more continuous costly labour than is at present spared for American farming, are on a very restricted scale. They are more grown in the cooler, moister parts of Canada, where Indian corn cannot be so successfully raised.

The hay crops have lately been extending; they occupy nearly 27,000,000 acres; the area of 1878 was 20 per cent in excess of 1877: more than one-fourth of the total, 40,000,000 tons, is grown in the States of New York and Pennsylvania. More fodder is yearly needed for the increasing number of horses, mules, and cattle used in the larger cities. In the eastern older States much of it is cut from meadows laid down to grass, or from clovers planted in rotation. In the west it is taken from the natural prairies, plains, and parks. There it is still to be had almost for the cutting, is worth only 10*s*. per ton, and I have seen flour-mills and thrashing-engines run with such rough prairie hay.

The annual value of the grain, potatoes, and hay of the United States in 1878 reached 264,630,000*l*. It was still greater in 1879 and 1880. Adding tobacco, cotton, and fruit, the agricultural produce makes a grand total of about 340,000,000*l*., or more than double the value of the corresponding produce of the United Kingdom.

The subjoined summary from the Report of Mr. Charles Worthington, the able statistician of the Department of Agriculture, Washington, gives the acreage of the principal farm crops, and their produce and value in 1878. Detailed returns of later years are not yet published. The values given in dollars I have converted into pounds sterling, taking 4*s*. 2*d*. as the value of the dollar:—

	Bushels, lb. or Tons	Acreage	Value in £
Wheat, bushels	420,122,400	32,108,560	67,769,285
Indian corn, ,,	1,388,218,750	51,585,000	91,730,780
Rye ,,	25,842,790	1,622,700	2,828,565
Oats ,,	413,578,560	13,176,500	21,289,166
Barley ,,	42,245,630	1,780,400	5,096,663
Buckwheat ,,	12,246,820	673,100	1,340,824
Potatoes ,,	124,126,650	1,776,800	15,111,825
Total	2,426,381,600	102,733,060	205,167,108
Tobacco, lbs.	392,546,700	542,852	4,621,484
Hay, tons	39,608,296	26,931,300	59,462,750
Cotton, bales 450 lbs.	5,216,603	12,266,800	40,380,928
Grand total		142,474,010	309,632,270

The yield of most crops in the United States is considerably less than that of corresponding crops in the British Islands. No comparison can, of course, be made as to sugar, tobacco, cotton, and other plants of almost tropical climates. We have no crop so widely grown and so generally useful for man and beast as Indian corn. We cannot compete in quantity and variety of fruit. On a given area we raise, however, double the amount of wheat, oats, barley, or potatoes, and in proportion to acreage our farms produce and feed much more than twice the amount of live stock. High rents, augmenting rates, and expensive labour enhance the cost of production in the old country. Droughts, locusts, Hessian fly, scourging cropping and imperfect cultivation are the farmer's chief enemies in the New World. The acreable value of the purely agricultural crops of America are small compared with those of Great Britain. They do not reach one-third the price which would remunerate the English farmer, but cheaply grown on cheap land they generally leave a margin of profit. Taking the official statistics for 1878 the principal crops in Massachusetts, Rhode Island, Connecticut, and California are valued at about 4*l.* per acre. In New York, Pennsylvania, Delaware, Maryland, Ohio, and Michigan they range from 2*l.* 10*s.* to 3*l.* In Kentucky, Tennessee, Indiana, and Wisconsin, they are about 2*l.* The crops of Illinois, Minnesota, Missouri, and Kansas average from 30*s.* to 32*s.* per acre.

Taking the official statistics for nearly twenty years, the average wheat yield of the United States is little over 12 bushels an acre. The yield per acre of the last three years, exceeding former averages, are 13·9 bushels in 1877, 13·1 in 1878, 13·7 in 1879. The winter wheats in many States have been more productive than the spring. In Illinois and Indiana and also in Minnesota, well-authenticated cases occur where 40 to 50 bushels per acre have been reaped. The British wheat yield ranges from 24 to 28 bushels. Without any considerable outlay, and despite drought and other conditions which cannot be controlled, American agricultural returns would be largely augmented by the more careful preparation and cultivation of the soil, by the occasional use of portable manures and dung from the yards, by the more frequent recurrence of clover and other restorative crops grazed with sheep or pigs, and by the judicious selection of seed suitable for the climate and locality.

The official report of the Statistician to the Department of Agriculture furnishes the subjoined table, which exhibits the average acreable yield, the price per bushel, pound, or ton, and the cash value of the several farm products for 1878, which may be taken as a fair average of recent years :—

	Yield per acre	Price per bush., lb. or ton.			Value per acre		
		£	s.	d.	£	s.	d.
Wheat, bushels	13·1	0	3	3	2	2	7
Indian corn ,,	26·9	0	1	4½	1	17	0
Rye ,,	15·9	0	2	2	1	14	6
Oats ,,	31·4	0	1	0¼	1	12	1
Barley ,,	23·6	0	2	5	2	17	11
Buckwheat ,,	18·2	0	2	2¼	1	16	10
Potatoes ,,	69·3	0	2	5¾	8	11	10
Tobacco, lbs.	723·1	0	0	2¾	8	5	0
Hay, tons	1·47	1	10	9	2	4	2
Cotton, lbs.	191·4	0	0	4	3	3	8

The magnitude and growth of American agriculture is strikingly illustrated by the numbers and rapid increase of the animals of the farm. The Statistician of the Department at Washington gives the following estimate of their number and value in January 1879 :—

	Numbers	Value per head	Total value
		£ s. d.	£
Horses	10,938,700	0 18 4	119,451,000
Mules	1,713,100	11 13 6	20,000,000
Milk cows	11,826,400	4 6 4	53,560,000
Oxen and other cattle	21,408,100	3 4 2	68,708,000
Sheep	38,123,800	3 8 7	16,464,000
Swine	34,766,100	0 13 3	23,044,000
	118,776,200		301,227,000

All classes of farm animals are steadily increasing, not only in numbers, but very notably in usefulness and quality. Horses multiply at the rate of half a million annually. Careful selection and the use of stout English thoroughbreds, Percherons, and Clydesdales is advancing the standard of excellence amongst the various breeds. Especially throughout Canada, New York State, and in Kentucky, English dealers obtain increasing numbers of stylish carriage horses. Very few hunters with good shoulders and manners are, however, to be met with ; cobs and hacks of the stamp to command a high price in this country are rare ; fast-trotting buggy teams are plentiful. The farm horses are lighter and cleaner limbed than those of Great Britain, and resemble the stoutest of the animals used by the omnibus companies. Upwards of 5,000 horses and 4,000 mules are annually exported.

Enumeration of Herds and Flocks.

During recent years the milk cows have multiplied annually to the extent of more than half a million. Owing to the low prices made by dairy produce during 1878 and the first nine months of 1879, the number of milk cows has, however, been again reduced. The Texans, rough, leggy, with imposing horns, descended from the Spanish cattle imported upwards of 300 years ago, the Cherokees and cattle of the western scrubs, are not bountiful milkers, do little more than rear their calves, but are improved both in dairy and feeding capabilities by crossing with better sorts. Shorthorn grades are generally preferred on account of their usefulness in the dairy and their subsequent value to the butcher. Dutch and Channel Islanders are common, especially in the Eastern States. The oxen and other cattle, enumerated in 1877 at less than 18,000,000, now exceed 22,000,000, and more careful selection and the use of well-bred sires are steadily determining more weight, quality, and earlier maturity.

These rapidly multiplying herds are ever-increasing sources of national wealth. One-fourth of the oxen and one-seventh of the cows are probably slaughtered every year, yielding 7,000,000 carcases, averaging 600 lbs., and, at 3$d.$ per pound, worth 7$l.$ 10$s.$ each, making an aggregate value of 52,500,000$l.$ The hides at 3$d.$ per pound, the fat at 2$d.$, with other offal, may be moderately computed at 30$s.$ per head, or 10,500,000$l.$ Besides other slaughter-house products, all carefully utilised, such subordinate articles as neat's foot oil, and parings for glue, are estimated at

2,000,000*l.* Rapidly although the exports of cattle from the United States have developed since they began in 1875, they are small compared with the enormous supplies. Allowing for live cattle deported through Canada, about 100,000 beasts are annually exported; about the same number are exported dressed; whilst more than another 100,000 are exported salted or canned. The live and carcase exports represent picked cattle, averaging, when dressed, about 700 lbs.; the preserved meats come from rougher animals weighing 400 lbs. to 500 lbs. dressed. The 300,000 cattle annually exported do not represent one twenty-third part of the total supplies. There still remain for home consumption 6,750,000 carcases, averaging 600 lbs. each, and representing an annual allowance of 84 lbs. of beef for every unit of the 48,000,000 of the States. Adding to the beef, mutton, bacon, and pork, and allowing for live and dead meat exported, the available animal food of the United States amounts to 160 lbs. per head per annum. The corresponding British supplies from all sources amount to 98 lbs. Although consuming the largest proportionate amount of animal food of any people in the Old World, we are not so liberally supplied as the Americans.

The milking cows of the United States, mustering 12,000,000, contribute dairy products worth 83,000,000*l.* annually, or a return of nearly 7*l.* per head. Increasing steadily year by year, in 1878 they made a bound of 30 per cent., with the effect of running down prices lower than they have been since

1861. The annual manufacture of butter reaches 1,000,000,000 lbs. A good deal of it is of inferior quality, the best is made in creameries, which are general throughout most States. Americans are great butter eaters, their consumption *per capita* is about 20 lbs. annually. Only 2 per cent. is exported. Cheese made on the farms and in the factories totals up 300,000,000 lbs. a year. It is generally of uniform and excellent quality. With abundance of other albuminoid food, Americans, however, use much less cheese than Englishmen; their average annual consumption *per capita* is about 4 lbs., or two-thirds the English consumption. The export of cheese now reaches 40 per cent. of its manufacture. Each unit of the American population consumes annually upwards of 100 quarts of milk, which is everywhere of excellent quality, and retailed at about half the price it brings in this country. Valuing the butter at 9*d.* per lb., the cheese at 3*d.* per lb., and the milk at 1½*d.* per quart, the dairy industries of the United States represent annual earnings which amount to 83,000,000*l.* They are more than double the value of the cotton crop, two-sevenths more than the wheat, nearly one-third more than the hay, and only an eighth less than the Indian corn.

Sheep increase at the rate of a million annually, and the Mexican and the Merinos, hitherto cultivated almost exclusively for wool, are being improved in weight and quality of mutton by admixture with Downs, Leicesters, and Longwools. Fortunately the system of crossing, which is enhancing the value of the mutton, and extending the demand for it alike in America and Europe, is also adding to the value of the wool. Cross-bred wools, which are in such request for the coarser cloths in general use, find of late years more ready purchasers than the finer merinos which were formerly in such demand for alpacas, or even than the long-stapled Cotswolds and Leicesters. From sheep the annual returns amount to 30,000,000 fleeces, averaging at least 4 lbs. worth 1s. per pound, and representing a value of 6,000,000l. One-fourth of the United States flocks, or about 10,000,000, are slaughtered annually. Most of the sheep are two and three years old before they come to the butcher. At present they probably do not average more than 64 lbs. dressed, but at 3d. per pound, or 16s. per carcase, this yields a total of 8,000,000l.

Pigs increase in the ratio of 2,000,000 a year; are chiefly of Berkshire, Yorkshire, or useful Poland-China sorts, and are quite as good and profitable as those at home. They are the most convenient and economical converters of bulky, unsaleable vegetable food into more concentrated saleable animal food. Cheaply reared on the pastures or in the woods, and finished off on Indian corn at 1s. per bushel, although they sometimes fall to 1½d. per pound gross weight, they pay their way. Multiplying rapidly and readily saleable at twelve to fifteen months, probably two-thirds of the total swine, or 23,000,000, are annually slaughtered. Their average weight in the great establishments where three-fourths of the hogs of the country are killed and cured, is about 217 lbs. At 2*d.* per pound this represents 1*l.* 16*s.* 2*d.* as the value of each hog, or an aggregate of 41,500,000*l.*; 60 per cent. of the hog products are now exported.

These facts and figures strikingly demonstrate the enormous mines of wealth which America has in her herds and flocks. Taking no cognisance of horses and mules, together worth 120,000,000*l.*, the annual sales of cattle, sheep, and hogs, and their produce, estimated at the above moderate values, may thus be summarised :—

	£
Cattle slaughtered, 7,000,000 at £7 10*s.*, carcases averaging 600 lbs. at 3*d.*	52,500,000
,, Offal at 30*s.*	10,500,000
Cows numbering 12,000,000, from which the dairy produce is estimated at	83,000,000
Sheep slaughtered 10,000,000, averaging 64 lbs. each, at 3*d.* per lb.	8,000,000
Wool from 38,000,000 sheep, averaging 4 lbs. at 1*s.*	6,000.000
Hogs, 23,000,000 slaughtered, averaging 217 lbs. at 2*d.*	41,500,000
	£201,500,000

This great production can be maintained and increased. There is still abundance of unoccupied or partially occupied land. There are plenty of well-watered summer grazings over which the wild herbivora still roam. There are vast areas available for Indian corn and hay, requisite for winter-feeding and fattening. Capital will continue to be attracted to the business; for although, during four years of industrial depression, prices of farm produce had fallen, cows and wool depreciating 25 per cent., and hogs 50 per cent., fair profits were nevertheless earned, and with extended industrial prosperity which set in during the autumn of 1879, prices and profits are again advancing.

The farm animals of Great Britain, although greatly more numerous per acre, and worth more than double the value per head, are few compared with those of America. Our agricultural horses are within 2,000,000, or one-fifth, those of the States. Our milk cows are less than one-third; our oxen and other cattle are about two-sevenths. With 32,000,000 of sheep we possess within 6,000,000 of the number of the American flocks, and with the extra weight of our sheep and their earlier maturity we annually produce a somewhat greater weight of mutton. In pigs, however, we are far behind, figuring up only one-tenth of the American census. The farm animals of the United Kingdom represent about one-half the total value of those of the United States.

CHAPTER III.

LAND, LAND LAWS, AND TAXATION.

AMERICA has almost inexhaustible supplies of the raw material from which farm crops and live stock are produced. She has profusion of land, much of it fertile, much of it in a good climate, much of it requiring no expensive clearing or tedious preparation to fit it for either arable or pastoral husbandry. In this closely peopled old country it is difficult to find a piece of ground without an owner, and whereon a man might squat undisturbed. On the American continent, however, there are still great tracts of unsurveyed land on which the enterprising pioneer may settle without so much as asking leave, and find, as in patriarchal times, food for himself, his herds, and flocks. Including Alaska, these unsurveyed lands now extend to 1,500,000 square miles. Of some eleven States and most of the territories considerable portions are as yet unappropriated. Less than half of California, not one-third of Oregon and Colorado, have hitherto been surveyed, disposed of, or settled. From the British possessions to Mexico, from the

Missouri river to the Pacific, lies a vast area of 1,000,000,000 acres of which not three per cent. is yet occupied in farms.[1] Eastward of the Rocky Mountains are thousands of acres of fertile slopes, sheltered valleys, and even of well-watered bottoms adapted for cattle or sheep, unclaimed and unappropriated. There are great tracts of uncultivated prairie in Minnesota, Iowa, Dakota, Nebraska, and other States and territories, which men and money at small expense are turning into fertile wheat and corn lands, or profitable pastures for cattle and sheep. The southern States lying between the Ohio river and the gulf of Mexico, between Delaware and the Missouri, including a territory four times as large as France, ten times the size of Great Britain, also present a great area of unused and very partially used land. Not one-fourth is yet actually farmed; not one-tenth is yet employed agriculturally; more than half is in wild pasturage adapted for cattle and sheep, and capable of carrying more than ten times the numbers now kept. Excluding the thirteen original New England eastern States which are more fully cultivated, it may be concluded that of the remaining area of five-sixths of the United States, not one-tenth part is at present appropriated, cultivated, or profitably made use of.

Over the Canadian frontier are likewise great tracts of useful, easily broken land awaiting settlement, and especially adapted for wheat. The

[1] United States Department of Agriculture : Message from the President U.S.A. relating to sheep husbandry, January 1879, p. 12.

northern portion of the Red River valley, the alluvial flats and bluffs of the Assinaboine and North and South Saskatchawan which flow nearly 1,000 miles from the Rocky Mountains into Lake Winnipeg, are now attracting European farmers. Any of these great river valleys when devoted to wheat might alone produce supplies sufficient to make good the annual deficit of the United Kingdom!

With such vast tracts of unappropriated and unused territory, no wonder that land in America is cheap. It is not as at home a luxury, indulged in by those possessed of ample means, and who can afford to invest capital to pay about 2 per cent. The land property of Great Britain is in the hands of comparatively few; one-fourth of the area is held by 1,200 persons; 600 members of the House of Peers hold rather more than one-fifth, and enjoy between one-tenth and one-eleventh of the total income derived from land.[1] There are many large estates in America, but the enormous area still leaves abundance for all who desire a piece of their own. In many of the Western States tradesmen, artisans, and domestic servants have an eighth or one-quarter section (160 acres) or even more land on which their savings are invested. Such purchases often pay very well, owing, however, rather to their steady appreciation than to their yielding a large annual return. In this country a rise of 1 per cent. per annum was con-

---

[1] *General View of British Agriculture*, by James Caird, C.B., *Journal of the Royal Agricultural Society of England*, vol. xiv. part ii. Second Series.

sidered a fair advance during the good times, which extended from 1855 to 1874. In America, where most things move with quicker pace, a great deal of land judiciously bought and fairly well managed undergoes an annual appreciation of 5 to 10 per cent., and in some States well circumstanced for railroads and other means of communication, thousands of acres have recently doubled in value within five years. The acquisition of land does not as in this country involve a heavy expenditure of capital, for which a low rate of interest is obtained. Securing the fee simple, the American yeoman not only has his annual profit, but the steady unearned increment in value, resulting from extending settlement and augmented wealth. Excepting in some of the Southern States, still paralysed from the sad conflict of eighteen years ago between North and South, and notwithstanding exhausting cultivation, land steadily becomes more valuable. Alike in the Eastern, Middle, and Western States, farms are constantly changing hands.

The possession of property so abundant and widespread as land is in America, naturally confers less consideration and homage than a good pile of 'the almighty dollars.' It secures fewer privileges and less social prestige than it does in the old country. The laws and customs relating to it very closely resemble those applying to personal property. The reform of our own land laws, which cannot long be deferred, must take this direction. The artificial, antiquated distinctions which have gradually grown in Great Britain between so-called real and personal property must be entirely or greatly reduced.

As might be expected in a new country, the land laws are simpler than those of England, and the acquisition and sale of land is more readily and cheaply effected. The title conferring the fee simple in the first instance comes from the National Government. At the general land office at Washington, and at district offices throughout the States and territories, are the survey maps and records of property, begun as early as 1785. The unoccupied lands have of late years been surveyed and set out in townships six miles square. Each of these is subsequently divided into thirty-six sections, each containing one square mile or 640 acres. These plots are arranged like the squares on a chess board, the straight boundary lines running north and south and east and west. Stones, stakes, or other distinguishing marks, indicate the corners of the sections, which are all numbered. In the newer States two out of the thirty-six sections are reserved for elementary and other educational purposes. The sections are sometimes sub-divided into halves, quarters, and eighths. The public lands undisposed of and scattered widely throughout nineteen States and eight territories belong to the United States Government, but Texas has reserved its own public lands. Railway companies, in consideration of their building lines of iron roads, have received large tracts generally in alternate mile sections, extending ten, and sometimes even twenty miles on each side of their line. Of these lands they gradually dispose, giving the purchaser for the sale and transfer a brief 'warranting deed,' which passes through the local register office, is duly vouched, and the transaction recorded.

Somewhat on the same system as obtains in Middlesex and Yorkshire, the details of every transaction connected with the sale, settlement, or mortgage of land, are duly recorded at the district register office. In these official documents stand recorded the names of the 'grantors and grantees,' the description and number on the plan, and acreage of every parcel of land purchased, the price, nature and date of instrument, with its date of acknowledgment and filing. When a sale is made, the registrar gives a certificate that the title of the lands dealt with 'is correct as the same appears upon the original records.' The clerk of the district court affixes his signature and seal to an appended certificate, attesting that he has examined the records and files and 'finds that there are no judgments therein against any of the within-named parties.' The county auditor further certifies whether or no taxes are due upon the land. In the absence of the deeds of conveyance, the records referring to any lot or parcel of land, as set forth in the books of the district register office, are held good evidence of ownership. Authenticated certificates of such records are procurable for a small fee. In the district office are also recorded all mortgages on land, and as they take precedence in order of their registration, no time is lost in their being officially entered. Very conveniently in the same office is likewise kept the

Entail and Primogeniture.   31

valuation of the whole of the landed estates of the district, made every five years, and in some cities revised at intervals of three years. These arrangements simplify and cheapen the purchase and sale of land. They obviate tedious and costly investigations of title or the drawing of voluminous deeds. Estates are sold and conveyed almost as easily and as promptly as bank or railway stocks.

Powers of entail and settlement for one life and twenty-one years, as in England, are recognised by United States law, but are seldom acted upon, and Americans can scarcely believe that half the land of Great Britain is held by strict entail. The custom of primogeniture, so common in the disposal of British landed estates, is rarely adopted. When a widow survives, after payment of legal charges, she is entitled during her lifetime to one-third of all real estate. In Kansas she claims one-half. After provision for the widow, the property of the father is generally equally distributed amongst the children. The property of an intestate landowner is divisible equally amongst his children or his next of kin. These laws and the custom which gradually moulds itself upon them interfere with the aggregation of large estates.

The public lands, of which there are still thousands of acres unoccupied in the Western States and territories, are divided into two classes. Some are to be bought on cash payment of 1 dollar 25 cents per acre. Others, more conveniently situated, for double that amount. But 160 acres of these cheaper, or 80 acres of the dearer, may be acquired under the

Homestead Acts on still easier terms. Any citizen of the United States, or any one who declares his intention of becoming a citizen, over twenty-one years of age, whether male or female, who will settle upon and cultivate these lands during five years, on payment of fees or commissions, varying according to situation or extent acquired from 30*s.* to 90*s.*, is entitled to a patent endowing him, his heirs and assigns, with the fee simple of the land. Cultivation for two years of five acres of forest trees under the Culture Acts of 1873–8, in most of the States, further entitles a settler, after three years and on payment of small office fees, to 80 acres of land. Ten acres of trees similarly cultivated secure a patent for 160 acres.

Increasing advantage is being taken of those cheap, easy processes for the acquisition of land. The official records[1] testify that 5,260,111 acres have been acquired under the Homestead Acts in 1879, the largest amount ever taken up in any one year, and nearly double the area acquired in 1869. Under the Timber Acts 2,766,574 acres have been acquired in 1879, or more than five times the area thus obtained in 1875. Eight million acres thus entered upon partially cultivated and planted in one year strikingly illustrates the rapidity with which the Western world is being settled. Many of the grants would be lots of 40 to 80 acres, but even supposing all amounted to 160 acres, here would be 50,000 new farmers

[1] American Almanac for 1880.

settled within twelve months. This continued ever-widening colonisation goes on every year, and this estimate takes no cognisance of the thousands of acres disposed of by railway companies, corporations, and private speculators, formerly void, but now being settled and brought into some sort of cultivation. Thousands thus going forth and cultivating the waste places of the earth augurs well for the future abundance and cheapness of food.

The assessed value of the real estate of the United States as set forth in the return of the last census of 1870 was $9,914,780,825. Personal estate is figured at $4,204,205,907. The true value of the two forms of property is given at $30,068,518,507. Since 1870, steadily recovering from the shock received from the civil war, the value of the land and personal property of the States is believed to have nearly doubled.

The land scheme of the United States aims at multiplying freeholders and erecting homesteads, which it also generally protects from forced sale. By federal law no homestead can be seized for debts incurred previous to the obtaining of a patent for such homestead. In thirty-two out of thirty-eight States the homestead is protected against execution from all debt, excepting for taxes. This protection has frequently been abused; it has proved a temptation to the taking up of land by men who had no capital with which to cultivate it; sometimes it unfairly shields the debtor from payment of his just debts. Most States now wisely limit the exemption to a certain acreage, to enumerated articles, or to chattels of specified value. In Vermont the homestead reserved must not exceed $500, with growing crops, clothing, furniture, farm animals, and sundry stores; $200 in teams, $200 in professional library. In New York State the value of the homestead reserved from seizure may be $1,000, with personal property, consisting of mechanics' tools to the value of $25, furniture, instruments, library, &c. In Kentucky the exemption consists of land, with dwelling, to the value of $1,000, with furniture, clothing, and domestic animals valued at $100. In California the fortunate debtor may reserve homestead to the value of $5,000, $200 of furniture, and a multitude of special articles. The house of the town debtor, sometimes with a quarter, and even half an acre of land, is exempted from seizure from debt. The husband cannot alienate the homestead without the consent, in writing, of his wife.

So long as land belongs to the United States there are no land or house duties, no stamps, or Schedule A of the Income Tax, which, in the United Kingdom, together collect 8,500,000*l.* and constitute 12 per cent. of our total taxation. The general Federal Government of the United States is supported by heavy customs duties collected on an import of nearly 100,000,000*l.*, and by internal revenue derived from spirits, fermented liquors, tobacco, banks and bankers, penalties and adhesive stamps. Spirits produce one-half, and tobacco one-third, of this excise. The revenue goes to meet the 20,000,000*l*. still required to pay annual interest on the National Debt, and maintain military and naval establishments, pensions, public works, the administration of justice, &c.

The states and territories raise for their own use about 12,500,000*l*., which is chiefly expended on public works, bridges, and roads, administration of justice in county courts, maintenance of prisons, lunatic asylums, education, and bureau of agriculture. Of these local taxes about one-half is derived from real estate. Land and houses are rated not as with us on annual rental, but on value determined at intervals, generally of five years. In different States, according to their necessities and the amount of their debt, the assessment varies considerably. It averages about one-half per cent. In Texas and some States it is provided by statute that the taxes on real estate shall not exceed one-half per cent. In Illinois the rate s about 3*d*. per acre. In Pennsylvania real estate is exempted from all taxation.

Land is taxed whether it is void or occupied, unless belonging to the United States Government or situated in Pennsylvania or other favoured districts. This somewhat discourages speculators holding land unprofitably idle waiting a rise. The revenue officers are prompt to take account of all improvements. The assessment made is the first lien on the land; interest accrues when it is unpaid; it constitutes almost the only description of debt for which in many States a homestead can be sold. The municipalities, besides paying their own city charges, unlike the English arrangement, usually also contribute their share to the country expenditure. Government, desirous to favour small freeholders, exempts from taxation in many States land under 200 dollars. In some Western States encouragement is given to clothe the bare prairie with trees, by exempting for seven years payment of taxes on land of which one-fourth is planted with timber trees.

More than half the local taxation is derived from personal estate. The assessment embraces horses and other live stock, steam engines, carriages of all sorts, implements and machinery, household furniture, including pianos, watches, clocks, jewellery, &c. A poll tax of 1 dollar is levied in some States. Professional men, merchants, and all manner of traders pay licence to practise their avocation. Railroad companies are generally charged one-half per cent. on the value of their property, and the same amount on their gross earnings. Boarding and eating-houses, as well as billiard-rooms and theatres, are taxed. Liquor merchants have usually to pay a graduated tax on sales. In some States stallions and jackasses contribute 10 dollars annually. Livery-stable keepers frequently are assessed at 15 dollars, and half a dollar for each stall. These licenses and taxes on personalty collect annually upwards of 6,000,000*l.* or one-half of the local assessment. The system has the recommendation of raising revenue from all sorts and conditions of men. Those who have most pay most. Professional men, traders, and those living on realised property (of whom, however, there are very few in America) are taxed according to their means. Local taxation is thus equitably spread over a wide area, and is drawn from every description of property. The farmer and the land are not so heavily mulcted as in Great Britain. The American agriculturist pays on an average about 1 per cent on the valuation of his land, plant, and personalty, which, presuming it to be valued at from 2*l*. 10*s*. to 5*l*. per acre, would place his local taxes at 6*d*. to 1*s*. per acre. The administration of the taxes is much better managed than it was a few years ago. Instead of increasing, as in England, they are gradually being reduced. Universal suffrage seems to keep down local expenses. In the West, owing to liberal grants of State lands, the cost of gratuitous education is minimised.

CHAPTER IV.

LANDOWNERS, FARMERS, AND LABOURERS.

THE United States census of 1870, out of a total population of 38,600,000 (which has now mounted to 48,000,000), represented 12,506,000 adults as engaged in various occupations, and of these 5,922,000 were employed in agriculture. The number must now exceed 7,000,000. Allowing to each bread-winner two non-workers, nearly half the population of the United States are directly concerned in agriculture. In the Trans-Mississippi States more than three-fourths of the people are engaged in agriculture. In the Southern States lying between the Ohio and the Gulf of Mexico two-thirds are occupied in rural pursuits.[1] Of the population of the United Kingdom about one-fifth are interested in agriculture as landowners, tenant-farmers, and labourers. The United States statistics in my possession do not show, as those of Great Britain do, the relative numbers of the three great classes engaged in agriculture, but farmers owning the soil still outnumber the other agricultural

[1] Report of the Commissioners of Agriculture on Sheep Husbandry, January 1879.

classes, and constitute more than half those engaged in agricultural industries. In Great Britain the farmers are six times as numerous as the landowners; the labourers are greatly more numerous than both put together.

No Domesday-book indicates the area of American estates; some of them, however, measure hundreds of square miles. As in this country, a good deal of land is in the hands of nominal owners, who have obtained advances upon it, who have not the means or the wish to employ it to the best advantage, but often await a sufficient appreciation to justify their partitioning it for sale. There are few old family estates. Almost all are for sale at a price. Land changes hands much more frequently than in England. Many elderly men now in the Western States began life on small New England farms, migrated to some of the Middle States, spent some years in improving property there, and, tempted by a remunerative price, sell and re-invest farther West. Numerous pioneers of colonisation push ahead of their fellows, acquire land cheaply, break up, cultivate, and after a few years sell out and move onwards with the sun. Of unoccupied, uncultivated land there must still be abundance for all comers for many years. In the enterprising States of Minnesota and Iowa, with admirable railway facilities, within three or four miles of a station, prairie land, requiring no costly breaking, can be bought at 25*s.* an acre. In older States, such as Pennsylvania and Kentucky, which have been occupied for a hundred years, farms are still purchased at 5*l.* to 6*l.* per acre. Whilst in Virginia within fifty miles of Washington and in Georgia, and other Southern States, are many fine estates belonging to gentlemen whose fortunes were wrecked in the struggle between North and South, who are unable to find the means for improvements or for farming profitably, and who, untrammelled by entails or settlements, would gladly sell their property at low prices.

By far the most numerous of the agricultural classes is the yeoman who cultivates his own land. So much is done by himself or his family that his hired labourers, who in this country are fully four times as numerous as the farmers, do not in America amount to half their number. With abundance of cheap land, easily worked and rising in value, labourers aspire to be farmers, and the farmers naturally prefer to own the land they till. This is especially the case in the West. In Minnesota and Kansas the moderate demand for land to let is evidenced by the fact that school lands, and those of absentee proprietors abounding in prairie grass, and well watered, are let at the moderate figure of two cents, or even one cent per acre, and no restrictions are made as to cutting hay or removing the produce. In the Eastern and Middle States many farms are let on shares, the owner, for his land, house, and buildings, usually receiving one-half of the grain grown. The tenant finds labour and seed, and besides his proportion of the grain, usually also earns a profit from his cattle and pigs. Many men of limited capital in this way make their first start in farming. On fruit and dairy farms a similar division of profits is often made between owner and occupier. It is the old principle, once common in this country, of payment in kind. Considering the abundance of land, it appears rather paradoxical that American landlords, when they do get a tenant, manage to have as their share nearly half the produce, whilst the British landlord has to be content with about one-fifth the gross yield of his land.

Farms are let occasionally by agreement from year to year, or on improving leases, the tenant of unbroken land stipulating to bring so many acres into cultivation annually. Sometimes, as with fruit and vegetable farms, leases extend for ten years, or even for longer periods. Simple leases and deeds of agreement, usually remarkable for their directness and brevity, are generally procured for 4$s.$ to 8$s.$, whilst 2$s.$ is the common charge for recording a lease or agreement. An indifferent tenant is not got rid of by a simple notice to quit. He must be served with a writ of ejectment. In most States distraint for rent is prohibited. The landlord has no hypothec or preferential claim. In most States, as already remarked, personal goods, farm implements, tools, and live stock to a stipulated value, are protected from seizure for debt.

The amount of capital employed in British agriculture, inadequate although it often is to secure the fullest returns, is enormously in excess of that required in ordinary farming throughout the States.

Agricultural land in England and Scotland in its natural condition, without any equipments, may still be taken to be worth about 30*l.* an acre. Farm-house, cottages, draining, roads, and fences cannot be furnished for less than 10*l.* an acre. The tenant's investment for machinery, implements, horses, cattle, and sheep should reach 10*l.* This total of 50*l.* an acre is a very moderate estimate of the amount of capital invested by British landlords and tenants. It is, however, ten times the amount hitherto employed in farming in the Western States, or in many of more recently settled parts of Canada. Throughout the great Trans-Mississippi wheat-growing regions, where about one-half of the wheat of the continent is now raised, good land is still purchased at 25*s.* to 30*s.* an acre. In the great stock-raising regions west of the Missouri, south in Texas, or north towards and beyond the Canadian boundary line, grazing lands are bought at 5*s.* to 15*s.* an acre. House and buildings cost less than half the amount expended upon them at home. Great tracts of country are in little need of artificial drainage. Where frost for three months secures an adamant way of ice, and summer drought for a still longer period gives firm transit over meadow and prairie, expensive roads are little needed. The herd law, in force throughout many States, forbids cattle being turned out without a keeper, and diminishes the need of fencing. These conditions obviously economise outlay. For 2*l.* an acre American farmers are generally supplied with the requisite buildings and permanent equipments which here cost

10*l*. On equally moderate terms the farmer possessed of the requisite ready money buys his lighter machinery and implements, and his lower-priced live stock. Many settlers on 320 acres calculate under this category to start with 1*l*. an acre. Even if double this sum is used, the total capital invested in the fee simple of the land, in its equipments, and in the farm stock, is but 5*l*. 10*s*., or little more than one-tenth the amount contributed by the British landlord and tenant in starting ordinary farming. On the British investment of 50*l*., if 5 per cent. over head is to be earned, the first charge on each acre will be 50*s*. This estimate may, however, be considered figurative —at any rate, it is very rarely obtained. The landlord, if satisfied with 3 per cent. on his investment of 40*l*., would claim 1*l*. 4*s*.; the tenant on his 10*l*., somewhat precariously invested in an uncertain vocation, should earn 7 per cent. or 14*s*. per acre, making a total for rent and interest on capital of 1*l*. 18*s*. per acre. Money, more valuable in a new country, must pay 10 per cent., and the American farmer's charge on his investment of 5*l*. 10*s*. would accordingly be 11*s*. an acre. This aspect of the land question accounts in great part for the low cost of agricultural products in America, and explains how wheat can be profitably grown, although it takes two acres to raise the amount obtained in England on one. With land so abundant and so cheap, and equipped and stocked at such moderate cost, farmers naturally prefer to own the soil they till.

Farming, like most other businesses in America,

is done with energy and with a determination to overtake as much work as possible. Labour is largely aided and hastened by ingenious, light, easily worked machinery. The land is generally level, friable, and free from stones. But so much is often attempted, that it is seldom thoroughly done. As often happens at home, the farmer has frequently too large an area under cultivation for the capabilities of his capital, his horses, or his hand labour. He grudges especially the employment of costly helps. A good deal of American farming, accordingly, lacks the polish, finish, and attention to details which distinguish the best British culture. Headlands, corners, inaccessible or indifferent portions of a field are seldom tilled. The returns of maize crops are thus minimised. Indian corn, missing frequent timely stirring, yields only half as much as it might do. On imperfectly prepared land, insufficiently hoed and not ridged up, potatoes are often less than half a crop. In many States reiterated growth of wheat, without any restoration of the annually extracted plant food, has impoverished many good soils. In the newer Western States, except amongst careful farmers, the bulk of the straw is wastefully burnt in heaps as it comes from the thrashing machines. Such treatment has gradually exhausted the fertility of much land throughout the Eastern and Middle States, and observant farmers are generally adopting a wiser system, are not growing wheat so frequently or continuously, are adopting some kind of recuperative rotation, are taking care of and applying the manure made, and are keeping more live stock. Good managers are realising the truth of the Spanish proverb which declares that 'the hoof of the sheep is gold.' The severe winter and dry summer are unfavourable for the growth of weeds, and notwithstanding the small attention paid to hoeing, many farms are tolerably clean.

Although the farmer is generally his own landlord, he works fully as hard as any British tenant, and as hard and for fully longer hours than many British labourers. He employs fewer hired helps; on all, excepting the largest occupations, the Boss and his household have their full share of the drudgery. The wife and daughters toil almost as hard as the father and boys. They usually do the milking and dairy work, and I have occasionally seen young women riding the sulky ploughs. The truth of the couplet is very generally illustrated:

> Man's work proceeds from sun to sun,
> But woman's work is never done.

Labourers have good wages, especially during summer, and all food is cheap; house accommodation is not, however, so good or so moderate as it now is in England, and there is often difficulty and uncertainty in procuring employment during winter. The average wages of ordinary farm men are $1, or about 4s. per day exclusive of board. Double that amount is given in harvest. Owing to the boom of increased prosperity which bountiful harvests have secured for the States, during the past year wages both of farm labourers and of artisans were advanced, and as compared with several previous years that of 1880 represents a rise of 7·25 per cent.[1] The summer wages range from $9·60 per month with board in South Carolina, to $12·62 in Vermont, and $16 in the Mississippi Valley. Although becoming more uniform than formerly, they are higher near towns than in purely rural districts. They are highest in Montana and the mineral districts. They are lowest in the Southern States, where there is on the whole less enterprise and demand for labour, and where a freed negro population is numerous. On most large farms the hands are engaged from March 1 to November, earn 3*l*. 10*s*. to 4*l*. a month, are housed in barracks or bothies, are well fed with meat thrice daily, and work twelve or thirteen hours. For unmarried men this arrangement answers well enough, but very few farms are provided with sufficient cottage accommodation for married men and families, and the wives and children have often to maintain a separate establishment in some neighbouring town or village.

Artisans have generally good remuneration and plenty of work. Carpenters, masons, blacksmiths, shoeing smiths, wheelwrights, and machine makers, without board, can earn $2 to $3 per day. They are most in request and best paid in Colorado, Oregon, and other Western States, where they command $3 to $4 daily.

In northern latitudes, towards and beyond the Canadian frontier, during the long bitter winter, when the land is bound in the adamant grip of frost, no outdoor agricultural labour can be effected. The care

---

[1] Statistical Report, Department of Agriculture, 1880.

of the live stock is the only work of the farm. Not one-half of the regular summer labour is required. The want of sufficient work for the agricultural population during winter is a serious evil, leading to constant changes amongst the labourers, leaving some in enforced demoralising idleness, necessitating their migrating in quest of lumbering, pork-packing, or other such work, driving many into the towns, where their summer earnings melt away. When severe winter extends, as in Manitoba, for nearly six months, spring brings the necessity for extraordinary effort. In the north and north-west, the spring wheats, where used, have to be put in with all haste, often while the frost is slowly relaxing its hold of the deeper soil. Haymaking in such a dry climate certainly causes less anxiety than under our dull, showery skies. Except where Indian corn is properly cultivated, there is little trouble or expense with hoeing. Wheat harvest again calls forth every effort. Under a blazing sun the ripened crop, unless promptly gathered, suffers great loss from shake.

Drought is the untoward condition which more than anything else minimises American grain crops, and especially wheat. It accounts for the small shrivelled berry, but if not excessive, confers the thin skin and richness in albuminoids. Notwithstanding deep good soils, it is the chief factor in bringing down the yield to 12 or 13 bushels an acre, or less than one-half the estimated acreable produce of Great Britain. We suffer from excess of rain and deficiency of sunshine; they have too little rain and too much sunshine. Drought in early spring sometimes interferes with regular germination or growth. Scorching weather as the grain is maturing sometimes shrivels it up, reducing in 1879 the yield of wheat in Kansas to 11 bushels, in Texas 7½ bushels per acre. In various Southern States and in California irrigation is essential for arable cultivation.

Locusts (*Caloptenus spretus*) have frequently committed great devastations. From their indigenous breeding districts in Montana, Wyoming, and part of Colorado, they have frequently extended in all directions over other States, reaching throughout the Canadian dominions, proceeding north as far as Ohio and south into Kentucky. In swarms measured by hundreds of miles the hoppers have travelled, darkening the air, stopping railway trains, devouring every green blade, leaving fields, gardens, and orchards bare and blackened, as if they had been swept by fire. They are no new plague. There are records of their devastations in 1858. Their most serious recent widespread eruptions were in 1875 and 1876, and throughout many parts of Kansas in 1877.

Another insect pest which causes serious loss is the small Hessian fly (*Cecydomia destructor*), which deposits its eggs in the tender leaflet of the autumn wheat in September, or of the spring cereals in April. The maggots, hatched in five to ten days, live on the fresh juices of the plant, starve, shrivel, and kill it. Later generations of the fly attack the cereals even when they have shot to the second and third joints.

Size of Farms.

Some of these serious drawbacks to American farming will doubtless be gradually abated. Planting, as pointed out, will increase and equalise the rainfall; irrigation will be more widely used in drier regions; thorough cultivation will extirpate insect pests, or limit their devastations; growth of clover, green crops, and their consumption on the soil, will maintain and increase fertility; selection of better seed, more suitable for special localities, will ensure a more uniform and better yield.

The farms of the United States as set forth by the official returns (no cognizance being taken of farms under three acres) averaged 190 acres in 1860, fell to 153 acres in 1870, and are still diminishing. They are under 100 acres in the New England States; in Utah, with its irrigated gardens and tidy orchards, they only reach 30 acres; the largest holdings are in California, where the acreage is set down at 482 acres, and where there are several arable farms of over 20,000 acres; the cattle ranches of Texas present an average of 300 acres; the cotton plantations of Georgia average 338 acres. The average acreage is greater than in the United Kingdom, where 70 per cent. of the farms are under 50 acres, and only twelve per cent. range from 50 to 100 acres.

Alike in England and America an important practical question arises, What size of farm pays best? In proportion to the amount of capital invested, the arable farmers who in America are making the most money are undoubtedly the industrious owners of 80 to 160 acres. A great proportion of their work is done by themselves and their families; their expenses are small; their wheat has recently paid well; they are generally diversifying their culture. With abundance of capital, the best of machinery, and systematic intelligent supervision, the large arable farms in California, the Red River settlements, and elsewhere, have lately paid well. Hitherto, however, they are too dependent on wheat; a good crop throughout Europe and America might seriously cut down their profits. Capitalists engaged in the great cattle ranches and sheep runs of Central and Western America are less liable to disastrous fluctuations of price. They have been making handsome returns, often reaching 25 per cent. on judiciously expended capital, and there is no near prospect of diminution in their returns. The wheat production of the world now readily suffices to find bread for her population, but the meat supplies, especially for the Old World, are yet inadequate to the wants of the people, and there is still ample scope for the production of beef and bacon. American dairy farmers have not generally done so well as the graziers or feeders. For a couple of years until September last good cheese has been selling at about 2*d*. per lb.; the cheese factories of New York State have repeatedly reduced their price for the farmers' milk; occasionally it has fallen to 1*d*. per quart. As at home, those who sell milk or butter have done better than the cheese makers. Owing to the large amount of capital embarked in the business, and the higher price of labour in the Eastern and Middle States, unless the farmers have taken up market-gardening, fruit-growing, or other specialty, they are not generally so prosperous as their brethren out West. Western competition, with some reason, is said to affect them as seriously as it has done the British farmer. Nor has agriculture been particularly prosperous in the Southern States. The free negro has not yet settled down to steady industry. Although not paid much more than half the wages given for white labour in the North or West, work is virtually more costly, whilst markets are not so numerous or accessible.

Compared with their British brethren, American farmers have certain other advantages. They are untrammelled by old-world restrictions. They can buy and sell land with as little expense and delay as if it were government or railway stocks. Their homestead or implements cannot be seized for ordinary debt. Excepting during close time, without licence or permission asked or given, they shoot and sport over their own and also over their neighbours' property. When land is let, the landlord does not dictate as to the mode of cropping or the sale of produce. There is no prejudice or clinging to antiquated systems; but a readiness to modify practice according to soil, climate, circumstances, or markets. Around the cities market gardens and orchards are rapidly multiplied, and dairy farming is prosecuted. This American adaptiveness is especially worthy of imitation in the present unremunerative condition of British agriculture.

CHAPTER V.

THE CHEAP MOVEMENT OF GRAIN.

A KEEN appreciation of novelty, a readiness to adopt improved processes, and the extensive application of machinery constitute important elements in the industrial successes of the United States of America. In the preparation of the soil, the harvesting of the crops and their transit by rail or water, these principles are strikingly illustrated. Time, labour, and consequently expense are hence economized. With a pair of smart horses, two acres are readily ploughed daily: the Western farmer, except when turning, mounts comfortably seated on his sulky plough. Reapers have long been universal, and are now superseded by the combined reaper and binder. On the great Dalrymple farm in the territory of Dakota 120 of these useful combined machines were at work last season. Portable steam machines thrash and clean the grain. In sacks, carried in light vans or waggons, it is delivered to the railway depôt or to the canal or river barges. A handy crane usually hastens the unloading and emptying of the sacks.

Grain delivered by the farmer even at remote western depôts is examined by the sworn inspector, is generally winnowed by steam, water, or wind power as it passes into the bins of the elevator. It is weighed 60 lbs. to the bushel instead of 63 lbs. as is general in England: 480 lbs. constitutes the quarter. The inspector grades both the varieties as No. 1, 2, 3, or 4 winter or spring. According to this official estimate, which is rarely questioned, the farmer is paid in conformity with his bargain or in accordance with current price. The memorandum of the transaction received by the buyer constitutes an order for the delivery of so many quarters of the specified quality. Unless, however, under special arrangement, not a particle of the same wheat to which the order actually referred is delivered to the buyer. The delivery note, especially in speculative times, is sold and resold repeatedly. Each purchaser deposits a small percentage to protect the vendor from loss in case of a drop in value. The ultimate buyer, although he does not receive the grain actually bought, has its equivalent of the stipulated grade set forth in his delivery order. Without this simple deferential system it would be impossible to conduct the great grain business of the Western World.

Nearly half the wheat grown in America now comes from the great Mississippi valley 1,000 miles west of New York, and from the vast alluvial prairies and plains which extend thence 500 miles, and away beyond the Missouri, embracing an area fifteen times as large as Great Britain.

The handling and transport of the grain from this great region, as elsewhere in America, is cheaply and effectively managed. Lakes, rivers, canals and railroads contribute ready and cheap transport. There are in the States 86,497 miles of iron roads; they have doubled their mileage twice in ten years; 4,721 miles were laid down in 1879. Over the great level western prairies they are built at the rate of 3,000*l*. per mile. The trucks or cars contain 400 to 500 bushels or 10 to 12 tons. The grain in bulk, and graded as described, does not require to be kept in small separate lots; the trucks travel full. The rail roads out west, where competition is small, charge, however, relatively high for transport. From St. Paul to Chicago, for example, a distance of 450 miles, the tariff is usually about 5*s*. 6*d*. for 480 lbs. From Kansas city (280 miles) to Saint Louis, the charge is about 4*s*. From grain centres such as Chicago, Cincinnati, or St. Louis, to the eastern seaboard, or to Great Britain, the cost of transport is, however, proportionally less. During the summer of 1879, owing to competition between the five railroads which run east from Chicago, thousands of quarters of grain were carried at 3*s*. 4*d*. per quarter, and even lower rates were given to Philadelphia and Baltimore. A similar moderate charge forwarded the quarter of wheat to British ports. But these are exceptionally low rates, probably 50 to 70 per cent. below what may be regarded as a fair standard during an average of years. Long distance charges are relatively sometimes absolutely lower than those for shorter distances. For other goods as well as for grain low rates are obtained.[1]

[1] New York Produce Exchange *Report* for 1879 and 1880; Messrs. Read and Pell's *Report on American Agriculture*.

From Chicago to New York, which, according to the route taken, varies from 800 to 900 miles, the cost of transport of a barrel of flour of 214 lbs. has ranged during the last five years from 50 to 80 cents (2s. 2d. to 3s. 4d.) Pork, beef, and lard have varied from 42 to 57 cents per 100 lbs. Tinned meats in cases, falling as low as 18 cents, for three years have had a steady maximum of 45 cents per 100 lbs.

Fully one-third of the grain sent east is carried by water, over all or part of the route. The canal or river barges stow about 1,000 quarters, and strings of twelve or sixteen, hawled by a steam-tug, are despatched at very cheap rates, over the great lakes or down the canals or rivers to the seaboard. From S. Louis 1,000 miles down the Mississippi to New Orleans, grain is often conveyed at the rate of 3d. per bushel. From Chicago *via* Buffalo or Oswego to New York, a distance of 1,400 miles, the freight for 1878 was $4\frac{1}{2}d$. per bushel; that of 1879 is about 5d. per bushel. The average cost of transport of 480 lbs. of wheat during the last five years has been 3s. 5d. The transport of a quarter (448 lbs.) of Indian corn has been 3s, 1d. Equally moderate rates are charged for the transit of grain from the interior to other ocean ports. By fixed or floating elevators it is transferred from the barges, and weighed by Fairbank's standard scales, as it is 'dumped' at the rate of 2,000 or 3,000 bushels an hour into the bins for storing, or into the hold of the vessel that carries it to Europe. Of the 152,000,000 bushels of grain and breadstuffs annually brought to New York, 44 per cent. is by water carriage, and somewhat similar proportions are carried to the other Atlantic ports.

Even in a country where everything is on a large scale, the grain traffic of the great railway companies, encouraged by these low rates, by numerous intersecting local lines, and by facilities for movement, 'bulks tolerably big.' New York has 54 per cent. of her grain and breadstuffs by rail. Fully 31 per cent., or about 50,000,000 bushels, is annually forwarded by the New York Central and Hudson River rail; $14\frac{1}{2}$ per cent. by the Erie; upwards of $9\frac{1}{2}$ per cent. by the Pennsylvania. The two latter lines are erecting at their depôts at New Jersey City elevators to facilitate the movement of the grain. Four years ago the New York Central and Hudson River Company, following the spirited example of Chicago, erected at their terminus at Fifty-ninth Street two gigantic warehouses with elevators, capable of storing 1,250,000 bushels, built on piles driven into the bed of the Hudson, and commanding 25 ft. of water for the mooring and loading of vessels. Each of these buildings is about 300 ft. long, 100 ft. wide, and 150 ft. high; and so rapidly is business extending, that it is said a third warehouse is required. Each building contains upwards of 100 bins; each bin is capable of holding 5,000 to 8,000 bushels. They are 12 ft. square, and 50 ft. to 55 ft. deep; their walls are made of 6 in. battens, 2 in. thick, spiked together, and further strengthened by a few iron rods passing across the bin. These bins are filled by 20 large elevators, which can take up grain simultaneously from ten

American Grain Warehouses.   57

trucks, unloaded on the ground floor within the building, or from barges, discharged from the wharfs on either side. An engine of 700-horse power drives the gigantic 4 ft. belt, 300 ft. long, which moves this unique machinery, the wheels, shafts, and working parts of which are conveniently fixed in the top stories of the building.

. Wheat and Indian corn constitute the bulk of the grain received, and about half of it is on through bills for Europe. Most of the oats go for the home trade. The grain is chiefly collected 1,000 miles to 1,500 miles west; the cars carry 400 to 500 bushels, or an average of 10 to 12 tons. The stuff is examined and graded on transit by qualified inspectors appointed by the State. Of the several grains there are about forty grades; of spring wheat, for example, there are first, second, third, and fourth grades, and rejected. Unless distinctly stipulated for in the bills of lading, consignors' lots are not kept separate; grain of the same grade is, however, strictly kept by itself; and indiscriminately from a bin of 6,000 bushels may be drawn the 1,000 bushels belonging to six small consignors. Separate bins reserved for small lots would entail much extra trouble and cost.

Three hundred cars, containing 120,000 bushels, are sometimes unloaded daily. In lots of 8 or 10, they are run under the elevators and rapidly emptied in 12 or 15 minutes. Two men, with respirators to keep the dust out of their lungs, enter each truck armed with a shovel, which consists of a board or tray, about a yard square and without any handle. To each of these shovels is attached a rope, which passes over a roller, conveniently placed several yards above the truck and worked by steam, which winds up the rope until it pulls the shovel and all the grain before it towards the door of the car, where it falls into a receiver below. The roller then automatically reverses its motion and unwinds the rope, thus enabling the workman to retire to the far corner of the car, when the roller again reverses, and the process is repeated until the car is emptied. The ropes are so arranged, that while one of the men is guiding his loaded shovel forward, the other is retiring for another charge. From the receiver, the grain is raised to its destination by an endless band, provided with the ordinary tin buckets. By arrangement of shoots each elevator is in communication with twenty-six bins. If it is desired, the grain on its way to the bin, at a cost of 1d. per quarter, can be run through one of the six winnowing machines with which each building is provided. The perforated shakers keep back stones, straw, or other rubbish: the air blast drives out very light grain, chaff, and dust, which, by a pipe, is conveyed into the Hudson. Every parcel passing through the elevators is weighed automatically by Fairbank's scales, which accurately weigh a bushel or a lot of 10 to 14½ tons. The charge made by the railway company for this transference from car or barge to the bins and re-delivery to the vessels is one-half of a cent per bushel; and this includes ten days' storage. Longer storage is charged at the rate of 1d. per quarter for ten days or any part thereof. At any time the grain can be turned, not laboriously by men with shovels, but by machinery, from one bin into another ; and for less than 1*d*. per quarter. Unsound stuff is charged extra rates. If grain is sacked and the sacks loaded on cars or barges, the charge is 4*d*. per quarter. Most of the grain within ten days is usually discharged from the bins into lighters for delivery to the steamers. or direct into the ship carrying it to Europe. Down shoots of about 12 in. in diameter the grain rushes through the hatches, and is firmly packed to prevent shifting. A steam-worked shovel, similar to that used for emptying the cars, might be here effectively employed. A handy vessel, with convenient hatches, is loaded with 60,000 to 80,000 bushels in eight hours. A steamer frequently receives on board in one day her freight of 90,000 bushels.

Without the fixed railway elevators and their steam-floating prototypes it would be difficult to load up and export every week, as is often done, from New York, upwards of 2,500,000 bushels of grain. Without them it would have been hopeless to handle the unprecedentedly large export of 13,676,000 bushels which were despatched for Europe during July 1880.

These ingenious useful appliances, so interesting to the mechanician and so considerably reducing the cost of the movement of grain, are not yet sufficiently used in Europe. In Great Britain the only public elevators are those in the grain docks at Liverpool. The handy floating elevators, costing about 6,000*l*., so constantly employed at all the American ports to transfer grain from the barges to the larger ocean-going vessels, are now likely to receive a fair trial in this country. An elevator built by the New York elevator construction company for Messrs. Edward Power & Co. has for twelve months been working successfully on the Thames. The adoption in this country of these American labour-saving machines has been retarded by many vessels bringing grain having besides other cargo on board, and hence discharging at docks remote from the grain warehouses. The general distribution of grain in sacks instead of loose, as it is in America, also limits the general use of elevators. The grain warehouses in many older ports are besides often placed too far from the wharfs to allow the grain being raised direct from the ships into the warehouses. At many of the newer ports, and where granaries have recently been erected, their convenient proximity to rail and water, and the introduction of elevators have most unaccountably been overlooked. The economy of such appliances is, however, very strikingly demonstrated in the tedious and expensive discharge of grain vessels at European ports. The vessel which had her cargo of 80,000 bushels put on board in bulk at New York in a single day, at her European destination is unloaded by tardy, costly hand labour; every bushel is painstakingly weighed and sacked up, often carried ashore on men's shoulders, and ten or twelve days are sometimes occupied, entailing, besides expensive labour, an unnecessary outlay of at least 10*l*. daily for detention of the vessel.

CHAPTER VI.

NEW YORK MEAT SUPPLIES.

THE sale, preservation, and distribution of animal food are somewhat differently managed in England and America. From American practices may certainly be learned various useful lessons; notably in the cheap transport alike of live cattle and of meat, in the sale of cattle, sheep, and pigs by weight, instead of by the guess system so generally prevalent in this country, in the use of convenient central abattoirs, in the adoption of cold storage chambers; and in utilising every portion of offal. The marketing, slaughtering, and shipping arrangements at New York illustrate these, and perhaps other practical lessons.

New York, with her million of population, attracts to her markets every week nearly 12,000 cattle for slaughter, 160 to 200 cows, about 30,000 sheep, 32,000 swine, besides variable numbers of calves and lambs. Twenty years ago New York, in twelve months, slaughtered 150,000 cattle, or about one-fourth of her present requirements. From Chicago, Philadelphia, and elsewhere, she further receives large consignments of dead meat, some of it for consumption, some of it for transmission to Great Britain.

The live-stock supplies are tolerably equally divided between the yards of the New York Central and Hudson River Company, at the foot of Seventy-Second Street, and those of the Stock Yard Company at New Jersey City, on the opposite side of the Hudson, but readily reached from New York in fifteen minutes by the huge ferry boats, carrying buggies, coaches, loaded carts and vans, as well as passengers. The swine are assigned separate quarters, at Fortieth Street, New Jersey City. The commoner cattle, narrow, leggy, brindled or yellow, with enormous formidable horns, direct descendants of the Spanish stock imported into Mexico 350 years ago, come 2,000 miles from Texas and New Mexico, weigh alive 1,000 lbs. to 1,200 lbs., and yield 52 lbs. to 54 lbs of beef for every 100 lbs. of live weight. More compact and shapely, nearer the ground, and with less offal, are the steers from Colorado and Wyoming. Many lots, varying considerably in quality, are made up from Chicago, St. Louis, or Cincinnati. Improved by selection, and 'graded up' by crossing with Shorthorns and Herefords, but seldom reaching one-sixth of the whole, are consignments from Kentucky and Illinois, forwarded direct from the pastures, or in winter and spring from the yards where they have been fed, mainly on Indian corn and hay, averaging four years old, reaching 1,500 lbs. to 1,800 lbs. live weight, and yielding 56 to 60 per cent. of beef. As everywhere in America the beasts are sold, as they should be in this country, by weight, the beasts bought pass, as they from the pens are run on to one of

Fairbank's ubiquitous weigh-bridges, where, inclosed within gates, their weight is recorded by a market official. These useful scales cost 70*l.* to 100*l.* Generally the animals are disposed of by live weight, or on the hoof, as it is termed; but at New York they are sold on the estimate of the carcase weight. In recent markets good and extra bullocks have sold at 5*d.* to 5¾*d.* per pound, and lower qualities at 4*d.* to 4½*d.* per pound.

In the great cattle-breeding territories, west and south of the Missouri, three and four year old cattle in good condition are worth less than 2*d.* per pound live weight. In early spring thousands are driven north and east, often for several hundred miles, to the railroad stations, grazing on the sparsely occupied, or unoccupied lands. They are usually travelled steadily, at the rate of ten miles a day; when well managed they improve, often gaining 1 lb. of weight daily; with considerable droves, 2*d.* per head per day covers all travelling expenses for men and beasts. Reaching their destination at the railway yards, they are allowed to feed and rest, are packed 16 to 20 in large well-constructed covered cars, and by special trains are forwarded east. The large operators have staffs of experienced, steady men, who take pains with their charges, with long poles keep them on their legs, prevent quarrelling, and have very few casualties. Every 300 or 400 miles, at intervals of 18 to 24 hours, the cattle are unloaded, fed, watered, and rested from 24 to 30 hours. Hardy and accustomed to roam at liberty in wide pastures or large yards, American cattle lose less weight in travelling, either on foot or by rail, than English cattle would do under like circumstances. A journey of 1,500 miles by rail generally pulls off 100 lbs. to 150 lbs., from a beast of 1,200 lbs. or 1,500 lbs., but three-fourths of this loss is fluids.

American transport charges are very moderate. From Cheynne, Julesburg, and other stations on the Union Pacific, 1,200 miles west to Chicago, the freight charge is under 30*s.* for each beast. From Chicago (900 miles) to New York, it is 16*s.*, the charge usually made in this country for one-eighth of the distance. From Chicago to Baltimore the rate is 20*s.* The charges are so many dollars per car load, nominally of ten tons; but so long as no cruel senseless overcrowding occurs, the companies are not particular in restricting the weight to ten tons. There is no ridiculous difference, as in this country, between the transport rates for live animals and for dead meat; both are charged, as they should be, by weight. The rates vary from $\frac{1}{2}d.$ to less than $\frac{1}{4}d.$ per lb. per mile. On short journeys higher rates are charged, concerning which there are many and loud complaints.

Mondays and Thursdays are the busy days at the New York and New Jersey stock yards, but sales are made daily at both; 150 to 200 car-loads of cattle are frequently forwarded in one day to each of these two stock-yards. Sheep and pigs are brought in double-decked trucks which, like those for the cattle, are double the size of those used at home. Hay is furnished at 1*d.* per lb. Officers of the Society for the

Prevention of Cruelty to Animals are in constant attendance. Cases of cruelty or neglect are punished. Whips and long sticks are used to separate and drive the animals; dogs are seldom employed. The railways discharge the animals direct into the stock-yards, each of which accommodates 6,000 cattle, and three times that number of sheep, which, forwarded mainly from Canada and the Northern States, are most numerous in the New York mart. The avenues between the stock-yard pens are 20 feet wide. The pens are 70 feet by 30 feet, mostly enclosed with six-barred iron hurdles, conveniently holding two car-loads, or about forty animals, and furnished with water-troughs and racks for hay, which is fairly supplied. The salesmen begin work at 5 A.M. They receive 2s. as commission on cattle, and 1s. on sheep and hogs. They furnish consigners the weight of the animals they sell, as ascertained by Fairbank's scales; they also give the price obtained, and the name of the purchaser—important particulars which salesmen in this country do not always vouchsafe. Animals disposed of at the stock-yards, whether of New Jersey City or those of the Central and Hudson River Railroad Co., if required, are conveyed by floats to any of the river slaughter-houses for the small charge of 10d. each. The charge for similar service on the Thames is 4s. per head.

Adjacent to the New York Central and Hudson River Stock-yards, at the foot of Seventy-Second Street, are the commodious slaughtering and cold storage premises of Messrs. T. C. Eastman and Co., the most extensive slaughterers and fresh meat exporters in America. Mr. T. C. Eastman was the first to open the fresh meat trade with England in 1875. His shipments of cattle and sheep alive and dead sometimes reach 1,000 per week. Now that the business is a success he expresses astonishment that it was not done long before. It is not, he remarks, uniformly conducted with profit. Numbers of those who have embarked in it have lost heavily. Owing usually to bad weather, sometimes from other causes, for several weeks together, a glut occurs in the English market, and prices fall 1*d.* and even 1½*d.* per. lb. Not only are profits sacrificed, but freight and insurance are lost. In summer the live animal pays better than the dead meat. About 6½*d.* obtained at British ports yields good remuneration to shippers. American meat, he says, could be afforded at less money if the present restrictions at the port of landing were dispensed with and the beasts allowed to be moved alive to inland markets. Mr. Eastman is a decided free trader: he says we cannot supply England nor any other part of Europe with provisions unless we are prepared to take manufactured articles in return. Politicians, he says, will have to fight out the question of tariffs, but the American people want free trade.

Mr. Eastman further informs me (May 29, 1880) that 'throughout the American continent there are now more good fat bullocks ready for the market than the home and export trade can use, and prices accordingly are falling off. The agricultural resources of the country are such that the supply can

Mr. Eastman's Establishment.

be kept up and almost any reasonable demand made good. Stock steers two to three years old are cheap and plentiful. They weigh about 1,100 lbs.; good grass or hay, and about 80 bushels of Indian corn, raised at an expense of 8*d.* to 1*s.* per bushel, will make them up to 1,500 lbs. A small portion of our rich western lands,' he continues, 'are really under cultivation. You may calculate that this country can furnish cattle delivered on British soil for an almost unlimited time at prices lower than are being realised at present.'

Mr. T. C. Eastman's premises are conveniently connected with the Hudson River stock-yards. The slaughtering and storage buildings are 150 yards long, 80 wide, and mostly four storeys high. Here 5,000 cattle are sometimes received, killed, and distributed in one week; 2,000 are sometimes remitted alive to other eastern cities; 500 are occasionally despatched to Europe. The chief proportion are slaughtered for the great Washington and Fulton dead meat markets. The commoner sorts are forwarded to the beef canning establishments. Three to four hundred men are employed, earning 6*s.* to 12*s.* a day. From the adjoining stock-yards the cattle are driven down the central passage into separate pens. Suspended from a revolving shaft are a series of stout hempen ropes, terminating in a hook, which is placed round one or both hind fetlocks of the beast. Automatically by steam the rope is slowly wound up. The bullock, at a loss to comprehend the unwonted process, seldom makes much resistance, is steadily raised off the ground, swung clear of the pen, and with a vigorous thrust of the knife the large bloodvessels of the neck are severed, and also the gullet, which ensures cleaner dressing. The blood rapidly drains away, and is collected in tanks, dried for sugar-refining, or, with the entrails, goes for manure-making. Four or five men are promptly to work with knife and cleaver removing the hide, which in summer is slightly salted to secure preservation. The heads are removed; the tongues go for pickling, the tails for soup. The kidneys find their way to the restaurants and hotel-keepers. The heart and liver are sold fresh or for sausage-making. The best of the fat, carefully washed and kept cool, is secured by the oleomargarine manufacturer. The refuse fat and that stripped from the entrails is used for soap and candle-making. The feet go for glue and gelatine. Within fifteen minutes the beast is killed and dressed; twenty are generally finished off every hour. Suspended from pulleys, run on stout iron rods overhead, the carcases are passed into a cool, darkened chamber, where at a temperature of about 40° Fahr. the natural heat is in great part dissipated. In from eight hours to twenty-four they are transferred to the adjacent cold storage chambers, in the centre of the building, with double walls of $1\frac{1}{2}$-inch boards, kept an inch apart, so as to reduce conduction, with an accurately fitting door on the same non-conducting principle. In these refrigerating chambers, with several hundred tons of ice overhead, and fans moved by steam, the dry air, at a temperature of 34° to 38°, is kept continually circulating amidst the suspended carcases, which remain for twenty-four to thirty-six hours, or in the case of meat intended for shipment to Europe, until the steamers are ready to receive it. The total cost of killing and dressing each bullock, including rent and interest on plant, Mr. Eastman informs me, is 3s. to 3s. 6d. But during summer, when the carcases are kept several days in the refrigerating chambers, the cost is nearly doubled. These expenses are, however, covered by the 6s. or 7s. obtained for the offal, of which the best is made. The blood dried, and in bags weighing 175 lbs., contains about 17 per cent of ammonia, and is bought for nurserymen and cotton planters at from $35 to $40 per ton of 2,000 lbs. The remainder of the offal, including heads of oxen and sheep, is reduced in steam-heated, close-covered vats, the grease skimmed off, the ground bones added, and a useful well-dried manure made, which contains about 6 per cent. of ammonia, and 25 of phosphates, and is disposed of at $26 per ton.

Mutton is not so much used in America as in England, nor is the quality generally so good. Sheep have been kept almost exclusively for their wool, but crossing the native Mexicans and half-bred Merinos with well-selected rams of approved English breeds, is steadily improving the weight and quality of the mutton. The best sheep brought to New York come from Kentucky, Michigan, and Ohio, and from Canada; 500 to 600 are sometimes killed and dressed in a day; their average carcase weight is 50 lbs. to 60 lbs., but picked lots, such as are forwarded to Great Britain, reach 65 lbs. to 80 lbs. The wholesale carcase price is 4*d.* to 5*d.* per lb.

Messrs. Sherman and Gillett have large abattoirs connected with the New Jersey Stock-yard, supply the trade in the Washington and Fulton markets, and elsewhere, and forward 250 to 300 carcases every week to England, besides about the same number of sheep and pigs conveniently disposed amongst the quarters of beef. Animals of different grades are killed for different purposes. The best, yielding 56 to 58 per cent. of beef, and weighing dressed 750 lbs. to 800 lbs., are forwarded over the Atlantic. The system of slaughtering is much the same as at Mr. Eastman's. Six men work together 'on the bed,' with a seventh as a subordinate to wash and tidy up, and have 2*s.* 6*d.* for each beast. The hides, weighing in the horns and hair of the tail, range from 56 lbs. to 96 lbs., bring $3\frac{1}{2}d$ per lb., are salted, and many exported to France. The head fetches 2*s.*, the tongue 2*s.* 6*d.* The kidneys bring 2*s.*, the heart and liver are worth 1*s.* 3*d.* The fat, of which 100 lbs. are got from a ripe beast, is worth $2\frac{1}{2}d.$ per lb. The feet, valued at 1*s.* 3*d.* to 1*s.* 6*d.*, are taken by the stock-yard company as rent of premises. The bones are sold at $1\frac{1}{4}$ cents per lb. Sheep skins are worth in October 6*s.* to 7*s.* each. After hanging for a few hours in an airy, cool, darkened shed, without any laborious carrying, suspended from pulleys gliding along iron rods overhead, the carcases are run into the refrigerating chambers, where, with ice and sometimes with salt, the temperature, even in the hottest summer weather, is maintained at 34° to 38°. The average cost of this thorough effectual cooling during summer is 7s. 6d. to 8s. per beast. The carcases intended for the English market usually remain in these refrigerators during two to four days. They are quartered and the quarters sewed in stout calico. The sheep and pigs whole are done up in cloths, and transferred to the cold storage chambers of the ocean steamers.

A large proportion of the meat slaughtered in New York is concentrated in the Washington and Fulton dead meat markets, whence it is distributed to retailers or bought by the public. In these large markets the price of the best joints is, however, high, compared with the first cost of the animals in the stock-yards, whilst in the retail shops in New York, and indeed throughout many cities especially of the Eastern States, the price of the best meat is as high as it is in London, Liverpool, or Edinburgh. Although the first cost is certainly $1\frac{1}{2}d.$ to $2d.$ per lb. less than it generally is in Great Britain, the best cuts are not obtained under 1s. per lb. Amongst almost all classes throughout America the prime parts, especially the tender loin, is in great request; boiling pieces are even more at a discount than in Great Britain, and their price does not reach one-half that given for the sirloin, ribs, or rump. A considerable proportion of the forequarters, the thin flank, and other inferior parts, disposed of with difficulty to retail consumers, goes to the canning trade.

The manufacture of oleomargarine and oleomargarine butter in America has now assumed large proportions.

There are eleven manufactories in various parts of the States. The New York factory alone turns out from 40,000 to 50,000 lbs. per day of this new butter in tubs and pound prints, which, according to law, must bear distinctly the stamp 'Oleomargarine.' Notwithstanding this brand, which the dealers in milk butter insisted on, and believed would prevent the sale of the oleomargarine, it has steadily gained the approval of all classes, and especially those who cannot afford butter at 1*s.* 6*d.* to 2*s.* per lb., and who freely purchase this new product at 9*d.* to 1*s.* The manufacture is conducted with great care and more regard to cleanliness than obtains in many dairies. The fat, fresh, well washed, and in summer iced, is forwarded from the slaughter-house to the works in covered vans daily and sometimes twice a day. It is again carefully washed and trimmed, cut finely in a sort of mincing machine, and then melted in jacketed kettles, when the melting fat gradually attains a temperature of 120° to 130° Fahr. When thoroughly melted, it is allowed to stand and settle, all fibrous tissues going to the bottom, and a yellow, sweet, and odourless oil remaining on top. In the earlier experimental trials, made seven or eight years ago, a little carbonate of potash and some rennet or portions of calves' stomach were introduced, but this is not now regarded necessary. The oil is run off from the top into tanks, allowed to cool gradually, and then iced. It is packed in clean cloths holding about 2 to 3 lbs. each, and exposed to hydraulic pressure. A clear, sweet, and golden oil, 'Oleomargarine,' is expressed.

Stearine in beautiful snow-white flakes remains in the towel, and is used for candle-making, and to give consistency to lard in hot weather. Fully 50,000 tierces, about 17,000,000 lbs., of the oil are exported annually from New York alone, and in London and elsewhere are made into butter, and sold seldom with any 'oleomargarine' brand. The making of the butter from oleomargarine oil is effected by churning in the same manner as for ordinary butter, adding a little milk for flavouring and arnatto for colouring. The product is salted and packed in the usual way. The orthodox and oleomargarine butters have closer resemblance than most prejudiced persons suppose. The cream oils from the milk and from the solid fat differ slightly. The butter from the two sources has the same melting point; the microscope discovers little difference; dissolved in ether and allowed to stand until the ether evaporates, the residuum of the oleomargarine butter exhibits a flavour of beef suet, whilst that of milk butter emits a distinct lactic flavour.

CHAPTER VII.

FRUIT AND VEGETABLE CULTURE.

TAKING advantage of suitable climate and soil, the cultivation of fruit and vegetables steadily extends throughout the United States. In no country is such food so largely used in such variety by all classes. Orchards, vines, and small fruit, it is estimated, occupy 5,000,000 acres; apples alone take up fully two-fifths of this area. Not including figs, oranges, olives, and almonds, California has 70,000 acres of vineyards, 45,000,000 vines yielding annually, besides grapes and raisins, upwards of 12,000,000 gallons of wine. Good wines are now also extensively made in Missouri, Ohio, and elsewhere. Of oranges alone Florida produces annually 100,000,000, worth about 300,000*l.* The total value of the fruit of the United States in a favourable year reaches 30,000,000*l.* sterling, or fully two-fifths of the value of the wheat crop. I do not find any recent statistics of the number of acres devoted to each description of fruit, but the government estimate made for the centennial in 1876 gives the number of trees of different sorts as follows: apple 112,000,000, pear 28,260,000, peach 112,270,000, grapes 141,260,000. The estimated value of the fruit was given as follows: apples $50,400,000, pears $14,130,000, peaches $56,135,000, grapes $2,118,900, strawberries $5,000,000, other fruits $10,432,800; making a grand total of $138,216,700. Encouraged by horticultural and pomological societies, which are particularly serviceable in indicating the best sorts for particular localities or circumstances, so soon as provision is made for bare life, the wheat planted, and a farmhouse and barn run up, the settler proceeds to enclose his orchard and garden. Illustrating the widespread anxiety to grow and make use of fruit, Messrs. Read and Pell in their report remark: 'More than 5,000,000 peach trees blossom every spring on the lands between the Delaware and Chesapeake bays and the interoceanic regions of the Northwest. In the Middle States and New England, hundreds of families get an income from the gathering and sale of the wild strawberry, raspberry, blueberry, ruckleberry, blackberry, cranberry. These small fruits are mostly consumed at home. In the Genesee valley peaches were carted about in waggonloads, and orchards of pears and peaches were universal. So eagerly are they cultivated here, that the graveyards are covered with these plantations.' (P. 6.)

The abundant varied fruit of favoured spots is widely distributed in a fresh state, often being carried 1,000 miles in refrigerating cars. In discovering and making a market for these, and indeed all other commodities, Americans are remarkably ready and enterprising. From the Southern States strawberries and peaches are obtained in May, and from later localities continue to be forwarded till the season is far advanced.

Spreading from Baltimore, where the business was begun twenty years ago, the preserving and canning of fruit is extending in many cities of the fruit-growing States. Carefully gathered peaches, plums, and the finer pears are boiled with sugar in steam-heated pans and bottled or tinned. Tons of small fruit are similarly preserved. An extensive industry is occupied in the systematic drying of many varieties of fruit in a succession of chambers, each of which is hotter than the preceding. Fully three-fourths of the natural moisture is thus removed without injuring colour or flavour. These fruit-preserving establishments also can vegetables and put up oysters during winter.

At Spencer Port, New York State, is a good typical evaporating establishment, where in the autumn of 1879 and in the following winter 13,654 bushels of apples were dried. The fruit is pared, cored, and sliced in one operation. One girl works the machine, a second trims the slices and places them one and a half inches thick on trays of galvanized iron wire holding a bushel each. Two girls prepare 20 to 25 bushels of fruit in a day of nine hours, receiving 6 cents a bushel. The trays filled with fruit are bleached by brief exposure to burning lime and introduced into the evaporator, which consists of a brick tower or chimney constructed with hollow brick walls 16 feet high and 5 feet square, at the base of which is placed the furnace. Up each side of the tower runs an endless chain, with cross bars 5 inches apart, on which the trays are run. One after another, at intervals of $7\frac{1}{2}$ minutes, to the number of thirty, they are placed in the evaporator at a temperature of 230° and in the order in which they are put in reach the second story, are removed, cooled, and packed usually in boxes containing 50 lbs. Five evaporators are now erected. In busy times the work proceeds day and night ; 700 to 800 bushels are dried daily: 60,000 to 70,000 in the season. Large consignments of the preserved fruits are forwarded to Russia. Here, as in so many other American establishment, every care is taken of so-called waste products. The refuse fruit, skins, and cores are dried for cider and vinegar making.

In this growing and preserving of fruit the British public are becoming more and more interested. The fruit exports of America have increased one hundredfold in five years. A large proportion comes to the United Kingdom. In 1861 the exports were valued at 54,000*l.* ; in 1871 they were 102,000*l.* ; in 1877 they mounted to 590,000*l.* The two last seasons not having been so generally favourable for fruit growing, the exports have declined 25 per cent. In 1879 the ripe apples, which generally reach 1,000,000 bushels, were valued at 200,000*l.* The dried apples, many of them pared and cored by machine, sometimes sliced and dried in the sun, were valued at 60,000*l.* ; other fruits, green, ripe, or dried, are set down at 50,000*l.* Preserved, bottled, or canned fruits reach 80,000*l.*

For 70 miles around New York market gardening and fruit-growing are important and increasing industries. Long Island for sixty miles from the city is devoted to vegetables, or 'trucking' as it is locally termed. The plots vary from five to twenty-five acres, and are generally owned by the cultivators. A great variety of articles are raised in order to insure against failure; or rather against markets glutted with some specialities. The fertility of the light, sandy soil, twenty-five years ago almost worthless, is developed and maintained by liberal doses of manure carried out in the vans which deliver the vegetables, or in barges, and by guano and other concentrated fertilisers. The most successful men do a good deal of their marketing personally. For distances of twelve or fifteen miles the produce is taken into town in the cultivators' own vans; but heavily laden trains night and morning deliver the produce of more distant districts. Up the Hudson, throughout many parts of New Jersey State, in Delaware, and on the rich, deep loams around Philadelphia, gardening and fruit-growing are industriously cultivated. As elsewhere, these farms usually range from 10 to 50 acres, and are owned by the occupiers. Only a very few are mortgaged. On some the peaches, pears, and other trees are found and planted by a more successful neighbour, who, for a term of years, reserves half the produce. One successful nurseryman at Morristown, New Jersey, has thus a lien over and good profit from about thirty orchards. The value of these vegetable and fruit farms varies according to nearness to New York and other local circumstances, and ranges from 20*l.* to 700*l.* an acre.

Many parts of New Jersey State illustrate satisfactorily the advantages of the 'little farm well tilled.' Taking advantage of proximity to New York and other large markets, the farmers go in largely for vegetables and fruit. They cannot compete with the West in wheat or maize, nor even in the cheap rearing of cattle and hogs, but successfully cultivate the most perishable produce which does not bear long carriage. On these farms, which seldom exceed 10 acres, more labour is often employed than on twenty times the area devoted to ordinary farm crops, and the profits also are often more satisfactory, especially where the grower, as is common, takes his share of the work, and does most of his own marketing.

For the cultivation of early potatoes and cabbage, the land is well ridged up in winter. As early as practicable in April it is ploughed and harrowed. With a two-horse plough furrows are drawn $2\frac{1}{2}$ feet apart and 8 inches deep. Fully 20 tons of well-rotted compost, made of farm and horse manure, fish refuse, and street sweepings, are generally applied. The early rose potato is a favourite sort. Large seed is cut usually to two eyes. Spring growth is so rapid that it is not necessary, as in Lancashire and elsewhere in this country, to start the sets before planting. They are covered in with a one-horse plough. The crop is usually hand-hoed twice, horse-hoed three or four times, and left well ridged up They are dug towards the end of July; 300 bushels of marketable potatoes are frequently grown per acre, worth 2s. to 2s. 6d. per bushel.

Cabbages generally pay well. For the staple crop, Drumhead and Flat Dutch are largely grown. Twenty to thirty tons of well-made manure are used. The plants are set out, often after an early crop of peas, throughout June and the first week in July; they are horse-hoed every week, and weeds cut out by hand; thorough frequent stirring of the soil is approved of, especially if the weather is not too dry; 3,000 to 4,000 marketable heads are got per acre, producing a gross acreable return of 30*l.* to 35*l.* From collards, brocoli, cauliflower, peas, and tomatoes still better returns are made. Lettuce, radish, cress, and other green stuff, for salad, are widely and profitably grown, and are largely used by all classes. It is the masses of the population throughout America that are the best customers alike for vegetables and fruit.

Fruit trees, as in England, are often grown on lands laid down to grass, apples, pears, damsons, and cherries being generally mixed. This is the practice followed on the large holdings remote from the towns. On the ten acre and smaller farms, under the fruit trees are usually planted gooseberry, raspberry, and other bushes, whilst strawberries and vegetables occupy the intervening space, which is constantly kept under the plough or spade. Exempt from the late white frosts which so often blast the prospects of English fruit-growers, and with a higher summer temperature, larger and more certain fruit crops are obtained. Mr. P. T. Quinn, of Newark, on one quarter of an acre has sixty-two Duchesse d'Angoulême pear trees, from which in 1878 he had, besides 10 bushels of small inferior fruit, 155 bushels of prime sold at $1·75, representing an acreable return of 74*l*. The same successful fruit-grower records that from twenty-six Caufield apple trees, occupying about an acre, he has a full crop every alternate year, and had last season 557 bushels, the best hand-picked selling at 8*s.* a barrel of three bushels, the remainder, disposed of for cider at 1*s*. 3*d*. to 1*s*. 8*d*. per bushel, yielding a total return of 40*l*. per acre. The growth of apples, as of all fruit, steadily extends. Besides a very great home consumption, 1,500,000 barrels of apples in a good year are said to be exported from New York alone. New Jersey State produces splendid peaches, but they are not so largely and generally cultivated as on the peninsula of Delaware and Maryland, where, in the prolific season of 1876, it is estimated that upwards of 7,000,000 baskets were gathered. Currants are usually an easily grown and good paying crop. They thrive even on heavy clays. They are usually planted on land prepared for potatoes, are set out 4 feet by 5, and potatoes planted between the rows. The sets cost $5 per 100. In the second year potatoes or beans are again grown in the intervening spaces. In the third year each bush is expected to produce 1 lb. to 1½ lbs. of fruit, saleable at 6 cents per lb. When in full bearing 3 lbs per bush is reached, which, allowing 1,200 bushes for the half acre, would realise $216, or at the rate of 95*l*. an acre.

The New Jersey State Agricultural Report for 1878 publishes the following particulars of the successful growth of strawberries by Mr. P. T. Quinn of Newark:— After a crop of early rose potatoes, heavily manured, dug, and marketed in the end of July and beginning of August 1877, furrows half-a-yard apart and 4 to 5 inches deep were opened with the plough. Between August 15 and 22 strawberry plants of the Charles Downing and Green Prolific sorts were set in these furrows 15 to 18 in. apart; weeds were kept down by two turns of the cultivator between the rows and twice hoeing. In December the plants were covered with a light, well-decomposed compost, made of sweepings of the vegetable and fish markets and some horse manure. Towards the middle of April the coarse portions of the manure were raked from the plants and left between the rows: salted hay was laid under the now luxuriant leaves to prevent undue evaporation from the soil, and to keep the fruit clean. The yield of strawberries was 5,487 quarts, the gross receipts were $795·61. Deducting commission and expenses of picking, the net returns for the acre were $626·60 or 125*l*. In 1879 equally good results were obtained. Mr. Henry Jerolaman, Irvington, Essex county, applies about 40 tons farm manure to his dark strong loam on the usual yellow clay substratum, sets out Durands and Boyden No. 30 strawberry plants, 3 feet apart and 1 foot from each other in the rows, keeps down weeds with horse and hand hoe, applies for winter covering protecting nutrient mulch, and obtained in 1878 from 1 acre 231 sq. feet. 4,568 quarts of superior strawberries, disposed of at 1*s.* per quart, and realising 225*l.* New York, like other cities, is most bountifully supplied with strawberries. During the height of the season, chiefly from New Jersey State, from Delaware, and the New England States, 10,000 bushels are sometimes received in one day.

Cranberries are largely and increasingly grown in New Jersey State. Low-lying moist ground is selected and usually flooded in the winter. One prosperous grower has his best crops in an old mill pond which he floods throughout the winter, running off the water early in May. 300 to 600 bushels of the long-shaped bell berry are obtained.

Grapes, often of the Concord variety, are grown on trellises about 5 ft. high, the rows 3 ft. apart. Compost is applied liberally in winter, weeds are carefully cut or pulled, but cultivation is avoided, as it injures the roots. Some of the prize lots of $\frac{1}{4}$ of an acre yield 1,500 lbs. and sell at 2*d.* per lb.

From these American successes useful home lessons are surely deducible. The American of a certain type has an instinctive aversion to the pursuit of an unprofitable calling; he has a wonderful capacity for accommodating himself to circumstances. If wheat-growing does not pay, he tries dairying or gardening, and, failing that, will cut down lumber or split rails, keep a store, or 'run a hotel,' or even make politics his profession. A successful New York merchant, referring to the readiness of the race, exclaimed the other day, 'I guess if a thoroughbred Yankee gets into a tea-kettle, he pretty quick kicks a hole and lets himself out.' Such extraordinary smartness and versatility are scarcely to be expected of those 'not to the manner born.' But British farmers certainly are not compelled to pursue unprofitable practices. They need not go out of their own vocation; they cannot cultivate the profusion and variety of vegetables and fruit produced in America; they may find it difficult to keep themselves and families and clear regularly, as many of the Long Island 'trucksters' do, 100*l.* a year from ten acres of vegetables and fruit; but they can profitably grow many of these useful articles, and the demand for them well deserves to be encouraged as a means of increasing the health and advancing the sobriety of the British public.

CHAPTER VIII.

FARMING IN THE NEW ENGLAND STATES.

TRAVELLING from New York to Boston, a distance of 240 miles, by way of Newhaven, Hartford, Springfield, and Worcester, ample evidence is obtained of the industrial prosperity of these and other thriving cities. Mills and factories are running full time; the unemployed labour which was common during 1878 and the earlier months of 1879 is absorbed; most firms have orders booked which will keep them occupied for months; and it is reported that several houses which were wont to take Government work have demurred to send in tenders, on the plea that they have as much general business as they can profitably overtake. It is well that these iron, textile, and other industries are prospering, for this seaboard portion of the New England States is not of high agricultural importance. The limestone and granite rocks are thinly covered by a poor soil; great boulders dot the surface, as they do on the Scottish and Cumberland mountains. The pleasantly undulating country is varied by lakes, rivers, and huge arms of the sea, and abundantly clothed with moderate-sized, sometimes with poor, scrubby timber, including oak, elm, and the various firs familiar at home. The timber is chiefly used for firewood. Neither winged nor four-footed game are found in the woods. Fences seldom enclose this line of railway, which passes unprotected along the streets of towns and villages, by country roads, and through unenclosed plantations, the boom of the loud bell or the hoarse screech of the engine whistle warning away trespassers. The houses in the villages and on the farms are small, mostly built of wood, and annually lime-washed, to protect them from the glaring summer sun, which is also kept out of the rooms by green-painted Venetian blinds.

Reclaimed from the woods or taken up along the river banks are scattered here and there small farms, which are often under 20, and rarely exceed 50 acres. The fields, usually 4 or 5 acres, not always very symmetrically shaped, are enclosed by rudely-built low walls, made with the stones so superabundantly piled about. Indeed, in such profusion are these stones, that a man industriously gathering and grubbing them up, if he clears an acre is said to require another acre on which to run them! Indian corn is the crop chiefly cultivated; wheat, oats, and small patches of turnips and potatoes are occasionally seen; clover and timothy grass are grown, and thrive for several years. Around the house is usually a small garden, not always as tidy or productive as it should be, and often flanked by a few fruit trees, seldom worthy the title of an orchard. About the farm premises and in the valleys are portions of permanent grass, mown for hay and subsequently grazed.

often in want of draining, and seldom made the best of. As in England, a good deal of the hay, notwithstanding the use of the canvas caps for the cocks, has been spoilt by rain and flood. The chief business of these small farmers is the production of milk and butter, which are disposed of in the neighbouring towns and villages, the milk bringing 1½$d.$ a quart, the butter 9$d.$ or 10$d.$ a lb. The cows are nondescripts, often with a considerable dash of Holstein, and susceptible of much improvement, whether as producers of milk or of beef. A few goats and pigs are kept; but during the 500 miles travelling *en route* to Boston and back to New York by one of the coast lines I never saw a sheep, although a great deal of the light land appears more adapted for sheep than for cattle. As already indicated, the greater part of this district is poor and sterile, and even under the best agricultural management, and although generally owned by the occupiers, the land will never yield very satisfactory returns; while the more promising industries in the towns and the farms of the west attract the best of the young men.

Nearing Boston the land is more bountiful, the farming better, the farmers more prosperous: several assure me that their average annual profits run from 10 to 15 per cent.; in this calculation household expenses are generally placed against their own personal labours. In a zone extending from 30 to 60 miles around the intellectual capital of America, as Boston is sometimes styled, ordinary farming lands are still to be bought at $15 to $25. Few farms reach 60 acres, many are not half that area; most are owned by their occupiers, and are devoted to the production of milk, butter, poultry, and eggs, and occasionally vegetables. The farmer and his family do most of the work; hired labour is uncommon. The household lives mainly on what is produced on the farm; expenses for butcher's meat, groceries, and clothes are not greater than those of an English agricultural labourer; but, unless in sickness, not a cent is spent upon beer, wine, or spirits; any cider made is sold. But with all their thrift, the milk farmers lately have not done well. Milk, and indeed all dairy produce, has been lower than at any period for thirty years. During summer, when their supplies are at their height, prices fall sometimes as low as 1d. per quart, owing to the town dealers being overstocked. The most hopeful relief of this state of matters is the introduction of separators, such as those used by the Aylesbury Dairy Company, London, or the somewhat similar apparatus being perfected in America. If the unsold milk is passed through these separators the thick cream, of which the last particles are extracted, is in an admirable condition for butter-making, whilst the skim milk, deprived of its spores and green slimy albuminoid matters, has its keeping properties improved. Waste is thus in great part averted and a better price consequently afforded for the milk. In many localities throughout the New England States, as well as elsewhere in America, following on the tracks of the cheese factories, butter factories or creameries are established, are furnished with skilful managers and modern appliances, handle the milk to the best advantage at a cost of 1 cent per quart; turn out a uniform high quality of butter, and pay farmers 1½ cents for every quart of milk they send in. To some of these establishments the cream only is forwarded, the skim milk being usually reserved for home use amongst calves and pigs.

In the distribution of milk and cream in Boston and New York, glass and porcelain jars and bottles, with stoppers and caps, are coming into use, as they have done in Paris. They are more easily cleansed than the metal cans, and the milk kept in them is less apt to sour.

The most successful dairymen are thoroughly alive to the importance of liberal management. They provide big barns in which are kept from November until April, not only the fodder but the live stock of the farm. These ungainly erections, very similar throughout all parts of the States, have often a foundation of stone or brick carried up a few feet from the ground, occasionally reaching as high as the first storey, the upper portions are built of boards; on the principals of the roof boards are nailed, on which are tacked shingles, made of parallelograms of thin wood about the size of ordinary roofing slates. These barns run from 60 to 200 feet long, 40 to 50 feet wide, and 40 to 60 feet high. In Massachusetts and various Eastern States under all, or a part, of the barn there is usually a cellar 6 to 8 feet high into which the manure is passed, and in which the pigs are kept. The ground floor partitioned into stalls and pens is occupied by cattle, horses, and sometimes sheep. With about 10 feet of head room on stout wooden supports, comes another floor reached from outside by a raised roadway, and into which loaded waggons are driven, and fodder, roots, and other food are stored and thrown as required down shoots to the animals beneath. In the larger barns communication between the several stories is effected by a rude staircase or by ladders. An inside casing of boards several inches from the outer wall is sometimes provided to keep out the biting frost and keen winds. Lumber is sensibly said to be cheaper than fodder. The cattle, and especially the milking cows in the severe winter which continues here from November to April, cannot thrive without warmth. Ventilation of the cattle pens and piggeries is secured by cylinders of boards 2 to 3 feet in calibre extending to the eaves sometimes with a diaphragm within them.

Hay costing $7 to $10 per ton of 2,000 lbs., and corn stalks worth about one-third that price, are the staple winter fodder for cows, the daily allowance ranging from 12 to 30 lbs. To those in full milk eight or ten quarts of cut mangel and swedes or purple turnips are given. Two quarts of oat or corn meal are usually allowed twice a day. This is considered a fair dietary for Ayrshires and Jerseys giving 12 to 20 quarts of milk. Bigger Shorthorn grades stand more forcing, and, where hay and roots are scarce, liberal supplies of concentrated food are used. Many Massachusetts dairymen give such cows when in full milk 12 to 14 lbs. daily of a mixture of oatmeal, shorts bought at $16 per ton, and cotton cake at $26. In winter the cattle are usually watered twice daily, when they drink rather less at a time than if water is given only once, and hence they are not so liable to suffer from chill. In some localities they are turned out of the barns for an hour or two in fine weather.

The summer pastures are helped by corn and cake, and by cut ryegrass, Hungarian millet, and green Indian corn, which when liberally manured produces several tons an acre of valuable fodder used chiefly throughout August and September. The cows are generally shorthorn grades; some herds have a good deal of Jersey and Guernsey blood; others a strong infusion of Ayrshire, said to be specially suitable for cheesemaking; others have conspicuous black and white Holstein markings. Most dairymen can tell you the weight of their cows, which they generally have scaled once a month. A record is often kept of the milk each cow yields. A very ordinary milker produces 1,800 quarts a year, or during her ten months' service. The Wanshakum and Miles herds of Ayrshires, of which a record has been kept respectively for eight and three years, have given overhead an annual yield of upwards of 2,500 quarts, whilst several good Jersey herds vary in their annual production from 2,200 to 2,300 quarts per cow per annum. The yield of butter from each cow per week throughout the height of the season is 9 lbs. to 10 lbs.; 300 lbs. should be produced in the year. Careful managers once or twice in the season test the amount of butter which each cow produces. These weighings and measurings, troublesome as they may appear to a

British dairyman, afford much valuable, practical, profitable information. Selection is improving the milking capabilities of many herds. Without fresh purchases of cows, by breeding only from the best milkers, many farmers within ten years have doubled the butter got from each cow. Milking is done at 5 A.M. and 5 P.M. Deep tin setting pans are generally preferred; in summer are often set on a floor laved with running water, keeping down the temperature to 50°, and in winter are placed in the cellar, which is essential in all American houses for tempering extremes of summer heat and winter cold. The cream is taken off generally in twenty-four hours and churned usually in the ordinary dash churn twice a week. An ounce of salt is added to every 3 lbs of butter. During winter the finest qualities bring 2s. per pound and occasionally more. Vermont butter, especially that from the Green Mountains, has the highest reputation throughout New England. The successful dairyman takes pains to keep the milk house at all seasons at 55° and scrupulously clean, and when the butter is being made up, to get rid by washing and often by the use of wooden paddles of every particle of milk.

Increasing attention is paid to sheep, of which Massachusetts musters 61,000, most of them of diversified character. They are now cultivated for mutton as well as for wool. The coarser wools are thrice as numerous as the fine. Notwithstanding the expense of housing or yarding during winter, necessary for protection from cold and wet, the flocks when properly

Sheep Management. 93

managed yield good profits, which might be still larger but for the numbers of unowned and dangerous dogs, which kill or seriously maim about 2,000 sheep annually. During winter the flock receives hay or good corn stalks night and morning, a few roots and half a pound of corn, or a mixture of corn meal, cotton seed meal, and a few oats. Sheep consume about 3 per cent. of live weight daily. Properly selected and fed they are expected to add 25 per cent. to their weight in four months. They generally go to grass late in April, cotton seed meal and corn are still sometimes supplied upon the pasture. They clip 4 to 5 lbs. of wool worth about 30 cents per lb. Near the cities a considerable number of early lambs are reared, realising $4 to $6 if brought out in May or June, but double that price if ready for Easter. Six months' winter feeding of ewes is estimated to cost $2·50. The summer keep, including salt-washing and shearing, is covered by $1. The estimated profit of breeding, and feeding over the whole flock of Massachusetts is stated to vary from $12 to $15 per head per annum, but many smart managers are believed to make more.[1]

Very good Berkshire pigs and middle-sized Chester Whites with a few Magie or Poland Chinas, are met with. They graze the orchards or pastures, clear up the refuse vegetables of the market gardens, and when it is desired to finish them off receive several pounds daily of corn meal, with occasionally a few oats or some barley. One bushel of corn meal is

[1] Report of Massachusetts Board of Agriculture, 1878, p. 304.

estimated to make 10 lbs. of pork, and when corn is 60 cents a bushel, bacon and pork to be profitable should realise 6 cents per lb. Placing a moderate value on the manure, New England farmers expect that the fodder and corn used in stock feeding pays twice its ordinary market value. The liberal management of the live stock, their enforced winter housing, and the judicious use of the manure made, as Mr. Mechi wisely insists, under cover, secures here, as elsewhere, satisfactory returns of grain and hay. The restorative treatment gives the New England farmers better returns than their brethren in the Middle or Western States. It is only in Massachusetts, Rhode Island, and Connecticut that the annual average of the farm crops reaches 4*l.* an acre. In New York State they are 2*l.* 13*s.*; in Kentucky 2*l.* 4*s.*; in Missouri and Kansas 1*l.* 12*s.*

Vegetable and fruit gardens flourish where there are good markets, good soil, and abundant capital. These three favourable conditions concur in the neighbourhood of Boston. Within six miles of this fine old aristocratic city are admirably managed market-gardens, worth 250*l.* per acre, employing capital to the extent of 100*l.* an acre, applying 20 to 30 cords of rich town manure, and producing all round an average yield of 200*l.* an acre. Mr. William D. Philbrick, of Newton Centre, thus describes the cropping of these gardens:[1] 'The vegetables mostly grown are spinach, kale, radish, dandelions, beet-greens, beets, early cabbages, lettuce, onions, to be followed upon the

[1] Massachusetts Agricultural Report for 1877 and 1878.

same land by the late crops, which are melons, squashes, eggplant, peppers, cauliflowers, celery, horseradish, beets, carrots, and parsnips. The only crops which occupy the land for the whole year are rhubarb and dandelions; and some gardeners grow a crop of onions set on the same land with their dandelions. In the management of these various crops so as to meet a profitable sale, and also not to crowd and injure each other, the skill and experience of the gardener are shown. To accomplish his purpose many ingenious devices are used for forcing early crops and for storing late ones; so as to keep up an unfailing supply the year round. In general only two crops are raised upon the same land in a season; but instances are not uncommon where three and even four crops a year are taken from one piece of land; thus winter spinach sold in March was followed by onions, sets, melons, and celery on the same land, all full crops; again, winter spinach sold in April, was followed by bush beans, melons, and spinach again.'

Success mainly depends on careful selection, usually of home-grown seed, on heavy manuring, skill in devising cheap effectual hot-beds for forcing early crops, the management of celery pits and spinach houses, the careful storing of roots and plants in winter, and dexterity and tidiness in packing for market. The demand for almost every description of vegetables and fruits steadily grows. Massachusetts is believed to produce 200,000 bushels of tomatoes, and 400,000 bunches of asparagus;

part of which are cheaply grown under field culture and kept clean by horse as well as hand hoeing. In a good season her 3,500,000 bushels of apples are worth 300,000*l*. New varieties both of apples and pears are being cultivated to take the place of the good old sorts which are degenerating. In many directions strawberries are largely cultivated. Around Norfolk-Vermont their production sometimes reaches 3,000,000 quarts a year, employing 10,000 pickers. One grower has 185 acres. In Boston alone there is received throughout the season 20,000 bushels of this fine fruit.

Hops, a few years ago, were an important crop in some of the New England States, which raised nearly 1,000,000 lbs.:[1] but for several seasons they have not paid, and production, as in England, is decreasing. The old yards running out in many quarters are not replaced. The total acreage approximates that of England, which in 1879 was given at 67,671 acres. The State of New York in 1877 was believed to have 36,000 acres, and to produce 20,000,000 lbs. Wisconsin comes next in hop cultivation, and although the growth is considerably restricted, especially owing to low price and attacks of lice, the yield is believed to reach 4,000,000 lbs. At Madison, New York, the average cost of raising hops is stated to be 12 to 14 cents per pound. The average yield ranges from 300 to 800 lbs. Prices during the last few years have been irregular and unsatisfactory, varying from 10 to

[1] Report of the Statisticians, Agricultural Department, for 1879, p. 276. Washington.

15 cents, and not paying the cost of production. Indeed in some yards the low price has caused growers to leave the crop unpicked. The statistician of the department of agriculture, Washington, in his report for 1878, remarks that a convention of hop-growers in New England appointed three different committees to estimate the average cost of producing hops. 'Committee No. 1 allowed $100 per acre for the average value of the land; cost of poles, fertilisers, and cartage, $44·10: labour in cultivation, $18; harvesting and curing, $64·36; insurance and marketing, $11·83; boxes &c., $2·98; total, $141·27. A crop of 1,000 lbs. would at such a rate average $14\frac{1}{8}$ cents per pound. Committee No 2, allowing $80 per acre as the value of the land, estimated the average cost of 1,000 lbs. at $12\frac{1}{4}$ cents. Committee No. 3 at $100 per acre, and with a yield of 800 lbs., made the average cost $12\frac{1}{8}$ cents per pound. The average total cost of producing hops in Kent, England, is estimated by a local authority at 5*l*., or $24. 30 per cwt. (not quite 22 cents per pound).'—P. 278.

Owing to diminished production, the export of hops, which in 1877 amounted to 95,000 bales, has now fallen to less than one-third; but the deficit in the home growth has been in part made up by importations from Bavaria.

Maine, the most north-easterly State of the Union, appears to keep well in the van of agricultural improvements. She has a State college, where gratuitous instruction in the principles of agriculture is given to youths born in the State; and where outsiders have similar advantages at very moderate charges. At experimental stations on the best German plans, investigations are conducted as to manures, varieties of seed and culture, and the relative value of feeding stuffs. Agricultural, horticultural, and pomological societies are doing good work. Interesting reports recording observations and progress are published annually. Besides creameries, there are throughout the State sixty cheese factories, some of them in operation during six months of the year, extracting 1 lb. of cheese from 8·75 lbs. to 10·5 lbs. of milk, and disposing of the produce at 11 cents to 14 cents per pound. The cows of the State are enumerated at 170,000; the other cattle at 202,000. The State has 3,000,000 acres of improved land, and about the same amount of unimproved. The farms, which average 98 acres, are worth about $110,000,000, or 30 per cent. more than they were in 1860. The average value of the crops as set forth by the statistical returns is fully $12 per acre, or about double the value of the yield in such Western States as Iowa and Nebraska. English practices and opinions prevail. Liberal good management is alone believed to pay. Not only is the home-made manure taken care of, but ashes, fish-scraps, bones from the glue and soap works, and concentrated fertilisers are in use. The general tendency is to plough less, graze more, and improve the grass land. Good breeding and care all the year round are the precepts inculcated by their successful dairymen.

The summer pastures with little trouble pay best, but a good deal of winter dairying is now practised;

the cows being warmly kept in barns, receiving 10 lbs. to 15 lbs. of hay, which should be cut early in July, a peck of roots, with several pounds of bran, oatmeal, or cotton cake. The best managers feed liberally, and declare that the more you pour into a good cow the more she pours into the bucket, and the more goes into the dairyman's pocket. Cows well fed, from 10 lbs. of milk produce 1 lb. of butter; 9·2 lbs. of milk produce 1 lb. of cheese. At a meeting of the Maine Dairymen's Association, Mr. H. M. Smith Orrington, who sells his milk at Bangor, gives the following account of his operations:[1]—' He keeps from twelve to fifteen cows, and feeds 4 quarts of shorts, and 2 quarts of cotton-seed-meal per cow daily, in two feeds, with extra early cut hay. He uses green food all summer, planting fodder-corn in large quantities, which he never wants to become over six feet high. His cows produce 3½ gallons of milk per day. His dry cows he feeds but half the above quantity of meal. Early in the spring he burns off the dead grass in his pastures as the grass starts, and on such spots the cows obtain their first feed, the ashes stimulating the growth of grass. His choice for cows is a cross of the Shorthorn and Jersey. His cows go dry two months. Upon an average in the year it costs $60 to keep a cow, and her income will average $110. His milk sells from 6 cents to 7 cents per quart. His provender is fed dry. Mr. Flanders said his cows fed on good hay would give from 20 lbs. to 22 lbs. of milk per day. Leonard Robinson considers that dairy-

[1] Twenty-third Annual Report of Maine Board of Agriculture, p. 112.

ing during the past thirty-five years had been the most profitable business with him. He top-dresses his land, using five cords per acre, once in three years. He thinks highly of oat and pea meal as a feed.'

Fewer trotting horses and more cattle and sheep, it is said, should be reared. The sheep, usually graded Merinos with varying admixture of Cotswold and Down, during winter are generally housed and get oat straw, a few roots, and the feeding flock some meal and fish pomace, which they soon learn to eat. Too many unowned dogs are stated to roam on some districts, disturbing and sometimes killing the sheep. Wages, which previously have been high throughout the New England States, during the period of depression from 1876 to 1879 fell 25 per cent. In Maine agricultural labourers hired by the month receive $18·25 without board, $11·08 with board. Temporary hands get a dollar without board, and about half as much more in harvest. Carpenters, blacksmiths, and other artisans earn from $1·40 to $1·47 per day. The estimated cost of growing wheat in Aristook county [1] is 25 cents per bushel, barley 35, oats 25, potatoes from 12 to 24 cents according to season; hay carted to the barn cost $3 to $4.

Freedom in America, as in well-ordered old countries, is hedged about by reasonable restrictions, and hurtful licence is jealously guarded against. In Maine and other New England States, every farmer is bound to keep in good order his fences, generally consisting of rails or stone walls. Fence-viewers are

[1] Twenty-third Annual Report of Maine Board of Agriculture for 1878, p. 155.

Laws as to Sale of Portable Manures. 101

appointed, to whom appeal can be made against careless neighbours, and who are bound to see that repairs are promptly done. Animals straying are impounded; trespassers are punished; the wilful or malicious killing, wounding, maiming, disfiguring, or poisoning of any domestic animal is visited by imprisonment or fine. The State enacts stringent laws against adulteration and sophistication of all articles of food. Beef, flour, and other commodities in bags or barrels must be branded according to quality. Standards of weight are fixed for the sale of all produce. No hay can be trussed and sold without the grower's name and place of abode being distinctly marked upon it. All portable manures sold at more than 1 cent per lb. and put up in bags of 50 lbs. or upwards must have specified on a printed label the maker's name and address, and the percentage they contain of soluble phosphoric acid, insoluble phosphoric acid, and ammonia. For any mis-statement the vendor is liable to a fine of $10 for the first and $20 for subsequent offences; and any purchaser receiving manure which does not come up to the specified standard is entitled to recover compensation. British farmers would gain by such a guarantee of the manure they purchase, and by enactments punishing fraudulent vendors.

Boston, like most other American cities, is well provided with markets. The meat is forwarded from the Brighton abattoirs, which also furnish supplies for Portsmouth, Concord, Manchester and other adjacent towns. Here 3,000 to 5,000 beasts and as many sheep are slaughtered every week. Several of the salesmen kill for exportation. Some of the cattle are useful and well fed, showing a large amount of short-horn character, weighing on the hoof 1,400 to 1,500 lbs., and forwarded from Illinois and Ohio. Others, chiefly of Texan extraction, have a great predominance of horn, thick hide and offal, and stand much in need of grading up. Their price varies according to quality from $4\frac{1}{2}$ to 5 cents per lb. ($2d.$ to $2\frac{1}{2}d.$) live weight. Kentucky sheep, from 130 to 150 lbs. live weight, or reaching about 20 lbs. a quarter dressed, constitute about 7 per cent. of the mutton supplies, and bring nearly $1d.$ per lb. more than the poor scraggy Merinos or half-breds, which average about 4 cents live weight. The best Kentucky, Ohio, and Canadian sheep, which are generally superior grades having several crosses of Cotswold, Leicester, of Down on Merinos or native breeds, average 6 cents live weight, and, as at home, the dressed weight is about four-sevenths of the live weight. Good lambs, from June 1 to July 1, are worth 8 cents ($4d.$), and later in the season fall to 7 cents.

At the Brighton abattoirs everything is handy and well arranged; the water-supply is abundant; refrigerating chambers preserve the meat for exportation or home use. The fat, assorted according to quality, is milled in large vats. The shin-bones, after extraction of their oil, and the hoofs, are exported to Europe for making buttons. Cattle hoofs, in growing demand for making other dress ornaments as well as buttons, now sell at $50 per ton. The blood, refuse, and bones, after digestion, are transferred to an adjacent building and converted into Stockbridge fertilizers; a great chimney gets rid of all disagreeable odours. For the refuse materials Messrs. Bowker & Co. pay the Abattoir Co. 8,000*l.* a year. Here, as at most of the stock-yards, dogs are little used. For moving the beasts the drivers use long sticks and whips, whilst the sheep are led from the cars and guided into pens, or wherever required, by docile flock leaders, picked specimens of their own race, whose readiness and intelligence belie the common belief that all sheep are either stupid or wayward.

Besides the meat consigned from the Brighton slaughter-houses, a large amount, of which no record seems to be kept, is forwarded to the Boston market from Chicago and also from New York. In the city markets beef sells from 6*d.* to 10*d.* per pound; the butchers here as elsewhere complain that inferior cuts are in such indifferent demand that a clearance has to be made at very low prices. Mutton brings from 4*d.* to 8*d.*; superior Canada and Kentucky hams fetch 6*d.* In the principal shops prices are, however, 25 to 30 per cent. higher. The best butter is forwarded from the factories, and during summer brings on an average 1*s.* per pound.

The winter price sometimes reaches 2*s.* The receipts of butter in Boston market during 1879 amounted to 750,000 packages, one-tenth being boxes 8 to 12 lbs. weight, the remainder averaging 50 lbs. each; 230,000 boxes of cheeses were forwarded averaging 58 lbs. These supplies, some of them drawn from creameries and factories 1,000 miles distant, besides supplying the city, are distributed to various parts of the State; about one-sixth of the butter and one-third of the cheese are exported, and these exports are steadily increasing.

Railroad cars kept cool with ice chambers are in general use for forwarding not only butter but the finer fruits for long distances. The vegetable and fruit markets are profusely furnished with an astonishing quantity, quality, and variety. Grapes, peaches, melons, and pears in their season are abundant and cheap; half a bushel of peaches is procured for a couple of shillings. On stands at almost every street corner, as well as in shops, at railway stations, and in the trains themselves, fruit is offered for sale, and the chief purchasers are the labouring classes. Owing to the great and growing taste for good vegetables and fruit, which has enormously increased throughout America during the past ten years, market gardening and fruit culture have paid better than most other departments of farming. Early supplies come from Florida and the sunny States laved by the warm waters of the Mexican gulf, which begin to forward strawberries in April, while Maine, in the north, contributes hers in July; and throughout this vast continent, with its varied climate and circumstances, some portion is enjoying its harvest season and distributing its surplus to customers hundreds of miles distant.

CHAPTER IX.

PENNSYLVANIA FARMING.

THE Pennsylvania railroad, starting from New Jersey city and running west 354 miles to Pittsburg, with its many branches, covers about 5,000 miles, and is in direct communication with the Great Western and Southern roads. The main line is thoroughly ballasted three feet deep to prevent disturbance from frost; the sharp curves, astounding to English travellers, are very safely negotiated by the long, heavy cars; over the light bridges the pace is always moderated; the travelling is smooth and easy, reaching on the main line 35 miles an hour. The trains are now well-filled and very punctual; once a week or oftener a line indicator car is run, and by means of ingeniously arranged wheels and indicators, on a sheet of paper, on a scale of 4 ft. to the mile, is accurately pencilled the condition of the permanent way. An ill-laid or started rail infallibly makes its mark on the chart, and as the instrument dots every mile, the whereabouts of any fault is thus readily noted.

The Pennsylvania and other great railroads are steadily developing their carrying, wharfage, and storing capabilities. Each year extends their mileage and their business. During ten years they have nearly doubled. Satisfactory as was their trade during 1879, that of the present year greatly exceeds it. Both the east and west bound traffic is increasing. On the four great trunk lines—the Pennsylvania, the New York Central, the Erie, and the Baltimore and Ohio—there has been, during the first eight months of 1880, an increase over the corresponding months of 1879 of 10 to 40 per cent. Under the 'pool' system, which institutes uniform rates and abolishes unfair discriminations, the charges are tolerably satisfactory alike to consigners and to the railways. The increasing steady business handled with the economy inaugurated during bad times is being done with profit. Compared with 1878 the interest paid on the funded debts of American railroads has slightly advanced, now averaging nearly 5 per cent. The average dividend has also improved, reaching 2½ per cent. Such results point to economy in running expenses. It is got out of more business better done. Freights all round are cheaper than they were a few years ago. The Pennsylvania, for example, which has the heaviest goods traffic of the American lines, moved 9,211,234 tons of freight in 1873, earning $19,608,555, In 1879 its goods tonnage grew to 13,680,041, but the earnings from the goods traffic declined to $17,017,080. It earned 1·41 cent per ton per mile then, it earns 0·79 cent now. The experience of the other lines is about the same.

About New Jersey City the land lies flat and low for several miles: the country is wet and swampy, producing mainly sedges and poor grass. Soon, however, it becomes more undulating and better wooded; straight, wide roads are tidily enclosed with stout rail fences. For 25 miles, until approaching New Brunswick city, the light red marl soil is mainly in plantation and scrub; not one-tenth of the land is cultivated; the sparse crops are poor; a few dairy cattle and young horses are on the pastures. Milk-selling, which is started here with a very restricted capital and the purchase of a few cows at 7*l.* or 8*l.* a piece, is the chief farming. This is not at all a favourable aspect of New Jersey State, but proceeding south-west the soil becomes deeper, drier, and more productive. The fields are symmetrical, usually measuring six to eight acres, enclosed with post and railing and occasionally with hedges. The Indian corn, reaching 4 or 5 feet high, is (Sept. 15) being cut and shocked. With active horses, such as at home are used for van or omnibus purposes, the wheat stubbles and clover leas are being ploughed; a single plough, drawn by a pair of horses or mules 16 hands high, turns a wide furrow about 4 inches deep, and overtakes an average of two acres daily. Wheat is being drilled; a bushel to a bushel and a quarter is the usual seeding; in some fields the wheat is up and already looking well; potatoes are being ploughed up. Near Trenton, the capital of New Jersey State, is Mr. Smith's stud farm, conspicuous with its nicely-arranged, commodious buildings, large fields, and tidy, clean cultivation, and doing good service by the breeding and distribution of superior male animals.

Near Bristol, Pennsylvania is entered—one of the richest of the Eastern States, with a history of more than a hundred years. Of a tolerably perfect rectangular shape, about 360 miles long and 200 broad, its western counties are the thriving strongholds of the coal and iron trade, while in the north among the Alleghanies flow the oil wells, which discharge their unsavoury treasure so bountifully that the oil is not worth on the spot over a cent a gallon. Although Pennsylvania embraces an area of 29,440,000 acres, not one-sixth of it is under tillage. Even here, so near the Atlantic seaboard, amidst a settled population, there is plenty of land which might be brought into cultivation and much more susceptible of improvement. The agricultural returns indicate that this State produces 1,473,000 acres of wheat, with an average acreable yield, however, of less than 15 bushels; 1,259,000 acres Indian corn, yielding 35 bushels per acre; 1,166,000 acres oats, bulking 32 bushels; 245,300 acres of rye, casting only 15 bushels; 26,050 acres barley, giving 26 bushels; 154,500 acres are devoted to potatoes, producing 70 bushels per acre, grown at much less cost than in Great Britain, and usually selling at 1*s.* 6*d.* to 2*s.* per bushel; 2,650,000 acres are mown for hay, and 19,000 acres are devoted to tobacco. The number of milk cows is figured at 828,400; the number of oxen and other cattle is the same; the average price of cattle is 7*l.*; sheep exceed 1,500,000, and are valued at 12*s.* each; there are nearly 1,000,000 hogs, worth about 28*s.* each. The population of Pennsylvania being at present about 4,000,000, the State could annually supply each of her citizens with about $5\frac{1}{2}$ bushels of

Vegetable and Dairy Farms.

wheat, 11 bushels of Indian corn, 9 bushels of oats, with fully 2½ bushels of potatoes: if all the tobacco were used at home, it would give 4½ lbs. per capita; the produce of the cows would represent a liberal daily allowance of nearly 2 quarts of milk; while the other cattle and sheep would contribute nearly a pound of meat daily. For each unit of the population, the hogs would further supply nearly one-third of a pound of bacon or pork daily. Pennsylvania may therefore be regarded as producing more than she requires for her own support.

Around Philadelphia the soil is a kindly working loam 15 to 20 inches deep, some of it 3 feet, generally on a clay subsoil interspersed with marl and limestone rock, requiring little drainage and that little being done with pipes or stones and at the depth of 2 to 4 feet. Vegetable farms are common, varying from 10 to 50 acres. Twenty or more different sorts of vegetables in their seasons are raised, chiefly for the Philadelphia markets. These market-gardeners own the land, manure it liberally, keep it as clean as the best gardens at Hitchin or Evesham, pay 4*s.* or 5*s.* per day for the men they require, and about half that for the women; but the day's work generally extends to 12 hours. Many farms of 70 to 200 acres are occupied in dairying. From some the milk is night and morning brought into the town and disposed of either directly to the customers or to the dealer who distributes it; 3*d.* to 4*d.* per quart is the winter price, 2*d.* to 3*d.* the summer. On other farms butter is the chief object, and some of the finest in America is produced here, the best bringing 20 cents per pound. Cheese is rarely made, except for household use.

The successful butterman usually has a spring-house of solid stone built by the side of the stream. Several inches from the floor, on stone slabs, the shallow vessels, usually made of tin, are filled night and morning with the fresh milk; the water turned on, flows constantly through the house, laving the milk vessels and keeping down the temperature. After twelve hours the milk is skimmed; the cream is still kept in the 'spring-house;' churning is done twice a week; scrupulous cleanliness is observed. The skim-milk is either sold in the town at half the price of the new milk, or is given to the calves or pigs. The cows are usually Channel Islanders or descended from such dams. Black-and-white Holsteiners are also used. As at home, the biggest and best show several crosses of shorthorn, and these not only milk the heaviest, but make afterwards the best carcass of beef. The cows are home-bred, or bought in, usually in the autumn, at 6*l.* to 7*l.* Their winter food consists of corn, flax seed, a little unthrashed corn, hay, and a few roots. The summer fare is grass, with a small quantity of oats and maize. Most of the dairymen give the cows all they grow, excepting a small amount of the wheat and the produce of the orchard. The pigs are generally kept for home use, and with poultry, eggs, vegetables, and abundance of fruit, constitute the farmers' fare. Accounts are not kept, and it is a little difficult in a hurried visit in an utterly new country to ascertain correctly the amount of expences and profits; but, after paying for everything, the dairyman seems to have a net profit of 2*l*. or 3*l*. per acre. I am assured by merchants and bankers in Philadelphia that within a radius of ten miles round the city there are plenty of dairymen who twenty-five years ago began with nothing, but have gradually acquired 80 to 100 acres, and, besides their land and stock, are now worth 2,000*l*. or 3,000*l*. In thus building up comfortable homes and securing a competency, these farmers, many of them from Vermont, have been greatly helped by industrious and thrifty wives. In many of these homely households education and refinement flourish along with laborious toil and careful saving. The young men as they grow up often migrate West, where a small capital acquires more land, where profits are larger, and there is a great margin for advance in the value of landed property.

Mr. J. E. Kingsley, of the Continental Hotel, Philadelphia, besides other business, has within a mile of the city a farm of 950 acres, which is a good type of these milk farms. He has from 60 to 70 cows, which supply daily to the hotel 400 quarts of milk and cream, and admirable butter. The cows are mostly Channel Islanders and crosses with shorthorns. Ten or twelve heifer calves are reared to recruit the herd, making a total cattle stock of 85 to 95. The rich grass is the chief summer food. About 100 acres of grass are mowed, yielding two to three tons of hay, which is the principal winter dietary, the milking cows besides receiving a ration of corn, meal, and bran night and morning. Besides the hay required for the cattle and 14 farm horses, about 100 tons is generally sold at an average of 4*l.* a ton. Thirty acres of Indian corn are grown, and are now being harvested, some being used green for the table, the bulk stacked for the winter food of the cattle, and yielding 150 bushels of corn in the cob, or 70 bushels of shelled corn. Twenty acres are devoted to millet, Hungarian grass, and sugar cane cut for summer foddering. A good deal of bran is used for feeding. Twenty acres are in potatoes and small vegetables used for the hotel. The land appears in too high condition satisfactorily to grow wheat. The 150 acres of pasture, consisting of clover and timothy, is allowed to remain down for four or five years, and when ploughed up is followed by maize. The farm is worked by eight or nine men, their average wages being 4*s.* a day; 25*l.* a week pays all the labour bills, including the foreman and his wife, who look after the cows. Mr. Kingsley and most of his well-to-do neighbours make free use of the best machinery, such as mowing, tedding, and unloading machines.

Even as recently as eight or ten years ago many of these farms were only worth 10*l.* and 12*l.* an acre, but would now realise double that value. I was shown, three miles from the city, a useful dairy-farm of 80 acres, said to have been purchased ten years ago at 15*l.* an acre; it has since been well but not extravagantly managed, has paid its way, and is now regarded as worth double its former purchase-money. Picked farms within five miles of Philadelphia, thoroughly equipped with house and buildings, roads and fences, and much cleaner and in higher manurial

Land free from Taxation.

condition than many are at present in England, may be bought at 30*l.* an acre. On such purchases money can be had to about half the value of the land at 5 to 6 per cent. Nor are investments limited in number or to a narrow area. For 50 miles around Philadelphia, in almost any direction, the land is an easily-worked fertile loam, adapted to any description of farming, well watered, and with reasonable prospect of a steady advance in value.

Land in Pennsylvania rejoices in immunity from taxation. Personal property moderately valued pays at the rate of 30 cents per $100; but the chief revenue is derived from taxing public corporations, stocks, coal companies, foreign and insurance companies, banks, and from succession duties, licences, and a small income tax. The affairs of the State have been wisely and economically managed; its moderate debt is diminishing. Its gratuitous public-school system works admirably, and shows its fruits in the general intelligence and knowledge of every class. Labourers, artisans, and small farmers met with in the cars and elsewhere exhibit more general information and readiness to converse and exchange ideas than people of the same condition in the old country.

The farmers show considerable versatility. Besides dairying, vegetables and fruit growing, and sometimes cultivating tobacco which is extending, many good managers address themselves to buying half-fed or lean cattle at 3*l.* to 4*l.*, feeding them in summer with grass, green oats, or other fodder, or in winter with a little beet or turnips, and with corn and hay, and after four or six months realise double their first cost. Others buy sheep from Ohio, Canada, or elsewhere in the north at 15*s.* to 20*s.* and, feeding them in a similar manner and for about the same period as the bullocks, dispose of them at 20*s.* to 28*s.* Others obtain, usually from flocks which travel eastward from Ohio, common graded Merino ewes at 13*s.* to 20*s.*, place them with a southdown ram, dispose of the lambs in May and June at 16*s.* to 30*s.*, secure about 5*s.* for the fleece of the ewe which speedily follows the lamb, realise several shillings more than cost price, and, besides manure, thus earn a handsome, quickly turned profit. The farmer of this district has a good choice of markets. In Philadelphia beef brings about 10*d.* per lb.; choice mutton, 6*d.*; veal, 8*d.* to 10*d.*; and early lamb, upwards of 1*s.* per lb.

The stock-yards at Philadelphia, as in other American cities, are commodious, contiguous to the railroads, and well managed. Useful cattle are selling at 6 to 7 cents per lb. live weight, ordinary half-bred Merinos and western sheep bring 4 to 5 cents, but well-fed Downs are worth 6 cents per lb. live weight. The stock-yard charges, including lairage and weighing, is 1*s.* 8*d.* for cattle, and 2½*d.* for sheep and pigs. Hay is provided at 1*d.* per lb.

Philadelphia five years ago commenced the export of dead meat to Europe, and Messrs. Martin, Fuller, and Co. are now extensive exporters both of live cattle and of dead meat. Live animals are sent during summer, dead meat is the chief winter trade.

They collect from the grazings of the far West, and from the feeding yards of Illinois, Indiana, and Ohio, good heavy cattle from 1,500 to 1,800 lbs. on the gross. The dead meat they consider pays for export better than live cattle, on which the transport charges are again increasing, 5*l.* per beast being now taken by the best shipping companies, and the heavy landing dues, especially at Southampton and Victoria Docks, London, being complained of as cutting seriously into profits. Their admirable premises at Philadelphia provide for the slaughter of 800 cattle and as many sheep daily; cold storage chambers, kept at a temeperature of 36° to 38° Fahr., economically preserve the meat and the best of the offal whether for home use or for export. The ice usually costs 10*s.* 6*d.* per ton. The carcases for British markets hang in the cold chambers for about forty-eight hours; in refrigerating cars, as yet not introduced in England, they are usually forwarded to New York; 1,000 quarters sewn up in stout calico are sometimes despatched by one steamer. Allowing for all expenses, Messrs. Martin, Fuller, and Co. concur with other shippers in declaring that 'a living profit' is earned if the beef and mutton in this country make. 6*d.* per lb. Owing, however, to glutted markets, they have sometimes, even for a couple of weeks, an unsatisfactory return of less than 5*d.* Pork pays if sold at British ports at 5*d*:

Mr. John Miller Hickory, of Washington County, West Pennsylvania, is the thriving owner of 400 acres of useful land, is superior in education to most of his compeers, a successful breeder of good Devons, and a prize-winning exhibitor at many State fairs. One hundred acres of his farm are in wood, hitherto only used as a source of fencing and fuel. He grows about 40 to 50 acres of Indian corn, which he has reaped towards the middle of September with the prospect of getting 100 bushels an acre of grain in the cob, or half that amount when shelled out. The shelled bushel of corn weighs 56 lbs. The stalks and leaves are the chief winter provender for the cattle. Throughout September and October, the corn stubble is ploughed, oats are sown in early spring, reaped in July, and yield 50 bushels an acre of about 33 lbs. to the bushel. In August the oat stubble is turned over to the depth of three or four inches. Wheat is sown in September, is reaped in July, yields 30 bushels, and is sold usually to dealers, who fetch it at an average of 90 cents. or 3*s.* 9*d.* per bushel. Along with the wheat in autumn timothy grass is sown; when the wheat is harrowed in the succeeding spring, clover is sown. The seeds are mowed in June, produce two and a half to three tons of hay, a second cutting is sometimes taken, and they remain down during three to five years. By the help of machinery, which, like so many American farmers, Mr. Hickroy uses to full advantage, he overtakes the seasonable working of his land with the assistance of four light-limbed, active horses, and three men, the principal of whom has 70*l.* a year, a cottage, and milk; while the other two have each 40*l.* and are boarded. The master, his family, and men live almost entirely on the produce of the farm; their animal food is bacon or pork; they kill an occasional sheep, have plenty of home-raised vegetables and fruit, drink nothing stronger than milk, water, tea, or coffee, are very seldom ill, but pay the doctor an annual retaining fee of $15 (3*l.*), and for this moderate sum command his attendance when required. Besides the few well-bred Devons, 20 ordinary milking cows, repeatedly crossed with Devon bulls, are kept, worth 6*l.* each when five years old, and used for breeding and making a little butter. The heifers produce their first calf when two years old; when longer grace is given they become too fat and breeding is uncertain. The smart steers and heifers, with their compact Devon type, weigh, when fed at three years, 1,200 lbs. on the hoof, and are worth 7*l.* to 8*l.*. With a larger breed more food would obviously be consumed, but considerably heavier weights would be scaled. The sheep stock appears to be more profitable than the cattle. One hundred and fifty Merino ewes produce 120 lambs; some of the selected ram lambs realise 5*l.*; the majority are not worth more than 3*l.*; the ewes do not fetch quite so much, ordinary ungraded stock ewes are not worth more than 20*s.* These Merinos, however, are still prized; they shear 6 lbs. to 7 lbs. of (unwashed) wool, saleable on farm at 1*s.* per pound; the clip becomes heavier as the sheep reach maturity. Some picked Merino hogs have shorn 15 lbs. to 20 lbs. Mr. Hickory had an old ram that produced 37 lbs.; these, however, are unwashed fleeces.

An approximate valuation and balance-sheet bring out the following figures:—

Capital Account.

	£	s.	d.
400 acres with buildings, roads, &c. at £20 .	8,000	0	0
Machinery, implements, and four horses .	1,000	0	0
60 cattle	200	0	0
350 sheep	1,000	0	0
	10,200	0	0

Expenditure.

	£	s.	d.
Interest on capital above detailed, £10,200 at 6 per cent.	612	0	0
Taxes and rates	20	0	0
Labour bills, 3 men	180	0	0
Own labour and superintendence . . .	100	0	0
Incidental expenses	20	0	0
Balance excess of income over expenditure .	8	18	9
	940	18	9

Income.

	£	s.	d.
Wheat, 45 acres, yielding 25 bushels at 3s. 9d.	210	18	9
Wool	130	0	0
120 sheep	400	0	0
20 cattle	140	0	0
Butter, poultry, hay, &c.	60	0	0
	940	18	9

This represents a meagre money profit: but planting fruit trees, draining, and other improvements have increased expenses without bringing as yet any adequate returns. On many farms Mr. Hickory believes as much produce might be got from 250 acres as he gets from 300 acres. While supporting himself and his family, he is, however, satisfied that consuming so large a proportion of his produce—

keeping so much stock and taking care of the manure —is steadily adding to the value of his property, which represents 1,000*l.* more than it would have done five years ago. In thus building up the value of their farms the profits of many good Pennsylvanian agriculturists are in great part invested.

During ten days, beginning September 8, 1879, in the Centennial buildings in the large and beautiful Fairmount Park, amid permanent art and manufacture exhibits, the Pennsylvania Agricultural Society held its annual show. A couple of hundred horses were collected, comprising several indifferent Clydesdales, a handsome Percheron stallion, owned by D. Walters, of Baltimore, well-bred sires for general purposes which did not reach a very high standard, and some useful mares, foals, and yearlings adapted for carriage or quick farm work. The cattle included pedigree shorthorns in good condition forwarded by Mr. D. Selsor, London, Ohio; half a score of smart, shapely, Bates-looking bulls and cows contributed by Mr. L. H. Long and Son, Mason County, Kentucky, descended from good sorts bred and imported by Mr. Abraham Renick and Mr. R. A. Alexander; and a number of superior grade shorthorns—that is, cattle not qualified by four crosses of pure blood for entry in the American herd-book. These shorthorn grades are rapidly extending and improving, and their size, weight, and good thriving testify how the general western stock may be steadily improved. Ten shorthorn-graded oxen, mostly roan, weighing on hoof 1,600 lbs. and selected from a lot of

64, were exhibited by the butcher who had bought them in Ohio, and would have done credit to any English agricultural show. In a dairy district Channel Islanders, as might be expected, mustered in force, and with grades contributed upwards of 100 entries; there were a dozen Ayrshires, the same number of black and white Holsteiners, and some very useful Devons, belonging to Mr. J. M. Hickory and Dr. C. Morris. There was a fair show of sheep, Merinos, Cotswolds, Oxfords, and other Downs; the grades and crosses were generally better than the pure breds. The pigs, both black and white, were very good. The poultry were not in as fine condition as at most English exhibitions.

Proceeding westwards from Philadelphia the land for fifty miles is pleasantly undulating, well enclosed, only sparingly wooded, and very fairly cultivated. The farms vary from 50 to 150 acres; very few exceed 200 acres, and the owners are almost invariably the occupiers. In rare instances the farm is run on shares, the landlord, in addition to soil and buildings, occasionally finding the implements and machinery, and even the span of horses, the tenant only furnishing labour, each party taking a proportion, usually half, of the takings of the concern. Desirable, well-equipped farms even 50 miles from Philadelphia sell at 20*l.* to 30*l.* an acre. Many of these thriving Pennsylvanian agriculturists or their fathers have come from Vermont; most are industrious and thrifty, bear up well against summer heat; nearly all have laid aside money, and started their sons either in adjacent farms or sent them farther West. Beyond the limits convenient for the production and sale of dairy produce and vegetables for the Philadelphia market, many farmers, for both summer and winter feeding, buy store bullocks from Colorado, Texas, or other Western States, paying for them $15 to $20 (3*l.* to 4*l.*) They are kept four to six months, getting the while grass or hay, according to the season, with Indian corn; 80 to 100 bushels of corn is generally estimated as the winter feed of an ox, and also help along the pigs. With good waiting on, the beasts in five or six months nearly double their value. Other managers purchase sheep, usually brought from Canada or the Northern States, bought in at about $3 (15*s.*), and sold out, after four or five months, at a profit of 5*s.* or 6*s.* As at home, most of the best cattle and sheep are bred on the farm, and not quitted until disposed of to the butcher.

Along the line of rail neat wooden station-houses are provided, and smart flower beds rival in taste and colour the pretty shows made at many English roadside stations. The familiar milk-tins are seen on many platforms; deliveries of wheat are being busily made, although growers and dealers complain that the carriage from their stations is so high that Mid-Pennsylvania competes disadvantageously with Chicago and the West, favoured as they are with cheap through rates. It is particularly gratifying to note bags of guano, phosphates, and other fertilizers, as well as lime, in the goods sheds; while evidences of a restorative system of farming also declare themselves in the carting out of yard-made manure by the bullock teams, and by small doses spread here and there. Neither straw nor stubble is now burnt in the State; nor, as formerly, is the stream turned through the yards ruthlessly to get rid of the manure. Taking advantage of the fine autumn weather, ploughing is being pushed along; the active horses, usually decorated with nets, doing fully an acre and a half a day, with the ordinary short and rather ungainly, but good working plough of the country made with wood stilts and beam, but iron working parts. A good deal of wheat is up (September 20), and more is being sown by light nine-furrow pair-horse drills. The clovers look well, and in the pastures and elsewhere white clover springs naturally, feeding kindly on the *débris* of the lime and clay slate rocks. In gardens and fields tobacco is cultivated, the large clammy leaves being cut and dried first on wooden horses in the fields, and subsequently in sheds and warehouses. Passing Elizabeth Town, where many Germans are settled, and the wooden houses are mostly painted of a warm brown red, the country becomes more undulating; the distant hills are well-timbered, and the larger enclosures and thinner limestone soil suggest recollections of the Gloucestershire hills. But soon, amid rugged hills, on which lie giant boulders, among the closely-growing timber, we reach the slow-running Susquehanna, winding through shallow lagoons, floating down quantities of timber, and driving numerous saw-mills. Approaching Harrisburg, the capital of Pennsylvania and situated in the centre of the State,

Mineral Wealth.

cultivation again improves; several large and well-managed farms are passed. Some considerable herds of Jerseys are kept for the milk supply of the city, which has rolling mills and an extensive manufactory of railway passenger cars, turning out, it is said, fourteen daily.

For 250 miles from Harrisburg to Pittsburg the country is generally wild, rugged, and mountainous. But although poor agriculturally, the country abounds in mineral wealth, mostly in coal and iron ore. On the eastern slopes the hard anthracite is found, and the soft bituminous is equally plentiful on the western slopes. Beginning the ascent of the eastern foot hills of the Alleghanies, the farming is confined to small scattered patches of cultivated land and some useful orchards. Amidst grand and varied mountain scenery for many miles the railroad winds along the beautifully-wooded banks of the Susquehanna, crossing and recrossing the river, which at several points is half-a-mile wide, plunging into darkly wooded ravines and running parallel with the road, canal, and river, forcibly recalling the Vale of Llangollen. Again, among barer rounded hills, and valleys down which the burns dance, with picturesque white cottages relieving the solitude of 'mountain, wood, and stream,' the mind reverts to the Peebleshire scenery.

Altoona, 327 miles from New York, is the resting-place for the night. It is a reproduction of Crewe or Swindon, with roaring forges and busy workshops; for here the Pennsylvania Railroad Company have their chief factory for engines and carriages, and for repairs of rolling stock, and generally employ 3,000 men.

Amidst mountains and woods, and at a high altitude, Altoona and its neighbourhood have not, however, much agricultural interest. Oats are grown in preference to wheat; maize is only produced of the smaller sweet sort cultivated for table use. There are not many cattle or sheep kept, but beef and mutton in the market here are bought at 4*d.* per pound, spring chickens are 1*s.* each, eggs two a penny, and vegetables and fruit varied, plentiful, and cheap, as they are almost everywhere throughout America. On the heights are settled numbers of the Donkers, who are allied to the Memonites, abhor war and litigation, and are thrifty, industrious people.

From Altoona, with three powerful engines dragging eleven cars, we slowly creep up the steep mountain ascent, with the grand forest trees just beginning to assume their wondrous varied autumn tints of red and brown, pink and yellow, proceed around rocky ravines overhanging the valleys and river, sweep round the sharp curve of the horse-shoe bend, pass along the wild wooded heights for fully twenty miles, and drop down on Johnstown. Thirty years ago, before the railroad was made, this journey was undertaken in favourable weather by canal, the boats, placed on wheels, were laboriously dragged by horses up a timbered road, were returned to the water when the more level plateau was reached, and made the descent on the other side by tedious locks. The journey of 200 miles from Harrisburg to Pittsburg,

Pittsburg, Centre of Coal and Iron Trades. 125

now accomplished in five hours, then occupied five days.

Pittsburg lies on the western base of the Alleghanies, at the confluence of the Alleghani and the Monongahela rivers, which here unite to form' the Ohio. It is the great centre of the Pennsylvania coal, iron, steel, glass, and petroleum industries. It is in the midst of the bituminous coal fields. The veins, conveniently near the surface, sometimes broken and upheaved by subterranean force, occasionally lying vertically instead of horizontally, are about five feet thick, are often worked without shafts or lifts, being quarried as stones usually are in this country, and loaded at once on tram cars. It is very free from sulphur, is prized for smelting and making iron; and a great deal is forwarded to New York and other eastern cities for household use.

The purification and export of petroleum is one of the important trades of this part of Pennsylvania. The oil was struck in the Alleghanies as recently as 1859, and has since been a continuous increasing mine of wealth. Produced from the gradual decay of vegetable matters, it exudes from the black shales, or is found in subterranean chambers into which it has filtered. When these are tapped by the borer, the oil is forced to the surface, and sometimes thrown out in jets. The borings or wells are 1,000 to 1,300 feet deep. When a well fails or runs short, another is dug. The supply seems never failing, and the region over which it is found is measured by several hundred miles. Expensive pumps are unnecessary, and would scarcely pay, as the oil at the wells is worth only ½d. per gallon. From its source along the Alleghanies it is carried by its own gravity in iron pipes, thirty or forty miles, to the various cities where it is purified and barrelled. Fifty-thousand barrels containing 45 gallons each are put up daily in the State of Pennsylvania alone. The largest proportion of this is done at Pittsburg by the Standard Oil Company, under the able presidency of Mr. J. D. Roekefiller. The extent of the operations of this company in illuminating and lubricating oils may be gathered from the fact that 40,000 tons of hoop iron are annually used for the barrels. Mr. R. G. Waring, one of the directors of this important corporation, informs me that three-fourths of the iron purchased in 1879 was bought by him in England.

It was in Pittsburg that Horace Greely and sixteen determined and zealous spirits, upwards of twenty years ago, met and organised the Republican Party, inaugurated the first decided stand against slavery, and insisted that it should not be introduced into any of the new States. The citizens of Pittsburg pride themselves that on the eve of the great struggle between North and South, they first brought under notice of the Government the depleting of the arsenals of the North, and obtained orders for the interception of cannons and military stores which were being transferred to Southern depôts.

CHAPTER X.

AGRICULTURE IN OHIO.

SOME of the Middle and Eastern States, settled for a hundred years, exhibit the aspect and methods of farming of the old country. In the contiguous States of Kentucky and Ohio are farms with house, buildings, fields, stock and general arrangements of a familiar English type. Ohio has an area of 25,500,000 acres, it is about one-sixth less than New York and Pennsylvania, half the size of Kansas or Minnesota, about one-seventh the extent of Texas, about three-fourths that of England. Fifty years ago Ohio was largely covered with forests, a considerable amount of which has been cut down with much labour. Upwards of 5,000,000 acres are still, however, under wood, which with thinning and management might pay better than it does. Evidences of the 'forest primeval' are still conspicuous in the old stumps standing several feet out of the ground in the pastures and even in many arable fields. A younger growth of plantation and scrub has risen in many localities, and even on lands which had been cleared and cultivated, which have been run out by exhausting cropping, and allowed to revert to their natural wild state.

According to the statistical returns more than one-third of the State, or about 9,000,000 acres, are in cultivation. About 6,000,000 acres are in pasture. Three million acres are devoted to Indian corn; nearly 2,000,000 acres each to wheat and hay, and 1,000,000 to oats. The yield of corn is stated at 35 bushels per acre, wheat at 15 to 18 bushels, oats at 36, hay at $1\frac{1}{2}$ ton per acre. Flax is not so common as it has been; tobacco is on a more limited scale than in Pennsylvania; sorghum extending in Minnesota and Missouri is uncertain, on account of frosts. About 500,000 acres are in orchards, producing in a fair season 10,000,000 bushels of apples, 500,000 bushels of peaches, and 100,000 bushels of pears. About 10,000 acres are in vineyards, annually increasing at the rate of 10 per cent., producing 12,000,000 lbs. of grapes and 500,000 gallons of wine.

Real estate in Ohio is assessed at $1,091,116,952, personal at $461,460,552.[1] The State taxes amount to 2·9 mills. per dollar. Besides State taxes there were levied in 1879 county taxes amounting to $16,429,629, and town, school, and city taxes amounting to $15,398,441. To these levies not only the land contributes, but all manner of personal property, all implements, machinery, and furniture, the animals of the farm, and dogs. Taking all into account, the taxes in Ohio range from $1\frac{1}{2}$ to 2 per cent on the fair valuation of the farm. Supposing the land worth 10*l*.

[1] *American Almanac*, by A. R. Stopford, for 1880, p. 186.

an acre, and bearing, as it does at home, the bulk of the burdens, these would amount to 4*s*. an acre. As in the old world, taxes are amongst the farmer's grievances. It is complained that the railroads do not contribute their quota. They take 12 acres per mile, occupy in Ohio about 4,000 miles, and hence represent property to the value of $1,500,000, which at present escapes taxation. Game, being public property, pays no rates. It is hunted or shot by any one. No proprietor forbids the sportsman ranging where he pleases. The only game laws are those preventing sporting during close time. Many farmers, especially near towns, would gladly have some enactments preventing the public, on Sundays as well as week days, tramping over their fields in pursuit of game, or fishing in their rivers or lakes, without so much as saying 'By your leave.'

Englishmen in Ohio, as in many parts of the Continent, will find some inconvenience from extremes of summer and winter temperature. The summer heat ranges from 70° to 75°: the winter from 28° to 34°. The rainfall at the capital Cincinnati, which lies low and attracts a good deal of moisture from the broad Ohio, on an average of twenty-five years, is 44·87 inches. At Cleveland on Lake Erie it is 37·6 inches. Draining and cultivation have removed the causes of malaria which some years ago was common.

In a great Republican country, where it might be supposed that the interests of agriculture would be left to individual enterprise, it is satisfactory to find that almost every State paternally enacts for its benefit laws, some of which in an old country might be regarded as arbitrary and unduly interfering with the liberty of the subject. The General Assembly of Ohio has laws regulating the ancient industry which in America is the first and great source of wealth. A State board of agriculture was formed in 1846, with laws as to public exhibitions, or 'fairs,' as they are termed. At these shows, as at home, prizes are given for live stock, for implements, and for labour competitions, in which both farmers and their men frequently join. Arrangements are made for the collection of statistics, the management of county societies and clubs, the prevention of contagious diseases amongst animals, and the construction of ditches, water courses, and drains. An Agricultural College is subsidised by the State, and does good work in disseminating information relating to the principles and practice of agriculture. A like technical teaching is also very generally given in the advanced schools in rural neighbourhoods.

Good farm houses and buildings are met with of modern and convenient structure, often of stone or brick, the shedding usually of wood. Draining is done to the extent of 35,000 miles, and 1,000 miles of drains are stated to be put down every year.[1] On clay subsoils, drains are made 3 feet deep and 3 rods apart; pipes have generally superseded stones and timber; in Lorain county, 2-inch tiles cost $10 per 1,000; 3-inch, $15; 4-inch, $20; digging and laying

[1] *Ohio Agricultural Report* for 1877, p. 10.

are charged at 25 to 30 cents per rod: the total cost per acre varies from $18 to $27.

Farms vary in size in different parts of the State, but according to the official census average 111 acres. By far the greatest proportion of the occupiers are their own landlords. With recent good harvests and improved trade the mortgages of former years have generally been extinguished, more spirited and diversified cultivation extends, and land is advancing in value. Around Rochester and Salem, in the Eastern portion of the State, good farms now cost 10*l.* an acre, and if sold valuation would besides be made for house and buildings. In some localities farms are run on shares, the landlord usually stipulating to have five-eighths of the land in grain, and to receive one-half of the grain produce.

The herd law, which is general in Western States and territories, and which compels the grazier to tend his animals, and keep them out of his neighbours' crops, is not recognised in Ohio, or other older States. The farms are fenced, and the fields divided by fences. In well-wooded districts where timber is still abundant, a six or eight rail, zig-zag or snake fence, is common; the heavy roughly split rails are laid one over the other, and, although without posts, this zig-zag fence is strong and holds back both cattle and pigs. Elsewhere, the more familiar morticed posts and split rails are used. Oak or locust posts, six inches square, cost about 1*d.* each. Some locust posts put in top end down, in which position they are most lasting, were shown me in fair condition, although they had been standing for thirty years. Split rails are procurable at $12 to $14 per 1,000. Inch pine boards are often nailed to posts, as is done in Scotland, and such railing costs less, and lasts longer than the railing with morticed posts. In the cleared open country where timber is becoming scarce, wire, sometimes barbed, is used; the posts are placed 32 feet apart, but such fencing is apt to flop in very hot weather, and contract and break when the temperature falls, as it often does in winter, to 20° below zero. Thorn and osage, or wild orange, are extending; both grow well, make capital fences, are sometimes allowed to run up 12 to 20 feet; are sometimes splashed as in this country, and kept tidily trimmed two or three times a year.

Eastern Ohio, the earlier settled part of the State, has a steady, hardworking population, largely consisting of Quakers, formerly drawn from Maryland. It exhibits some good mixed farming, and is in convenient proximity to markets. The better wheat crops of the last few years have infused more spirit amongst farmers. Land is more enquired for, and brings a better price. Useful farms five miles from any considerable town are to be bought at 5*l.* to 8*l.* an acre. During the last ten years neither the arable nor pastoral products of this part of Ohio have sufficiently increased; indeed, in some districts they have actually retrograded. An old Scottish settler remarks that 'the men farm as if they had only an annual instead of a permanent interest in their holdings.' A few farms are held by tenants, most are farmed by their owners. A few years ago many were heavily mortgaged, the advances, often to half the value of the property, being made at 7 and 8 per cent. The recent better times have, however, gradually reduced these encumbrances. As is common elsewhere, many with means sufficient to farm 50 acres, profitlessly endeavour to farm 150 acres. It appears, however, to be generally admitted that any man with capital, judgment, and industry should still be able to make a fair livelihood from farming.

Wheat in Ohio is chiefly sown in autumn. It is got in during the latter part of September and early in October, and grows rapidly and vigorously. Generally it follows clover, roots, or oats. Wheat-growing in Ohio and other mid States costs much more than on the cheap virgin soils of the West. Rent, or interest on capital, and rates are nearly three times what they are in Minnesota, Iowa, or Dakota. On lands long farmed manure is required, and at a moderate computation adds 10s. an acre or 6d. a bushel to the cost. Ploughing is rather more costly than farther West, reaping, thrashing, and other charges are about the same. Subjoined is a statement of the average cost of an acre of wheat in Ohio :—

	£	s.	d.
Rent or interest on capital of £10 at 10 per cent. .	1	0	0
Rates and taxes	0	4	0
Ploughing	0	8	0
Manure	0	10	0
Seed	0	6	0
Sowing and harrowing	0	3	0
Reaping and stacking	0	10	0
Thrashing	0	5	0
Delivering and incidentals	0	3	0
	3	9	0

This is less than half the cost of wheat-growing in England, but it is nearly double the cost of production in the cheaper Western States. In growing wheat the yeomen of Ohio are almost as heavily handicapped as the farmers of Great Britain; for several years eighteen bushels has been the yield in the best districts of Ohio; grown at 3*l*. 8*s*. an acre, if it is to pay expenses it must be sold at 3*s*. 9*d*. a bushel. On the cheap, unmanured lands of Minnesota, eighteen bushels, which is a fair acreable yield, are obtained for 2*l*. 2*s*., and can hence be sold without loss at 2*s*. 4*d*. per bushel. This difference in the cost of production more than counterbalances the advantages the Ohio farmer possesses in nearness to markets and to the eastern ports. Besides in many parts of Ohio, wheat-growing is eminently uncertain. In eighteen years it is said that there have been only six full crops.[1] A few days' scorching drought when the grain is ripening, or subsequent high winds and storms, seriously jeopardise results. The farmers of these middle States, like those of England, discovering that extensive wheat-growing is seldom profitable, are wisely bestowing more attention on the more certain Indian corn and the rearing and feeding of live stock.

Indian corn is produced at less cost than wheat. With good cultivation more than double the number of bushels is obtained from an acre. Where forty bushels are reaped the first cost will amount to 1*s*. 6*d*. to 1*s*. 9*d*. per bushel. It can generally be sold to

---

[1] Messrs. Read and Pell's Report: *Agriculturist Interests Commission*, p. 14.

secure a small profit, but still more advantage results when, as is the practice with most good farmers, it is converted into beef or bacon. Half a bushel per day is the usual allowance for a three-year-old beast when first put up, but more is given as fattening advances. The 80 to 100 bushels sufficient for feeding a beast is expected, besides adding to the value of the manure, to make about 50 per cent. more in beef than it does when marketed as corn. The fodder, which is the equivalent of English hay and roots, is used alike for cattle, sheep, and pigs. In the yards for each beast two pigs are kept as scavengers. Ten pounds of corn make one pound of bacon. On clover and timothy grass the live stock, including pigs, are run from May until October, and from these Ohio pastures come a considerable number of the best bullocks which during the late summer and autumn months are landed at our ports. From the yards in winter are consigned many of the animals weighing 1,600 and 1,700 lbs., which are slaughtered at the eastern ports and sent to England.

Dr. Black's farm at Pickaway is a good type of the management in the pleasant Scioto valley: 371 acres represent $15,000 of outlay in purchase and improvements, or 8*l.* an acre: 150 acres are devoted to corn, rye, and clover, in rotation: 140 acres of cleared land grows Kentucky blue grass: 65 acres is in woodland, furnishing, however, a good deal of herbage: 5 acres are in woodland producing no grass: buildings and roads occupy 3 acres. The expenses range from 40*s.* to 50*s.* an acre. In 1874 they were 713*l.*

The receipts were 1,075*l*., leaving a profit of 365*l*., or fully 12 per cent. upon the investment. In 1875 the expenses were 970*l*., the receipts 1,467*l*. The profits 496*l*. or 16 per cent. In 1876, expenses carefully looked after were reduced to 634*l*. The receipts, owing, however, to the previous wet season and the consequent indifferent thriving of the stock, were only 760*l*. the profit of 126*l*. being little over 4 per cent. upon the outlay. The expenses of 1877 were 632*l*.; the receipts 1,069*l*. The profit 435*l*., or 14 per cent. 1878 and 1879 exhibit still more satisfactory results, and the profits of Dr. Black's six years' farming exceed 12 per cent. per annum; which is nearly double the amount which most British agriculturists, even in the best of times, are able to obtain.

Dairy farming is the chief industry of the clay and shales of the Northern part of the State and of the Western reserve, occupying the chief portion of the counties of Ashtabula, Trumbull, and Geauga, with considerable portions of Portage, Summit, Medina, and Lorain. Although involving more trouble, if properly attended to, dairying is believed to pay better than feeding. Of the 1,624,286 cattle of all descriptions enumerated in Ohio on January 1, 1880, nearly one-half were returned as milk cows. As has happened in Cheshire, Buckinghamshire, and other parts of Great Britain, twenty years' dairying, with continuous disposal of the phosphate-containing milk and no adequate return of plant food, has, however, deteriorated the pastures and reduced the amount of clovers and fine grasses, which sprang spontaneously and flourished for a time on the cleared forest land. Neglect of draining and allowing cattle and horses to stray over these heavy soils in wet weather, has further determined their deterioration. The productive capacity of the pastures is stated to have been reduced one-third; four acres instead of three are now required to maintain a cow. An average farm of 100 acres generally carries ten or twelve cows; three or four heifer calves are reared annually to recruit the stock. The land is worked by a pair of horses. Fifty acres are required for pasture, which, as a rule, receives no manure; 21 acres may be devoted to timothy grass, which lasts three years, and hence necessitates 7 acres being sown down annually. Fully 21 acres will be ploughed every year, one-third being Indian corn manured, one-third oats, one-third wheat, for which some manure is often spared, and amongst which the timothy is sown. Eight acres will be occupied with garden, orchard, and buildings. Besides the yield of the seven acres of wheat there is little to sell excepting the dairy produce, which reaches 4*l.* or 5*l.* per cow; 800 to 1,000 quarts is the annual average yield of milk per cow. The cows are chiefly Shorthorn grades, a few have an infusion of Ayrshire, Guernsey, or Holstein. At the cheese factories and creameries the price paid for the milk rarely exceeds 1½*d.* per quart, and the farmers who make their own butter and cheese presumedly do not realise any better price. Generally throughout America, in all the larger markets butter is now carefully graded; the common qualities, unfortunately most abundant, sell tardily at 9*d.* or 10*d.*, the best readily make 1*s.* 6*d.* to 1*s.* 8*d.*, and in winter considerably more.

The annual yield of butter in Ohio exceeds 50,000,000 lbs.; that of cheese is 30,000,000 lbs. By more careful selection of cows of good milking families, by better feeding, and by draining and manuring the exhausted pastures, the yield of milk and the profits of the dairy may be considerably increased.

Profits on cattle-feeding are being augmented by more careful breeding and handling. Well-selected animals with two or three crosses of Shorthorn or Hereford are easily fed at three years, whilst the commoner, plainer, heavier-boned, restless natives do not come out until four or five. The better bred more shapely animals with one-fourth less food reach heavier weights, and realise 1 to 3 cents per pound on the hoof more than the commoners. To this more profitable standard the home-bred Ohio beasts are being steadily raised. Good Shorthorn herds throughout most States, annually distributing thousands of pure bred and graded bulls at prices varying from $50 to $300, are increasing the beef-producing capabilities of the great American herds.

Ohio does not breed nearly all the cattle she requires to consume her heavy crops of corn. From Cincinnati and Chicago, railed thence 1,000 miles from the great western branches, are brought every autumn thousands of three- and four-year old bullocks. They are placed in large yards, 70 to 100 are usually seen together, but they agree tolerably amicably. They eat daily 10 lbs. to 20 lbs. of hay at 40*s.* per ton, as much corn cobs and stalks as they can clear up, and 20 lbs. to 30 lbs. of corn or corn meal. A little bran at 30*s.* per ton is sometimes given; salt is placed within reach, but roots are too scarce to be used. The beasts are weighed in during October at 1,100 lbs. to 1,300 lbs., and go out in spring at 1,600 lbs. to 1,800 lbs. Farmers who cannot buy bullocks frequently have their yards filled, and their hay and corn consumed by animals consigned to them by their more prosperous neighbours. The cattle are weighed over to them on the stockyard steelyards, and they receive $2\frac{1}{2}d.$ to $3d.$ for every pound of gross weight gained. Good beasts well managed are expected to make 4 lbs. daily addition to their live weight.

Hogs are readily and cheaply reared, and fed chiefly on grass and clover in summer and in winter in the yards amongst the cattle and finished off on corn. They would need to be inexpensively kept, for sometimes they realise very low figures. They fell during 1878 and the first nine months of 1879 to $3 and even to $2·50 per 100 lbs. gross. In 1866 and 1867 they made $7. Their present value is about $5 per 100 lbs. live weight. Prices are sometimes lively; following a sudden jump of sometimes $2 per 100 lbs. in the value of pork, live hogs will run up too fast for the buyers. Well posted by his smart paper, the seller is ever on the alert to benefit by any rise. In every exchange room and marketplace the latest quotations of the values of all agricultural commodities are posted and eagerly read and commented on, not only by merchants and farmers, but by drovers and errand boys. Throughout America, alike in town and country, the young idea is uncommonly precocious, and shows early aptitude for business. On January 1, 1880, 1,974,868 hogs were enumerated in Ohio with the low average valuation of 15s. per head. Being taxed, however, according to their value, this is returned as moderately as the conscience of the owner permits. Ohio packs annually upwards of 100,000 hogs, or 12·5 per cent. of the whole of the States. Of this amount Cincinnati does one-sixth. Like so many American cities, Cincinnati is a great and growing entrepôt for all descriptions of agricultural produce. During twelve months she now receives about 1,000,000 hogs, 250,000 cattle, and 600,000 sheep. The weight of the hogs slaughtered during five years averages 217 lbs., or about the general average of the States. They yield 37 lbs. of lard. Averaging $2\frac{1}{4}d.$ per lb., each fat hog accordingly realises a trifle under 60s. Hog cholera has occasionally done even more devastation than in England. During twelve months to April 1877 it destroyed 15 per cent of the whole hog crop of the States. The mortality was double that in Missouri; in Florida, Alabama, Kentucky, and Illinois it was 20 per cent.; Ohio fortunately got off with a loss of 7 per cent. A somewhat analogous complaint has sometimes decimated the poultry yards.

Ohio has long had a high reputation for sheep. With the exception of California and Texas, her flocks are more numerous than those of any other

State. Steadily increasing, they numbered on January 1, 1880, 4,595,462. Until recently most of the best flocks were Merinos, cultivated exclusively for their fine lustrous wools. Thirty years ago many were largely crossed with Saxony sheep, contributing light, fine wools. Subsequently the fibre was shortened by infusion of Silesian blood. Latterly Spanish or American Merinos, often from Vermont, have been used, with the effect of adding to the weight both of carcase and of fleece. The ewes clip 5 lbs., the wethers 6 lbs. or 7 lbs. Some of the best managers have received for years 40 to 50 cents per lb. for their choice wool. The average price for ordinary clips is about 1*s.* per lb. Many flock-masters still untidily shear the unwashed wool. Some of the best Merinos yield for one year's growth $3\frac{1}{2}$ inches, and occasionally $3\frac{5}{8}$ inches, of wool. Some of Mr. Andrew M'Farland's sheep have produced wool, the fibre of which, equalling the best Saxony, was only 1·1250th of an inch in diameter. A heavier fleece and more mutton is now very generally aimed at and obtained by crossing the Merinos and Merino grades with English longwools and Oxford Downs. Many of these crosses at two years old dress 60 lbs. to 70 lbs., or are 10 lbs. to 15 lbs. heavier than the Merinos. As in the North-eastern States, some of the sheep in Ohio are housed during the severe winter months. This is necessary with Merinos kept in exposed situations. Such flocks in consequence suffer from foot-rot. Extremes of heat and cold telling on a somewhat delicate constitution occasionally produce scrofulous abscesses and tubercular diseases of the lungs, with anæmia, of which one form is popularly termed 'paper skin.' Flock masters in Ohio, as in other States, are subject to a loss from which British breeders are exempt. Notwithstanding the tax upon 184,035 dogs, many appear to roam in a semi-feral state, and kill annually 28,000 sheep, seriously injuring nearly 20,000 more. Official statistics indicate a further mortality amongst sheep to the extent of 1·6 per annum; the mortality amongst horses is 1·44, and amongst cattle 1 per cent. per annum. Texas fever has occasionally been introduced, usually amongst beasts from the Mexican Gulf States forwarded from Chicago. The mortality amongst the new comers has generally been serious. Dry food has proved the best remedy. In these cooler States the disease fortunately does originate and does not spread.

Besides the sheep bred in Ohio, numbers are brought from the West and from Canada for feeding on grass and clover in summer, or corn and bran in winter. These sheep, chiefly Merino grades, in the fall cost two and a half to three dollars. Occasionally early lamb is reared, but, although dropped in January, chiefly house-fed, and disposed of in March, only 5d. or 6d. per lb. is said to be got for it—a price which can scarcely be remunerative. In autumn lamb weighing 30 lbs. to 35 lbs. per carcase is only worth 4d. per lb., and veal 80 lbs. to 140 lbs. is selling at 2$\frac{1}{4}d$. to 3d. Some of the most useful mutton-producing sheep, having a look of the Cheviot, were said to be homebred and probably descended from imported stock. The ordinary flocks are not winter-housed, and do not produce their lambs until April; the earlier lambs are apt to suffer from cold and want of green food. The amount of roots grown appears insufficient for successful sheep-breeding. Many of these Ohio sheep-farmers declare, however, that they get along 'considerably well.' They own the land they farm; twenty or thirty years ago most of them began with a few dollars; they have brought up families, and many are well-to-do; some with buggy and pair of horses and a comfortable, well-built, nicely-appointed house, of much the same style as would be occupied by the 200-acre farmer at home.

Throughout the State the number of labourers to the acreage is much smaller than at home; a great deal more systematic hard work is done by the farmer himself and his family. Even the labourers work with a refreshing heartiness satisfactory to observe. No man worthy the name has time or inclination in America to idle or trifle. In all classes there is a vigorous determination to be up and doing; even the rural labourer appears similarly inspired; the idler and dullard is either drilled into better ways or thrown out of the running. Wages vary from 4s. to 6s. per day—the latter amount being given in busy seasons. Regular hands are engaged for the eight or twelve months at 12s. to 16s. a month, with lodgings and board. Many farm men during the winter months go off to the lumbering or timber business, which is a great interest in Upper Pennsylvania and Ohio. Provision for education here, as elsewhere, is admirable;

school grants have been liberally made ; even in the more thinly populated districts a school and good tuition is generally found within two miles of every house. This parochial teaching throughout America is gratuitous, but not compulsory.

CHAPTER XI.

AN AGRICULTURAL EXHIBITION IN MICHIGAN.

THE Michigan Agricultural Society held their tenth annual exhibition during the week beginning September 15, 1879, at Detroit, on the western banks of Lake Erie—fifty years ago a village with less than 2,000 inhabitants, now a thriving city with a population of 125,000. The show-yard is fully a mile out of town and covers 60 acres. In large, airy, well-lighted wooden buildings, many slated and permanently kept for the annual show, are collected attractions even more numerous than grace the Bath and West of England polyglot exhibitions—pictures by native artists, china, porcelain, carpets and rugs, with skins and furs, which are brought here in enormous quantities from Canada and the West, woollen and cotton goods, specimens of the artistic walnut and oak furniture for which South Bend is so celebrated, carriages and waggons, which figure prominently at all American county and State fairs, handsome nickel-plated stoves for heating rooms and corridors, and kitchen ranges wonderfully and economically fitted up by the Michigan Stove Company, who employ 1,300 men. Different counties of Michigan, which comprises 36,000,000 acres, and produced last year 31,000,000 bushels of wheat, contribute interesting specimens of their special agricultural, garden, and fruit produce. From Saginaw are forwarded specimens of the salt which, over an area of twenty-five miles, is found in abundant brine springs from 800 ft. to 1,500 ft. deep, is pumped up, evaporated in large hollow wooden vats heated with steam-pipes, and distributed widely throughout the country in bulk or in barrels at 1*s*. 3*d*. per five bushels, weighing 280 lbs. Two million barrels are thus annually disposed of. Messrs. Pingree and Smith import into a large building some of their ingenious machinery for making boots and shoes, and have a dozen men and about the same number of women cutting out, sewing, firmly securing the soles with brass wire cut as a screw, and deftly finishing off some dozen varieties of boots and shoes. In this temporary factory within twenty minutes the measure of a lady's foot was taken and a handsome boot made and ready for use. This business has been established at Detroit thirteen years, employs 400 operatives, and turns out daily 1,500 pairs, which are chiefly sold in the South and West. Averse from crippling their customers, Messrs. Pingree and Smith wisely denounce the very absurd fashions of narrow toes and high heels.

Butter, cheese, and vegetables occupy several sheds. The flower show is specially great in gladiolas and asters. The fruit exhibition is particularly worthy of commendation. Various local pomological societies and many private persons forward collections of six or eight different fruits, while numerous varieties of common fruits are well illustrated. From one single orchard, Mr. Bidwell, of Plymouth, sends 50 different sorts of apples, and avers that he has other 50 not here represented. On account of the excessive summer drought, which scorched up the immature fruit, the Michigan apple crop is not so abundant or good as usual. The sorts most prized are the Baldwin, a ready cropper capital for household use; the Red Canada, a superior keeper, a basket of 1878 produce being tabled in beautiful preservation; the Golden Russet and Rhode Island Greening, for dessert; the Wagner, for the western pioneers, as it begins to bear in three years. Another beautiful variety much grown for autumn use is the Maiden Blush. Fifteen pence a bushel is the present value of the best apples here; but by May Day they are usually worth double that price. Prime pears cost 8s. to 10s. a bushel; those of the finest colour and quality come from the northern parts of the State; the varieties most esteemed are the Bartlett, Flemish Beauty, Duchesse d'Angoulême, and the little Sheckels. The western shores of Erie produce the finest peaches: Crawfords, early and late, and Old Majors being favourites. Grapes grow readily almost everywhere; in Munroe tons are made into wine; the Iona are regarded the finest flavoured; the Concord are hardy; the Delaware are good, but small. Plums of thirty varieties are shown from many northern parts of the State. Tempting specimens of jellies and preserved and canned fruits adorn the tables, and this trade, as well as the consumption of fruit in the growing towns, still encourages the planting of orchards

In every farmhouse fruit in its natural state and cooked is also in daily use; cider, however, is not generally made; but in seasons of great superabundance large quantities of fruit are eaten by cattle and hogs.

Along either side of two shafts, each 200 ft., are mowers, reapers, and self-binders, shown in motion. Although the Michigan Society this year awards no premiums for such implements, Walter A. Wood's, M'Cormick's, and other combined reapers and binders were daily exhibiting their capabilities surrounded by admiring crowds. A score of light portable engines, from four to fourteen-horse power, were at work. Several were adapted for burning straw as fuel: most were suitable for wood fuel. The vertical construction is adopted by several makers, who declare that by bracing up and supporting the boiler tubes they have succeeded in combining durability with lightness, handiness of setting, and low price. Among other objects are windmills and the wonderful combinations of levers, screws, and hydraulic presses constituting the house-raising machine which was so extensively used in lifting so many edifices in Chicago. American thrashing machines are now generally made with winnower and folding straw elevator all in one. A serviceable combination implement of this sort is turned out by Messrs. Aultman and Co., of Canton, Ohio, driven by an 8-horse engine, thrashing and cleaning 800 to 1,000 bushels of wheat in ten hours, delivering the straw 20 to 24 feet from the machine, and costing 90*l.* Ploughs from many factories are here, short in beam, mould board, and handles not extending 8½ to 9 feet in length, made to turn over a furrow usually about 6 inches deep by 12 or 15 inches wide, and costing, according to style and finish, from 2*l.* to 3*l.* Ample margin of profit is obtained at these figures, for one extensive manufacturer informs me that machinery and subdivision of labour enabled him to turn out a superior article for less than 10*s.* The Gale 'Chilled Plough,' hailing from Albion, Michigan, of which 20,000 are said to be made annually, and which brought a gold medal from the Paris Exposition, has one of its several varieties, with a beam of three wrought-iron rods; by nuts screwed up or down on one or another of these rods more pitch or land is given; the single wheel is not attached to the beam, but to the clevise. Numerous light, durable horse-rakes are exhibited, weighing 200 lbs., several with wheels 4½ feet high, with seat for the driver, malleable steeled teeth, and costing 5*l.* The 'Farmer's Friend Grain Drill,' manufactured for 26 years at Dayton, Ohio, appears to be largely used. It is made of various sizes, delivering from nine to fifteen rows; is adapted for all descriptions of grain and grass seed, regulates and registers the amount of seed per acre, and has zigzag attachment so that half of the feed-hose can be thrown out of gear. This light and simple drill was awarded two medals at the Philadelphia Centennial and one at the Paris Exposition. The same firm also make combined grain and fertiliser drills, for which, however, there has been hitherto scarcely any demand in America.

The live stock, although this year perhaps unwisely restricted to exhibitors living within the State, comprises 500 entries of horses, as many of cattle, 700 sheep, 200 pigs, and a good many pens of poultry—Cochins and Bramahs appearing most numerous—but none shown either here or in market in the plump good condition which characterises superior English poultry. Horses are classified under nine divisions, as thoroughbreds, horses of all work, roadsters, gentlemen's driving horses, road, waggon, draught horses, carriage and buggy horses, breeder's premiums for roadster and thoroughbred stallions, breeder's premium for mares and geldings, and sweepstakes for stallion, with six of his own get, which brought forward half a dozen competitors. These classes are subdivided as to age and sex; 600*l.* is offered in premiums. Several indifferent heavy draught animals are shown—a description of horse which in America stands in great need of improvement in style and shape, and which will be much amended by crossing with such useful, active Percherons as the five-year-old shown by Mr. Hiram Walker, of Detroit, winner of twenty-seven first prizes and a Paris gold medal, and just arrived in this country along with two grey and a black mare of the same breed. At present, in Detroit and other towns, the railroads, coalmasters, and manufacturers usually employ horses of the stamp seen in the London omnibuses, and demur to the economy of the slower, heavier-limbed sorts.

Thoroughbred and roadster stallions were more numerous, and fully as good a muster as at an English county show. In a class of seventeen, Mr. E. H. Lyon, of St. John's, stood first with a very strong, handsome, 16 hands, dark bay, showing very level good action, and of Marquis and Messenger descent. Of hunters, cobs, and other riding classes there are none. The trotting horses, emphatically an American institution, are, however, in great force, exhibited in pairs, in four-wheeled waggons weighing 60 lbs. to 100 lbs., or singly in racing sulkies of 50 lbs. to 75 lbs. In some competitions speed entirely determines the awards, and the prize winners, if 'good ones to go,' are sometimes 'rum ones to look at.' However, at Detroit the Judges sensibly took into consideration symmetry, style, soundness, and manners as well as speed. No Norfolk or other English horse comes up to these American trotters in speed. We may demur to a somewhat ungainly appearance and wide gait behind, but they lay themselves down to their work and tool along at an alarming rate. All the best running strains come more or less directly from the grey thoroughbred Messenger imported from England in the close of last century. By careful selection and training speed steadily increases. In 1830 the maximum pace was 2·50; for many years before Flora Temple's day 2·40 was the trainer's height of aspiration; now six cracks have done their mile in 2 minutes 15 seconds; and Maud S. at Chicago covered the distance in 2 minutes 10¾ seconds.

The prevailing shortcoming of most American horses is the upright placing of the shoulder; hence it is rare to see the long sweeping action which distinguishes a first-class English hunter or carriage horse. Judicious admixture with stout thoroughbreds, or with the best English roadsters, might, however, improve the shoulder conformation, and impart more level, all-round action, without interfering with the speed which in America is here so highly desiderated. All the horses, even the stallions, are singularly tractable, are driven with snaffle bridles, both in the show-yard and the streets. Many are reined up with bearing bridles, sometimes passing over their heads and thence to the hook on the pad. Although often having hard mouths from hurried bad bitting, and requiring full 56 lbs. tension to steady them, they stand quietly hitched, or sometimes even loose, on the road or street, in a way that could scarcely be expected of high-couraged English horses in good condition. Double teams of carriage horses, owned and driven by the exhibitors, brought nine excellent entries of well-matched nice steppers, several of them worth $1,000. For a pair of strong, shapely, dark bay stallions, which did their mile over the heavy track, sodden with recent rain, within four minutes, $3,000 was vainly offered. Several of the horses trotting singly, notwithstanding the heavy state of the course, covered the mile in 2 min. 30 sec.

In Michigan, as well as in the neighbouring States, there are a considerable number of shorthorn herds. Mr. Curtis, of Hillsdale county, and Messrs. Avory and Murphy, of Port Huron, two of the oldest and most successful breeders, are not this year represented, but will doubtless again compete when the lists are open to all comers. Mr. Brooks, of Brighton, Livingston county, has descendants of some of the shorthorns which his father upwards of thirty years ago selected from Mr. Tanquery's. For himself and the State Society twenty-five animals were bought in England, but several unfortunately died on the passage; some of the remainder were unfortunate. To make some restitution Mr. Tanquery subsequently sent Mr. Brooks a young bull and two Gwynne heifers. Good bulls, bred in Kentucky, usually by Abe. Renick and Mr. Alexander, have kept up the successes of this early good beginning.

Ten exhibitors of pedigree shorthorns have each half a score entries, and some smaller herds contribute lesser numbers. There were seventeen competitors for the prizes for three-year-old bulls. For the family group of a bull, cow, and three of her progeny, there were eleven competitors, a larger entry than would readily have been got together at any British show. The first premium and the third were awarded to Messrs. G. and T. Phelps, Webster, Washtenaw county, who make also a sweep of many of the class prizes, and stand in for the first place with their four-year-old bull, Duke of Hillsdale, by Duke of Wicken, bred by Lord Penryhn at Wicken-park, Bucks, England. The second prize bull, Mazurka Duke II., has more size and grandeur than his successful competitor, and is, after Mr. Alexander's 23rd Duke of Airdrie, a Bates tribe much esteemed both in England and America. Such facts testify to the determination and zeal of American agriculturists to improve their cattle and emulate British stock-owners in producing profitable, early matured animals. Without exception, the breeders of these pedigree shorthorns are well satisfied with the business they are doing. There is a good and growing demand alike for young bulls and for heifers: fancy prices are not often got, but yearling bulls are readily sold at 25*l*. to 40*l*., and the pick bring more. These sires are distributed far and wide; some are carried hundreds of miles west; mated with the cattle of the district, they produce the so-called grades which, at the Michigan and other shows, and in the stock-yards, constitute an increasing proportion of really good cattle, and which in a moderately good herd, after two or three dips of the improved sort, are scarcely distinguishable from it. So great is the demand for good red or dark roan young bulls for the Western States, that many graded animals with only two or three crosses are saved. One informant tells me that he could sell 'cartloads' if he had them; that since he used good shorthorn sires he has never had any trouble to dispose of his stock. He never takes them to market; the dealers hunt him up. He makes quite the top figure; has cash down and no credit; and is clearing out both bullocks and heifers fat at about two-and-a half years old, the bullocks averaging 1,300 lb. on the hoof, and worth $3\frac{1}{2}$ cents to 5 cents per pound. The best of these cattle will dress 56 lbs. to 58 lbs. to the 100 lbs. live weight.

Besides shorthorns and shorthorn grades, the Detroit meeting presents good specimens of Herefords, Holsteins, and Channel Islanders. The pure Herefords, although not making much pretension to milk, are useful, thriving beasts, chiefly descended from English-bred animals, or those brought from breeders of repute in New York State, or from Mr. F. W. Stone. Guelph, Ontario, long favourably known as an importer and breeder both of shorthorns and Herefords. The Holstein and Channel Island stocks, although very well adapted for dairy purposes, do not grow big enough or lay on beef quickly and kindly, nor do they appear to mix satisfactorily with the indigenous sorts.

Sheep at the Michigan show, as elsewhere in the States, are not so good as the cattle. The housing of the flock throughout the severe winter in Canada and various of the Northern States interferes with their well-doing. . Nowhere in America is mutton in such demand as beef; in most markets it is 2*d.* per lb. lower. Sheep hitherto have been cultivated almost exclusively for their wool. Merinos and Merino grades are greatly in excess of all other breeds. In Ohio, Michigan, and other States, English sheep are, however, being tried, and at Detroit there are some good pens of Cotswolds, Leicesters, and Oxford Downs. As at home, the first crosses, produced by mating these improved sorts either with the indigenous breeds or with Merinos, are particularly good; but it is difficult satisfactorily to proceed further. At the Michigan fair, as at other such exhibitions, official reports are prepared setting forth the weight and age of all the prize animals, their mode of feeding and other particular records, which afford valuable information regarding the capabilities of different breeds and sorts of animals, and the economy of the several methods of feeding.

In this district sheep-breeding is carried on in conjunction with cattle-raising, and the growth of a limited amount of grain and fodder for winter feed and a little wheat for sale. Mr. E. J. Hardy, of Livingston county, who shows some of the best Merinos at this State fair, has a useful farm, which represents the general mode of proceeding among the better class of successful cultivators. He owns 580 acres, of which 160 acres are wood. His flock consists of 400 Merinos derived from Vermont, whence from time to time he obtains fresh blood. Like many of his neighbours, he hails from New England. He has 200 breeding ewes; they produce their first lamb when three years old. The lambs are dropped throughout April, sometimes as late as May; unless housed, they could not stand the earlier spring cold; 150 to 180 is the annual crop. Twins are not common, and are not desired: one good lamb is declared better than two poor ones. The ewes continue breeding until they are seven or eight. Ewes and bucks for stock are readily sold at 1*l.* to 5*l.* The fine fleece weighs 12 lbs. to 16 lbs. of unwashed wool—some of the rams have given 35 lbs.; the price, now steadily advancing with other things, varies from 10*d.* to 13*d.* Along with the sheep Mr. Hardy at present runs four pedigree shorthorn cows and ten good grade cows, rears his calves well, and sells the two-and-a-half year bullocks, weighing 1,200 lbs. to 1,500 lbs. Fifty to 100 acres of wheat are grown. The yield varies from 20 to 30 bushels—this year it is 22; $1 per bushel is the average price obtained for it. Clover and timothy grass, sown with the wheat, remain down for three or four years, and are mown the first and sometimes the second year. The grass is sometimes ploughed up early and a sort of fallow made. Indian corn is planted from the 12th to the 25th of May, as soon as risk of frost is over. One hundred bushels of corn in the cob are a fair return. Oats follow, drilled as early as possible in April, and producing 30 to 50 bushels. The farm is worked by himself, two sons, three men in winter, and five in summer, the helps receiving about 1*l.* a week, with board and rations. Four or six horses, harnessed, of course, in pairs, do the ploughing, overtaking each team 1½ to 2 acres a day. Mr. Hardy, with just pride, says he has worked for all he has. His land fifty years ago cost about 10*s.* an acre; some has since been added at 6*l.*; but house and buildings have been put up, roads and fences made, and the farm is now worth 15*l.* an acre.

The pigs generally are as good as can be seen at any English show, although not exhibited in such a state of helpless obesity. Berkshire are most popular, numbering 60 pens. Fisher Hobbs's Essex breed is also much appreciated. Suffolks and white Chesters contribute many good entries, while Poland Chinas, a less familiar breed, are distinguished by their black and white colour, somewhat scooped jowls, rather long fine noses, good frames, and lightness of offal.

A few of the show-yard arrangements at Detroit, as at other such agricultural gatherings, appear capable of improvement. The want of catalogues renders it difficult to find what one wants, and leads to many things which one would gladly examine being overlooked. Entries being made up to the opening of the show, and animals and implements forwarded apparently with little or no notice, there is not time to prepare detailed catalogues. Another proceeding which seems inexpedient is the grouping together of each person's exhibits, so that except when the objects are placed together for judging, it is difficult for the enquiring public to estimate the number of competitors or to gauge the relative merits of the implements or animals making up the class.

The general exhibition arrangements at Detroit, as elsewhere in America, are, however, conducted with spirit and good effect. The presence of President Hayes, his wife, General Sherman, and Staff, added to the *éclat* of the proceedings. On the Thursday the President gave an address setting forth the progress made in this and other States. On Friday he drove and walked through the yard, spending several hours examining the more interesting objects and chatting to many friends. Forty to fifty thousand people were on the ground daily, but so judicious were the arrangements of the active executive committee, that not a hitch or accident occurred. American agricultural shows present more variety and bustle than corresponding exhibitions in the more sedate mother country. With a licence costing a few dollars, cheap jacks, itinerant doctors, acrobats, and jugglers have their stands and their circle of admirers. Private and other carriages by the score traverse most of the wide avenues. Advertising, which is advanced almost to the position of one of the fine arts, is pushed in the most varied and telling manner, neatly got-up circulars being distributed by officers in all manner of costumes, as well as from carriages and balloons. A line of railway runs into and through the showyard for the delivery, unloading, and loading of implements and live stock. Such helps to the ready movement of heavy goods carried throughout the yard might have been of signal service at recent Royal shows. Booths, refreshment stalls, and vendors of fruit are ubiquitous and numerous, but not a drop of intoxicating liquor is sold in the yard. With their plates of beef and pork, their tea, coffee, fruit, and lemonade, visitors of all classes made, however, good cheer, and appeared most thoroughly to enjoy themselves.

CHAPTER XII.

CHICAGO GRAIN AND CATTLE TRADES.

CHICAGO illustrates well the activity, enterprise, and progress of a young American city. Fifty years ago it was a fishing village, boasting of seventy inhabitants, on the swampy edge of Lake Michigan. It has twice been burned, and has twice risen bigger, busier, and more bumptious than ever. The capital of Illinois, the queen and metropolis of the West, the home of 500,000 people, the centre of a network of some sixteen railroads, she attracts the growing agricultural produce of the West, North, and South; she draws her supplies of grain and live stock for 1,000 miles. By four great lines, as well as by lake and canal, she cheaply transports to the eastern seaboard, 900 miles distant, the varied produce she receives. Substantial and handsome public buildings have been erected; fine wide streets with stone and brick buildings in varied styles of architecture have been symmetrically laid out; two sumptuous parks have been enclosed, planted, and intersected with carriage roads, trotting tracks, and shady paths for foot-passengers. With screw jacks and hydraulic apparatus, the houses in some quarters have been raised many feet, and the levels of streets and their sanitary state improved. Planked footways are elevated two to four feet above the central roadways, which in Chicago, as in too many other American cities, are often uneven and worn, whilst in some of the second-rate streets no attempt has been made at storing or putting any foundation into the roads. Convenient tram cars run in most of the principal thoroughfares. Two miles out from the lake shore the water supply of the city is drawn and distributed by two engines of 1,000 horse power. Admirable arrangements are made for the early discovery and putting out of fire. Besides the well-trained official brigade, there are squads of efficient private firemen in connection with all the great establishments. The main pipes of most of the new buildings constitute one side of a ladder, which, although not at all conspicuous, is serviceable for rescue in case of fire; but also appears to afford considerable facilities for burglarious entrance of the upstair premises. With the adoption of our handy fire escapes, which do not seem to be used in America, these fixed ladders would be less needful. The sewage question is a most important one in America, as at home, and was for some years a puzzling problem here. By a great cutting of several hundred feet, extending for several miles, the streams which bore these polluted waters are made to run what was formerly uphill, and now discharge some miles distant into the Mississippi. These costly improvements, some of which have not always been judiciously or economically undertaken, led some years ago to a heavy floating debt, which has, however, been extinguished; the bonded debt reduced to 13,000,000*l.*; and the municipal expenses are met by a rate of about 3 per cent. on the valuation of property throughout the city. Considerable complaints, however, occur concerning the inequalities of the valuation lists, which, including real and personal property, exhibit an aggregate of $117,970,035.

Everybody in Chicago appears actively occupied, earnest in his work, and bent on making money. Gentlemen are at their business offices or in their stores by eight, and some of them earlier; and with an hour, or often less time, for dinner, they work steadily on until six or seven. As elsewhere throughout America, telegraphs and telephones are in general and constant operation. One firm sometimes receives daily 500 messages, of which a considerable number are from Europe. There are in Chicago upwards of 1,000 subscribers to the Telephone Company. The labouring population is mostly steady and industrious. Lager beer is the chief drink. Although there is more dissipation than is good for the unfortunate victims, there is much less than in most cities of the like size in Great Britain; and it will be a long time before half the artisan and labouring population, as in Chicago, live in their own houses. There is a large German population, eminently industrious, but decidedly Socialistic in their views, and so opposed to decent Sunday observance that they have gradually secured the opening, not only of museums and art galleries, but of concert halls, theatres, dancing saloons, and public-houses. Sunday afternoons and evenings in

Chicago are accordingly the special seasons of most festive merry-making. They are sometimes also devoted to hard work. One Sunday evening, straying out of the Grand Pacific—one of the biggest, most sumptuous, convenient, and economical of hotels—I found several hundred men at work, taking up and relaying the wooden pavement of one of the principal streets. Operations had commenced at dusk on Saturday; during the night the work progressed admirably, under the cheering influence of an electric light at each end of the section under repair; with relays of workmen toiling uninterruptedly, several hundred yards of new wood pavement, without hindrance to business, were ready on Monday morning. Although we might dispense with the Sunday labour, something of this promptitude of official action and consideration for public convenience would be very advantageous at home.

The Produce Exchange at Chicago is one of the most stirring in the world. An immense amount of business, real and speculative, is effected; hundreds of operators are ready to buy on forward delivery, wheat, corn, canned meats, mess pork, or anything which promises a rise. A wholesome arrangement insists, however, that each purchaser on forward delivery shall provide at his banker's a margin to meet any drop in the value of his purchase. Just outside the Mercantile Exchange is a large well-frequented saloon, thronged by a still more speculative crowd, where several auctioneers, throughout the long day and well into the night, proclaim and sell the odds on English races, Manchester pedestrian competitions, Paris cock-fights, chess tournaments, and all manner of sport and gambling enterprises throughout the world. Unsuccessful efforts have been made to put down this wholesale public gambling. To do so would, however, consistently necessitate some sweeping alterations in the management of the Produce Exchange, which it might, at present, be difficult to arrange. The spirit of gambling, too rife throughout young America, is further displayed in the offices, found in Chicago and other cities, where a dollar or other small amount can be invested in wheat, lard, railway, or other stocks. On the chances of 'making a pile,' shop boys, artisans, and many women last autumn were going in for speculations of this sort.

The general business of Chicago is great and rapidly expanding. She received during 1879 about 1,333,333 tons of coal, valued at from 10*s*. to 30*s*. per ton. The 1,469,878,991 feet of lumber, and 700,000,000 roofing shingles, about half of which are used in the city and suburbs, testify to the activity of the building operations. Nearly 50,000,000 lbs. of wool and upwards of 61,000,000 lbs. of hides are annually despatched. One and a half million barrels of salt are brought in for meat-preserving. Yearly there is now made up and sent off 110,000 packages of beef, 354,000 barrels of pork, 835,000,000 lbs. of cured meats, 250,000,000 lbs. of lard, 50,000,000 lbs. of butter.

The grain business of Chicago reaches large dimensions. She controls, buys, and sells yearly up-

Enormous Grain Business.

wards of 4,000,000 barrels of flour, 4,000,000 quarters of wheat, double that quantity of Indian corn, 2,500,000 quarters of oats, upwards of 1,500,000 quarters of barley, besides rye and buckwheat. Besides what is delivered by lake and canal, the railways bring in annually about 250,000 car-loads of grain, each car averaging about 400 bushels. Of this great amount of grain nearly one-half is brought forward by two lines of railroad—the Chicago and North-Western, and the Chicago, Burlington, and Quincy. It is graded by sworn officials, red, winter, and spring wheat being each divisible into three classes, and rejected; a large proportion passes through the elevators and store-houses of the city; a small amount is retained for home consumption; about one-half is forwarded to the manufacturing and commercial Eastern cities, and for export by lake and canal; the remainder is transported by rail, the Michigan, Central, and Lake Shore and Michigan Southern conveying the largest proportion. Competition between the several railroads and the various water routes secures cheap transport from Chicago to the Atlantic seaports and to Europe, a fact which very materially affects the price of bread in Great Britain. During the last few years the transit charges have been very moderate; 100 lbs. of grain have been forwarded 800 or 900 miles to the eastern seaboard for an average of 1*s*. 3*d*. by rail, and little more than half that amount by water in steam-tugged barges down lake and canal; 100 lbs. of provisions are carried for 1*s*. 5*d*.; McCormack's reapers, manufactured here, ploughs, and other machinery, are conveyed to New York or Boston at about 1*s*. per 100 lbs. These charges doubled represent the usual cost of forwarding the goods on through bills of lading to the seaboard and across the Atlantic to British ports. During 1879 freights for grain from Chicago to Liverpool varied considerably; in June they fell as low as 6*s*. per quarter, but in November and December were doubled. The freight of the large grain exports forwarded to Antwerp during the winter was about 12*s*. per quarter. The combination or 'pool' formed by the leading railway companies was inaugurated in June 1879, to secure more uniform rates, to discourage the special charges hitherto so commonly made in favour of large operators, certain sorts of traffic, and certain localities, and to prevent the ruinous competition which has frequently occurred between different lines. The railway interests in America are powerful, they are now well 'organised;' whilst the combination holds together, ruinously low tariffs such as have sometimes ruled will be impossible. But competition between rail and water routes, improved transit facilities, and the steadily expanding trade, render unlikely any material or permanent advance on the present moderate transport charges. Grain, as now, will probably continue to be forwarded from Chicago to Liverpool or London at about $\frac{1}{4}d$. per lb., whilst goods in cases or otherwise will come at less than $\frac{1}{2}d$. per pound.

 The grain business of Chicago could not be overtaken with its present expedition and cheapness without the great elevators, of which there are now upwards of twenty, with a storage capacity of 17,000,000 bushels. The first grain elevators in America were built at Chicago eleven years ago by Messrs. J. and E. Buckingham; the plans adopted have been tolerably closely adhered to; and here, as well as elsewhere in America, they effect enormous saving in the handling of grain. They are generally built on piles by the side of a lake, river, or canal, to enable barges, and even vessels of considerable tonnage, to come alongside. They vary from 200 to 400 feet in length, 100 to 150 in breadth, and reach 150 feet in height. The ground floor is arranged for the reception, unloading, and loading of the railroad cars, in which the grain is almost invariably carried loose. Outside is generally a wharf, against which the barges are brought up. The foundations and walls as high as the first story are of substantial masonry, but above this they are generally of timber, cased with slates. To lessen the risks of fire, and limit if possible its destructive effects, brick walls are sometimes carried up from the ground separating the building into sections.

The interior of the building is mainly occupied with a series of bins, which in a large warehouse sometimes exceed 300; they are 10 to 15 feet square, 50 to 75 feet deep, hold 2,000 to 6,000 bushels, their walls are made of six-inch battens two inches thick, securely held together with nine-inch pins, strengthened by a rod of iron passing across them, with a little ladder in one corner for cleaning out, and hoppered in the bottom, from which their contents are drawn. These bins can be put in connection with one or other of the ten or fifteen elevators which raise the grain from the cars, or with the shoots which discharge it into cars or barges. The elevation is effected by india-rubber belts, on which at intervals of 13 inches block tin buckets are fixed with strong flat-headed iron screw-bolts. The belts taking less power are preferred to the worms used in many English mills. From the cars the grain is shovelled into receivers through which the belt runs, and in ten to twelve minutes the load of 400 bushels is moved by one elevator. As it is passed along to the bin reserved for it, it is weighed automatically. In some warehouses the stuff, if desired, can also be winnowed. The discharge of grain is effected even more rapidly than its reception. From a shoot twelve or thirteen inches in calibre, the grain rushes into the cars or barges. Using several shoots simultaneously, 80,000 bushels can readily enough be shipped in a day. This amount of work, involving in a considerable concern the movement of several million bushels in a year, is effected with a minimum of labour and expense. Engines of 300 to 400 horse power drive the machinery; the few hands employed adjust the elevators and shoots to the different bins to be filled or emptied, take the weights automatically registered, and credit or debit the amounts run in or out.

Besides the earlier elevators put up by the Messrs. Buckingham, Messrs. Munger, Wheeler and Co. now have six at the depôts of the Chicago and North-

Cheap Handling of Grain. 169

Western Railroad, and Messrs. Armour, Dole and Co. have four in connection with the Chicago, Burlington, and Quincy Lines. That built last summer is large and substantial, 425 feet long, 120 feet wide, 140 feet high. The stream beside which it is placed has been dredged so as to command 16 feet of water; it contains 326 large and 72 smaller bins; it has storage for 2,000,000 bushels; it cost about 80,000*l*. On the double track 24 cars can be brought within the building, and, if need be, might be emptied simultaneously by the 24 elevators. There are 13 spouts by which cars can be loaded, and nine to fill the barges at the wharves. The charges for receiving the grain at these elevator warehouses, storing it for ten days, and delivering it again, is $1\frac{1}{4}$ cents. per bushel. For every additional ten days or part thereof the charge is $\frac{1}{2}$ cent. As a deterrent to the forwarding of indifferent stuff, it is charged at higher rates. If the grain when received is condemned by the inspector as unmerchantable the charge for the first ten days or part thereof is two cents., whilst for each additional five days or part thereof $\frac{1}{2}$ cent. is further added.

Mr. Charles Randolph, the obliging Secretary of the Board of Trade, informs me that Chicago business is expanding in all departments. Specie payments have increased confidence and circulated ready money. Better cultivation and more money spent on the farms are producing better returns. Land is advancing in value; the poorer farmers are getting out of debt; those who have been hitherto paying their way are saving money. The cost of wheat-growing in Illinois and adjoining States he gives as follows :—

	£	s.	d.
Rent of land worth £5 bearing interest at 6 per cent.	0	6	0
Taxes at 2 per cent.	0	2	0
Ploughing and seeding	0	7	0
Seed, 1½ to 2 bushels	0	6	0
Harvesting and stacking	0	10	0
Thrashing and cleaning	0	5	6
Delivery to railway station	0	2	0
	1	18	6

The winter-sown variety in Illinois constitutes six-sevenths of the wheat grown, and with fair cultivation has recently reached 18 bushels an acre. This gives 2s. 2d. as the price per bushel or 16s. 8d. as the price per quarter. Where 25 bushels an acre are reaped the cost of production would be reduced to 12s. 6d. per quarter. Taking 13 bushels the recent general average of the whole of the States as the acreable yield the price per quarter is advanced to 24s. Mr. Randolph sees no reason to suppose that the cost of wheat-growing will increase, nor does he believe, railroad pools notwithstanding, that transport charges will advance. Indeed, as the country becomes more closely peopled, freight charges, both by lake and railroad, will be reduced. Improvement of the lake and Canadian water routes would reduce transport charges to the seaboard. The exports of 1879 have been tolerably equally divided between the United Kingdom and the Continent of Europe.

The Chicago stock-yards, four miles to the south-west of the city, are the largest and busiest in the world. They are owned by an enterprising company, were opened in 1865, and occupy 370 acres. They have convenient access from 13 different lines of railroad. They comprise nearly 500 open cattle yards, nearly 700 hog and sheep pens mostly covered, 300 chutes and pens, with houses and barns for the storage of hay and corn. There are 15 of Fairbank's scales, on each of which 50 tons of beasts can be weighed at a time. In this stirring live-stock centre are the business offices and premises of 200 firms, and immediately connected therewith are 26 packing houses, which slaughter about 2,000 cattle and 20,000 hogs daily. At the yard is published every day a well-conducted stockman's journal and market bulletin. There is a capital hotel with 350 rooms, built at a cost of 20,000*l.*, endowed with a good garden and a dairy of 25 cows. The drovers, who receive 5*s.* to 8*s.* a day and are employed by the quarter, half, three quarters, or whole day, are capitally provided for, have a bright clean luncheon bar, ornamented with hanging baskets and great pots of flowers, and opening into courts beautified with shrubs and flowering plants. Three artesian wells furnish a capital supply of water. The annual receipts of live stock at this great centre during 1879 amounted to 1,210,732 cattle, 6,539,244 hogs, nearly 500,000 sheep, 10,000 horses; representing an aggregate value of 30,000,000*l.* sterling. The numbers of the stock have doubled since 1872. With the exception of 8,176 cattle and 2,321 sheep, all these animals are delivered into the yards by rail. Nearly half the cattle and sheep received and one-fourth of the hogs are forwarded east alive or dressed.

In these stock-yards occur admirable opportunities of studying the diverse sorts and conditions of the bovine race. Belonging to Mr. Walker and Mr. Sharman and housed here, presumedly for instructive contrast with less improved specimens, were on the occasion of my visit September 1879, 16 fat three-year-old shorthorns, most of them weighing over 2,000 lbs., one very good two-year-old shorthorn, scaling 1,800 lbs., a five-year-old scaling 3,500 lbs., two grand massive Herefords, and several good Devons. Outside in yards, many of them 60 feet long and 20 wide, with provision for food and water, amongst the daily arrivals are lots of superior grades, showing the ameliorating effects of several crosses of well-selected Shorthorn or Hereford sires. Useful beasts are forwarded from Minnesota and Iowa, where some capital herds have been established. Strong-limbed tolerable-looking steers come from Montana, where the grass is good and the cattle grow big and strong, but appear to have a tendency to get too far from the ground and lack quality. Compact sires such as could be picked from some well-bred herds in this country or in Kentucky should, however, remedy these shortcomings. Several good lots were pointed out from Oregon—not so large, but with more of the shapely form, levelness, and coat, distinguishing ordinary Yorkshire or Lincolnshire beasts. Some very serviceable lots were from Colorado, shapely animals, of fair quality with two or three Shorthorn or Hereford crosses, generally three years old, worth $3\frac{1}{4}$ cents. per lb., live weight reaching 1,000 to 11,000 lbs. and dressing 56 lbs. to the 100 lbs. But here, as in other great Western markets, the large proportion, especially during summer and autumn, are Texans—rough, flat-ribbed, leggy, Spanish-looking subjects, narrow in the back, open in the loin, usually with immense horns, often of a yellow colour, weighing alive, or 'on the hoof' as it is termed, 900 to 1,200 lbs.

The cattle are all branded permanently and deeply, the brand being made with a hot iron, when the animal is a calf, and sometimes repeated annually. Besides having the disadvantage of cruelly punishing, this branding deteriorates the hide. A handy sufficiently permanent mode of identifying animals straying widely over plain and prairie is a desideratum. The bulk of the cattle are reared on the great plains of Texas, amidst the beautiful valleys of Colorado, in the parks and glades of Wyoming, or on the western side of the Rockies in Oregon or Washington. By far the larger proportion of the summer and autumn supplies have journeyed over 1,000 miles, have probably been driven some hundred miles to one of the stations on the Union or Northern Pacific railroad, and loaded seventeen to twenty in a car. In transit they are very well attended to, and are fed, watered, and rested three or four times. Their travelling expenses for 1,000 miles add about 30*s*. to the value of each beast. The stores in Chicago average 1*d*. to 2*d*. per lb. live weight. Thousands are purchased in the autumn by the farmers in the Mid and Eastern States to be fed during winter, mainly on hay and Indian corn. These corn-fed beasts, ripe and well-matured, are forwarded to the winter and spring markets. Useful fat beasts, 900 to 1,500 lbs, at Chicago, vary from $1\frac{1}{2}d.$ to $2\frac{3}{4}d.$ per lb. live weight, and produce according to their condition, from 50 to 60 lbs. of beef to every 100 lbs. of live weight.

Sheep from Colorado, Montana, and even from the arable farms of adjacent States, show a great deal of Mexican and Merino blood, and realise about the same prices as the cattle. The cattle and sheep are generally classified as 'shipping or export,' and 'butchers;' the store cattle are described as 'stockers and feeders,' the lowest grades are 'through Texans,' 'common natives,' and 'scrubs,' averaging 700 to 900 lbs. live weight. The hogs are very good, vary from 150 to 300 lbs. and range in value from $1\frac{1}{2}d.$ to $2\frac{1}{2}d.$ per lb., and are classified under the several designations of choice packing, good shipping, selected heavy, Philadelphias, light bacon, singers with culls, keps and graziers.

All cattle, sheep, and hogs are sold by live weight; from one to a score or more are run on to the Fairbank's scales; the seller endeavours to secure their being first fed and watered. Officers of the Society for the Prevention of Cruelty to Animals are constantly in attendance to report upon and prevent cases of cruelty or neglect. As hay is procurable at 40s. per ton, and corn at 1s. 6d. per bushel, the animals are fairly supplied with food. The stock-yard

All Animals Sold by Weight. 175

charges are 1*s.* per head for cattle and horses, and 4*d.* for hogs and sheep. The salesmen, of whom there are 100 connected with the stock-yards, charge 1*s.* for commission on the beasts, and about 6*d.* on the sheep and hogs. Consigners are much more satisfactorily dealt with than they are at most British marts. Their memorandum of sale sets forth the exact live weight of the animals, the value paid, and the name and address of the purchaser. Store stock and even milk cows are all sold by weight; the stores are generally one to two cents. per pound less than the butchers' beasts. Good grades, two to three years old, are generally preferred for fattening. Both cattle and pigs have steadily improved, especially during the last ten years. The better selection of breeding stock, and their more judicious management, continue to bring from the great breeding regions of the West still increasing numbers of more shapely and economical animals.

Too wide a margin often exists between the price that the farmer receives for his cattle and sheep and the prices that the beef and mutton are sold to the British public. Profits are sometimes swallowed up by unnecessary multiplication of middlemen; waste and expense are frequently incurred by slaughtering in inconvenient private killing houses; from the want of cold storage chambers a great deal of meat during hot weather is spoiled, whilst much of the offal is also wasted or misapplied. Such losses injuriously affect alike producers and consumers. The American methods of slaughtering, storing, and distributing the meat and offal are generally preferable to our own.

At large public abattoirs, which are almost universal in all considerable cities, and which commend themselves both from an economical and sanitary point of view, the slaughtering is effected rapidly and cheaply. Cold storage chambers ensure thorough cooling and preservation of the meat; the whole of the offal is systematically made the best of. The abattoirs and beef and pork packing establishments of Chicago exhibit in successful operation mechanical appliances, smartness, and systematic arrangement, much of which might be advantageously imitated in this country.

At the Union Stock-yards Mr. Nelson Morris has a large establishment where upwards of a thousand cattle are killed and dressed daily. Carcases, sides, or quarters are distributed to the retail butchers of the city. The canning and packing establishments take 700 to 1,000 carcases daily. Three or four car-loads are despatched most days to Boston and other eastern cities. Every week about 700 carcases are forwarded to England, in winter in cloths, in summer in refrigerating cars and chambers; and, so carefully cooled and managed is this Chicago slaughtered meat, that it is often eaten in London a fortnight later in as good condition as that killed only a day or two previously in the metropolis itself. For the different departments of the trade various animals are used: only the best pure breds or superior grades, weighing when hung up 700 to 750 lbs., are sent over the Atlantic. A proportion of these are also used by the home butcher. For the canning business four-year-old Texas and Colorado bullocks, weighing net 450 to 500 lbs., are chiefly used. The beasts at Nelson Morris vary according to quality, season, and supplies, from $1\frac{1}{2}d.$ to $2d.$ per lb. live weight; for every 100 lbs. of live weight they yield 52 to 60 lbs. of beef; the price per lb. of the carcases is thus about double that given for the live animal.

Communicating with a great common yard is a series of ten pens into each of which a couple of bullocks are driven. From a platform overhead the operator dexterously drops his pole, armed with a steel blade, which severs the spinal chord just between the first and second cervical vertebræ; the first thrust almost invariably takes effect; the animal drops instantaneously dead. The quivering movements sometimes seen have been ignorantly supposed to evidence suffering, but are purely involuntary muscular movements. So soon as the victim drops he is fixed by the horns to a revolving chain passing along the floor, worked by an engine, set in motion by the movement of a lever, and dragging the carcase out of the slaughtering pen some twenty feet to the great shed, where he is dressed. The large vessels of the neck are cut to allow thorough bleeding; the horns are promptly removed by a circular saw worked by the engine and set in motion as required by a spring on the floor; the skin is removed; the trees are applied in the usual manner and the carcase strung up. Eighteen cattle are killed and dressed in fifteen minutes. Seventy-five are sometimes turned into the cooling chambers in an hour.

Without laborious lifting or any heavy manual labour, the carcases, from the sheds where they are dressed, are swung along on wheels running on stout iron rods overhead, and ranged in the cooling chamber. The tongues are forwarded to the packing houses for preserving; the internal organs, carefully washed, are converted into sausages; the tallow is assorted, the best of it, worth $3\frac{1}{2}d.$ to $4d.$ per lb., goes for oleo-margarine; the second qualities are used for soap and candle-making; in eight large vats the heads, bones, and refuse are digested and made into manure; the blood is preserved for the same purpose; the hides are generally salted to ensure preservation, but here as elsewhere there are loud complaints of the damage done by the deep rude branding. The workmen receive from $5s.$ to $8s.$ daily. So promptly is everything done, so handy are the arrangements, so systematic the supervision, that the killing and dressing of each beast is profitably effected at less than $1s.$ Several hundred sheep are killed and dressed towards evening, remain in the cool chambers throughout the night; the carcases, even in hot weather, thus thoroughly cooled keep well, and are not liable to the green decay which is so liable to affect the deeper textures of our summer-killed, imperfectly cooled British meat.

Messrs. Libby, McNeil, and Libby are the most extensive and successful of the Chicago beef-canning firms. They have been engaged in the business nearly six years, and for five years have sent their goods to British markets. They have large convenient premises four stories high towards the southwest of Chicago, where the meat is received from the slaughter-houses, cooked, salted, canned and packed. The tins and boxes for its transport are made on the premises. In capacious cool cellars, where 20,000 packages can be stored, the temperature is maintained at 35° to 40° by iced brine constantly circulating throughout coils of galvanised pipes. Handy elevators connect the several stories. The railway cars are brought to the sides and rear of the building. Fifteen hundred hands are employed; the men receive from 5s. to 10s. a day; the girls and women have 12s. to 18s. a week; everything is done by day work, but each department is under thorough supervision and a full turn out of work is expected and got. The cans of two, four, seven, and fourteen pounds are made on the premises: 40,000 to 50,000 are turned out daily; about one half being of the 2 lbs. size. The tin and also the lead for solder come from Great Britain. Twelve machines are at work cutting and blocking the tins. Ingenious devices are adopted in their rapid soldering. To secure economical packing all the beef tins approach the square form. The two pound tins cost $3\frac{1}{2}$ to 4 cents; the 14 lbs., 11 to 12 cents; the substantial deal cases in which four dozen 2 lbs. cans are packed cost 17 to 18 cents.

Chiefly from Mr. Nelson Morris's slaughtering establishment are received during the busy summer and autumn months 900 carcases of beef daily. During 1878 and 1879 the carcase price varied from $3\frac{1}{2}$ to 4 cents per lb. Like most other commodities;

it has during the last few months advanced in price. In the great hall, cooled as above described, the carcases are received, cut up, and distributed for different purposes. The hams pickled for thirty days and dried are worth 7*d*. to 10*d*. per lb., and are packed in barrels containing 220 lbs. The flanks, generally boned, are salted, sometimes smoked, are largely used in the lumbering and North-west States, and are usually sliced for cooking. Beef in brine is employed for ships' stores, keeps a few months, is worth 4*d*. to 5*d*. per lb.; but is not a very satisfactory or increasing trade. The canning is the great and growing business; 150 tons of beef go daily for this department; all bone and gristle are removed; 2 lbs. of beef in the carcase are required to yield 1 lb. of tinned meat; a large proportion is put up as corned beef. It is partially cooked in baths of which eighty-two are usually in operation, each holding six barrels of beef. In suitable pieces it is transferred to the tins, which are wheeled to another set of baths, in which they remain from two to seven hours; and are gradually cooked without any loss of the natural juices or aroma. Air escapes through a puncture in the lid. Removed from the baths, three men are constantly occupied soldering this aperture in the tin. A scrubbing machine and several alkaline baths effectually cleanse the cans from grease, and economise the labour of about 300 girls by whom the tins are papered and packed. Sample tins are taken daily into the test room and examination made for leakage or for evidences of faulty keeping. The

Beef-packing.

business rapidly extends. For nearly a year Messrs. Libby, McNeil, and Libby have been unable to overtake their orders. The canned corned beef is in chief demand; the 14 lbs. tins go for restaurants and public institutions, but the largest trade is in the 2 lbs. tins; the beef is much preferred to the mutton, of which only a limited quantity is put up. Besides the articles mentioned, ox and pigs' tongues, ox tails and cheeks, are also canned; turkeys and chickens carefully boned are conveniently put up along with tongue; minced collops in 2 lbs. tins are in growing favour in Scotland. A great quantity of capital soups are prepared, and are coming into general use not only amongst private families in England, but in many of the great restaurants and hotels. The tallow is carefully rendered and disposed of. The marrow from the bones is tinned, much of it coming to England, where it is used as a substitute for butter, and for pastry making. All the refuse is preserved for manure making. Although each pound of meat averages only 4d. to 5d., the weekly takings amount to about 15,000l. About one half the canned meats are sent to Europe on direct bills of lading, at a cost of less than one halfpenny per lb. for transport; about one fourth of the total output is consumed in the United Kingdom.

Besides other packing concerns the Wilson company does a large and growing business. They started in 1874; their works now occupy seven acres in the west of the city; they employ nearly a thousand people; they preserve and put up daily the meat of several hundred cattle; in 1879 they turned out 8,000,000 tons of meat.

Chicago is the great metropolis of hog-packing. Two-thirds of the American hog-packing is done in the west: 70 per cent. is overtaken in the six cities of Chicago, Cincinnati, St. Louis, Milwaukie, Louisville, and Indianapolis; more than half are handled in Chicago, where, as already stated, nearly 7,000,000 hogs are annually concentrated and 5,000,000 are slaughtered.

The business has quadrupled since 1872; it has doubled since 1875. More pigs are killed in twelve months in Chicago than in the whole of the United Kingdom. Owing, however, to the diminished hog crop of 1880, packing has been on a more moderate scale than in 1878 and 1879.

Twenty-five firms are engaged in the trade, employing about 20,000 hands. The three principal, disposing among them of 2,500,000 hogs annually, are Messrs. Armour and Co., the Anglo-American Packing and Provision Company, and the Chicago Packing and Provision Company. The hogs selected from western markets and from the adjacent stock yards where 60,000 are sometimes pitched in a morning, are shapely, of good quality, well fed, but with more lean meat than distinguishes our pigs. They are Black Berkshires and Essex, a white sort analogous to our middle breed, and a useful China hog with light offal. Four consecutive good corn crops have increased their numbers, improved their quality, and also lowered their price, which in 1879 ranged from 1½d. to 2½d. per pound for live hogs. They vary from 160 lbs. to 260 lbs. net weight; the heavier are killed in winter.

Hog-killing was wont to be chiefly confined to the winter months, but with ice and refrigerating chambers two-fifths is now done during the summer months from March 1st to November 1st. The packing business formerly consisted in pickling and putting up the meat in barrels; now only 15 per cent. is dealt with in this way, the great trade is in dry-salting the bulk of the carcase and sugar-curing the hams. Science and skill are brought to bear on the several processes. Different cuts and modes of treatment are adopted to suit the taste of various markets. Quite recently Mr. Lorenzo Fagersten, of the Union Stock Yards, has been experimenting with boracic acid salts and especially with biborate of soda, which proves so serviceable as a tasteless antiseptic in the preservation of butter and other dairy produce. He finds that the hams, before being sewed up in calico, if moistened with the boracic solution, or better still if dusted with the dry salt, travel without suffering so much from the green mould which is apt to affect them, whilst a drop of the solution in the shank bone prevents fermentation and souring of the marrow.

To do a big roaring business is the ambition of these western packers. Their success is demonstrated in their enormous output, which for the year ending March 1, 1879, was valued at 14,700,000*l*.[1]

[1] *Twenty-Second Annual Report of Trade and Commerce of Chicago*, by Charles Randolph.

The results of the winter packing for the six months to March 1, 1879, was made up of the following products :—

	lbs.
Middles of various cuts	235,000,000
Green, dry, and sweet pickled shoulders	60,000,000
Backs and bellies	12,000,000
Singed bacon	1,115,125
Hams of various sorts	60,000,000
Barrels of pickled pork, 242,232 averaging 200 lbs.	48,446,400
Barrels of pigs' tongues, 7,091 averaging 200 lbs.	1,418,200
Barrels of hocks, 1,915 at 200 lbs.	383,000
Lard, 395,659 tierces containing 300 lbs.	118,697,700
Grease, 9,683 packages varying from 300 to 500 lbs. each	3,873,200
Total products of winter packing	540,933,625

This is, however, only the winter produce. The summer manufacture adds two-fifths to this amount. The grand annual total of Chicago's hog products approaches 900,000,000 lbs. More than 60 per cent. of it is exported to Europe; nearly half the export goes to the United Kingdom. The shipments have recently increased at the rate of 20 to 30 per cent. per annum. The daily despatch averages eighty carloads of twelve tons each.

The general procedure in most of these great hog-packing establishments is much the same. To one of the largest and most flourishing, belonging to Messrs. Armour and Co., I paid two visits.

Messrs. Armour handle 1,000,000 hogs annually at Chicago, and have similar establishments at

Milwaukie and at Kansas City, at each of which upwards of 400,000 are slaughtered and packed. From small beginnings in 1860 their business has steadily increased; within six years it has doubled. At the Chicago works at the stock-yards, 10,000 pigs are frequently killed daily in summer; 20,000 constitute a full day's slaughtering in winter. Two thousand tons of meat are sometimes despatched in a single day from the railway sidings which are conveniently brought into the premises. The works cover 14 acres; the buildings are four stories high, and are being constantly added to. In convenient carpenter's, blacksmith's, and engineers' shops skilled artificers are employed in repairs, alterations, and additions. Throughout the works and to the city offices telegraphic and telephonic wires are laid. There are six lifts, and hydrants and fire hose are fitted at convenient points on every story. A trained fire brigade is recruited from among the operatives, and a dozen well-drilled steady workmen always sleep on the works. The premises are insured for $1,000,000, the annual premium on different parts of the works varying from 1 to $1\frac{3}{4}$ per cent. Gasoline, prepared from oil stored in underground tanks, is used for the 700 lights requisite in the short but busy winter days. Two thousand men are employed in summer, and 3,500 in winter. Everything is done by day work, but all is so systematically and effectively arranged that no man can shirk his duty. Incompetence or idleness cannot be tolerated, for one man's trifling might stay the work of hundreds. The wages vary from 6s. to 8s. per day of 10 hours for ordinary labourers; but the butchers and skilled operatives, numbering about 500, including the men who cut up, attend to the salting, prepare the sausages, or otherwise exert special skill, energy, and care, earn 10s. to 15s. a day. Wages are higher in winter than in summer, and payments are regularly made every Wednesday.

The raw material which keeps this great establishment moving is conveniently found in the contiguous market, where 60,000 hogs are sometimes pitched in a morning, and on one occasion last summer the number ran up to 80,000. On one of Fairbank's standard scales, which will weigh 40 lbs. or 40 tons, the purchased pigs are duly weighed. They are selected for various markets and purposes from 6 to 18 months, ranging from 150 lbs. to 250 lbs. The average weight of the summer pigs is 218 lbs., of the winter 246 lbs. Messrs. Armour have large pens and yards where their purchases are fed and watered until required. No fasting is practised as in England. The grunter has his breakfast even if he is doomed before dinner time.

On the afternoon of September 19, Berkshire and Essex hogs, varying from 250 lbs. to 300 lbs. live weight, were being driven along the ascent and over the 'Bridge of Sighs' into the third story of the building in which the slaughtering is conducted. About a score are enclosed together in a catching pen. Around the victim's hind limb just above his dew-claw a piece of chain with a tolerably large ring at either end is passed. From a roller overhead is lowered a chain, terminating with a hook, which is deftly passed into the ring on the limb; the long chain is steadily wound up by steam. When the pig's head is about five feet from the ground, another hook, suspended from a wheel, is fixed into the ring round the limb. This wheel runs on a stout $1\frac{1}{2}$ inch iron rail, which is carried onwards through several large rooms for 100 yards, always at an incline, down which the pig is carried by its own gravity. The hog, astounded at being raised heels first from the ground, makes little resistance, and is swung over the wall of the catching pen. With one sweep of a sharp short knife the executioner severs the arteries and veins of the neck, occasionally penetrating to the heart itself. The blood flows through a grating into the premises below; every half minute the foremost of a row of some six or eight, now perfectly dead, by the touch of a spring is unhooked and plunged into a vat of steam-heated water, where he remains for about three minutes, and where nine or ten are immersed together. Every thirty seconds, or oftener, at the lower end of the vat, a great, curved, rack-like gridiron lifts a smoking hog on to the table, along which passes an endless chain, by which, fastened by the nose, he is drawn among ingeniously conceived and accurately working spring scrapers, driven by steam, and invented by one of Messrs. Armour's chief engineers. On each of seven cylinders are placed forty-eight steel blades, and so exactly and effectually do they work that in ten seconds the hog emerges from the machine thoroughly denuded of hair. Any slight oversight is made good by handscrapers wielded by a couple of men on each side of the bench. Necessity, as usual, led to the discovery of this handy machine, which saves the labour of ten men. The scrapers, who were making $3 a day, struck. They thought that at any sacrifice they must be retained. They reckoned not that machinery could supersede their laborious manual service, which at other places I have seen done by eight or ten stalwart negroes, usually working stripped to the waist. Here, as everywhere throughout the works, perfect order and cleanliness obtain. Vulcanized indiarubber hose hang suspended over the table, and jets of water, as required, are directed over the carcass, removing any adhering hair, scurf, or dirt. Again the hog is raised, this time by the nose; steam, as before, doing the lifting. Down the inclined rail he swings. Detained for a few seconds over a bench, he is disembowelled, each portion of his viscera being carefully separated, cleansed, and set aside for use. The lungs, heart, and liver are forwarded to the sausage department; the stomach, cleansed, also follows, to be used as a bag in which to pack some of the sausage meat, of which more anon. The intestines, stripped of fat, are scalded and form cases for the sausages. From England there have recently been enquiries for fresh or carefully preserved livers which it is not generally known, are the chief ingredient in mushroom ketsup. Over the next table the head is cut off, and removed for the lard tanks; the tongue, a dainty morsel preserved in sweet pickle, is exported in barrels and sold wholesale in London at $3\frac{1}{2}d.$ to $4\frac{1}{2}d.$ per lb, or nicely cooked is done up in tins disposed of at $9d.$; the ears are canned for home use. Still suspended from the iron rod, down a long passage, guided by a small boy with a long pole, and round a corner into a big cooling room swing along six hogs at a time. Here, to insure thorough cooling, they are cleft down on each side of the backbone, and again run along, still hanging from the ceiling, and arranged in battalions of several scores. The time taken to catch the hog, slaughter, cleanse, dress, and deliver him in this cooling chamber, is fifteen minutes. When two sets of executioners are employed double baths and two sets of scraping machines are at work, upwards of fifteen hogs are killed every minute and promptly and systematically subjected to the succeeding operations.

In the lofty cooling room, at a temperature during autumn of about 40° F., the air kept in motion by overhanging punkahs and blowers, the hogs hang five or six hours. To hasten cooling they are then divided down the back, the two sides only held together at the neck, and are moved, still wheeled on the iron rails, dependent from the ceiling into the ice-chamber, which is 400 feet long and 200 feet wide, located in the middle of the building, and maintained at about 38° F. by a 20 foot stratum of ice stored overhead. In this chilly atmosphere, darkened to economise ice, with a boy stationed at every entrance to insure rapid closure of the doors, the hogs remain about thirty hours. On the thoroughness of this cooling depends the success of the whole operation of summer hog-packing. Although in winter little ice is requisite, the summer demand absorbs 3,000 to 5,000 car-loads, each containing about 14 tons.

Firm and dry, the carcass, still suspended on the labour-saving rails overhead, is run to the door of another long room, is separated into two sides, and now for the first time is moved by manual labour. By a strapping fellow each side is seized, carried a few yards to a solid bench, where, with a powerful chopper, with a blow that would astonish a Mameluke, the ham is severed; as accurately the shoulder and underlying ribs are cut off, leaving a rectangular side of bacon. A gentler blow separates the feet, which are canned, pickled, or passed into the lard tanks. These skilful swordsmen, who never maul, and cut to a hair's breadth, receive 14*s*. a day in summer and 16*s*. in winter. The sides of bacon have the backbone partly or entirely removed; the tender loin or fillet, being more difficult to cure, is taken out, and sells readily for immediate use. The sides of bacon, averaging about 56 lbs., are removed on trucks to the salting house, thoroughly rubbed with salt, the Canadian and Liverpool being preferred, and a very little saltpetre. Each side takes up 2 lbs. to 3 lbs. of salt. In a dark, cool store-house these sides are piled to the number of 16 to 20, one on the top of the other. After the lapse of a week they are turned over and again rubbed. Occasionally they go out in twenty days; but if intended for long keeping they require double that time. Every piece, as it passes from the salting-house, is examined, a tester thrust in to ascertain if any taint has accidentally been incurred. It is then washed, scraped, dried and packed. Large boxes, containing eight to ten sides of bacon, or 500 lbs., are almost daily being put up for European markets. Messrs. Armour have large contracts with the United States Government, and, at a push, 150 of these boxes can be put up in an hour. Even in this country of cheap lumber these boxes cost 56 cents. each. The bacon bought unpacked goes at nearly a cent less per lb. Of those sides of bacon and shoulders, which are treated in much the same way, Messrs. Armour turn out yearly upwards of 80,000,000 lbs. weight. So economical and systematic are the arrangements, and so carefully is the best made of everything, that the sides of bacon and shoulders can with profit be disposed of, even at the present enhanced price, at 4½*d*. to 5*d*. per lb. In Liverpool and many other United Kingdom ports large quantities of this bacon are purchased, washed, nicely smoked, and disposed of at a handsome profit as 'Prime Wiltshire' or 'First-rate Yorkshire.'

In imitation of the British home-cured, singed bacon is now produced. The hog is swung from the slaughtering pen on to a hearth, where it is singed among straw and wood shavings, and its pachyderm rendered more tender. The belly pieces from smaller hogs, pickled in great vats, constitute a growing trade. Of this pickled pork 40,000 casks, each containing 200 lbs. to 300 lbs., are put up annually. These used to go chiefly to the lumberers, the sugar and rice plantations, and the West India Islands, but now a great demand has grown in this country, in France, and in Belgium; and of the carefully prepared New York bellies worth 54*s*. to 56*s*. per cwt., many tons are used in London, served up with Ostend rabbits.

The hams are of especial interest, for a very large proportion come to England of sizes and cuts to suit various markets. They are sold under many *aliases*, and are recognisable in Bond Street and other fashionable London shops, where their Chicago origin is not conspicuously set forth. Messrs. Armour last year turned out upwards of 5,000,000 lbs. of hams. Their London house alone received during 1879 nearly 300,000 hams, averaging 12 lbs. to 14 lbs. each, and sold wholesale at about 6*d*. per lb. In a sweet pickle, made with salt, sugar, and saltpetre, the hams lie in vats for sixty to seventy days, and are changed over three times. After trimming and scraping some are hung for three days in the smoking-room, amidst empyreumatic, antiseptic vapours of maple sawdust, are sewed neatly in calico, stamped, and packed thirty to forty together in a box with a partition down the middle, to insure ventilation and lessen the risks of bruising. In summer for air they come in crates. The breakfast bacon—the light bellies from pigs six or eight months old, in handy, shapely pieces of 8 lbs. to 10 lbs.—is treated much in the same manner as the hams, and, when smoked, brushed, and cleaned, is transferred to a packing-room, where each piece is rolled tidily in gray paper and sewn in calico by men who manage the needle with cleverness that a seamstress might emulate. In this department I saw twenty men busy, but in winter 100 are often occupied. Each is expected to put up 200 to 250 parcels for his day's work; the pay varies from 6s. to 8s. a day, but extra money is given for extra work or for extra hours. The breakfast bacon thus neatly sewn up for the American market is brushed over with a solution of chrome and riceflour to prevent access of flies; but the British public naturally object to this coating of the yellow poisonous lead salt.

The composition and manufacture of sausages are frequently a subject of suspicion and ridicule; but the materials and making here are above all doubt. In five large vats the steam-driven mincers are constantly reducing to a fine pultaceous mass portions of meat, trimmings from the sides and hams, with the heart, liver, and internal parts. From the usual machines, 29,000 lbs. of sausages are generally put up daily, and are readily cleared off by the pork butchers, hotelkeepers, and others, at about 5 cents. per lb. Extra work is often required from this department. Several descriptions of sausages are made —liver, blood, and pork, Frankfort, which is partly cooked and smoked, and keeps a week; Bologna, prized in Germany; 'the lion,' which is chiefly sent to France, and keeps a year. A new manufacture has recently been begun. The soft parts of the heads, cleansed and minced, are flavoured with salt, pepper, and spice, chiefly coriander seed, carefully cooked, canned in 2 lb. and 6 lb. tins; are ready for immediate use, or will keep ten years, and are becoming very popular under the names of collared head or brawn.

The American hogs yield about 5,000,000 cwt. of lard. The summer killed average 34 lbs., the winter 37 lbs. Messrs. Armour, buying hogs above the average in condition, have a yield of fully 45 lbs. of lard from their summer and 54 lbs. from their winter hogs. In 50 tanks, heated by worms from ten boilers, the fat and other refuse, melted during ten to twelve hours, are drained off in different grades. The first quality, made from leaf and trimmings, is recognised as 'prime steam lard.' The intestines and refuse yield a lower quality, known as No. 2 lard, a large proportion of which goes to Europe. Some of the bristles are conserved for brushes and for the cobblers, but the bulk of the hair is sent to this country in bales of 5 cwt., and, mixed with horsehair, is used for stuffing railroad and other carriage cushions. It is now worth 14*l.* per ton. The blood, dried in revolving steam-heated cylinders, contains about 14 units of ammonia, and is sold for \$28 to \$30 per ton to the sugar-refiners and manure manufacturers. For this latter purpose enquiry is now made for 1,000 tons to be delivered in the Thames at 9*l.* 10*s.* to 10*l.* per ton. The bones, after crushing and passing through the lard tanks, and the refuse from every department, are dried, pressed to get rid of grease and water, exposed for 15 minutes in a 25 foot steam-heated revolving cylinder, and constitute a valuable fertiliser, containing 8 units of ammonia and 21 of phosphates, sold at $16 per 2,000 lbs., and in growing demand among gardeners, nurserymen, and cotton planters.

Whilst a big wholesale and export business is the main concern with Messrs. Armour and Co., it is pleasing to find attention paid to the wants of their numerous employés, their families and neighbours. Adjacent to the office is a large shop, where hog in countless forms is sold at little over prime cost, for which a few oxen are also killed, and where the daily takings sometimes reach 500*l*. As if this pork business were not enough for one concern, Messrs. Armour have recently been directing attention to beef, and are now putting up compressed beef which contains all the juices and is not hard or fibrous.

In the Chicago office, Mr. Phil. Armour presides over the financial and business arrangements of this growing concern. Like some other Chicago merchants, he is usually at his office at 7 A.M., surrounded with correspondence, telegrams, and cabled price lists, while regularly every morning comes the statement of the London bank account of the previous afternoon. Telegrams from London, Liverpool, Belfast, Paris, Antwerp, and other parts of the world come in all day, often numbering several hundreds. Forty clerks are fully occupied in this representative Chicago pig-packing concern. Doing a big business, Mr. Armour rightly declares that he can work for a small profit. He says he has got rich by selling cheaply. He insists on ready-money transactions, and makes, accordingly, no bad debts. To use his own expression, his agents go with the goods in one hand, and get the money in the other. More than half their production is exported, and of this export more than half is taken by Great Britain. For sugar-cured hams and fancy goods England is their chief and increasing market. With through rates the produce is forwarded to United Kingdom ports at three-eighths of one penny per lb., and during the past two years tons have been sent at half that figure. Occasionally Mr. Armour has boldly obtained control of the bacon, pork, and hams of the West. During the summer of 1880 he has had on 'shows' and 'option' 40,000,000 lbs. of winter cut meats, and, squeezing the rising markets, is understood to have made 500,000*l.* by this big corner on pork.

CHAPTER XIII.

THE RED RIVER.

THE Red River Valley, extending for 350 miles from Breckenridge to Winnipeg, is destined to be one of the great wheat-producing regions of America. Its southern extremity lies in the State of Minnesota; it passes north through Dakota and Manitoba; nearly one-third is within the Canadian Dominion. Narrow at first, it widens to nearly 100 miles. It is bounded on the east by a chain of hills, but on the west the rise is gradual, the second ridge is as fertile as the Savannah, and several valleys debouch into that of the Red River. In a former era of the world's history, this extensive basin was evidently a great inland lake, within which was deposited with great uniformity a bed of diluvium, now represented by 12 to 30 inches of black earth, rich in vegetable fibre, friable, and perfectly free from stones, reposing on 50 to 60 feet of soft soapy argillaceous deposit, containing vegetable *débris*, while underlying this is a bed of gravel, amid which are small fragments of granite, porphyry, and limestone. These facts are disclosed by the wells which are sunk on many farms, and which generally supply a rather brackish water, apt to disagree with men and animals unused to it. This extensive tract of level prairie is occasionally interspersed, especially along the banks of the rivers and near the numerous lakes, with plantations and scrub; more frequently it extends with unvarying monotony for miles. The yellow and red prairie grasses are relieved occasionally by a piece of stubble; rarely is Indian corn attempted; oats and barley are only grown for home use. At far intervals are seen simple log huts, a few small ricks, or heaps of straw which there has not yet been time to burn. The valley is traversed by the Red River which is navigable as far south as Fargo, and by the St. Paul and Pacific Railroad section completed in 1878, running parallel with, and about 10 to 15 miles eastward of, the river.

At Fort Abercrombie in the southern part of the valley the rainfall averages 16 inches, the temperature of the three summer months is 71°: the three months' winter average is only 8°; the annual mean temperature is 40·34°. At Fort Burford in Dakota, west of the Red River, at an elevation of 2,210 feet, the average rainfall for ten years from 1868 is 12·36 inches; the heaviest rainfall, in 1872 and 1873, reached 20 inches. May and August appear to be the rainy months; thrice during this decennial period the May rains have measured 4 inches; in 1873 they reached 6·60 inches and caused much flooding. In August 1875 and 1876 the August rainfall was respectively 3 and 3·95 inches.[1]

The United States, although famous for great

[1] U.S.A. Agricultural Reports for 1878, p. 550.

undertakings, have not many large wheat-growing farms. Throughout the Eastern, Middle, and even the North-Western States the ordinary grain farmer seldom possesses more than 200 acres. But at Casselton, in Dakota Territory, in the valley of the Red River, is a striking exception—a farm of 75,000 acres held by Mr. Oliver Dalrymple. Four years ago this enormous farm was a portion of the far-reaching prairie wilderness. No evidences of human life were visible. Prairie fowls, snipe, jack rabbits, the prairie squirrel or gopher were the inhabitants; while wild ducks and geese congregated in creeks or marshy spots. A few years previously buffaloes and badgers were common, and on many spots of the untilled prairie their whitened bones still lie scattered. Some of the directors of the Northern Pacific Railway had acquired these lands and wisely appointed Mr. Oliver Dalrymple their manager, with a half share in the concern. Mr. Dalrymple brought to his serious task a goodly experience, acquired in successfully farming 6,000 acres at Lake Elmo, near St. Paul, Minnesota.

On Friday, September 26, 1879, the members of the Royal Commission, Messrs. Read and Pell, and a party under the guidance of Mr. James H. Drake, assistant manager of the St. Paul and Sioux City Railway Company, were most hospitably received by Mr. Dalrymple; were driven for miles over this vast prairie farm; examined its dark, friable, alluvial soil, perfectly free from stones, varying from 12 in. to 20 in. deep, resting upon an argillaceous stratum rich in vegetable remains; gathered information as to the cost of wheat production, and speculated on the permanence of continuous wheat-growing. The arrangements of this great farm are well considered and systematically and effectually carried out. Minor details receive more attention than on most farms of 100 acres; time and labour are everywhere economized. On one of the subdivisions of the property telephonic communication, at a cost of only $300, is established between the superintendent's office and those of his foremen; and this rapid and direct system of control is being extended throughout the whole estate. Substantial and economical wooden buildings have been erected at suitable points, consisting of houses for superintendents, sleeping and dining rooms for the men, stables, granaries, and sheds for the storing of the numerous and valuable machinery and implements, with blacksmiths' and carpenters' shops. Handy to the several buildings, wells, varying from 50 ft. to 80 ft., have been dug into the sand and gravel bed which underlies the clay. On one farm avenues of trees are planted out. A bookkeeper and two clerks have constant occupation in keeping accounts, checking off stores, arranging the vouchers without which no payment is made, and attending to correspondence. Amid such modern equipments and good cultivation it is difficult to realise that this busy, profitable settlement was six years ago lonely, barren prairie.

This Dalrymple property cost from 40 cents to $5 per acre. There are no federal taxes; rates, mostly for school purposes, amount to 10 cents per acre. The

Mr. Dalrymple's Big Wheat Farm.

estate is partitioned into divisions of 5,000 acres, each under the management of a divisional superintendent, who has under him two foremen, one of whom, on horseback, accompanies his 15 or 20 teams to work, sees to the ploughing or drilling, observes and reports as to the behaviour of the men, the condition of the animals, and the efficiency of the machinery. Each division has two or more sets of buildings, and in connection with the principal homestead of each farm are the quarters for the men—large wooden barrack rooms, comfortably warmed with stoves, where 50 men sleep in busy times two in a bed. Hard by are the kitchens, each with the capacity to provide for the wants of 100 men, presided over by the cook and his mate, who, on requisition through the foreman, draw supplies from the stores—flour for bread, puddings, and cakes, beef which costs fresh fully 3*d*. per pound, pork, bacon, cheese, and butter, tea and coffee, and other good things. But the stores, liberally provided with necessaries and luxuries, including some of the best butter and coffee we ever tasted, wisely dispense neither beer nor spirits. Three hot meals a day are provided: before 6 A.M., at noon, and at 7 P.M.; meat, bread, puddings, cakes, tea and coffee are supplied without stint.

All payments are made by the bookkeeper on vouchers signed by the foreman. Men can draw their money as they please. Some take it weekly; a few spend it at the beer saloons at Casselton; others, more provident, allow it to run on for weeks, or even for half a year. The rate of wages varies with the season. With board during the spring $18 a month (18*s*. a week) is given; during harvest wages advance to $2·25 a day; during the thrashing season the rate is reduced to $2; during the autumn months the pay is $25 per month. No piecework is adopted, but so thorough is the superintendence that full work is obtained from both man and beast. There is no difficulty in obtaining extra hands, amongst whom are many Norwegians, Scandinavians and Germans. During harvest and thrashing, which is done in the field, as many as 600 men are frequently employed. Even with this great accession of labourers, work proceeds systematically and harmoniously. No rows occur; brawling and fighting are extremely rare, but when they do occur it unfortunately is usually on Sunday. Dismissal for insubordination is scarcely known. Men injured or sick from causes beyond their own control are nursed and have medical attendance gratuitously. Extra men in harvest and during thrashing only receive pay for the hours they labour. So soon as frost prevents ploughing, the whole of the force on the farms are dismissed, with the exception of the divisional manager and about ten men, who each look after about 40 mules or horses, feed and water them, and turn them into a yard for a quarter of an hour's exercise night and morning. Hard as such wholesale dismissal would be in Great Britain, it is no hardship here, for these men readily find lumberwork in the forests. It is obviously an enormous boon thus to get rid of men whom the farmer cannot profitably employ during the five winter months. Many an English wheat grower would gladly practise this retrenchment and send most of his staff to other vocations during the short days and bad weather of mid-winter.

Twenty thousand acres are already under cultivation; 5,000 acres are broken up annually. The uncultivated portions are chiefly used in growing prairie hay and grazing the milch cows. During autumn four hundred mules or horses are daily engaged ploughing the stubbles, or back-setting or cross-cutting the land broken up from prairie during the early summer months. The sod of ages is readily disintegrated; the prairie grass, previously cut short by the mowing machine, is rotted. The stubbles are left of about the same length as they are in England; but since the straw is burnt it would save expense, both in reaping and thrashing, to leave a longer stubble and burn this and any weeds among it before the ploughs went to work. In one field we come upon nine double-sulkey ploughs; the ground being hard owing to a month's dry weather, four mules are allotted to each. The driver mounts comfortably, as on a reaping machine, guiding his four-in-hand with reins. Instead of a coulter, these ploughs, made by John Deer, Illinois, and costing $60, have a cutting wheel. The working parts are of steel; the shares are sharpened every third or fourth day. Each of the two ploughs turns a furrow 15in. wide by 5in. deep. In another field a dozen mule teams are similarly employed. Two and a half acres are at present turned over by each team daily; but when the ground is softer fully three acres are overtaken. The teams walk 17 to 20 miles daily, turn out at 6 A.M., are in the stable and fed for an hour at noon, and have four to five hours' work in the afternoon. The fields are conveniently laid out in squares of 100 acres. Some are fenced with oak posts and two strands of barbed steel wire, which keeps back cattle and horses, but not sheep and pigs, and has the disadvantage of lacerating any animal coming forcibly into contact with it. To prevent idly walking several miles to work, the teams going and returning invariably plough along the intervening fields, the twelve teams each time they go out or return contributing a broad strip of nearly 30ft. of ploughing.

The breaking up of the level prairie is neither tedious nor costly. No stones or tree roots cause breakage or delay. With the single hand ploughs and a pair of horses, or three abreast if the ground is very hard, a stout furrow, usually measuring 12 in. by 4 in., is turned. An acre and a half is easily overtaken in the May or June day of ten hours. Mr. Dalrymple estimates that the breaking up, allowing for wear and tear of plough and sharpening of the steel shares, which should last two seasons, costs him fully two and a half dollars. The stubble and cross-ploughing are computed to cost $1·75. Even in this newly-settled country small farmers and others can be hired to do the ploughing, furnishing a man and pair of good horses at the cost of 12*s*. daily, and doing regularly their 1½ acre in a workmanlike manner.

Mr. Dalrymple and Mr. Dutton, one of his intelligent and able divisional superintendents, both prefer mules to horses on account of their hardiness, endurance, equable temperament, and freedom from disease.

With about an equal proportion of mules and horses they have in four years used up 16 horses, but the whole of the mules are still serviceable, excepting one, which was accidentally injured. The mules are bought chiefly at St. Louis, at five or six years old; they are $16\frac{1}{2}$ to 17 hands, weigh 1,100 lbs. to 1,200 lbs., are well broken, steady workers, good-tempered and quiet, and cost on an average $140 (28*l.*), while the transit of 1,000 miles from St. Louis home puts about $10 (40*s.*) more on their price. Mules and horses do not differ much in value, and are managed and fed alike. They are housed in good lofty stables, accommodating about 50, standing in pairs in 9 ft. stalls. Racks and mangers are used as at home. They are tied by halters or head-stalls. The light harness, used indifferently for plough and wagon, costs $23 for each animal, and is expected to last ten years. The feeding, carefully attended to by the stable 'boss,' consists of 12 quarts daily of mixed home-grown oats and barley, and 15 lbs. to 20 lbs. of prairie hay. During winter the amount of corn is, of course, reduced, and this five months' rest and some days' lighter labour between seasons accounts for the good looks and condition of the teams and their standing satisfactorily at busy times 11 hours' work daily.

Towards the end of March the working staff are again got together. The lumbering is finished up, and men are ready for farm work. A few of the hands of former seasons return. The gang foremen, selected for intelligence and promptitude, are appointed. The whole of the land intended for crop has been ploughed in autumn; the newly broken, as indicated, has had a second furrow, which keeps down weeds and insures more certainty of result. So soon as the frost has left the first six inches of soil, which is generally by April 1, the seeding of the wheat commences. Scotch Fife, a good, hard, thin-skinned red variety, is used. The seed is selected from the newly broken-up land; if any cockle or other weeds are observable, they are carefully winnowed out. No dressing or pickling is adopted. During autumn or winter, in 1⅝ bushel lots, the seed for each acre is bagged up. Whenever the weather permits, seeding commences. The seed is distributed by broadcast machines, 100 being at work daily for three weeks. Two hundred sets of harrows complete the operation, two or three turns being required, and Mr. Dalrymple jocosely states that he orders it 'to be well done, and then give one turn more.' Four harrows, united by chains, work in a set, cover 20 feet., and are drawn by four mules. In each harrow are 72 round teeth; the set costs $14 to $15. Immediately after wheat seeding, the oats and barley grown for horse provender are put in.

No horse or hand hoeing, no weeding, or any further expenses are incurred until harvest. Seasonable showers usually occur during June and July; heavy dews restore part of the moisture removed during the warm noontide. For four years the seasons have been propitious. The drought during July 1879 occasioned, however, considerable apprehension. Prayers for rain were offered in the churches, while

Automatic Self-binding Harvesters. 207

English farmers were imploring fine weather. Another week of scorching drought would have shrivelled up the soft, milky ears : but the much longed-for rain came seasonably. Drought is probably the chief cause of uncertainty in the American wheat yield. Hailstorms and tornados, abounding further south, are unknown here. No wire worm, weevil, or fly interfere with Mr. Dalrymple's crops; mice and rats have not yet made their home in Dakota; sparrows, larks, and rooks are equally rare. Grasshoppers did some injury in 1876, probably diminishing the yield by three bushels an acre; but Mr. Dalrymple considers that he is too far north to suffer much from the hoppers, and believes that they cannot do much damage on cultivated land, although why such marauders should spare the cultivated crops is not very evident.

Harvest begins about August 1, usually amid fine, settled Californian weather. About 300 extra men are engaged. One hundred and fifteen automatic self-binding harvesters are busily at work; 100 of these are Walter Wood's, the remainder M'Cormick's. Both are reported to do their work admirably; no objection is found to the wire binding. The grain is shocked, and cutting is overtaken in 12 days. No time or outlay is expended in stacking. No barns or granaries are required in this dry climate. Trusting implicitly in fine weather the whole of the grain is thrashed from the field, indeed sometimes the wheat is not even shocked. Seventy-one steam thrashing machines made by the Buffalo Company, and costing $600, with thrasher, winnower, and straw elevator in one, are placed at convenient points throughout the fields. Ten wagons, each with a pair of horses or mules, bring up the shocks and carry off the thrashed corn in three bushel bags an average distance of two miles to the railway cars. A gang of 25 men keep wagons and thrashing machines steadily going, and deliver at the station 1,000 bushels of wheat daily. An expert on horseback superintends two or three harvesters or thrashers, keeps everything in good working order, promptly repairs any breakage, and thus loss of time is guarded against. Each day the thrasher and engine, which is partially self-propelling and costs $800, is moved, so as to shorten haulage of the sheaves. Every busy day, 50 railway cars, each containing 400 bushels, are loaded, and stand ready for despatch, usually to Duluth, 254 miles distant, on the western corner of Lake Superior.

The crops of 1879 and 1880 Mr. Dalrymple states to be much the same as those of former seasons. They average 15 to 20 bushels an acre of 60 lbs. to the bushel. The natural weight is 59 lbs. to the bushel. As usual the produce of the newly broken-up land is best. The quality is fully as good as that of 1878. When run once through the winnower at Duluth, it will be graded No. 1 hard. Mr. Dalrymple usually sells as fast as he can deliver, but in 1879, holding for the rise, he had for some weeks the chief portion of his crops warehoused at Duluth. The oats are reported to yield 50 bushels to the acre and 38 lbs. to the bushel; last year 60 bushels were produced. The barley did not do particularly well in 1879; but generally runs 40 bushels. On each farm a few potatoes, cabbages, swedes, and other vegetables are grown for home use and for the cows which are kept to supply dairy produce; but wheat-growing is the great business of this great farm.

Now comes the important question of the cost of production. Mr. Dalrymple furnishes the following figures:—

	$	c.
Land valued at $12 per acre, interest thereon at 6 per cent.	72	
Taxes and rates	10	
Buildings, machinery, and teams, valued at $10, interest at 10 per cent.	10	
Ploughing	3	0
Seed . . , ...	1	50
Harvesting and thrashing	3	0
Total cost of growing an acre of wheat . .	8	42

Mr. Dalrymple thus produces an acre of wheat for less than $8.50, or 35s. 6d. per acre; indeed, he asserts that hitherto the actual cost has not reached $8, excepting in the case of the first year's crop, which the extra expenses of breaking and two ploughings advance to $11. For four years his acreable yield is said to have averaged 20 bushels. On the basis of this calculation the wheat would cost nearly 43 cents, or 1s. 10d. per bushel, or 14s. 8d. per quarter. On his own and other suitable wheat-growing farms, in favourable seasons, Mr. Dalrymple declares that the crop does not cost more than 35 cents per bushel. Sold, as it readily can be at the railway station at Casselton, at 75 cents to 80 cents, a very handsome profit is obtainable. This return

P

approaches the Dutchman's 1 per cent., which on investigation proved to be a cent. per cent. return.

Forwarded to the United Kingdom, Mr. Dalrymple's wheat would further incur the following charges, and the quarter of 480 lbs. would be landed in Liverpool at 35*s.* 4*d.* For more accurate comparison with our English wheat weighing 500 lbs. one twenty-fourth would be added, bringing the cost to 37*s.*

	£	s.	d.
Cost of production of 480 lbs. wheat		14	8
Elevator charges at Duluth		1	0
Freight to New York		9	6
Ocean freight		6	0
Insurance, incidentals, and commission on sale		2	0
Landing charges		2	2
Total cost of 1 quarter of Mr. Dalrymple's wheat (480 lbs.) landed at Liverpool	1	15	4

Mr. Dalrymple's cheap production is, however, exceptional. His superior management, and the systematic manner in which the great business is conducted, secure results which are not attainable generally even on the best land of the Red River. Taking a considerable number of the best-managed holdings, and averaging these for a series of years, the bushel of wheat will be found to cost 50 cents instead of 35 cents, or 2*s.* per quarter more than it is favourably figured by Mr. Dalrymple. Even at this rate good profits remain for the grower, and with the transport charges above given, which represent a fair average of recent years, the quarter of wheat (480 lbs.) can, with profit to all concerned, be landed at British ports at 37*s.*

Important alike to producer and consumer, comes

now the question, will these crops and profits be permanent? At Mr. Dalrymple's no symptoms of deterioration are yet apparent. The land is clean; neither twitch, thistles, or docks appear. The chief weeds are wild cotton, barn grass, a sorrel with a yellow flower, and the Michaelmas daisies. The manure made from the stables lies about in heaps, which it is not yet thought worth while to apply. Excepting the small quantity of straw used for littering the animals, the whole produce of the 20,000 acres is burnt. The spots on which these heaps burn show no obvious difference from the rest of the field, indicating that the unassisted soil still contains phosphates and potash sufficient to grow full crops. How long the continuous corn-growing can be profitably persisted with is somewhat difficult to foretell. On similarly good land in various parts of the country fields are pointed out from which, without any restorative treatment, twenty consecutive crops of wheat have been reaped, and neither quantity nor quality as yet undergoes obvious diminution. Mr. Dalrymple is, however, too prudent a farmer to draw too long or deeply on the resources of his land. By ploughing year by year an inch deeper he brings up fresh plant food; by growing at intervals probably of four years, as he purposes doing, a crop of clover, rolling it down and ploughing it in, he intends cheaply to maintain fertility. By these means and by selection and change of seed, as well as by an occasional crop of oats or barley, Mr. Dalrymple's superior management will doubtless secure a continuance of good crops for many years.

The fame of Mr. Dalrymple's success is bringing settlers from Northern Europe, from England, and from Canada to aid in developing the resources of the Red River. There is less difficulty now than there was five years ago, in disposing of lands. Where reasonable judgment is used in making the selection, the untilled prairie, somewhat wet and forbidding, when broken up, proves a friable, deep, good soil, and both the soil and aspect of many parts of this level country forcibly remind one of the Cambridgeshire fens, the dikes, however, being absent. Long lists might now be made of successful cultivators. Mr. Dalrymple has near Casselton, a nephew, who last year grew 1,800 acres of wheat, and another with a section of 640 acres, most of it broken up. Mr. C. S. Barnes has had seven years' experience of the valley north of Glyndon, where five years ago no wheat was grown. He has this year grown 2,600 acres with an average of 15 to 20 bushels an acre, while on the poorer land he plants oats which cast 50 to 60 bushels an acre. But, perhaps, one of the strongest evidences of the extension of wheat-growing here is the fact that Mr. Barnes, in the prosecution of his corn-factor business, has during the last four years erected at various roadside stations throughout this country as many as thirty elevators, several of them worked by steam.

Mr. Hadwen, of Wheatland, near Casselton, Dakota, a near neighbour of Mr. Dalrymple, was born near Lancaster, England. He farmed for many years near Godridge, Canada, where he owns and lets a farm of 160 acres. He came to prospect this country

Extended Settlement. 213

in 1876, bought 730 acres close to Fargo, at $25 an acre, for which he is now offered $50, and also made a larger investment of 6,000 acres at Casselton, paying from $3.50 to $5. Of this he had 1,000 acres broken up the first year, and within 12 months had 19,000 bushels of wheat for sale. He now lets his town farm, receiving as rent one third of the produce, which has averaged nearly 27 bushels per acre. On his Casselton farm he has now 2,100 acres ready for planting his third crop next spring. A number of other farmers in the district have also done well. A blacksmith has invested his savings in 540 acres, lying close to the railway town of Fargo, and has had it for nearly three years entirely under cultivation. Besides other good stock he has a Percheron stallion, for which he paid $2,000, and for the use of which he gets $20, and has just completed a handsome two-storied house with dining-room and drawing-room. His son has 300 acres, and in his spare time hires himself and horses to plough for neighbours, receiving, according to depth and whether the land has been previously ploughed, from two to three dollars an acre.

The frontier towns and villages in this new region of cultivation and civilisation exhibit wonderful illustrations of rapid growth. Fargo, now a flourishing place with 2,000 inhabitants, in 1873 was a bare tract of Indian reserve, from which white men were warned off. From the Eastern States and Canada as well as from Europe, people of all nationalities have come in. Besides connections northward with Canada and with St. Paul and Chicago, by the St. Paul, Minneapolis, and Manitoba railroad, Fargo is on the main line of the Northern Pacific, which is opened west to Bismark on the Missouri, and is thence being pushed on to the Yellowstone river, opening up a country rich in coal and other minerals and bringing forward the cattle from Northern Wyoming and Montana. In Fargo, built of stone and brick, there are already three good hotels, and another in contemplation; rather too many bars and drinking saloons; a concert and ball room, where recently a grand subscription ball was given for which gentlemen's tickets were stated to be $25. There is a court-house and two portly courteous judges, and a provost marshal or commandant of police, all these important officers holding their appointments from year to year; a successful daily newspaper, two corn-merchants, a thriving school, while preparations are being made for building churches. An Opéra-Comique is in successful operation, where the nightly attractions consist in dramas, nigger and other songs, and dancing. I can vouch for the fun and humour and never-flagging spirit of the performances, for the goodness of the singing, and taste and capabilities of the orchestra. An imperturbable, irrepressible Irishman was represented as effectively as he could have been at the Haymarket or Olympic. I do not wonder that from an area of many miles the dark-visaged farm-fellows with slouch hats, many with blue guernseys, some lumberers in red flannel jackets, and occasional Indians, and many half-breeds, congregate in large numbers to this opera-house at Fargo. In the wide streets the population is busily occupied.

The immense and varied collections of agricultural implements are strikingly indicative of the breaking in of new lands. The light waggons are drawn by horses, mules, and oxen, but the ox teams are rather the most numerous.

But Fargo is a metropolis compared with the 'primordial cells' of towns budding at roadside stations, some in more advanced condition boasting of a hotel, beershops, dry goods store, post-office, and even a bank. Occasionally more imposing houses with at least two public rooms are noticed. Ploughs, reapers, and other implements lie at the stations, indicating more extended settlement, presaging more food for man and beast.

At this autumn season the land generally is dry, or only wet in the hollows and so easily broken up that teamsters can be hired who will bring horses and ploughs, pitch their tent, and turn up the virgin soil 4 or 5 in. deep at less than $3, or 12s. per acre, overtaking 3 to 4 acres daily with the double plough on which the man rides. This should be done in June; two or three months later the sod will have partially rotted, and cross-ploughing or back-setting is undertaken at a cost of 8s. The land remains thus roughly set up throughout the winter. So soon as the weather permits, often indeed while the deeper soil is still ice-bound, the seed, of which a bushel and a half is allowed to the acre, is sown. It comes up in a few days, and requires no further labour or expense until harvest, which begins early in August; is rapidly overtaken, and costs, with thrashing, about $3 per acre (12s.)

The whole expenses of raising even the first crop of wheat, in this locality hence do not exceed 40s. an acre, and subsequent crops do not of course require the expensive preliminary ploughing. The yield varies somewhat, but many wheat-growers with whom I have talked declare that they got over 20 bushels an acre, and on an average of years can count on making on the spot 75 cents per bushel or $15 an acre, and thus secure a profit of $5, or fully 20s. an acre.

Four years' experience of the country having been satisfactory and many farmers having done well and made money, settlers are coming in rapidly. Near the stations quarter claims of 160 acres are taken up, for which payment is made of $3 to $10 according to proximity to the railway or other circumstances. On favourable terms another 160 acres can be had under a homestead claim, and another equal portion will be given the claimant free of all except land office fees of about 15 cents an acre, if he plants on 160 acres ten of trees, and takes care of them for five years.

Mr. George C. Reis, a successful ironmaster from West Pennsylvania, has located himself pleasantly at Edna. Since taking possession in April he has built a capital house barn and premises for 32 horses, has 1,000 acres broken up and cross-ploughed ready for wheat next April, and from his hall steps can count fifty houses or cottages, while on his first visit to Edna twelve months ago, as far as the eye could reach, only five buildings of any description could be seen. Assuredly, the wastes are being peopled. I have repeatedly seen the bullock teams trudging along over the prairie, the wagon laden with the tent, ploughs, a few handy tools, some simple furniture, and mounted aloft the wife and children, while the procession is usually brought up by one or two cows, and sometimes by a few pigs. Like a good man of business Mr. Reis determines not to depend upon one resource, however promising. He intends growing cattle as well as wheat, and has his hay of prairie grass stacked upon pillars and raised sufficiently from the ground to allow the cattle to draw underneath and take advantage of shelter from the winter blasts. West of Edna, the Grandin Brothers have a large wheat farm, but they also divide their chances by a heavy investment in a cattle-ranche at Mayville.

Forty miles north of Fargo, the Red River receives an important tributary—the Goose River—which runs north-west through a very fertile country, into which many Norwegians have recently penetrated, where weeds 10 ft. high spring when the soil is stirred, where the luxuriance of the first wheat crops frequently causes them to be much laid, where $8 cover the total cost of an acre of wheat, and whence in wagon teams the grain is often wearily brought seventy miles to Fargo. But this serious disadvantage will shortly be remedied by the branch railway which the Northern Pacific purpose pushing north from Fargo along the west bank of the Red River. The St. Paul and Manitoba Company also contemplates a line from Crookston passing over the river and proceeding north-west to the Pembina Hills.

Seventy miles north of Fargo on the Red Lake

River, about sixteen miles from where it flows west into the Red River, is Crookston, founded four years ago. Here, a few years previously, amid the pleasant woods, were buffaloes and wolves, and they still abound fifty miles higher up amid the pine forests towards the Red Lake. It is expected that this timber will shortly be handled and brought down the stream to Crookston, where a dam could be erected, an old river course used for the tail water, and sawmills put up. Three years ago Crookston was the terminus of the St. Paul and Manitoba Railway, with four houses; now there are two streets, many wooden and some good substantial stone houses, and a population of 1,500 souls. A good school-house in the autumn of 1878 was erected to hold 120 pupils, but the schoolmaster, who had been in office a year, informs me that he is already overcrowded, with 200 children on his attendance roll. Three churches are organised and about to be built. Two bishops have already been down to look after building locations. Last winter is described to have been cold but dry. The schoolmaster, who had formerly wintered nearer the Atlantic, states that he prefers the bright winter sunshine of Dakota, which continued during 100 days and prevented any inconvenience being felt even when the thermometer went down to —30° Fahr. A grain elevator and crane are put up; the sidings are overcrowded with agricultural implements; all summer the railway vans arrive with new citizens, their families and baggage. Near the town the land has been taken up chiefly in quarter lots of 160 acres.

Dining Stations.

Warren, the dining station on this road, dates from the summer of 1878, but has not yet advanced beyond the wooden hotel with two dining-rooms and half-a-dozen cottages, one erected at a cost of 15*l.* owned by an old lady born at Newcastle-on-Tyne, with experiences as a settler in Australian goldfields, and now owning several town lots at Warren, while her two sons and a daughter have pre-emption and homestead lots not far distant. In anticipation of extending cultivation, two grain elevators are already erected. On several occasions thrashing was done, and engines were moved readily by a pair of horses or oxen, the engine helping the moving. Several farmers assure us that their yield of wheat this season varied from 30 to 40 bushels per acre; while their potatoes, which were sound and good, reached 300 bushels. A prairie fire was seen, but the previous night's rain and light wind prevented its extending far. The rough prairie grass in many places had been cut and cocked for winter fodder; mowing machines evidently were in general use, but near St. Vincent, on the Canadian frontier, an apparent new comer was at work with his scythe. Proceeding north and entering Manitoba, the soil becomes heavier and wetter. Scrubby willow and aspen are the only apologies for trees. An occasional span of prairie fowls or a hawk were startled by the train as it leisurely proceeded through the prairie wilderness, where frequently the eye would vainly scan the landscape away into the far horizon without discovering evidences of human habitation.

Lone and sparsely occupied as the Red River

valley still is, it has immense capabilities. Including its upper third lying within the Canadian Dominions and constituting a portion of Manitoba, the valley, as has already been hinted, might alone provide the bread stuffs which Great Britain at present requires to import.

The valley, as already mentioned, is 350 miles long; comprising the Goose Lake and other valleys with which it communicates, and including its second western slopes, which are as good as any part, it may be stated to be 100 miles wide. Supposing that only one-half of this immense area were in wheat, and taking the yield at only 10 bushels an acre, there would be a total annual produce of 96,000,000 bushels, or 12,000,000 quarters. But such calculations are based upon certain somewhat unlikely conditions. The Red River soils, although deep and good, cannot go on yielding wheat indefinitely without the return of the more important elements of fertility. Ten or twelve years' continuous corn-growing even on the best of virgin soils causes such exhaustion that the reduced, starved crops will not pay. Deeper and more careful culture may postpone but cannot avert the day of reckoning. Clover crops and stock-feeding insure more permanent corn-growing. It is doubtful, however, whether stock-farming is likely to prove remunerative in most parts of the Red River Valley. The long, cold winter must add greatly to the expenses of stock raising. Still another disadvantage presents itself. The land, especially in the lower and upper portions of the valley, is wet. In

1859 and again eight years later, the country, especially about its southern extremity towards Breckenridge and Fargo as well as around Winnipeg, was for months under water, and such inundations may recur, interfering not only with stock rearing but with corn-growing.

CHAPTER XIV.

MANITOBA.

NORTH over the Canadian frontier are valleys as fertile and prairies as extensive as those of the Red River, some of them scarcely yet opened up for cultivation. Wheat of fine quality is grown in the Athabasca and Peace Valleys, which, although north of latitude 55°, are stated to have a genial climate, and produce flowers and fruits in as great perfection as localities many hundred miles south. The Peace River Valley is estimated to have an area of 100,000 square miles. The North and South Saskatchewan, which with rapid flow run a thousand miles from the Rocky Mountains into Lake Winnipeg, are described as traversing immense areas of alluvial soil, while along their banks are beautifully-sheltered well-watered spots adapted for stock-raising. Five hundred miles west of Winnipeg is the Prince Albert settlement, established about three years ago, now numbering 600 inhabitants, busily engaged in mixed husbandry, but in such a remote region sensibly devoting special attention to the raising of cattle, which, amid abundance of good grass, can be produced at little more than the cost of herding, and can tolerably

Great Wheat-producing Areas. 223

comfortably carry themselves to market. Starting also in the Rocky Mountains and likewise pursuing an easterly course, and discharging its waters into Lake Winnipeg, is the Assiniboine, which with many important tributaries, waters, especially on its northern aspect, an enormous tract of good country, which might absorb thousands of settlers, and when opened up, as is being done, by the Canadian Pacific Railway, and the often discussed lake, river, and canal system, might export millions of bushels of wheat. On the authority of the Legislative Assembly of Manitoba, it is estimated that the total wheat area of the North-West is about 380,000 square miles. The cheap land, one great element of this country's greatness, is here; the cheap transport, so necessary properly to utilise the cheap land, is being gradually secured.

At St. Vincent on the southern confines of Manitoba on the Canadian frontier, seventy-five miles south of Winnipeg, the good car Mineopa, so obligingly placed at our disposal by the managers of the St. Paul and Sioux railroad, and which for a fortnight was our comfortable home often by night as well as by day, was transferred to the line of the Canadian Pacific. Whilst this was being effected, prospecting in the neighbourhood of the station, we met several Indians. Some of the old ladies, rather forlorn and dilapidated in appearance, rigged out in garments of very motley description, were disposed to be friendly, and by unmistakable signs expressed anxiety to have something to drink. They looked as if they not infrequently wanted food as well as drink. They are reported to be harmless, although apt to help themselves to anything movable inadvertently left about. The men are not fond of work, and any small amount of tillage which is overtaken around their huts is done by the women. Almost all are stipendiaries either of the Canadian or United States Governments, receive five dollars a year, and draw doles usually on the approach of winter in the form of flour, pork, a few clothes and blankets.

At a steady pace of ten or twelve miles an hour, over the rudely constructed line of the Canadian Pacific, innocent of ballast, with oscillations and bumpings sufficient to produce sea-sickness and bring passengers to their knees, we are carried to St. Boniface, an old French colony on the right bank of the river immediately below the confluence of the Red and Assiniboine rivers. St. Boniface, founded in 1818, curiously still maintains its French character, appearance, language, and religion, and has a handsome Roman Catholic cathedral with a fine organ, several schools, and a convent and hospital.

The Red River, which here is as wide as the Thames at Westminster, is to be spanned by a bridge, when the authorities manage to agree upon the best point to build it. Now it is crossed by a steamer which carries carriages and horses as well as passengers. Immediately opposite to St. Boniface are Fort Garry and Winnipeg. The fort, with several stores and 500 acres around, belongs to the Hudson Bay Company, which by charter from Charles II. long exercised plenipotentiary authority throughout the great north-

Farming around Winnipeg.

west, governed well its vast domains, and treated its Indian and indeed all its subjects fairly. Agricultural development was not the business of the company; but it fostered a great trade in furs and skins, and prospected and opened up the country. When the charter grant expired in 1869 the great domains were secured by Canada, which paid the Hudson Bay Company 300,000*l.* and allowed it to retain her trading stations, 50,000 acres of land around them, and one-twentieth of the remainder of the land. As settlement extends the wild animals which sustain the trading business of the company diminish, but the great land estate proportionally increases in value. Judgment and tact will be requisite to develope this property. Hitherto the best has not been done with the 500 acres around Fort Garry. No sufficient effort has been made to dispose of it for town sites.

Contiguous to Fort Garry, and north of it, is the newer city of Winnipeg, in 1870 a poor village of 300, now mustering 7,000 tolerably prosperous people. It is nicely set out with its principal streets 132 feet wide, with three small parks, which will be serviceable when population becomes more closely packed; a trotting track and rifle range, two flour mills, a distillery, and some good stores. A comfortable club house was founded in 1874. Several hotels and twenty-three drinking saloons, each pay annually $240 for their licence, which is liable to forfeiture in case of misconduct. The town-hall, churches, and most of the best shops and houses are built of pleasant primrose yellow bricks made from the underlying clay. The soil is of more tenacious staple than in the upper portions of the Red River Valley. Door scrapers, apparently unnecessary in other districts, are universal here. Facilities of transit are the great desideratum. Coals, much needed in a locality where the thermometer falls frequently to —40°. Fahr., cost 3*l*. 10*s*. a ton. Timber, which is chiefly forwarded from Minneapolis, reaches 25*s*. to 35*s*. per 1,000 feet. Provisions generally are dear. Wheat, however, owing to indifferent means of transport, is 15 cents a bushel less than at Fargo. Difficulties occur as to the direction of the projected line of the Canadian Pacific, and as to the suitable site for the much-wanted bridge over the river. Useless surveys are made for which the Government or somebody has to pay; the railway enterprise is weighted with a host of officials who appear to hinder instead of hastening the work. Jobbery, nepotism, and party politics also retard railroad and general industrial progress.

The heavy clay land which extends for many miles around Winnipeg is generally wet. Most of it is wisely left in grass. Oxen are chiefly used both for ploughing and road work, and cost $120 to $160 per pair. Horses and good mules, weighing 1,000 lbs. to 1,100 lbs., reach nearly double that price. Cows are in good demand at $25 to $30; they are usually small, of shorthorn and Jersey grades. Oxen are generally bought by the butchers at 9 to 10 cents for the dressed carcase sinking offal. The sheep are not numerous, are narrow and poor, with a good deal of Merino character, and are worth $3 to $4. The hogs are not generally so good as those met with farther south.

Five years ago the resources of Manitoba were so imperfectly developed that the wheat, beef, and pork requisite for the western military posts, for the police and Hudson Bay stations, for the thinly-scattered hunters and settlers spread over the Riding Hills, and extending onwards towards the Rocky Mountains, were in great part forwarded to Winnipeg from the east. Now the 200 bullock teams which start thence in spring for their 1,000 miles' journey north-west to collect the furs, as well as the boats, many of 60 tons burden, which ascend the great rivers on the breaking of the ice towards the end of April, are mainly laden with wheat and flour grown and ground in the province, aud with home-reared beef and bacon.

Five miles from Winnipeg, at the Scotch colony of Kildonnan, founded forty years ago, are about 1,000 industrious agriculturists occupied in mixed husbandry, few of them with more than 160 acres, but all prosperous and contented. The land, a few years since, exhausted by wheat-growing, has lately been better managed, and, although not clean, grows 25 bushels of wheat and double that amount of oats. The hard yellow corn preferred by the distillers is successfully produced. Potatoes do admirably in the friable loam, swedes and clover flourish. The annual rainfall, including melted snow, is about 25 inches. The highest summer temperature is $95°$, the lowest winter cold is $-40°$, which proves sometimes rather trying, and the keen frost is apt provokingly to extend into April, preventing all agricultural work. On April 18, 1880, some of my friends crossed the Red River on the ice and ten days more elapsed before ploughing or wheat-sowing could be begun. The severe prolonged winter is quickly followed by a short, hot Norwegian summer; grain, fruit, and flowers, such as are familiar in England, flourish and come to perfection.

At Selkirk, a rising town on the Canadian Pacific line, where it crosses the Red River, twelve miles north of Winnipeg, the railway cuttings are furnishing capital lime-stone rock and brick earth and shingle, all of which are being freely used for building purposes. North of Selkirk, which stands high, and descending towards the lake, the country is not of much agricultural value, being chiefly divided between wood and prairie swamp. Here and around Shoal Lake, twenty miles farther north, many of the best farmers are young men from Ontario, who, although sorely tried by two wet seasons, are contented, generally doing well, and not finding the long cold winter more trying than in their former home. Besides full crops of grain, turnips grow well, producing 700 bushels an acre, while 300 bushels of potatoes are produced often with the small trouble of cutting the prairie turf partially with a stock axe, introducing the potato set, and again firming down the turf with the foot. Eighty miles south of Winnipeg, on each side of the Red River, are the settlements of the Mennonites, German Quaker emigrants from Russia, which they leave in large numbers mainly to escape the conscription, so irreconcilable with their principles. In this Red

River settlement 8,000 of these thrifty, industrious people are collected. They have not, however, been very fortunate in their location; the land is sadly in want of draining; and their wheat yield has consequently dropped to 10 or 12 bushels. Wheat-growing is at present their principal occupation, but it would be well if they were encouraged to multiply their resources. It can never answer to have all the eggs in one basket.

A much richer country opens west of Winnipeg, extending along the northern bank of the Assiniboine, peopled chiefly by English and Scotch half-breeds, descendants of the pensioners sent out by the British Government in the days of the Hudson Bay Company. This race furnishes more industrious, painstaking farmers than the French half-breeds, who show more of the restless wandering spirit of the Indian, who make good trappers and hunters, and who become more numerous about Baie St. Paul, so famous for its rich green, English-like pastures. Westward, to Portage la Prairie, 75 miles from Winnipeg, the country is a fine rolling prairie, the soil lighter, more kindly and productive than about Winnipeg. Good crops of wheat, oats, and barley are being harvested during the last week of September. The yield of wheat on the best farms reaches 35 bushels of 60 lbs. Barley, which is often put in as late as June, yields 35 to 40 bushels of 38 lbs. Oats cast 60 to 70 bushels of 34 lbs. Potatoes produce 300 to 400 bushels. A good deal of Hungarian millet is grown for fodder. Labourers with board get $15 a month, and $1·50 to $2·50 is given in harvest.

Even thus far north are abundant records of crops destroyed by locusts, hatching early in May, becoming winged, taking flight, and beginning their destructive attacks in the end of June or early in July, and clearing every green crop before them. Great losses were thus sustained in 1874 and 1875. Land varies much in value; for some well-placed holdings near river frontage $20 an acre is asked, but similar land farther back from the river can still be got at one fourth that price. Taxes, chiefly for school purposes, range from 10 to 30 cents an acre. Messrs. Read and Pell in their report mention, 'that a great portion of the land here is held by speculators and companies, and there is quite a rush of farmers' sons to the west to acquire land under homestead law and the right of pre-emption to the further quantity of 160 acres. The result is that instead of all the land being developed in this neighbourhood, three-fourths will remain as prairie until the far west is settled. The singular mixture of dirt and discomfort in the dress of the farmers and in the house and surroundings was enough to astonish anyone who was assured of the good and affluent position of the owners.'

The Lieutenant-Governor of the State, M. Cauchon, who, three years ago, came to Winnipeg from Quebec, is well satisfied with the condition and progress of this youngest province of the Dominion. Both the Governor and his son are extensive farmers. The town which has sprung up around Fort Garry, he informs me, contained only 700 inhabitants in 1871, and has now ten times that population.

Sales of Land and of Produce. 231

During the year ending October 31, 1876, 154,003 acres of land were disposed of at the Dominion Land Offices, at Winnipeg. During the year ending October 31, 1878, 682,592 acres were granted, bringing the total area of lands disposed of in Manitoba to fully 2,000,000 acres. The province is gradually becoming self-supporting so far as concerns the chief necessaries of life, though imports of foreign goods are rather diminishing, and for the year to June 30, 1878, stand at $1,171,105; while the exports, steadily creeping up, are valued for the same period at $725,898.

Bishop Tache, the Roman Catholic archbishop of this great domain, has resided for thirty-four years at St. Boniface. During many years a missionary amongst the Indians, he travelled much and gathered the valuable information set forth in his work 'Seventy Years of Missions in the North-west of America.' His experience, discretion, and large-heartedness have gained him great influence, not only amongst the community, where he has ruled as archbishop for twenty-seven years, but throughout the whole province and amongst his old friends the Indians. He has greatly helped to forward the cause of education, has several schools under his own special care, and was zealous in the establishment of the University of Manitoba, which represents the Episcopal College of St. John, the Roman Catholic College of St. Boniface, and the Presbyterian College of Manitoba. These bodies, wisely working in harmony, with other powers relating to education, grant degrees in arts, science, law, and medicine.

No one knows the country better than Archbishop Tache. He tells me that for growing wheat, oats, and barley an immense proportion of the land is as well adapted as any he knows in England, France, or Germany. What the country mainly wants, and is now gradually getting, is cheaper and more accessible communication by land and water. The Archbishop aptly illustrated the need of improved transport by the history of his cathedral bells, which some years ago came from London and were landed at Montreal. In their tedious transit by river, lake, and canal, they had to be transferred thirty-seven times. Unfortunately the belfry was shortly burnt; the fragments of melted metal were, however, gathered up and forwarded to London, the bells were recast and again hang in St. Boniface tower, after being again subjected to thirty-seven portages on each of their journeys. Good national schools, supported by liberal land grants and where education is provided gratuitously, are rising throughout the province. The different nationalities agree very well. The Archbishop reports the Irish to be steady and very fair settlers, but the young Canadians from Maine and New Brunswick, accustomed to farmwork and inured to cold winters, constitute the best pioneers and farmers. The communistic Germans, who infest Chicago and are met with farther south, are not numerous here. The high price of coal, often bringing $18 a short ton, his Grace justly observes, is a serious evil in the cold winter season; but wood is cheap, and coal abounds on the Saskatchewan and also south-west on the Yellowstone, and will prove a great boon when worked and deported throughout the country.

Mr. J. W. Taylor, United States' Consul at Winnipeg during the last thirteen years, and with previous extensive experience in various parts of America, confirms the generally entertained opinion that the quality of the wheat improves as the northern limit of its cultivation is approached, and declares that the spring wheats grown in Manitoba will always bring five to ten cents a bushel more than those raised 200 miles south. Minneapolis millers, anxious to secure wheat rich in gluten, he adds, are sending their buyers to Winnipeg, and in order to avoid the 20-cent duty levied on each bushel used in the States, are carrying it south in sealed wagons, grinding it in bonded mills, and exporting the patent flour to England.

Lord Beaconsfield recently extolled the resources of this portion of the Canadian Dominion. The amount of good land awaiting cultivation is certainly enormous. The whole of the tenants of an English county might be translated to the Assiniboine Valley, and supplied with the same acreage which they farm at home without appreciably reducing its great tracts of fertile land. The inducements offered by the Canadian Government are sufficiently attractive; even the railway lands can be bought upon favourable terms. But prudent, thoughtful emigrants, as already hinted, with reason, find serious drawbacks in the want of cheap, convenient transit. Their produce cannot be profitably disposed of. Wheat is often ten cents a bushel lower on the Canadian side than 100 miles south in the States territory. Coals at Winnipeg and throughout the district cost, as above-mentioned, $18 a short ton. Lumber for house building and other work is one-third dearer than it is 300 miles farther south. All household requisites are high. Until these disadvantages are removed by increased and extended railway facilities, this desirable region of Canada cannot be peopled and developed as it should be.

The enormous area of land both in Canada and the United States which, as I have endeavoured to show, is suitable for wheat-growing, its wide geographical distribution, its varied conditions of climate, lessen materially the chances of widespread failure, and justify the belief that for many long years no apprehension need be felt as to the abundance and cheapness of bread. Allowing for the exhaustion of land by continuous wasteful wheat culture, the fresh virgin soils will still last for several generations. On this continent, certainly not one-seventh of the land available for wheat-growing has yet been cultivated. Nor with the area of cultivation extending westwards will the cost of the wheat even when brought to Europe necessarily be increased. Cheap machinery and cheap transit will probably counterbalance this disadvantage. Cheap land and cheap transport are the two important factors which enable America profitably to make good the food deficiencies of European countries. Her capability to continue, or, if necessary, to increase, her exports of breadstuffs is undoubted. She now exports on an average one-third of the wheat, but only one-seventh of the maize, she grows.

CHAPTER XV.

ST. PAUL, MINNESOTA.

ST. PAUL, the capital of the State of Minnesota, is one of the most charming and prosperous cities in America. Its terraces of handsome stone houses rise along the left bank and elevated bluffs of the Mississippi. From many a commanding position the undulating wooded country, the beautiful valleys, the grand sweeps of the great Father of Waters, present a magnificent, almost matchless panorama. Around St. Paul are many famous haunts of the Indians, who, with a spirit of poetry often seen in savage tribes, have a strong appreciation of the picturesque and beautiful. St. Paul repeats the story of many Western towns. It has grown and developed with wonderful rapidity. In 1849 it had 30 inhabitants, now it has 50,000. Its aggregate annual trade is stated at $44,000,000. It is the centre of a growing network of railways. Its elevated position and fine climate attract many visitors, especially from the relaxing warmer Southern States. Limestone rock of beautiful quality and of three shades of colour in grand blocks is readily got out of the cliffs and ridges on which the town is built, and, used alike for public and private dwellings, gives a solidity and freshness which wooden or brick-built towns never possess. Villas as sumptuous and inviting as those around Kew or Richmond abound in the well-laid out avenues and extend into the suburbs.

Concurrently with this material growth education and culture have been well provided for. Churches and handsome public schools, quite as imposing as those of the London School Board, are numerous. But the cost of erection and maintenance fortunately come only in part out of the pockets of the ratepayers. One-eighteenth portion of the lands of the State has been set aside for educational purposes. The proceeds of lands sold are invested on bonds, and the interest divided amongst the public schools of the State in proportion to the number of their scholars. This endowment at present suffices to meet several weeks' school expenses. The balance required is made up from the one mill tax, and from the direct tax on the property of the district. The increasing value of the school lands will however, by-and-by, reduce the proportion to be drawn from taxation. Gratuitous education is given to every child; more advanced culture is also provided. A State University was eight years ago inaugurated near Minneapolis, five miles from St. Paul, where the President, William W. Folwell, LL.D., and twenty professors and tutors, give gratuitous instruction in literature, art, and science to nearly 400 students of both sexes, and of ages varying from fifteen to twenty-one. There are special curriculums for arts, for agriculture, and for mechanical science. On the occasion of our afternoon visit, a lecture on elocution was being given, other students were at geometric drawing, another class were busy at chemical analyses and investigations in the well-equipped laboratory, while small children, apparently from some junior school, without hindrance, were sauntering in an orderly way through the natural history museum, rich in elks, moose deer, and other western fauna, and unrestrained by college don or janitor. Another lot of plainly clothed youngsters were strolling in the conservatory and botanical museum, and evidently enjoying and making good use of their rights as citizens of the Great Republic.

On Saturday, the chief market day, the wide streets of St. Paul are thronged with buggies and waggons often to the number of four hundred ; wheat, hay, vegetables, and other farm produce are brought in ; lumber. and stores are the homeward carriage. The teams are chiefly active horses of the stamp of a London light omnibus nag, and weighing 900 lbs. to 1,200 lbs. Some of the farmers have driven in twelve miles ; more distant visitors have usually arrived by rail. Factors collect and despatch from St. Paul large and increasing quantities of wheat. Besides home supplies 2,000,000 quarters annually pass through the elevators for transhipment. By one railway 1,000 cars of Indian corn are forwarded from Omaha *viâ* St. Paul to Duluth at the moderate cost of eight or ten cents a bushel, the cars loading back with lumber. A large number of cattle grazed and fed throughout the State are railed to Chicago and New York, and during the past ten days three special trains, each containing 400 to 500 compact, useful, well-fed beasts, have been unloaded, fed, watered, and rested in transit from Northern Wyoming or Montana, where, at a cost of £3 or £4, they are picked up, quietly driven, grazing by the way, to Mandon or Bismarck, there loaded and forwarded by the Northern Pacific to Chicago, a distance of upwards of 800 miles, at a cost of about $3·25 or 13s. 6d. This is a comparatively new source of cattle for the eastern markets, and with the railway facilities is likely to be greatly developed.

Driving north eight miles over beautiful undulating downs of light sand and limestone soil, grazed by useful dairy cattle, with varied view of water, wood, and hill, Minneapolis is reached, famous for its great water-power flour mills. Between the two cities, which it is said will in twenty years expand and merge into one, there is ample choice of drives: one by the Mississippi banks is specially fine, and another, 60 ft. to 90 ft. wide, where not already fringed with timber, is being planted as a boulevard, and laid out in park-like fashion with racing and driving tracks and broad walks for foot-passengers. Here, on a capital Rotten-row of the far west, numbers of horsemen and horsewomen turn out in the fine autumn afternoon, and help to illustrate, as so much else does, that here in the centre of the American continent, where, within the memory of many inhabitants, Indians, elks, and buffalo roamed the wood and prairie, there have rapidly grown prosperity and culture undistinguishable from that of many English towns dating from the Norman Conquest.

The State of Minnesota comprises 53,459,840 acres: it approaches the size of New York and Pennsylvania together; it has two-thirds the area of the British Islands. One-third is occupied with timber, which abounds in the north-east, where the country is hilly and rugged and the soil thin and poor, yet capable of growing good oak, elm, and pine. Another belt of timber extends from St. Paul towards the south-western portion of the State. There are 7,000 lakes, most containing fish, the shallower frequented by wild ducks and geese, their bright clear aspect fully justifying the title of 'Minnesota,' or 'the sky-tinted waters.' In a primeval state these waters have generally overspread this and adjacent States, and on the Lower Silurian in the eastern parts of the State, and on granite and porphyry in the west, have deposited beds of limestone and cretaceous clay on which are imposed a diluvium of one to four feet of fertile loam. On many elevated positions huge boulders of blue granite, gravel, and rocks of foreign material have been deposited by glaciers. The level prairie surfaces, often extending for a stretch of many miles in every direction, are interspersed with more rolling country, and are drier and cut up by fewer 'slews' or gulleys than are met with in the Red River or Assiniboine valleys. These prairies are kept bare of trees by frequently recurring fires, which occasionally in spring, more frequently in autumn, devour every green thing. When they gather force and are impelled by a steady breeze, they advance in a V-shaped form at the rate of a mile in three or four minutes, the flames towering fifty feet, and extending two or three miles wide. These fires sometimes destroy houses, barns, and hay-ricks, sacrifice human lives, and leave on the blackened prairie the roasted carcases of animals unable to escape from the devouring element. The prairie traveller, always provided with a box of matches, when he sees the conflagration advancing, sets fire to the dry grass about him, and thus speedily clears a space on which he stands scatheless whilst the wall of flame turns aside. To protect homesteads, hay or corn ricks, or young trees from such danger, the land around for several yards is ploughed. Trees eight or ten years old stand the scorching. Rivers and lakes along their southern and eastern shores usually escape the fire, which travels with the prevailing north or north-westerly winds. These recurring fires get rid of coarse grass, continually furnish valuable plant food, and improve the herbage.

The extreme winter cold is probably the chief disadvantage of life in Minnesota; but although the thermometer sometimes falls as low as -40 deg., the atmosphere is dry and clear, the sun shines, and if care is taken that the ears are not frosted and one can move briskly about, there is less discomfort than in damper Eastern climates with the temperature 60 deg. higher. Keen cutting winds occasionally drive across the prairies; there is seldom much snow

—more would be acceptable. The summer heat in the shade reaches 90 deg.; 22 in. to 28 in. is the rainfall reported in various seasons and localities.

Farming in Minnesota is more diversified than in many other States, either to the north or south. As in Dakota and Manitoba, wheat is grown; the spring varieties are almost invariably preferred; the hard winter and sparse protection of snow prevent the successful planting of winter wheat. The ample crop of 1877 produced, according to the United States official returns, upwards of 33,000,000 bushels, or an average of 18·5 bushels an acre: but the scorching summer of 1878, and the dry spring of 1879 reduced the average of both these years. Although some successful managers secured 20 bushels per acre, a good many, unfortunately, had to content themselves with eight or ten. More generally satisfactory results were secured in 1880, and with the widening area of cultivation upwards of 42,000,000 bushels of wheat are now annually produced in Minnesota.

Indian corn, although not so largely grown or so luxuriant as in Nebraska, Southern Iowa, or Missouri, thrives capitally and pays well. The State is credited with 17,000,000 bushels in 1878, which is an average of 30 bushels an acre. Still larger returns have been obtained from the extending cultivation of 1879 and 1880. Probably three-fourths of the corn-crop is wisely consumed at home in the feeding of cattle and hogs. Half a million acres are devoted to oats. The yield is officially stated at 33·5 bushels; the produce does not, however, usually weigh over 32 lbs.

a bushel. The cultivation of barley is extending both for malting and for feeding. In many districts linseed is being tried, but although profitable use can be made of the seed, the fibre is not yet readily disposed of. Sorghum is grown in many counties, and yields an abundance of rich syrup, producing readily crystallisable sugar. For the preparation and refining of this sugar a manufactory has been established at Farribault, 40 miles south of St. Paul. Potatoes and other vegetables grow well.

Within the last few years cattle are being reared in increasing numbers, of improved quality, and with satisfactory profit. The chief difficulty and expense is providing a really useful bull. The cows run on the prairie or among the shaded shrubs. Water is abundant, and where lakes and streams are not accessible, a well of 20 ft. to 50 ft. reaches a good supply. No provision generally is made for roots or green crops to carry the stock over the winter; but hay is cut and cocked at the cost of $1·25 per ton, and is brought in for the stock as they require it in winter. In many districts hay well saved can be delivered to the farmers' stables at $2·50 to $3 a ton of 2,000 lbs. As three tons of this useful blue-joint hay, and 3 lbs. or 4 lbs. of corn, worth one-halfpenny a pound, will keep in improving condition a two-year-old beast throughout the four or five months of winter, some estimate may be formed of the moderate cost of stock-rearing. The summer feeding entails even less trouble and expense. A lad at $6 or $8 a month will take charge of 50 to 100 cattle on the prairie, on one's own farm, or graze them over unoccupied Government school or other lands, where the only fault of the grass is its luxuriant abundance, occasionally altogether concealing the stock grazing among it. For the privilege of such pasturage over the unoccupied lands of absentees rent is seldom asked or offered. One successful stock owner showed me, however, several Government sections which he rents for one cent an acre annually, and without any restriction as to mowing and carrying the hay on to his own land adjacent.

Sheep as yet are not much cultivated, are generally more or less of the Merino character; wool rather than mutton is still desiderated; the confinement of the stock during the long winter, and their restriction during that period to dry food, somewhat interfere with thriving. With cheap sheds, more yard room, a few roots or cabbages, which grow capitally, mixed with the hay and corn, and some attention to their feet, there is no reason why sheep should not answer well. Hogs are not so numerous as in the more purely corn-growing States of Iowa and Missouri, but are generally good. Indeed, I have not seen a thriftless bad pig since I landed in America. Horse breeding is receiving attention, and much need, for the horses are neither as big, shapely, nor as profitable as they should be.

The prosperity of Minnesota has been mainly fostered by the extensive and energetic development of her railways. The Mississippi, navigable for 90 miles above St. Paul, was originally the great highway, and still proves useful for the moving of lumber and some heavy goods. In 1862 the State had but 10 miles of railway; now she has 3,000 miles, and is laying down upwards of 300 miles annually. Through the level prairie, without any heavy cuttings or embankments, with only low wooden bridges, such lines are constructed and equipped at about 3,000*l*. a mile. The St. Paul and Sioux City and other enterprising lines do not always wait for the march of population westward; they obtain from the State a grant of every alternate section of one square mile or 640 acres for ten or twenty miles on each side of their approved line; they push their railway into the new, scarcely inhabited, country. There are no heavy Parliamentary expenses, no litigation with captious owners objecting to severance of their estates, not even a sportsman puts in a plea for the disturbance of game. Within six or eight months a line of 50 miles is often surveyed, staked out, and built, the iron rails laid, station houses put up every six or seven miles, and a steady fellow appointed, whose principal work for some time is in his garden. But as emigrants follow along, the man's importance and income speedily increase. He has a small percentage on the business done; he has something for showing the railway lands, which are soon picked up at prices varying from $4 to $8 an acre. Those three or four miles back from the railway are obtainable at less money. In Minnesota, the Government lands have almost all been taken up under homestead, pre-emption, or timber grants, and the various railway companies are hence the chief parties from whom good accessible lands can now be obtained. The price of land, as might be expected, varies considerably with its situation and other circumstances, beginning as low as $3 an acre. It is, however, steadily rising. Near railway stations, even 100 miles from St. Paul, a great deal bought or pre-empted at $1 or $2 an acre is now worth $10, and where buildings have been erected, trees and fences planted, and other improvements made, even purely agricultural sections sell for $20 to $25. Although a large proportion of the State has already been disposed of to settlers, speculators, and others, and although a considerable area is usefully occupied for grazing, not one-tenth has as yet been brought under cultivation, and of that cultivated portion certainly not one half receives the ploughing and other labour requisite to produce the best returns. The deep, good, easily worked soil which is so widely distributed in this State only needs more labour, capital, and steady industry to increase its production both of bread-stuffs and of meat.

Market-gardening, which flourishes on the light, friable loam around St. Paul, is pursued chiefly by Germans, who have recently been paying £30 to £40 an acre, and generally cultivate five to ten acres. Some have advances to about half the value of their purchase, accommodation for which they have to pay 10 per cent. Most of the smaller farmers also grow the commoner vegetables for sale in St. Paul and Minneapolis, succeeding particularly well with potatoes, which produce 200 to 300 bushels an acre, and sell at about 25 cents per bushel, with cabbages, which bring 4 cents or 5 cents per head, and with onions, which fetch 35 cents per bushel. There is nothing special to note in the management of these vegetables. These vegetable growers as yet are, however, the only farmers who appreciate the value of manure and find time to apply it. In the west it is still generally regarded as a waste product, to be got out of the way as cheaply as possible. When it accumulates several feet high around the buildings, a stream is sometimes turned on to carry it away, or the hovel itself may be moved. If the manure is carted, it is generally to fill up some hole or make a road. Wheat straw sells at $3 to $4 a ton in St. Paul, but a few miles out it is valueless and thousands of tons are annually burnt throughout the State. When the paper mills which are in contemplation in various districts are in full operation, straw may become of some value independently of its agricultural uses.

Owing to the abundance of common lands and grazings in the woods or on unoccupied prairie land rent free or at nominal rates, many cows are kept in the neighbourhood of St. Paul. They are seen in herds often numbering 100, and are looked after, as the law insists, by a lad. Some are turned out with their calves at foot. Many are decorated with a bell hung round the neck. All are brought in and distributed to their owners at night. Milk sells at about 10d. per gallon. Butter is of good quality, usually made rather salt, and worth 1s. to 1s. 4d. per lb.; cheese is rarely made. All the considerable dairy folks have 'spring houses,' usually built of stone, situated on some stream or lake, sheltered by a few trees, with the water flowing through rude clay, stone, or iron tanks, in which the tins of milk are placed so soon as drawn from the cow. All these people are comfortable and well-to-do. Their common history is 'ten or twenty years ago they had nothing.' Now they own, often without encumbrance, their land and what it carries.

Writing of corn and cattle, of land, its capabilities and its value, I cannot stay to describe this beautiful and varied country: the woodland drives by the banks of the Mississippi; the crystal bays of Minnetonka Lake, on which four large steamers carry excursionists; the delicate, lace-like tracery of the Minnehaha Falls, or the grand commanding position of Fort Snelling, built in 1819, 70 ft. above the meeting of the waters of the Minnesota and Mississippi, famous in many an Indian campaign, and now the chief United States fort of the North-west. Beyond this are wonderful upheavals of the displaced sandstone and limestone rocks. At Mandota, hard by, General Sibley forty years ago built the first private residence in the country, having no white neighbours, excepting in the fort, for 300 miles. No one has been more intimately concerned in the progress of this State than General Sibley, who informs me that his love of wild sports brought him here in 1834. As head of a great fur-trading company, he travelled widely over the North-west, with a faithful white servant; he lived much among the Indians, receiving from them uniform kindness, often supplied with the best their slender resources could furnish. In his hunting expeditions he constantly encountered herds of moose and buffalo. With Indian troubles looming, he was rightly regarded the fittest man to command at Fort Snelling, and more recently he was elected the first Governor of Minnesota.

Although the elk, buffalo, and other big game have retired before the advance of colonisation, there is still abundant sport in the woods and on the prairies, and from trains, from carriages, and when on foot, we have raised countless prairie chickens, grouse, quails, golden plovers, wild ducks and geese, great sand-hill cranes, weighing 20 lbs. and fat as turkeys at Christmas, with rabbits and hares, the latter oddly termed Jack-rabbits. A sportsman desirous of striking into new but pleasant quarters for either shooting or fishing might do much worse than come to Minnesota. He can reach St. Paul within 15 days from London, and at a moderate cost of £25. Solicitous to preserve good sport, Minnesota, in common with other States, has enacted game laws. There are no penalties against shooting or trapping on other people's land. The sportsman can shoot or fish where he lists. The small owner or tenant has himself to blame if any damage is sustained from game; but a close time is rigidly prescribed, and infringement of its provisions is punished by fine or imprisonment. It is unlawful to kill or traffic in the subjoined descriptions of game, excepting during the following periods :—Woodcock, July 4 to November 1 ; prairie chicken, August 15 to October 1; quail or partridge, September 1 to December 1; ruffled grouse or pheasant, September 1 to December 1; aquatic fowl, September 1 to May 15; elk, deer, &c., November 1 to December 15; brook trout, April 1 to October 1.

Two farms visited in the neighbourhood of St. Paul afford some idea of the farming of the locality. Mr. Smith, of the Meadows, owns 300 acres three miles from town; 140 acres were bought in 1867 at $20 per acre, but subsequent and more recent additions have cost from $25 to $40 an acre. The land is undulating, and was chiefly underwood and scrub, which has been grubbed at a cost of $20 an acre with $5 for clearing off the timber and $5 for the first ploughing. These items forcibly set forth the expenses of bringing woodland under thorough cultivation. About $10 an acre was however realised by the sale of the wood. The farm is enclosed and conveniently subdivided. Before it was enclosed 500 cattle occasionally strayed over it, devouring everything almost as closely as the locusts did in some districts in 1874 and 1875. Draining a few springy, wet places has been effected with 3 in. pipes placed 4 ft. deep. Eighty acres are still in wood, with a lake of ten acres, which it is proposed to drain. A stable and cattle shed, with a barn overhead, has been built of stone and timber, 100 ft. long and 50 ft. wide, covered with wooden shingles, or thin slips of wood cut and put on like slates. The building, which is 48 ft. to the eaves, is divided into two stories; the lower, eight feet high, partitioned the long way, allows four rows of cattle to be tied up. Accommodation is said to be provided for 110 animals; but such a number would necessitate close packing. The upper barn portion will store 200 tons of hay, with bran and meal, and through convenient hatches and shoots, and with very little manual labour, the horses and cattle below are fed. A well 20 ft. deep is sunk in the middle of the shed, and with pump and iron piping the water is conveniently distributed. A very nice, well-finished dwelling-house of wood, with ten rooms, has been erected at a cost of $2,000. Around the house evergreen shrubs have been planted, and several hundred apple trees, but many of these have perished from frost.

Mr. Smith frankly confesses that he would have had a much better return for his labour and capital had he gone to a western prairie, where, without clearing expenses and expenditure of time, he might at once have stuck in his ploughs; but with a liberal education, and anxious to attend science and other lectures at St. Paul, he preferred to remain near the town. The increased value of his estate, which would now sell for $60, would, however, repay outlay. About 100 acres are still under the plough, and 120 are in grass. The crops are good. On the newly-broken land Indian corn is first taken, producing 50 bushels of shelled corn, which is used for the stock. Wheat follows, sown in spring, and leaving 15 to 25 bushels an acre. Potatoes have occupied a variable but considerable breadth, do well on the peaty loam, help to clean the land, get rid of the prairie grasses, and bulk 250 bushels. Portions have been sown with oats, yielding 40 to 50 bushels an acre. No very definite rotation is followed, but Mr. Smith is gradually sowing most of his land with clover and Timothy, intending, for the present at any rate, to let it remain permanently, graze it with cattle, or cut hay and sell it in St. Paul for $5, which can be got for good samples of 'tame' grass, as the cultivated variety is aptly termed. The stock of the farm, reduced by recent sales, consists of seven horses, four two-year-old colts, five cows, about twenty cattle of various ages, and some good pigs; but there are no sheep. Four labourers are regularly employed at a cost of $1 a day for each, excepting in harvest, when rates are doubled.

Mr. Sam Deering, of Bluffdale, a mile from St. Paul, is a capital specimen of a Western settler. He came to his present abode as a tenant thirteen years ago with a waggon drawn by four bullocks, followed by seven small cows, and containing a poor stock of goods. By thrift and industry he now owns his 75 acres, has built good barns and premises, and is master of 120 good cattle, of which about 25 are superior pedigreed shorthorns. He has seven useful Gwynne cows and heifers; the older ones bought at Mr. Gibson's sale—one, Miss Gwynne, roan, of April 1873, following 2d Duke of Oneida, from Atlantic Gwynne, purchased by Lord Lathom at the famous New York Mills sale. Besides these are an old Princess cow and her smart roan heifer calf, and several prize-winning sorts of less notable pedigree.

Bull calves are sold readily at 25 to 50 guineas. The young stock are from the deep, massive, useful 3d and 5th Marquis of Oakland, the best of these two from a Gwynne cow sent to an Ardrie Duke. From the grade cows, now three and four times crossed with the shorthorn, the bull calves, no matter how promising, are wisely sent to the butcher whenever they are worth $10 or $12; a few heifer calves when two or three weeks old are disposed of to breeders at $25 to $30. The stock are well kept; none are forced, but all are doing well. Mr. Deering sensibly insists that nothing pays unless done well. Several ten-months heifers the useful steelyard shows to weigh already 700 lbs., and they are steadily gaining 100 lbs. a month. The cows are expected to produce 24 to 25 quarts per day; several calved six months are still giving 15 to 16 quarts; the milk is chiefly sold new at St. Paul for 5 cents a quart. The cows, mostly good grades, are milked at 6 a.m. and 5 p.m. So steady is the demand for the milk, even of 70 cows, that little butter is made. The annual milk sales reach $7,000; the sales for stock hitherto have been irregular, owing to the herd being steadily increased, but it has lately averaged $3,000; and as the pedigree shorthorns increase and more young bulls are sold at advancing figures, higher averages will be reached. Natural and artificial grasses constitute the chief food in summer, the heavier milkers receiving, however, a few pounds of bran and corn. Besides the farm of 75 acres, some common and woodland afford grass during summer. From November until March the chief food of the cattle is Indian corn—sown after the middle of May, put in thickly on land well manured, and producing the biggest crop of stuff I have yet seen in Minnesota. Reaching 6 ft. high, and thickly covering the ground, there seemed to me to be five tons of valuable fodder on every acre. On this corn, given in the straw, the cattle of all ages—the shorthorns as well as the grades, the milkers as well as the feeders—thrive equally well. A small quantity of clover (which, being also manured, yields fully three tons for the first cutting) and some prairie hay are also used. Eighteen tons extra of hay were purchased last winter, costing $3 delivered; but the chief extraneous food is bran, of which 200 tons are used, costing $3·75, or 15s., per ton of 2,000 lbs. I do not anywhere remember 75 acres of land producing such heavy crops of fodder and contributing so largely and profitably to feed 120 cattle and nearly as many hogs. What Mr. Deering has done others surely may do.

CHAPTER XVI.

THE MINNEAPOLIS FLOUR TRADE.

THE head-quarters of the manufacture of American patent flour is Minneapolis, the twin capital of the fertile State of Minnesota, where the mighty stream of the Mississippi pours over a precipice 50 ft. high, constituting the Falls of St. Anthony. They were discovered on July 3, 1680, by the Jesuit father Hennepin, named by him after St. Anthony of Padua, and described in his journal as 'a huge cadence of water.' Originally they were several miles lower down the river, and have been gradually receding for thousands of years, steadily wearing away a bed of blue limestone about 30 ft. thick which rests upon a soft sandstone. They have reached within 1,000 ft. of the upper edge of the limestone strata. To make the best of the ceaseless motive power and prevent further recession of the falls, the water is now carried over an immense apron or inclined plane constructed of heavy wooden crib-work filled with stone, and the whole floored over with timber. As there was great danger of the entire falls being undermined and swept away, the water having found a passage under the limestone bed, a subterranean concrete wall has been erected entirely across the river and about 50 ft. into each bank. This wall is about 100 ft. back from the brink of the fall, and fills a chamber cut in the sandstone commencing at the bottom of the limestone and going down 38 ft. into the sandstone. This work was done by the Government of the United States under the direction of Col. Farquhar, U.S. Engineer Corps. The total fall within one mile is about 75 ft. The head and fall at the Washburn Mills about 300 ft. below the falls is 40 ft. A short distance above the falls the Minneapolis Mill Co., which controls the water-power, has erected a dam 14 ft. in height, which turns the water into a canal 60 ft. wide and 14 ft. deep, which runs parallel with the river, and on either side of this canal most of the flour mills are erected, while upon the dam seven saw mills are also situated with a daily capacity to turn out 500,000 ft. of sawn lumber, distributed hundreds of miles to build settlers' houses and supply the wants of States less bountifully provided with timber.

Still more widely distributed is the flour ground by twenty-five mills, varying from three to eight stories high; their floors computed to occupy an area of one and a quarter million feet, and filled with superior modern machinery. This milling enterprise has grown rapidly. In 1873 there were but twelve mills, not worth more thon $50,000 each; now there are twenty-five valued at a low estimate at $75,000. Four have been built during 1879. Largest of all is one just constructed by ex-Governor Washburn, which has a daily producing capacity of 3,000 barrels. The

Washburn A mill has recently been completed and fitted up with 30 run of stones, 40 sets of rollers, and superior machinery and appliances at a cost of $350,000. With the Washburn B mill it has a daily producing capacity of 2,000 barrels of flour. The Washburn mills gained the first prizes for the finest flour exhibited at the great milling convention at Cincinnati in 1880. Among the other big concerns are the Crown Roller Mill, belonging to Messrs. Christian Brothers and Co., with a daily output of 2,400 barrels, and the several well-arranged mills of Messrs. C. A. Pillsbury and Co., who turn out 1,800 barrels a day, and whose brand secures the highest market quotations on either side the Atlantic. The Messrs. Pillsbury are constructing another handsome well-appointed mill with a producing capacity of 3,000 barrels a day. In 1860 Minneapolis turned out annually 30,000 barrels of flour. Her present producing powers would almost enable her to do this in two days. With a little extra effort she could nearly manage to furnish the 12,000 sacks (of 280 lbs.) which are said to be consumed daily in London. Her actual daily turn-out when all the mills are working is 12,000 barrels. She ground in 1879 upwards of $1\frac{1}{2}$ million barrels, and of this large produce nearly one-third (442,598 barrels) was exported. The only other place where anything approaching to this business is overtaken is St. Louis, where the flour produce of 1879 was upwards of 2,000,000 barrels.

The Minneapolis millers have formed an association through which all purchases of wheat are made which employs agents in various parts of the country, and distributes the supplies as required to the different mills in proportion to their run of stones or rollers. Settlements are made once a week. Every mill is provided with its elevators, so that the cars, containing 400 bushels, all loose, are brought up, unloaded, and are ready for despatch in fifteen minutes. The grain is usually winnowed several times, run through a smut machine, passed down a shoot, in which powerful magnets retain any portions of wire, nails or other metal, which, besides injuring the stones and rollers, are also a fertile cause of explosions, such as that which in May, 1878, destroyed Ex-Governor Washburn's large mill and killed fourteen persons. Flour and dust in a confined atmosphere are found to be almost as explosive as gun-cotton, and hence a spark or light often does incalculable damage. Even the running of the empty stones sometimes suffices to strike the fatal spark. Down copper tubes, enclosed in a jacket containing steam, the wheat passes to dry and toughen the skin and facilitate the separation of the bran. Between slack rollers the wheat is cracked that the bran may be separated with as little flour as possible attached to it. The stones to which it passes, unlike those which grind the soft winter wheats, are run at low speed. Using hard spring wheats, slow movement is found to produce the best quality of flour. The stones, as at home, are dressed with the diamond machine and hand-picked; but the dressing is generally better done by fewer hands at lower wages, while sharpness is maintained by the use of

Hungarian or Patent Flour.

solvents. From the stones the ground wheat is thrown on to the silken bolting cloths, which carry over their farthest end the husk or bran, discharge into other hoppers the tailings and middlings, in another channel run off the cheaper bakers' flour, which has occupied the central layers of the grain, while the germ, situate close to the hilum and containing oil, which discolours and spoils the flour, is also separated as an oily flake and made into the 'red dog'—the lowest quality of flour.

But at Minneapolis and many modern American mills where spring wheat is used still further separation and reduction are effected. The middlings are run repeatedly between stones, iron or porcelain rollers, and through the silk bolting cloths. These processes, first adopted in Hungary, and hence called the Hungarian process, are repeated four times, and in some mills as many as twelve times. From these repeated reductions of the middlings, which constituted the layers of the wheat berry immediately under the bran, and which until recently were almost classed with the refuse, are made the finest qualities of the highly albuminoid or patent flour. This flour has not hitherto been sufficiently appreciated in England. It has, however, much greater strength than the ordinary bakers' flour; it takes up more water; it makes lighter bread; a barrel of 196 lbs. makes 140 loaves of 2 lbs., while the same weight of ordinary bakers' flour turns out about 125 similar loaves. Forty-five per cent. of patent flour is sometimes taken, but this large amount reduces unduly the quality of the other grades, and most millers are satisfied with 35 to 40 per cent. of patent. The better qualities of spring wheat, graded Nos. 1 and 2 hard, produce the heaviest yields of patent flour. Preference is given to grain grown on tolerably fresh, unexhausted soils, and in a favourable, rather dry season. Both ex-Governor Washburn and Mr. Pillsbury, however, assure me that, with their improved machinery and repeated purifications, although the yield is not so great, they can now turn out of No. 4 wheat as good flour as was formerly made from No. 2. They believe that milling will still prove profitable when properly managed in America, provided wheat can be bought for what it is worth to ship out of the country, and has not its value artificially enhanced, as it has been during the last two years, by rings.

Very notable in these new mills is the extreme solidity of the whole structure, the absence of vibration, the abundance of air and light, the introduction of air between stones and rollers, and, by a powerful suction draught on the top story, the effectual riddance of the dust, so disagreeable and, as already stated, so dangerous in most older mills. In the upper part of the Washburn Mills are simple and ingeniously-constructed chambers, into which is received from the stones and cleaners the up-draught of dust-laden air, which deposits its burden on flannel webbing, which is swept and cleansed from time to time. The ubiquitous handy lifts render communication easy between the several floors, but increase the risks of fire spreading. The large amount of timber used in all American mills also greatly increases their liability to destruction by fire; while, placed near together, as most of the Minneapolis mills are, a serious conflagration would be alarmingly prone to spread. The precautions against fire are, however, admirable; cisterns of water, hydrants, and hose are on every floor: the men are well instructed and drilled, so as to act promptly in case of emergency. Patent safety gas lamps, enclosed in crystal globes, are always kept with a speck still burning, so that, without opening the lamp or the use of a naked flame, the light can in an instant be turned up.

An increasing proportion of flour is exported in sacks, which cost from 12 cents to 16 cents, according as they hold 140 lbs. or 200 lbs. The smaller being half the weight of the English sack, are preferable on account of facility of movement. In sacks, the flour is easily and cheaply packed both on car and on shipboard. The sack, moreover, costs less than one-half the price of the barrel. In sacks, moreover, the full weight of flour is likely to be insured. In the barrel, however, which costs 42 cents to 44 cents, and weighs 20 lbs., the flour is less likely to be injured by being placed in a dirty car or by sea water; while the stamped paper linings of Mr. W. H. Bailey of Sioux Falls Mills, if used, at a trifling cost per barrel, not only aid in preserving the flour, but prevent the common fraud of refilling barrels bearing a superior brand with flour of inferior quality.

For the water privilege the Minneapolis mills pay $1,260 for every nine run of stones, but some of the older concerns have more favourable terms. Many large, well-situated English steam mills do not pay much more for their motive power. Coals at 6s. to 7s. per ton are estimated to put 2s. on each quarter of wheat ground. Alike in a well-placed English, as in a similarly favourable circumstanced American mill, the total expenses for rent, interest on capital, water or steam power amount to about 2s. on each barrel of flour (196 lbs.).

British millers and bakers anxiously inquire whether these improved American processes pay. A few figures may afford experts the basis for their calculation.[1] At Minneapolis it appears that 285 lbs. to 300 lbs. of No. 2 spring wheat, weighing 62 lbs. per bushel, are required to make a barrel of flour. About 50 per cent. of this flour is the ordinary

---

[1] More exact figures regarding wheat grinding were furnished by Messrs. Pillsbury and Washburn to Mr. Robinson Greenwood of Blackburn, England, who accompanied Messrs. Read and Pell and myself to Minneapolis. The subjoined statement was published in the Report of the Royal Commissioners. The prices quoted were those current in October 1879:—

Messrs. Pillsbury.

	Currency dols.	£ s. d. Sterling.	£ s. d Sterling
196 lbs. flour at	5·55	1 3 1½	
94 ,, offal	·24	1 0	
	5·79	1 4 1½	1 4 1½
300 lbs. wheat, at 98 cents per bushel	4·90		1 0
			3 8½

This shows a profit for grinding and expenses of 3s. 8½d. per barrel of 196 lbs.

bakers' qualities; about 40 per cent. is the patent, worth about 30 per cent. more than the bakers'; about 10 per cent. is 'low grade,' sold at about half the price of the bakers' flour. Besides about 10 lbs. of waste, in the making of each barrel of flour, there is about 80 lbs. of bran and offal, worth 10*d*. to 1*s*., or sold at the mill at $5 to $5.50 per ton of 2,000 lbs. This low price of the offal is one of the American miller's disadvantages, which he has hitherto vainly sought to remedy by condensing the bulky bran into a portable form and thus profitably forwarding it to British markets, where it would be worth about five times the price it brings at Minneapolis. The transport of the flour to European markets, whether in sacks or in barrels, is, however, effected through

Messrs. Washburn.

	Currency dols.	£ s. d. Sterling.	£ s. d. Sterling.
196 lbs. flour at	5·55	1 3 1½	
79 ,, offal	·20	10	
	5·75	1 3 11½	1 3 11½
285 lbs. wheat, at 92 cents per bushel	4·17		18 2½
			5 9

This shows a profit of 5*s*. 9*d*. for grinding and expenses per barrel of 196 lbs.

Flour is reckoned as under :—

	Dollars.	£ s. d
40 per cent. patent at $7	2·80	11 8
50 ,, Bakers' at $5	2·50	10 5
10 ,, Red dog $2.50	·25	1 0½
	5·55	1 3 1½

bills of lading on terms very favourable for the American miller. By several routes the barrel of flour can be transported from Minneapolis to Liverpool, London, or Glasgow at 5s. to 5s. 6d.

The larger conveniently situated British mills have, however, nothing to fear from American competition. They purchase their wheat in a much wider market. The supplies of the whole world are on offer to them. Wheat off the coast is usually to be purchased on relatively easier terms than it can be bought from the farmer who has grown it or merchant who has stored it. The transport and insurance charges are about the same as those which the American miller will have to pay upon his flour. But the British miller of means has a further advantage. Many cargoes off the coast are for immediate sale; money has occasionally been advanced upon them; their sale being usually imperative within a few days gives the purchaser an advantage which may be estimated at about 1s. per quarter. The Americans have no monopoly of improved machinery. The ingenious and important improvements recently made by American millwrights and engineers are not confined to America. In many modern British mills these improvements are introduced. On two of the largest Lancashire mills American artificers are now at work perfecting and modernising the machinery and arrangements. As with wheat and meat, American competition in flour notably keeps down prices. British millers have to work for smaller profits. The business passes into the hands of larger capitalists, who work it systematically, and who, with a big turn-over, can afford to do with narrower profits. When the English market is dull and glutted with American flour, the British miller often buys largely, and makes handsome profits at the expense of his American *confrère*. Like his New World competitor, he has his wheat delivered on his premises by barge or rail. Being in bags, it is hauled up by cranes. Elevators are not used so frequently as they are for the loose grain in America. The grinding is done cheaply and effectively. By judicious mixtures of various wheats better results are usually obtained than where one sort only is used. The bakers say that in purchasing from the best English mills they have hitherto got a more uniform and reliable article than when they bought American flour. The British miller, brought into personal contact with his customer, moreover, better understands and supplies his wants; and, lastly, he has the advantage over the American miller in realising four times the price for his offal.

To the British public it probably matters little whether the staff of life is imported as wheat or as flour. The chief anxiety is to secure plentiful and cheap breadstuffs, and never was there better prospect of such plenty and cheapness. The British wheat-producing capacity is limited. On many British farms it is greatly more profitable to grow other produce, especially of a more perishable description and which cannot be so readily brought from abroad. Between one-third and one-half the wheat annually required in the United Kingdom must now be imported. Other countries, notably our colonies and the United States, can fill our deficit. For many years to come America from her surplus can supply not only the wheat we need, but various other agricultural produce. She has a vast extent of cheap good land. In the great trans-Mississippi zone, where nearly half the wheat of America is now grown, not one-fourth of the land available for wheat is yet cultivated or even occupied. Throughout these regions wheat, as has been demonstrated in these pages can be profitably raised at 22*s.* to 25*s.* a quarter. In many older States and on most farms a little more care in cultivation and in the selection of seed would profitably secure an increment of several bushels per acre over the present meagre 12 bushels—the acreable wheat average of the United States. Recent enhanced prices have greatly extended the wide area devoted to wheat alike in Canada and the States. With anything like favourable seasons, America will have bigger surpluses than ever to dispose of. Hitherto she has spared one-third of her great yield, or upwards of 18 million quarters. Future crops will doubtless provide still more if it is needed. The transport charges on the American continent and across the ocean add 50 per cent., and sometimes more, to the first cost of these cheaply-grown breadstuffs. Any permanent or considerable rise in these transit rates would obviously affect the price of bread in England. But such rise will be counteracted by the introduction of improved machinery and appliances in the several modes of transport, by competition among carriers by land and sea, by augmented trade insuring the loading of ships and cars going west as well as returning east, by the reduced wages and expenses induced by amendment or removal of the present costly duties which the United States levy on all imports. These considerations favour the conclusion that the present moderate charges are very unlikely to be advanced. A quarter of wheat (480 lbs.) is now carried on through bills of lading 1,200 to 1,400 miles by railway cars or barges and 3,000 miles over the ocean to British ports for about 15*s.* For 2*s.* 6*d.* landing, dock, and other charges are met. With a living profit to all concerned, American wheat can, therefore, be landed in the United Kingdom at 40*s.* to 42*s.* per quarter, and with tolerably favourable seasons and without the disturbing influence of American rings, or exceptional conditions, this price is not likely for any long period to be exceeded.

CHAPTER XVII.

LUMBERING AND PRISON LIFE.

STILLWATER is sixteen miles north-east of St. Paul, on the confines of Wisconsin, beautifully situated on the St. Croix River, which joins the Mississippi twenty miles below St. Paul. It is one of the most important and thriving cities of Minnesota, has a population of 8,000, is the capital of the lumber trade, and is notable for its saw mills, its flour mills, and its State Prison. The city has grown within thirty-two years, has handsome churches and four sumptuous schools supported in part from the lands set aside for the purpose by the State, and furnishing capital gratuitous education; a public library and court-house, hotels, an opera-house just completed, and intended to accommodate 1,000 people. There are good stores and shops built of Minnesota stone or of brick, the usual park and pleasure grounds, and the carefully laid out mile trotting track. From the precipitous cliffs, 110 feet above the river bed, stretching away beyond the lower town, are numerous villas, and a far-reaching magnificent view of the windings of the silvery St. Croix, of a picturesque undulating country, and of dense imposing woods. A pontoon bridge spans the

St. Croix, which is here about one-third of a mile wide; the central part swings out, making an opening of 300 feet for the passage of vessels or rafts. The river supplies capital fish—pickerel and pike, including the peculiar wall-eyed variety known as jack salmon, bass of three colours, the flat sun fish, sturgeon, and white and red trout, in the summer afternoon rising to the flies, and many of them 2 lbs. to 3 lbs. in weight.

The 'forest primeval' around the town has been felled, much of the undergrowth burned; a younger less vigorous timber arises, different from the original, principally consisting of a scrubby oak and poplar. The soil generally is light, consisting of gravel and sand. On the untimbered spaces and on cleared land farming has grown during the past twenty years. Owing to the improved demand for agricultural produce 3,000 to 4,000 acres of 'wild land,' during the last two years, have been broken in for crops. The farms average 150 acres. Corn growing, stock raising and dairying are pretty equally prosecuted, Stillwater itself absorbs the agricultural produce of the district. On the common land about the town many of the citizens keep their own cows. Within an area of two or three miles land is worth $50 to $100 per acre. In Stillwater beef sells at 6*d.* per lb.; poultry by weight makes the same price; milk is 2½*d.* per quart; potatoes, 1*s.* 3*d.* per bushel. Wheat generally sells at nearly 4*s.* per bushel, it is not considered to pay at less than 3*s.*; bakers' flour is worth about 20*s.* to 25*s.* per barrel of 196 lbs.; oats cost 1*s.* 3*d.*, Indian corn 1*s.* 6*d.* per bushel, hay

36s. to 45s. per ton, coal being 21s. per ton. A cord of fire-wood, 8ft. long, 4ft. wide, and 4ft. high, costs $4.

There are three flour mills at Stillwater, one erected as far back as 1856, now possessing eight run of stones, eleven sets of porcelain rollers, and two sets of iron rollers. Besides the supplies sent in by neighbouring farmers, 2,000 to 3,000 quarters of wheat are brought from a distance for grinding. The wheat of 1879 is reported better than that of the previous year, and as thin in the skin and producing flour of as much strength as the superior crop of 1877. Five bushels are used to produce the barrel of 196 lbs. of flour. About 30 per cent. of patent flour in two grades; 60 per cent. of bakers' or shipping flour; and 10 per cent. of a still lower grade are produced. In the manufacture of the patent flour the middlings are subjected to four reductions. There is a fair local demand for the bran at $5 to $5.50 per ton. Neither farming nor milling are, however, at Stillwater as important interests as lumbering.

For three hundred miles north by the banks of the St. Croix, and away to Lake Superior, are great forests, mainly of pine, oak, and poplar. Timber merchants and speculators purchase from the State great tracts of these forests at a cost very slightly if at all exceeding the value of the standing timber. The trees that will pay for transport are marked during the summer or autumn, and are sometimes barked for a couple of feet from the ground a year before they are felled in order to arrest circulation of the sap, and more quickly season the timber. Towards late autumn the lumberers are sent into the woods, build their log huts, lay in their stores of provisions, and proceed to cut down the trees marked for them. Faulty and worm-eaten timber is not regarded worth moving; every tree as it is felled is marked with the cabalistic sign of its owner. Along the hard frozen snow or ice they are readily rolled and dragged to the nearest stream. Mr. E. W. Hurant, of Stillwater, informs me that timber standing in the forest is worth $1.50 per 1,000 feet; it costs $1.50 to $3 to drag it out and place it on the stream one to three miles distant; and about $1.50 to deliver it to Stillwater. Brought down to the water, the trees are rafted, the raft frequently being 300 ft. long, and 30 ft. to 50 ft. wide. When deeper wider water is reached several rafts are united. In convenient shallow portions of the great rivers, as on the St. Croix, a couple of miles above Stillwater, booming of the logs takes place. Upwards of a hundred million feet of logs are here boomed at a time. Some three hundred lumberers, usually picturesquely dressed in red flannel shirts and blue serge trowsers, with long poles separate the logs belonging to perhaps three or four hundred different owners. Springing from log to log with the unerring precision which practice alone can give, finding firm footing on the bobbing, rolling trees, each man selects and brings together the brands of probably a score of owners. Down the St. Croix and its various tributaries two hundred million feet of timber sometimes come in one season, much of it is bound direct for Quincy and St. Louis, but nearly one-fourth is worked up at Stillwater. The timber in the rough is worth $10 to $12 per 1,000 feet.

At Messrs. Seymour, Sabine, and Co.'s saw mills 120,000 to 150,000 feet of timber are cut in one day, and 200,000 feet when the mills are running day and night. A stout platform, 120 feet long, with parallel rails, connects the saw mill and the bed of the river, and has a dip of about 20 feet. Down these rails, lowered by a great chain, a low car is run, is passed under the floating tree, which is wickered to it, and drawn steadily up the incline. The touch of a spring raises and guides great levers, which, with human-like precision and superhuman power, deposit the tree on the saw table, and adjust it as if it were a nine-inch batten. Circular saws square it, the outside slabs are automatically run out of the way. Without loss of time, with the slightest manual interference, but with the help of the levers by the side of the table, the squared log is removed to the upright saws of which 12 or 15 are constantly at work. Planks, battens, and boards are rapidly turned out. About half the refuse and sawdust, on endless webs, are run to the furnaces, which supply the motive power which drives the two 120-horse-power engines. The refuse not thus used is ground, and stored in large heaps for winter fuel.

The contiguous saw mills, belonging to Messrs. Schielenburg, Ralcker, and Co., also produce a large turn-out, and exhibit admirable labour-saving appliances. Every day, logs, to the number of 800 to

1,000, averaging 200 feet apiece, are cleverly raised from the river on strong toothed wheels, fixed on the endless chain which runs down the platform bridging the space between the saw mill and the water, and extending for some distance into the river. Over these formidably toothed wheels the log is guided, is caught and steadily held by them, is carried up into the mill shed, 130 feet from the river, making an ascent of about four inches in the foot. Whilst the chain moves upwards with its heavy creaking burthen, a web in the trough underneath moves in the reverse direction, and carries down into the river portions of bark, which the firmly-gripping wheel teeth tear off, and which, without this provision for its removal, would block the raising tackle or carry into the shed a great amount of rubbish. Deposited on the saw table, adjusted by the great levers, which start up and work like human arms, but more powerfully and untiringly, the tree is squared between circular saws, moved to a turn-table, on which it is deftly directed at right angles toward the upright saws, which reduce it to the desired planks or boards. Two trees, each 3ft. to $4\frac{1}{2}$ft. in diameter, are cut up simultaneously, by two sets of saws. The two lots of fifteen to twenty boards, by another set of handy levers, are rolled together, and wickered with a rope at each end. The ordinary hands employed in the mills have $35 per month. The men who file the saws have $5 to $6 per day, but find a lad to help them.

In making the roofing shingles so largely used throughout America, the dressed logs are cut into

T

blocks about 18 inches by 9 inches. These are carried automatically against rapidly revolving circular saws, which slice the tough wood as if it were a turnip. Down a hopper, into a lower chamber, the stream of shingles is delivered, and they are then edged, squared, tested, and bunched with hoop iron. They are usually made 15 inches long, 4 to 6 inches wide, 5-16ths thick; they cost $2 per thousand; 1,250 cover one square, i.e., 100 square feet. Laths of various sorts and sizes are made. Planing, tongueing, and mortising machines are at work; ledged doors, 7 feet by $3\frac{1}{2}$ feet, are turned out for $1.25. All the machinery is carefully covered in, and accidents are very rare. From these mills the timber is sent by rail and river often for 1,000 miles. The sawn stuff, in deals, battens, and boards, with lath, shingle, and lighter articles above, are made into rafts, often containing a million feet, and despatched fully 700 miles down the St. Croix and Mississippi to St. Louis, or still a thousand miles farther to New Orleans. Steam tugs are generally engaged to drag the raft, which usually takes twenty days to reach St. Louis. On their floating home, the men in charge generally erect their tent or hut.

The State Prison at Stillwater is a good specimen of an American Penitentiary. Five to six hundred male delinquents are placed here. Those committed for one year and life sentences are not separated; and, it is stated, no disadvantage results from the confinement of those committed for such variable periods. The penalty of death being seldom inflicted in the States there is a considerable number convicted of murder, amongst them a pleasant intelligent-looking fellow, a warder in the Hospital, and three brothers of good birth and deportment, who robbed a bank, boldly intimidated several considerable villages, whilst they harried the principal houses, shot several who endeavoured to resist their marauding, and for some weeks terrorised a large neighbourhood. Within a twenty-foot wall, where sentry boxes are placed at various points, and where warders day and night mount guard, with loaded rifle, the substantial stone prison is built. The cells are in three stories, the two upper entering from cast-iron galleries reached by iron staircases. The cells on the ground appear rather cold and damp, but, on the whole, are tolerably comfortable. The passages and cells are warmed with hot-air pipes; the chapel, hospital, and kitchens seem well arranged.

About the stone prison house are less substantial buildings and sheds for machinery and workshops, where thrashing and winnowing machines elevators, and barrels are manufactured. This industrial department is in the hands of Mr. Sabine, whose saw mills have just been described, and who furnishes machinery and appliances, and pays the prison authorities 1s. 11d. daily for every man who turns out to work. This arrangement has been in operation for some years, and will still continue. It goes a good way towards making the penitentiary self-supporting. In the carpenters', blacksmiths', painters', and other shops, the convicts have active healthy labour, which for robust subjects is preferable to the shoemaking, tailoring, brushmaking, and comparatively sedentary occupations chiefly pursued in our prisons. Associated with the convict hands, helping to train them, and maintaining a regular and high character of work, are 250 artisans who come into the penitentiary daily. This association of the criminal classes with those unstained by crime, the active busy life, the training in useful work which can be profitably pursued when freedom is regained, the good conduct earnings which often amount to 10*s.* per month, must exert an ameliorating influence on most characters, and prevent relapses into crime. With more extended scope for labour and less keen industrial competition, private traders in America do not suffer as they might do in this country from such employment of prison labour. Warders perambulate the workshops, the convicts are forbidden to leave their benches or duties, talking is interdicted, the men are orderly and respectful, insubordination and attempts at escape are rare, but occasional malingering occurs.

The ample supplies of cheap timber are a sufficient guarantee that only the best material is used. Throughout the works a great deal of labour-saving machinery is employed. Besides ordinary vertical and circular saws are saws working at various angles, and employed for notching. The tough ash axles are cut and blocked by machines, doing the work better and quicker than the twenty men they have superseded; they are shod with a cast-iron thimble, on which the wheel runs. Twenty thousand to 30,000 feet of planing, tongueing, and grooving are sometimes done daily. The oak used for the framework of the machines have their four sides planed at one operation. Axles and other parts are bored sometimes with seven holes simultaneously, and with much more accuracy than could be done by hand. The iron beaters for the thrashing machines similarly have eleven holes drilled at once. Numerous mortising machines are constantly at work. The wheel making is well and substantially done; nearly a hundred are tired in an hour, and a rivet is put on each side of every spoke. The thrashing machines, designated 'The Minnesota Chief,' almost every portion of which is machine-made, are carefully put together. The adjustment of the blast for winnowing each description of grain is well managed from the outside. The larger machines thrash 1,000 bushels in twelve hours. With horse power complete they cost $650; without horse power the price is $500; they are usually driven by a ten-horse portable engine, which may be bought for $1,400. Six or seven thrashing machines are tested and turned out on an average every day; and about the same number of winnowing machines and elevators, which, with about half the reach of the best English machines, cost about $80. A thousand flour barrels are machine-made daily, have seventeen oak staves; the champering and crozing are done in the same operation. The barrels are sold at about 1s. 9d. each. One of the most novel and interesting of the many arrangements connected with the Penitentiary is an exhaust tube 3ft.

by 2ft., which runs 1,300 ft. from the saw mills on the river edge, over the prison walls and up to the wood yard. Up this tube the refuse timber from the saw mills, broken into small pieces, is drawn by a huge fan, at the rate of a ton and a half an hour, and conveniently deposited in heaps for winter fuel. In the Old World Penitentiary, labour is a drug, and idle unprofitable service has often to be allotted to the uninterested inmates. Here, at Stillwater State Prison, there is as much activity and energy as in any free industrial private enterprise. Labour is as carefully economised, heavy toil is lessened by ingenious appliances, and production is multiplied and cheapened by the employment of the best machinery.

CHAPTER XVIII.

SOUTH-WESTERN MINNESOTA.

THE president and directors of the St. Paul and Sioux City Railroad graciously placed one of their saloon cars, handsomely decorated with the Union Jack, the Stars and Stripes, with fruit, grain, and other industrial trophies of Minnesota, at the disposal of the Royal Commissioners, Messrs. Read and Pell, of myself, and Mr. R. Cox, of Edinburgh. Accompanied by Mr. Horace Thompson, president of the St. Paul Bank and of an important section of the line, whose recent untimely death has proved a great loss to this country, by Mr. A. Young, commissioner of emigration, and several other gentlemen, and in charge of Mr. James H. Drake, the able and energetic secretary of the railroad, we started on Monday, October 6, for a week's survey of South-western Minnesota. Flying 'wild,' or 'special,' liberty was given to proceed along the main line and branches over full 600 miles of road, to stop when and where desired, and to use the carriages, as we freely did, not only for a tower of observation, but as a hotel on wheels, where at night twelve comfortable beds were frequently made up. Thus sumptuously provided, we had admirable opportunities of seeing the country pleasantly and rapidly. Steaming from under the rocky bluffs of St. Paul, bridging the grand Mississippi, winding along her beautiful banks, a wood country is shortly reached, extending north and south for about 100 miles, through which for 40 miles our well-appointed light train bowls along, travelling south-west. Amid an aftergrowth of smaller stuff are still standing noble specimens of 'the forest primeval.' Some have their death-warrant run round the stem 2ft. from the ground. A circle of bark being gouged out, the tree slowly dies, and the timber, when felled 12 or 18 months later, has become fairly seasoned. Besides trees familiar to English eyes are quantities of the rapidly-growing, moisture-loving cotton wood, a sort of black poplar, and the tamarack, which, although not of large growth, is prized for its toughness, and is used for fence posts and railway ties. Such supplies of wood prove valuable in a country where coal is not yet largely worked and the winters are long and cold.

In the open places in the woods and in rich marshy flats by creek or river large quantities of hay are cut, are cheaply collected into ricks, which, as in the English fen countries, stand until the ground is firmly frozen and transport is cheap. Such hay is cut usually with machines, and got together with rakes and elevators, at a cost of $1.50 to $2 a ton, and, delivered in St. Paul, sells during the winter at $4 to $5 per ton. Whether in the woods or in the more open prairie cattle are kept. They are becoming yearly more numerous and of better stamp; and in the sunny, bright October day, with the thermometer at 75° in the shade, are standing in picturesque groups to the middle in many a lake and stream.

On the edge of the big woods we pull up at the thriving town of Shakopee, where during the previous week a serious fire had occurred. A telegram was sent to St. Paul for an extra fire engine, which was run from the offices on a railway truck, a railroad èngine attached, and within an hour of the despatch of the message the fire engine was doing good work at Shakopee, 38 miles distant. The railway company has some engine shops here, and, driven by steam, lathes, punches, with other machinery, are working noiselessly. No British machinery of this sort is met with west of Philadelphia. The artisans are receiving 10s. to 11s. a day. Societies which are formed among the workpeople wisely restrict their duties to benefit purposes only. Strikes are unknown. Wages have advanced steadily and naturally with increased business. The societies give $20 to $30 at the death of their members, but no provision is made for the death of wife or children. Coal at present is chiefly brought from Pittsburg, and costs in large quantities $3.50 per short ton, but will be cheaper when the railway is pushed through, as it will shortly be, to the useful coalfields 150 miles south, at Fort Dodge.

The next important stopping place, 75 miles from St. Paul, is St. Peter, a town of 3,300 inhabitants, with wide streets symmetrically laid out and trees planted and protected by the side of the wooden footways; two large handsome school-houses, forming, as usual, the most prominent of the public buildings; a public library and book club, with numerous churches—for even here the Scandinavian population, which muster strongly, insist on having their particular dogmas duly represented. The land is light and sandy; the prairie rolling; the grass cropped short by cattle: the country has much of the appearance of the Sussex Downs. On the common lands which rise behind, cattle of the townspeople are herded. A mile further over the ridge the land is of heavier staple—a fine friable loam, 2ft. deep, growing 15 to 20 bushels of spring wheat, and although not manured, still shows no visible deterioration. Corn is, however, more certain; from 35 to 50 bushels are produced, and this secures the keeping of cattle and pigs, which are not affected by the locusts and drought that sometimes victimise the wheat crops of this and adjacent States. The dry, down-like lands are suitable for sheep, which in winter are yarded and fed on hay and corn, usually given unthrashed. There is no reason why flock-masters should not grow a few mangel and cabbage to diversify the dry food and insure the better thriving of the flock. Good land is with difficulty procurable within two miles of the town at $40 an acre. A quarter section of 160 acres, a little beyond that radius, on which a good stone house and farm premises have recently been built, is on offer at $30 an acre. As is almost invariably the case, the farmers own the land they cultivate; but here were 50 acres rented at $1.50 an acre, the tenant paying taxes. A few farms are run on shares, the owner, in addition to the land, sometimes finding half the seed, and contributing one-half towards thrashing, each party taking half the wheat, corn, and oats grown. Here, as elsewhere, are complaints that assessments are made annually, and that improvements barely completed, and for which there has been no opportunity of obtaining any return, are fully charged.

Two miles from St. Peter is one of the State asylums for the insane, commenced in 1867, and finished two years ago, costing, with furniture and appliances, 120,000*l.*, capable of accommodating 600 patients, and occupied by 520 persons of both sexes and various stations in society. Early in 1881 this handsome structure was unfortunately burnt to the ground. Throughout America private asylums are very properly discountenanced; the State asylums provide gratuitously for all classes; and here are representatives of all nationalities, their various languages and idiosyncrasies considerably increasing the difficulties of medical officers and attendants. As at home, drink proves the cause which most commonly carries patients to such institutions; but the lone dreariness of some of the sparsely-peopled western regions proves a common cause of melancholia. The wards, dining and sleeping apartments are particularly comfortable. Among the cases promptly sent to St. Peter a satisfactory proportion of cures is reported.

The asylum has a good farm of 410 acres, lying well sheltered under the bluffs, managed by the physician, details being carried out by his bailiff, an energetic emigrant from the north of Ireland, who has a high opinion of the capabilities of the farm, and declares that he has never failed to raise 60 bushels of 32lbs. of oats, fully 50 of Indian corn, and 150 bushels of first-rate potatoes. The 30 milk cows are useful. A superior well-descended short-horn bull is kept, and calves are reared. Several bullocks, three years old, brought in for three months' feeding, weighed 1,650lbs.; 100 hogs are bred and fed. The stone-built granaries, stables, and other premises are well and strongly constructed. Some of the feeding cattle are kept in the second story. By lifting a hinged plank in the floor all *débris* is twice daily swept down into the pig yard beneath. Water is distributed in iron pipes from a pump worked by wind. The manure is utilised in the capital gardens mainly cultivated by the patients. The drainage of the asylum irrigates the meadows a quarter of a mile below the terraced gardens.

Ten miles from St. Peter is Mankato, a prospering town on pleasant rising grounds, with hanging woods sheltering it from the north-west, the Minnesota river running below and affording convenient water transport, which has, however, been little used since the railroad was made. The soil is light and easily worked, and numbers of small farmers from the neighbourhood express themselves fairly satisfied with their position, although generally complaining of the disappointing yield of the wheat crop of 1879, which barely pays its way even at the low valuation of $8 (32*s.*), stated to be the cost at which an acre is grown.

Those who get the recent current rate of 80 cents for No. 2 spring wheat will not, however, be losers with the 10 bushels which they average. Although the spring was disastrously dry, oats and corn have done better than wheat, and cattle as elsewhere have paid. The Roman Catholic church and school stand conspicuously on the hill; two other schools, each capable of accommodating 300 children, are in different parts of the town; a normal school with an efficient preceptoral staff, capital lecture-rooms, and appliances, attracts 100 young people of both sexes, who have, as at home, a two years' curriculum before they obtain their certificates. Several capital dry-goods stores have a frontage and style more imposing than are met with in many English towns of four times the size and ten times the age of Mankato. In some of the grocery stores were Harvey's and Lea and Perrin's sauces, Cox's sparkling gelatine, and Colman's mustard, despite the 30 per cent. duties which handicap these ubiquitous luxuries. Beef and mutton sell at six to seven cents per lb.; poultry, $1.50 per dozen; milk at 4 cents a quart; eggs, 3 to 10 cents a dozen; potatoes, 25 cents per bushel; hay, $3 to $5 per ton; Indian corn, 20 to 25 cents per bushel.

Mr. R. D. Hubbard has completed a most substantially built flour-mill, with twelve run of stones, a capacity to turn out 500 barrels of flour daily, and all the modern appliances for producing a superior article. For cleaning there are two large separators and a smaller provided with magnets to remove iron nails and any portions of wire used in binding the sheaves.

Steam-heated chambers warm and toughen the grain to prevent its breaking. It is crushed between stones or rollers. The stones are still dressed by the old diamond machine; iron and porcelain rollers are also employed; the oleaginous germinal centre is carefully separated by silk screens. The crushed grain is ground, the bran stripped off, the flour bolted, separating middlings and leaving about 58 per cent. of bakers' flour, worth $6 to $6.50 in New York. The repeated reduction some four times over of the 'middlings' produces the valuable patent flour, which here constitutes about one-third of the produce, worth in New York $7.50 to $8.50. The clean middlings put through the purifiers leave about 7 per cent. of an inferior flour which is worth about $5. The bran at the mill realises $5, the finished middlings $12, the shorts $7 per ton of 2,000 lbs. Although 1,000 miles from the Atlantic seaboard, Mr. Hubbard has enterprisingly laid out $80,000 on this new mill. His machinery is driven by a 200-horse power horizontal engine, with 5ft. stroke and 2ft. cylinder. The waste steam is utilised to pump water for the mill at the rate of 400 gallons a minute, and, more important still, to drive a larger pump which raises 2,350 gallons a minute for the town, which, besides, has two artesian wells. The wheat graded No. 2 spring hard is bought at 75 to 85 cents per bushel of 60lbs.; 4¾ bushels weighing 185lbs. are required to produce a barrel of flour (196lbs.); a through freight transports the barrel from Mankato to Liverpool for $1.75, or 7s., while one cent more delivers it in London. British millers from these figures may form some conclusion as to the sort of competitor they have to cope with here in South-Western Minnesota.

Mr. Hubbard has also a linseed mill, which uses up the linseed grown tolerably freely in the neighbourhood. At a small cost of labour, 10 to 20 bushels of linseed are got per acre. There has hitherto been small demand for the flax fibre. The linseed averages 4*s.* a bushel. There is nothing special in the mode of manufacture : the seed is generally screened ; for containing the steamed pulp, long-wool cloth bags are regarded almost as good as the more expensive camel-hair bags. One bushel of linseed yields two gallons, or 15lbs., of oil, worth about 2*s.* 6*d.* a gallon, and 40lbs. cake, which, although pure and good, is here worth only $21, or 4*l.* 4*s.*, per short ton. It is carefully packed for the eastern markets and for Liverpool and Glasgow in bags containing 362lbs.

Mankato further possesses a brewery and a communicative German brewer, Mr. Bierbauer, who purchases the six-rowed barley of the country, which would be graded as No. 3, weighs about 34lbs., and costs 35 to 40 cents a bushel. Two and a half bushels of this barley make a barrel of 31 gallons of beer. On this is paid a duty of $1 (4*s.*), which is not, however, due until the barrel is sent from the brewery or sold, when it must have the dollar stamp, with which the brewer must provide himself, gummed over the spigot-hole. Beer of whatever strength pays the same duty ; no duty is paid on malt ; no interference occurs and no duty is charged on brewing small quantities of beer for home use.

Beer sent out for sale without the dollar stamp subjects the sender to a fine of $300. A deduction of 7½ per cent. is allowed on the stamps. Brewers manufacturing over 500 gallons annually pay besides a special tax of $100; those manufacturing less than 500 hundred barrels are charged $50. For the sale of beer a $20 licence is required, and $25 for a spirit licence. Round the bung-holes of both the larger and smaller barrels there is fixed a light iron casing, which prevents splitting.

Sorghum saccharatum is grown in this neighbourhood and yields a rich syrup. Mr. T. E. Reeves, of Le Ray, is stated to have got 400 gallons of syrup per acre. He and his neighbours are now busy crushing and refining. Mr. Reeves is turning out from his mill 60 to 100 gallons daily, expects to run 4,000 gallons before the season is over, and considers that amber syrup in suitable circumstances will yield double the acreable return of wheat. The sugar crystallised from the syrup is bright and good. A sugar refinery is talked of at Mankato.

Eighteen miles east of the town, at Janesville, is Messrs. De Graff and Hopkins's stock farm of 2,300 acres, of which 350 are under cultivation, and where a Clydesdale and several superior Hambletonian trotting-horses are kept, as well as a number of pedigree shorthorns and Jerseys, with some superior Cotswold and Southdown sheep and pigs, a collection of well-bred animals which should materially raise the character of the live-stock of the district.

South of Mankato is Blue Earth county, through

which the St. Paul and Sioux City Railroad surveyed a line in the spring of 1879. In six months after its commencement, nearly forty miles were finished to Winnebago, and in little more than a year a further extension will be made to the coal-fields of Fort Dodge, where coal can be put upon the cars at about 9*s.* per ton. At Winnebago the Southern Minnesota railroad has also a depôt. The land, much of it settled ten to fifteen years ago, is rich, deep, and full of vegetable fibre; the river banks are well wooded; the prairie stretches away north-west full 500 miles towards the Rocky Mountains, still affording location for some generations of settlers. The farms vary from 160 to 320 acres, are generally well laid out and enclosed, frequently, with the barbed wire fixed on maple posts so apt to lacerate stock running against it. An English colony of good farmers is established.

Land is all taken up, and is worth $40 to $50 an acre. Mr. Sherman, of New York, has 2,000 acres under capital cultivation. Messrs. Shaw and Bullis, who came out six years ago, went in for Hereford cattle, have a herd of 60 Pale Faces, and find a good demand for the young bulls. Four miles distant is the farm of Mr. Latimer, who, besides his arable sections, has 1,000 acres of well-watered grass, creeks, and timber bottoms, where he successfully keeps shorthorn graded cows, and has recently purchased a useful Percheron horse. From Winnebago, where twenty-five years ago the only live stock were antelopes, gophers, and prairie fowl, there has this season been forwarded direct to New York 170 carloads of useful fat cattle, and their production is everywhere on the increase.

Twenty miles west of Winnebago is Fairmont, seven years ago containing not a dozen houses, now a town of 1,000 people, the head-quarters of an English settlement, with substantial public buildings, a grist mill driven by wind erected at a cost of $10,000, and a cheese factory which uses the milk of several hundred cows, extracts on an average 1lb. of cheese from the gallon of milk, and does the whole work at a cost of 1 cent per lb.

About Winnebago, eastwards in the Fairbault county, and indeed in many localities throughout Minnesota, Iowa, and adjacent southern and western States, the cultivation of amber cane sugar is steadily extending. There has long been a considerable domestic manufacture of syrup from maize; but the sorghum saccharatum, or amber cane, is now deservedly preferred. It contains nearly as much sucrose as the sugar cane itself. It succeeds in a cooler climate and on a drier soil. In South-western Minnesota, 8,000 acres are now devoted to it. Sandy loams, whether prairie or timber, are chosen; properly matured unhybridised seed, as soon as spring frosts are gone, is deposited in drills on thoroughly stirred land. The plants are harrowed while they are coming up; like Indian corn, they should be worked with the horse hoe and plough repeatedly. The canes reach nine to eleven feet high; as they approach maturity they are apt, especially in a wet season, to shoot, and any suckers require to be lopped off, for the unrestricted growth of wood will often take 50 per cent. from the yield of sugar. The cost of growing amber cane is about the same as that of wheat: the harvesting, crushing and crystallisation of the sugar is more than double the expense of the field culture. Mr. Charles Eustis, who raised 40 acres in 1880, gives the following estimate of the cost of growing an acre of amber cane :—

	$
Ploughing	1·25
Harrowing	·50
Planting	·50
Hoeing by hand	1·75
Cultivation	2·00
Harvesting	4·00
Incidentals	1·00
	$11·00

A gentleman near Fairbault, who has had six years' experience of amber cane, gives the following estimate of the cost per acre in English money :—

	s.	d.
Ploughing	6	0
Harrowing	1	0
Marking	0	7
Planting	1	8
Rolling	1	0
Seed	1	3
Hoeing	12	0
Cultivating	8	0
Stripping	4	6
Cutting	6	0
Carriage two miles to mill	12	0
	£2 14	0

Crushing the canes, preserving the quality of the

readily fermentescible syrups and crystallising out the sugar prove costly operations, and are not always satisfactory, when conducted rudely on the small scale. An acre of canes weighing about 10 tons are crushed for about 60s. to 66s., this cost being tolerably equally divided amongst labour, fuel and interest on, or tear and wear of, machinery. In the neighbourhood of Fairbault, where thirty farmers are now successfully growing the amber cane, Dr. James Wilhelm has established a refinery with powerful crushing rollers, appliances for the preservation of the syrup, steam-heated pans with the heat under perfect control, where the whole of the operations can be effected with a minimum of waste and expense.

Under proper management the acreable yield of syrup ranges from 150 to 200 gallons, worth about 2s. per gallon. The lesser produce would realise a gross return of 15l. an acre; allowing 5l. for expenses of cultivation and crushing, a profit would remain of 10l. an acre. In many instances as much as 3s. per gallon is obtained for fine syrup. An acre of amber cane properly treated yields 1,000lbs. of crystallised sugar, and about one-half that amount of molasses, which, like the seed of the cane, proves useful food for cattle and sheep. Dr. James Wilhelm for several years has been investigating amber cane; he finds the amount and variety of sugar vary considerably in the plant in different stages of growth. Early in August the sorghum contains only six per cent. of cane sugar, but more of grape sugar: the latter, however, diminishes, and when maturity is reached in September, the cane sugar has advanced to 10 or 12 per cent. From every gallon of good syrup 6lbs. of superior well crystallised sugar is obtained. On suitable land and in fitting climate the growth of amber cane sugar must develop into a great and profitable industry, and might supply a large proportion of the sugar now imported from the West Indies and other sources and for which the United States at present pay annually 17,000,000*l.*

CHAPTER XIX.

PRAIRIE FARMING IN MINNESOTA.

WINDOM, in Jackson county, 150 miles south-west of St. Paul, is a town of 700 inhabitants, with a smart park laid out with trees—always pleasing in a prairie country—several busy stores, two railway stations, and a capital hotel, capable of accommodating thirty or forty people. As is very general throughout America, the townspeople sometimes, even with their families, board and even live at these hotels. Catering for the public is hence in small towns much better done in America than in England. At the refreshment stations even in remote western localities, and at these smaller hotels, on innumerable little *assiettes* at every meal, a varied and good repast is set forth, consisting usually of fish, several sorts of butcher's meat, and fowl, costing, of course, less than half what they do at home, usually fairly cooked, although frequently one hears the order: 'As rare as you can, and the gravy red,' while the beef sometimes proves refractory. Innumerable vegetables—potatoes, common and sweet, perhaps whole, and mashed, corn, beans, tomatoes, &c.—are presented. Pastry, puddings, and ice follow without stint; several descriptions of bread, of wheat or corn, are offered, with tea, coffee, and abundance of good milk, a glass of which is ordered even at dinner much more frequently than wine or spirits. At such hotels and refreshment rooms these meals are charged at the rate of 2s. to 3s. each. Drinking, if done at all, and it is rare among the western farming population, consists in a 'straight tip' of spirit before sitting down to meals, or of a 'nip' after supper.

Twenty miles north-east of Windom, near St. James, is Barden-Barden, on the line of railroad, with a convenient private siding close to the house. Here Mr. R. Barden, son of a New York State farmer, himself a wheat buyer as well as a farmer, has 2,100 acres, 1,400 being under crop. The farm was bought three years ago at $6 to $7 an acre. Three crops have been reaped, barns and stables have been built, and commencement has been made of a three-storied stone house, 150ft. long by 60ft. wide, in the excavated basement of which Mr. Barden purposes to feed in 3ft. stalls 200 cattle. Overhead, conveniently entered from a bank rising on one side, calves and yearlings will be accommodated, while the top story, which can also be reached by carts along a winding ascent, will be devoted to hay, roots, and grain, which will be sent down to the mangers by shoots. From a well 30ft. deep, worked by a windmill, water will be forced to a tank in the top of the building, whence it is conveyed throughout the stalling.

Mr. Barden believes that the management of land, generally successful in England, must be successful here. He approves of diversity of cultivation and rotation of crops; twelve or fifteen years' continuous wheat growing without manure would exhaust, he believes, the fertility of most land. With part of his wheat he purposes sowing clover and Timothy grass, which will be cut for hay or grazed, and after one year ploughed up. The newly broken prairie allowed to remain longer in grass is apt to run to weeds and coarse herbage. Curiously, however, both horses and cattle appear to be fonder of the natural prairie hay than of that made from clover and sown grasses. About 800 acres are prepared for wheat which is spring sown; 1½ bushels is a sufficient seeding. The total cost of the raising of an acre of wheat is stated to vary from $9 to $10, or 36s. to 40s. The average yield is 20 bushels; but, owing to the long spring drought, the crop of 1879 had not generally yielded more than 12 bushels at Barden. A hundred acres are devoted to corn, which costs about $7 or 28s. an acre, and yields 50 to 60 bushels of shelled grain, worth 20c. to sell, but still more to use for feed. A hundred acres of oats make an acreable return of 60 bushels, weighing about 34lbs. Barley grows about 50 bushels of 36lbs., but owing to the heavy dews gets more discoloured than our English barleys. Unlike most farmers here, Mr. Barden takes good care of his manure, and carts and spreads it on his land almost daily.

With convenient lakes and streams on his farm and considerable adjacent ranges of claimed but unoccupied Government and other land, which are grazed for nothing or for the moderate acknowledgment of 1 cent an acre, Mr. Barden is wisely availing himself of the opportunity of rearing stock. He has already 150 scrub cattle, more than half of them useful, profitable dairy cows, and purposes raising his herd of cows to 200. The cream of his cattle are 20 shorthorns, several bought at Colonel King's sale, at Minneapolis, and including the massive Rosedale from Lady Pigot's herd, unfortunately not likely to be of further use; Harriet Bates after 14th Duke of Thorndale, Emma Rose, a good four-year-old, from a Rose of Sharon cow, Australia 16th from Arizina, and other useful shorthorns. From the Rosedale cow, after 2nd Duke of Hillhurst, is a three-year-old roan bull, styled Rosedale Duke, with good flesh and hair. But the premier is a long deep stylish sire, Duke of Rutland, roan, nearly three, bred by Mr. Gibson, after 22nd Duke of Airdrie, dam by 3rd Duke of Airdrie, from a superior specimen of the Bell Bates tribe. Using these two sires, selecting his best grades, and steadily multiplying his shorthorns, Mr. Barden trusts speedily to have 200 cows, to rear annually 200 calves, to feed at least 100 steers, which at $2\frac{1}{2}$ years should make 1,300lbs. to 1,500lbs., according as they are grass or corn fed; and for which he trusts, as is often done elsewhere, to secure 2c. or 3c. a lb. more than is given for commoner qualities. At Barden, as in other herds, large numbers of cattle of various sorts and ages are run together. In one large yard into which during the summer and autumn they are driven at night, and where they remain without feeding for 10 or 12 hours, Mr. Barden has cows, heifers, and suckling calves to the number of 300; but they certainly agree well enough together. The weaned calves also appear to be run in big lots of variable size and strength, and would certainly thrive better if distributed in several smaller yards. More fortunate than British shorthorn breeders, Mr. Barden states he has no difficulty in selling his bulls when a few months old at $100 to $200, which, relatively to the cost of rearing, is equivalent to 100 guineas in England. Prices for young bulls of good lineage are said to be higher than they were two years ago. No bulls from graded cows are kept. The herd law is very properly stringent as to bulls being allowed to stray. Any Texan or underbred brute found at large can be taken up and 'altered.'

Mr. Barden has a taste for horses as well as for cattle. He has a useful, active Clydesdale and a number of fashionably descended trotting-horses of Hambletonian and Squales lineage; but owing to strangles having recently run through the stable, the foals and yearlings are not in showing trim. For these well-bred youngsters capital lofty, well-aired boxes are provided, 12ft. by 10ft., with approved spared partitions, iron rack and manger, and doors running on an iron rod overhead, no post or projecting object obtruding to tempt an idler to bite and crib.

As yet Mr. Barden has no sheep, but he purposes starting a flock, probably of the ordinary Merino graded stock of the country, and crossing them with Leicester or other well-established English breed. He has nearly 100 Berkshire pigs. The only purchased food used is bran, of which the annual consumption is about 100 tons, the price delivered at the farm being a trifle over $4. The corn and oats grown are all used at home, part being thrashed, most given in the sheaf.

Hitherto Mr. Barden has got a good deal of his work done by small farmers, who undertake almost any agricultural work. A man and a pair of horses can be hired at the rate of 1*s.* an hour. Ploughing has cost about $1.25 to $1.50 per acre, a furrow of 14in. by 4in. being turned over with two or three horses; two and a half to three acres are generally well ploughed every day. With an eight-feet broadcaster 10 to 12 acres are sown and about 14 harrowed over once. Unlike some other managers, Mr. Barden disapproves thrashing out his crops from the shocks in the field. It entails, he considers, a great deal of labour when the cost is at its highest; it increases the risk of injury from bad weather; it retards for ten days the men and horses getting at the ploughing of the stubbles; while it diminishes the value of the fodder for the stock. For thrashing wheat he pays four to five cents per bushel, the machinist finding three men, water, and fuel; the eight-horse engine and thrasher are capable of doing up 600 or 800 bushels a day. The average price of wheat delivered to the siding on the farm in 1878 was 70 to 75 cents; in 1879 and 1880 it has been fully ten cents higher, but the higher price has not paid for the diminished yield.

At present Mr. Barden employs twenty farm horses, several boys, but only ten men, who receive

$16 to $17 a month with their lodging and board, and are engaged from March 1 until farm work ceases in the end of October. About half the men will be paid off during winter; the remainder will receive $12 a month. Even with all the advantages of labour-saving appliances, and without any of the chaffing, root-cutting, mixing, or cooking which occupy so much time during winter on an English stock farm, it must take five good smart fellows and the manager's sagacious planning properly to feed and attend to 400 cattle and 100 pigs. Certainly both farmers and agricultural labourers work here with an energy, will, and purpose now rarely seen in the old country.

Driving with Mr. Barden over the prairie, flocks of wild duck and geese were raised from the small lakes; a sandhill crane was quietly fishing for its afternoon meal and flapped slowly away, apparently assured that we were unprovided with destructive weapons. By the side of Bingham Lake we came upon a herd of 40 useful cattle of all ages, belonging to a homesteader of 160 acres reared in New Brunswick, and a resident by this lake side during the last eight years. Unhampered by primogeniture or entail, Mr. Parsons had 12 months ago given his daughter and one-half of his estate to a steady young fellow, who has built on his dower a log house of two rooms and the indispensable underground cellar, has some tolerable corn potatoes and a few young cattle, and has been earning some hard cash by ploughing for Mr. Barden. Neither Parsons nor his son-in-law are, however, satisfied with the year's yield of wheat. They have between them upwards of 60 acres, but owing to the dry spring they will not get more than seven bushels an acre. Corn and potatoes have answered better. Some two-year-old steers have been sold for $15, which, although a small price, represents an outlay of little more than the wages of the lads herding them on the adjacent prairie and cutting for them from the same free land a few loads of hay for winter use. The poor yield of wheat has told in another way against Parsons's prospects. His thrashing machine has earned little money; the active wife cannot yet have the new house and smart furniture which were promised when times mended. But although the house is poor, the mistress is tolerably comfortable and independent. She and her family enjoy most pleasant, healthful surroundings; with flour from the neighbouring mill, and home-made yeast, manufactured from potatoes, hops, sugar, and ginger, she makes light, beautiful bread, the like of which we should thankfully have on many a London table; milk, butter, and eggs are plentiful. Things are admittedly brighter than they were during the 'hopper' visitations of 1874 and 1875. The cattle and pigs are growing into money, if the crops are not. Two sharp boys are at a good school not two miles distant, for in this, as in most Western States, wherever there are fifteen children over six years of age, school buildings and a qualified teacher must be provided at public expense.

From our comfortable head-quarters at Windom, some of our party made a diversion in favour of grouse, prairie chicken, ducks, and wild geese, which abound on the numerous lakes; while others, anxious to see more prairie farming, drove eight miles through rather a bare rolling country to Heron Lake, where Messrs. Thompson and Kendall have a farm of 5,000 acres, fully half of it reduced within two years to cultivation. The land is a strong loam, with the usual abundance of organic matter, the accumulation of successive crops of prairie grass; 2ft. to 3ft. down is the yellow argillaceous subsoil. Three years ago the land cost $4 to $7.

On prairie broken early in spring flax and buckwheat were put in during May—an old English preparation for wheat. The flax yielded only five bushels an acre, but as the seed made a dollar a bushel it more than paid expenses. Buckwheat proves capital feeding for horses and hogs, and is used during winter for cakes, which appear on almost every American table; but the crop was disappointing, owing to a sharp, early September frost. The flax and buckwheat stubbles, free of weeds, with the prairie sod well rotted, were on October 8 being turned up by two sulky ploughs, each drawn by three horses, the foremost ridden, as usual, by the driver, the second following without any guidance, excepting that at the end of his mile furrow the driver, after turning and entering his own plough, sprang off and turned in the second, which followed promptly alone. This is not a regular proceeding even in a country where labour is carefully made the most of, but is only an occasional economy when the driver is temporarily absent; but it testifies to the determination to keep moving.

On we go to another field where fourteen of 'Cassidy's Chill Plows,' drawn by three horses abreast, with the drivers riding, come down like a battery of artillery, turning over each a capital regular furrow 15in. wide by 5in. deep. In the soft, easily-worked, stoneless soil a land-side is dispensed with. The axle towards the land wheel is curved so that the wheel goes at an angle of about 60 degrees. Care is taken that the far-away fields are first ploughed, and the teams carry a furrow almost from the stable out, and bring another back as they return for their hour-and-a-half rest at noonday, as well as at night. Two and a half to three acres is the daily work of each plough. The 60 horses from the beginning of March receive about 24lbs. each of oats daily, or sometimes have an equal weight of corn substituted for the oats. Thirty big three- and four-year-old bullocks have been broken, and work capitally in pairs. Spring wheat, sown in March, is at present the chief product of the farm: it is harvested in July; the St. Paul harvester and self-cord-binder was last year chiefly used. With eight of these machines 2,130 acres were cut; the cord did admirably, there was never any hitch or slipping; even now, in examining the sheaves, they will not give way at the knot; a couple of mechanics from the works remained throughout harvest, to prevent any risk of breakdown or stoppage. Mr. Kendall, who has had much experience of both wire and cord self-binders, much prefers this cord machine. The two machines are the same in price. The cord itself is cheaper than the wire, and if made lighter, as it might be, would be reduced to about 1*s*. per acre. The corded sheaves do not require to be unbound for the thrasher. The cord is less apt than the wire to damage the machine, and cannot, even if eaten with the fodder, seriously injure the cattle.

Over several fields we drive to see the work of the Minnesota Chief thrasher with attached winnower and elevator, made at the convict establishment at Stillwater, costing $525, capable of thrashing out readily 1,000 bushels a day, driven by a 10-horse portable, fed with flax straw, the extra capacity of furnace required for the bulky fuel being extemporised by introducing within the furnace door a six-foot iron tube, into which the straw is packed, dried, and is pushed into the furnace. The produce of 36 to 40 acres is thrashed daily; 16 men, a pair of horses, and two teams of oxen do the work, including drawing water and taking the wheat to the granary, at a cost frequently within 60 cents an acre; but where weeds are numerous, sometimes entailing double that outlay. Mr. Kendall has a number of convenient portable wooden granaries, holding 1,800 bushels, moving on runners, costing $50, with ventilating tubes passing up from the floor, which is raised six inches from the ground. These granaries, much resembling the shepherds' huts used in many parts of England, would be still more handy for movement if their dimensions were reduced so as to hold 1,000 bushels, or one day's thrashing.

The cost of growing an acre of wheat is closely

calculated by many Minnesota farmers. Some absentees hire the whole of the work, including ploughing, seed and seeding, harvesting and thrashing, with delivery of the grain to the station, say, three miles distant, and get all fairly well done at $8 to $8·50 (32*s.* to 35*s.*) per acre. This does not, however, usually include interest on capital expended in the purchase of the property, or in permanent equipment, or taxes—items which cost fully a dollar or a dollar and a half, and which thus represent the acre of wheat to cost $10 or 40*s.* This closely agrees with the following detailed figures supplied by Mr. Kendall :—

Interest on cost of farm $6 per acre at 8 per cent.	·48
Interest on buildings, roads, fences, &c., $5 at 10 per cent.	·50
Taxes	·10
Wages of man ploughing 2½ acres daily	·28
Board of man	·15
Pair of horses at 45 cents per day	·24
Seed 1¼ bushel	1·50
Wages and board of man sowing 35 acres daily and harrowing 12 acres	·02
Interest tear and wear on teams valued at $300, harness at $25, ploughs $45, harrows $50, sowing machine $100 at 25 per cent.	·88
Cord or wire for binding	·50
Wages and board of men and horses harvesting 15 acres daily	·10
Interest and tear and wear of harvester $250	·58
Wages and board of men shocking and stacking	·86
Thrashing	1·15
Wear and tear of thrasher $525 and of engine $1,000	·12
Wages of stablemen attending horses	·20
Incidentals, foremen's wages, &c.	1·00
Freight of grain to market	1·30
Total cost of an acre of wheat	9·96

Regarding the foregoing careful estimate, Mr. Kendall remarks all board and wages are figured at actual cost taken from the books. Men's wages are $18 a month, with board, excepting in harvest and thrashing, when they are $2 per day. A man's board costs 15c. daily; a pair of horses, 45c., which purchases 1½ bushel of oats at 25c. per bushel, and hay at $3 per ton. Interest is figured at 10 per cent., but tear and wear of horses and most machinery is charged at 25 per cent. This does not apply to the engine, which is used during ten months for sawing and other work independently of the farm. Estimating the yield at 15 bushels an acre, which is within the average of the district during the past five years, the bushel would be delivered at St. Paul or Minneapolis at 66 cents (2s. 9d.), or 22s. per quarter of 480lbs. With a yield of 20 bushels, easily secured in favourable seasons, the cost price, leaving a fair working profit on the transaction, would be 50 cents, or 2s. 6d. per bushel, equal to 20s. a quarter. Freights vary somewhat according to route or season, but Southwestern Minnesota is well off for competing lines of railways, and 15s. commands a through rate over 1,300 miles of railway and 3,000 miles of ocean; marine insurance, commission, and brokerage take about 1s.; shrinkage and dock dues swallow fully 2s.; but, allowing for all charges, Minnesota wheat can be sold at British ports with a profit to all concerned at about 40s. a quarter.

Although wheat has hitherto been the principal produce of the Heron Lake Farm, it is wisely determined to multiply resources. Oats are encouraging; one piece last year produced at the rate of 70 bushels. Five thousand bushels of swedes are grown for calves, sheep, and pigs, and this area is to be extended. Clover and Timothy are to be laid down as a good preparation for wheat and a means of keeping more live stock. A smart useful black Clydesdale, with good back and joints, clean in his legs, and weighing 1,560lbs., has been imported. His service fee is $10, or $15 if a foal is ensured. Several Gwynne and other useful shorthorn cows have been purchased. Two hundred ewes of native breeds with a good deal of Merino character are being crossed with Cotswolds. The hogs are good Berkshires.

Messrs. Thompson and Kendall, desirous to compare the results of large and small farms and of farming by landlord and by tenant, on each of two lots of about 150 acres have built a house of four rooms, a stable, and granary, and let each on lease for five years to an American family. The owner pays taxes and insurance, does the first breaking-up, finds half the seed, requires that half the land shall be in wheat, and that he shall receive half the grain produce as it comes from the thrasher. One of these farms has this year produced from 41 acres 3,136 bushels of oats, worth 25c. a bushel; from 111 acres 1,165 bushels of superior No. 1 wheat, weighing 62lbs. With the advance in price, the wheat, at a dollar, will fully pay expenses; while the oats will leave a handsome profit. The other tenant is also prospering. In his spare time he has done for Mr. Kendall 45 days' team work, which earns him $3 a day; his thrashing has been overtaken at a reduced rate of 3c. per bushel for wheat, and 1½c. for oats; while he has 1,500 bushels of oats for sale. These tenants may be regarded to have done fairly, inasmuch as neither had any capital. Both have lived comfortably, and maintained their families during 18 months at Heron Lake; and, notwithstanding the poor wheat crop, each has made about 100*l.* out of his labour and his two crops.

Under this share system, which is practised to a limited extent in many parts of America, and which bears close analogy to our much-becalled plan of renting, an industrious man with 120*l.*, if set down on a fairly good arable district, may lease 150 acres of land, purchase horses, implements, and household furniture, and have sufficient to keep himself until his crops are reaped and his pigs fed and killed. His probable expenditure would be as follows:—Pair of horses, 25*l.*; plough, 4*l.*; harrows, 1*l.* 10*s.*; harness, 5*l.*; wagon, 15*l.*; small tools, 3*l.*; cow, 4*l.*; three pigs, 1*l.* 10*s.*; furniture, 20*l.*; maintenance, say, 20*s.* a week for 26 weeks, 26*l.*—total, 104*l.* His landlord would probably give credit for the seed; the broadcaster here generally used could be hired, or the grain hand-sown; the use of a reaper could also be obtained, or, if the crop justified, paid for out of the produce. Without outlay for purchase of land, or for building of a house or premises, with a limited capital, a steady energetic man has thus the opportunity of satisfactorily going into farming, of becoming acquainted with what may probably be a new country to him, and acquiring experience which will be of much value when he makes a purchase of land on his own account.

T. Moore has settled in comfortable quarters adjacent to Messrs. Thompson and Kendall. Having been two years in the United States Navy, he got his homestead patent for 160 acres, after two instead of five years' residence, and on payment of trifling office charges. He is a sharp active fellow with a good house and premises, has three horses and two foals, three cows and twelve young cattle, and the usual good hogs. He grows 50 acres of wheat, 10 of corn, 20 of oats, 10 of barley, and 20 of clover and Timothy. He manages this himself with the occasional aid of one man; but his farming is untidy, his land foul, and his implements, of which he has a good selection, as is generally the case, are lying about exposed to wind and weather, without even a cheap shed or covering of straw to protect them. During the seven years he has been here his best yield of wheat has been 32 bushels in 1877; his worst, five bushels in 1875, when the hoppers were so destructive. Now that the country is more generally cultivated there is not, however, much chance of their again doing such serious damage.

Twelve miles drive over rolling prairie brought us to Messrs. Thompson and Schurmeier's farm of 640 acres, beautifully situated at the head of Willow Lake, a mile long and half a mile wide. Although the land has only been occupied 18 months, the two young farmers have a capital house and stabling, are themselves putting up shedding for 230 half-bred Merino ewes, purchased at $3 each in February; the wool was sold at $320, the flock was increased to 400, and thus promises to pay even for the expensive and rather unnatural three months' confinement in yards necessary on account of the severity of the winter. Hay, which has been got together at a cost of $2 per ton, and bran, bought at $4, constitute the winter fare both of sheep and cattle. Before another year roots and cabbage will be provided. Five-and-twenty useful graded shorthorns of different ages are on the prairie by day and in the yards at night: a big growing shorthorn yearling is on service, and there are some capital sties of Berkshires. Half the farm has already been broken up, and borne wheat. The settlers on the dark alluvial soil which surrounds this lake are prospering, and Mr. Barrington, a brother of the Mayor of Dublin, has just taken up several sections on the lower margin of the lake and purposes settling with his family.

One hundred and sixty miles south-west of St. Paul, in the midst of a capital game country, is Heron Lake Junction, where the traveller and sportsman will find a capital hotel. From this point the Black Hills Branch of the St. Paul and Sioux City Railway is carried thirty-three miles to Woodstock, and is thence to pass through the Indian pipestone country, where the easily-cut and readily-polished ferruginous metamorphic clay lies in beds about a foot deep between intervening layers of quartzite. The Indians believe the soil to be coloured with the blood of their forefathers, visit the spot once a year, and reverently carry off supplies of the pipestone to be carved into various ornaments. Down this line will by-and-by be brought a portion of the varied mineral wealth of the Black Hills and the cattle reared in increasing numbers on the bluffs and valleys of the Dakota river. Five miles west of Heron Lake Junction, the town of Dundee is rising; and a few miles south, on the Southern Minnesota Railway, is Airlie, where Lord Airlie, I am informed, has property and has contributed handsomely towards town improvements.

Throughout these Western States lands are frequently pointed out belonging to Englishmen, who, to counterbalance the depreciation unfortunately going on in land property in England, are investing in desirable estates in America, which are destined to advance in value as railways and emigration spread westward. A quarter of a century ago settlers from the older States and from Europe were buying farms in Illinois and Ohio at $5 to $10 an acre. Although contemptuously said to be 'played out' and not always producing as much wheat as they did when first brought under cultivation, these lands, nevertheless, are selling at from $25 to $40 an acre, and some of the sellers are reinvesting in Minnesota, Dakota, Iowa, Missouri, or Kansas, confidently anticipating good interest on their investment and labour, and a similar steady increment in the value of their property. Of such promising investments there is an abundance throughout these Western States.

In the State of Minnesota alone on the 1st of

January, 1879, the official records reported upwards of 10 million acres unsurveyed and unoccupied belonging to the United States. Three million acres of surveyed lands belong to the United States, and about the same quantity is owned by the State of Minnesota. For these the appraised price is $2·50 per acre for lands situated within railway limits, and $1·25 for those without the 20-mile limits. A considerable proportion of the most desirable of these State lands has already been taken up under pre-emption, homestead, or timber Acts. Nearly seven million acres are still in the hands of the five competing railway companies, who have conveniently 'gridironed' the State of Minnesota with iron roads. For 10 and occasionally for 20 miles on either side of their lines they have received each alternate section of a square mile, and these sections they are disposing of at prices varying, according to eligibility, from $5 to $10. Credit may be taken for payment, which may usually be made at the rate of $1 or $2 per annum, 7 per cent. being charged on the deferred payments.

Some idea may be obtained of the undeveloped food resources of America when it is thus recorded that in this one State alone there are still about 20 million acres of unoccupied lands, while in several other States and Territories an equal or greater extent of unclaimed lands is to be met with. Here in Minnesota is an ownerless, unoccupied tract two-thirds the extent of England. Supposing one-fourth of this area were in wheat and produced only 13 bushels per acre—the average yield of the State during the last two unsatisfactory years of drought—there might here alone be grown 74 million bushels of wheat, or rather more than half the wheat exports of the United States!

Close to the railway, ten miles beyond Dundee, on a pleasantly rolling prairie, by a pretty lake-side, the zealous Roman Catholic Bishop Ireland is planting the township of Avoca. Seventy thousand acres have been bought from the State, and from the St. Paul and Sioux City Railway Company. The first pioneers arrived twelve months ago. Now there are 30 families, some still in tents; but a chapel, school, and store are built. Neither here nor in any other of Bishop Ireland's townships are any intoxicants allowed. 'Railroad,' 'Park,' and 'Grand Avenues' are staked out; thirty town lots, 22ft. by 150ft., are sold for shops; some residential lots of 66ft. by 165ft. have been also disposed of. The plans and site for a good hotel are fixed on, the Bishop with liberal spirit determining that his hotel-keeper shall be a Protestant. A park is reserved running down several hundred yards to the margin of the lake, about two miles long, around which it extends, and water is abundantly supplied from the lake and from wells 20ft. to 30ft. deep. Father Koebrel, who concentrates in his own person the functions of priest, mayor, architect, and surveyor of the new colony, expects within a year to have a hundred families comfortably housed. Some of the people are recently from Ireland, but most are from Canada. Several houses are finished and occupied; a dozen are in course of construction, most of them of two stories, measuring 24ft. by 16ft., with three rooms above and the same number below. Inch boards ready dressed cost $16 per 1,000; doors and window frames come ready to be put in; wooden shingles are used for roofing. The contract price for the artificers' and labourers' work is $33; the total average for the completed house is $250.

The Black Hills Railway, begun in the spring of 1879, before autumn extended 45 miles from Heron Junction, and is destined to be pushed along north-west 400 miles through the prairies, so recently the hunting-grounds of the Dakota Indians, over the Dakota river towards the Missouri, to tap the mineral riches of the Black Hills. Ten miles north of the railway runs the old Dakota track, along which are numerous settlements, and where wheat has been grown for twenty years consecutively on the same good soil.

Back we run to Heron Junction, where, although 900ft. above St. Paul, the land appears rather wet, but the sedgy lakes afford good lodging for wild fowl, and eighteen miles down the main line we reach Worthington, a place of 700 inhabitants, colonised from Oberlin College, Ohio, and determinedly upholding the Maine Liquor Law. Close by the railway is a flour mill, where the fuel used is hay and rushes, part of it cut during winter by running the mowing machine over the frozen prairie and lake banks. This readily-collected fuel costs $1·50 per ton, and the usual daily consumption is seven tons. At

Worthington I attended a county agricultural exhibition, which, although the first attempted, attracted a goodly show of stock, implements, and general farm produce. The live stock was not in the high condition usually seen at English county exhibitions; the horses showed most need of improvement; but there were some useful shorthorns and grades; a good red ten months shorthorn bull scaled 900lbs. Some of the grades were scarcely distinguishable from the pure breeds. The sheep were chiefly the produce of Gloucestershire-Cotswolds from the Norwegian-like ewes of the district, which are worth $2·50 to $3 each, and there were a few pens of Merinos and Merino grades which, although paying well with their fleece, are not profitable as mutton producers. Capital potatoes and tomatoes are exhibited, and several specimens of amber sugar cane, with its syrup and crystallised sugar, which is easily cultivated, and reported to pay $20 an acre.

One of the best farms I have seen in Minnesota is Messrs. Thompson and Warren's in Rock county, two miles from Luverne town and station, and comprising 23,000 acres. The first sod was turned in May 1877, and fully 1,500 acres have each year been brought into cultivation. A good house has been built, with barns, two lots of barracks, capable of accommodating 70 men, stabling for 200 horses or mules, with some shedding and pigsties. To break the wind, attract moisture, and beautify the estate, trees, mostly of cotton wood, are planted about half a chain apart around the roads which surround the sections. White willow hedges, which make capital fences, are also planted, and it is intended to follow the successful example of some of the neighbouring small holders and plant fruit trees. On the prairie sod turned in during May and June, Indian corn is sometimes immediately dibbled, and the hastily prepared crop usually yields 15 to 20 bushels an acre. On other portions of the newly-upturned prairie navy beans are drilled or dibbled about June 1, are pulled about the middle of September, and although only yielding three to five bushels, make about 5*s.* per bushel, and, like the corn, constitute a good preparation for the subsequent wheat. Here as elsewhere flax is also used as a preparatory crop.

These and other stubbles were being ploughed up. In one field were at work 25 'Casiday's sulky ploughs,' made at South Bend, Indiana, costing $65, and each drawn by four horses or mules. Three draught animals are often used; but two months' continued dry weather having hardened the soil, the ploughing is fair work for four. The working parts of the plough are of cast steel; a metal disc suffices instead of the coulter in the soft fen-like soil; the axle is bent, so that the wheel in the furrow goes at an angle of about 60°. Small skims turn in the stubble and any weeds, of which, however, there are few. Three acres are turned over daily by each team, which does, morning and afternoon, its five bouts of a mile out and in. Accompanying the plough is a foreman on horseback, hired for the seven or eight months at $50 a month. The ploughmen are engaged from April 1 to November 15, or until the end of the season, at $18 a month, with board. The dietary, which differs little at the three meals, consists chiefly of bread and butter, fresh and salt pork, fried or boiled, beef once or twice a week, baked or boiled potatoes and other vegetables, pickles, and fruit, with coffee and milk. A cook and his mate are attached to each of the two barracks. No beer or spirits are allowed on the place. Half the wages are paid every month, the remainder at the close of the season. For harvest, thrashing, and other work, extra men are engaged at a dollar, and occasionally at a dollar and a quarter, per day, with rations, which are valued at 25c. The men are rung up at 4.30 a.m., feed their mules, clean out stables, breakfast at 5.30, feed, harness, and start their own teams at 6; do about ten miles on the sulkys; stop at noon, and unless near home have troughs and nosebags for the mules at a field barn, where their own dinner is also forwarded. Out again at 1.30 p.m. they continue until 6, or when drilling, harvesting, or at other important work, until dark. On Sundays the men are not expected to turn out until 7. Excepting in harvest, no work is done on the day of rest unless it is the washing of clothes. Some of the men go to church. Others have an afternoon's shooting.

Mules, although costing quite as much money, are preferred to horses; they stand the heat and the annoyance of flies better; long days do not generally knock them up; they are always ready for their food, which consists of a mixture of two-thirds oats and one-third Indian corn, and of this they have 16lbs. to 18lbs.

daily, or nearly as much as they can eat. They do not use more than 10lbs. or 15lbs. of hay. Fly nets are employed in hot weather. The flies being so troublesome in June and the first fortnight in July, the mules paw and strike with their feet, and the ground being dry and hard they are sometimes shod in front. At other times shoeing is unnecessary. The mules stand 16 hands high, weigh 1,200lbs. to 1,300lbs., and cost about $120 in Missouri, whence it takes about $10 to bring them home. Several ox teams are kept. They cost per pair, when ready broken at three years old, $120 to $125, and last four years. A man and his pair of mules can be hired at $1·50 to $2 per day, the hirer feeding the man and his beasts. Autumn or Fall wheat is not used—the severe winter is apt to throw it out; but Mr. Warren purposes trying it, as is done in Illinois, along with one-third of a seeding of oats, which grow up vigorously and protect the wheat, although they perish in the service. Hard Minnesota wheat is put in with the broadcaster early in April, and is generally up in a week. The harvest begins about July 12, twenty-five cord self-binding harvesters are at work, and three machinists are engaged to superintend the harvesters. The grain is cut and carried within twenty days. The yield of 1879 varies from 7 to 15 bushels. That of 1880 was 25 per cent. greater. One field, owing to the spring drought in 1879, proved so indifferent that it was not harvested.

Indian corn is sometimes planted, as already stated, on the spring-ploughed prairie sod, but greatly better crops are produced when the land has lain ploughed throughout the winter, and the sod has thus been thoroughly rotted, or when the corn follows a crop of wheat. Dibbling is then done late in April or in May, usually with a machine which deposits two rows of seed at intervals of about three feet in rows, four feet apart. The surface is repeatedly harrowed, and, as with beans at home, may be again harrowed while the corn is coming up. As the crop is growing, it is cultivated several times between and across the rows, a lad and a pair of mules doing two rows together and overtaking 12 acres daily. Corn enjoys the singular advantage of remaining uninjured, no matter how long harvesting is postponed. Where the straw as well as the grain is to be used, it is cut, bound, and shocked, and often rather untidily left standing in the fields until it is required for the cattle in winter. Frequently the cobs are gathered from the standing corn at a cost of one dollar for 50 or 60 bushels, and the corn stems dragged out by an old iron rail 28ft. long, mounted on 6-inch wheels, and drawn by a couple of mules over the field. The corn stems thus pulled up are raked together and burnt, and if the cultivation has been effectual, the land requires no ploughing for wheat. On this Warren farm the yield of corn free from the cob is 50 and occasionally 60 bushels per acre. The cost of production is about two-thirds that of wheat.

A magnificent crop of clover and Timothy grass is found in one of the wheat stubbles. A hundred acres of seeds sown with the grain in April were (11th of October) strong enough for mowing, and in the subsequent spring would be grazed with pigs and horses, perhaps with sheep, of which Mr. Warren purposed purchasing 2,000 and feeding them throughout the winter, chiefly in yards, on corn, bran, linseed, and barley straw, which is here preferred to oat straw as fodder for stock. No cattle as yet are kept. The heaps of good manure from the stables are only used occasionally in the garden, where the vegetables in luxuriant variety amply attest the productiveness of the soil. So little value is attached to the manure that Mr. Thompson remarks, 'I would gladly give $100 to have 1,000 tons cleared out of the yards; for,' he adds, 'it does not at present pay to use it, and for years the deep good soil will require no help except from clean thorough cultivation.' Good cultivation has certainly demonstrated the capabilities of this soil, which if in England would grow four to five quarters of wheat, or would be anxiously looked after for market gardening. For portions of the estate which four years ago cost $6, $15 to $20 have lately been offered.

Five miles from the Warren farm are the wonderful 'Luverne Picture Stones.' From the bosom of the level plain a great hill, ten miles in circumference, appears to have been upheaved: the red ferruginous quartz rock, sand and wind worn, is thrown into quaint, weird shapes, larger, more numerous and varied than the remains on Salisbury Plain. Along the eastern rampart, pillars not unlike those of Samson's Ribs, south of Edinburgh, rise abruptly 100ft. In sheltered nooks are beautiful mosses, ferns, and cacti. From the elevated plateau a magnificent view, extending thirty miles in every direction, is obtained of the rolling brown prairie, diversified by the silver sheen of lake and stream, and the extending cultivated fields of yellow wheat and corn.

CHAPTER XX.

LAND AND CROPS IN SOUTHERN DAKOTA.

THE civil war which eighteen years ago disturbed all American industries, the Indian uprising and massacres of 1862, which jeopardised life and property in certain Western States, the raids of locusts in 1874 and 1875, and the want of railroad facilities retarded settlement in Dakota. But these troubles are over. Dakota Territory has now a population of upwards of 50,000, besides an Indian reservation on its northwestern frontier estimated to number fully 20,000 red men. There will, however, be elbow-room and to spare for some years to come, for the Territory embraces an extent of 96,000,000 acres, or exceeds by nearly 20,000,000 acres the area of the British Islands. Of her northern tracts, towards the Red River, I have already written. The more Southern portions are conterminous with Nebraska, Iowa, and South-Western Minnesota, which it much resembles. The prairies, however, are rather more rolling; between the several rivers which intersect the country are considerable hills. Along the Sioux River for a dozen miles east of Sioux Falls is a ridge of rounded limestone hills, covered with short sweet herbage, on which sheep should thrive—a spur of the range which runs 200 miles north-west to the Cheyenne. The climate, especially of the southern parts of Dakota, is good; the summer heat, greatest in July and August, very seldom reaches 95° in the shade; the winter cold rarely marks −20°; the winter atmosphere is dry; not more than 12in. of snow falls throughout the winter, and until the exceptionally severe winter of 1880–81, it has seldom lain long; the rainfall taken at the Observatory at Yankton, the capital, was 23·74in. in 1874 and 37in. in 1875; the average appears to be about 25in.; the chief rainfall comes when it is most required, from April to September.

Two-thirds of Dakota consist of useful farming land; most of the remainder is good stock land. Pine timber occurs among the Black Hills; and cotton wood, oak, ash, hackberry, soft maple, elm, and some black walnut are found along the Missouri, the Big Sioux, and other rivers of the south-west. For many miles which I examined around Sioux Falls the black loam soil is 15in. to 30in. deep, resting on an argillaceous subsoil, sometimes on beds of gravel, which in this climate are apt, however, to drain away the moisture rather too quickly. Water generally is readily found at 30ft. to 40ft.

Sioux Falls, a thriving town, 250 miles south-west of St. Paul, is an apt illustration of American urban progress; a few years ago an Indian trading post, in 1878 having 400 inhabitants, it now enumerates 3,000 souls. It is the centre of a wide area of fine country. It lies sheltered by surrounding hills; the river, an important tributary of the Missouri, rushes over the red quartzite rocks, which water and ice have worked into strange shapes. As in other western cities, the hostelries are numerous. Besides the Cataract-house, which was built at a cost of $11,000, and absorbed $16,000 for furnishing, there are a dozen places of public entertainment. Good shops, houses, and a school costing $16,000, are built, and now an opera house to seat 800 is being erected. The Southern Dakota Railway from Yankton, the capital of the Territory, seventy-five miles south of Sioux Falls, is arranging a joint station with the St. Paul and Sioux City line, and the southern Minnesota has its road brought into the town.

Here, as everywhere else in my travels, I met with most hearty welcome, and was cheerfully furnished with any information desired. Throughout these Western regions there is much kindly feeling towards England, and much hospitality extended to Englishmen. At many towns on our route, and even at roadside stations, gentlemen have come considerable distances to welcome ',the English travellers,' and volunteer all help and information. At Sioux Falls Judge Brookings, with a number of his townsmen, most courteously received our party, consisting of the Royal Commissioners, several other gentlemen, and the assistant-manager of the St. Paul and Sioux City Railway. Preceded by a band of music, we were conducted in carriages through the town, around the bluffs, to the falls, remarkable for their wild red rock scenery, and to the picturesque wooded island formed by a sweep of the river, where, in umbrageous retreat,

The Queen Bee Mill.

free from the annoyance of mosquitoes, many of the townspeople pleasantly spend their summer evenings.

The Big Sioux river close to the town makes a descent of 60 feet in three falls, within half a mile, and is estimated to represent about 1,040-horse power. This important natural advantage is being turned to several useful enterprises. Under the able practical presidency of Mr. James H. Drake, a company has been formed with a capital of 80,000*l.* A handsome substantial flour mill named the 'Queen Bee' has been built. Founded on the solid rock, the massive walls, five feet thick, ensure the requisite steady firmness and absence of vibration. The most recent scientific and mechanical appliances have been introduced. The latest inventions in rollers promise to secure from the fine hard wheat of the locality a yield of 65 per cent. of high grade flour. The mill will have a capacity to turn out 1,400 barrels daily, and running full time will require an annual supply of 300,000 quarters of wheat. An elevator adjacent is being constructed to hold 19,000 quarters of grain. A paper mill, linseed crushers, and amber sugar factories are projected. Excavating for the mill has disclosed the value and extent of the metamorphic sandstone fused into grand masses of a warm red colour, imperishable as adamant, so hard as to scratch even glass or granite, useful as emery powder for polishing steel and stone, and susceptible itself of a mirror-like polish. Besides being used for lapidary purposes, it promises to be of much value for table-tops, monuments, and pannelling, as well as for ornamental building; standing heat and acids unchanged, it is proposed as a lining for blast furnaces. This rock, especially valuable in a locality where stone is scarce, is quarried chiefly by the plug and feather process, and the water power is to be applied for dressing and polishing.

Judge Brookings informs me that the civil code of Dakota is identical with that of California. No land in this Territory has been granted to any of the five railway companies which are opening up her agricultural and mineral riches. Acquisition of her unoccupied lands is obtained from the Territorial authorities under the Homestead, Pre-emption, or Timber Acts. Any person, male or female, 21 years of age, a citizen of the United States, or who declares his intention of becoming one, under the Homestead Act, may claim 160 acres of unoccupied prairie or timber land. After filing his application at the local land office and paying his fees of $14, the homesteader proceeds immediately, or within six months, to build a house, take up residence on his claim, and carry out his breaking-up and other improvements. In five years, if he prove by two competent witnesses that he has lived upon his homestead and effected reasonable improvements—concerning which the authorities are not difficult to satisfy—he is entitled to his certificates patent and title to the land. The homesteader may, however, if he pleases, commute his residence of five years, and within twelve months obtain his patent and title, if, six months after taking up his claim and building a house—which may consist of the rudest log shanty —he chooses to pay $1·25 per acre for his land.

Some settlers adopt this latter course, and, having acquired their homestead, proceed to gain another quarter section by pre-emption.

Under the Pre-emption Act the settler, whether a recent arrival or one who has already secured his homestead, makes his claim to 160 acres of unoccupied land, and pays a fee of $2. He must immediately erect upon his claim a house, commence breaking and other improvements, and reside for two and a half years, when he is called upon to pay $1·25 per acre, and then receives his patent. A settler cannot at the same time be acquiring land under both the Homestead and Pre-emption Acts; but, having secured one quarter section under one of these Acts, he may proceed to claim a second under the other; while during the currency of either claim he may, under the Timber Act, acquire another 160 acres of Government land, contiguous to his own or otherwise, provided he pays $14, breaks up 1-16th part annually, devotes it if he pleases to crop, but subsequently plants on each acre 2,700 timber trees, and thus within four years sets out 40 acres of timber. Some hard wood trees should be interspersed with the soft, rapidly growing poplar, chiefly planted. The young shoots taken out of the plantations generally cost 5*s*. to 6*s*. a thousand; the railways usually forward them gratuitously. In many Western States the planting of 40 acres of trees, on each unoccupied section, excuses the owner paying taxes during five years. To secure these privileges of the Timber Acts, the trees have to be protected during eight years, and at the expiration of this period, if 650 thriving trees survive on each of the 40 acres, the Territory or State, grateful for thus clothing and beautifying the bare prairie, on payment of a final fee of $4, grants in perpetuity a certificate and title for the 160 acres.

With homestead, pre-emption, and timber lots, within eight years, a settler may thus obtain for himself 480 acres of land, for which he will have paid $254, or a little over 50*l.* Any members of his family over 21 years of age may acquire the same quantity of land in the like manner. Very similar laws, it should be remarked, regulate the acquisition of land in other Western Territories and States. As in the Australian colonies, all titles and transfers of land are registered at the district offices. There the records give the name of the owner of every estate and the burdens upon it. A purchase of land not registered is set aside in favour of a second sale which is recorded on the register. Mortgages on land and other property are also registered, those standing first on the register taking precedence. Property acquired under the Acts described, although liable for mortgages, cannot be seized for ordinary debt: nor are equipments or necessary tools or implements liable for debt. A husband cannot dispose of his homestead without the consent in writing of his wife. Women's rights further receive tender consideration in Dakota, and a married woman can hold property and conduct business independently of her husband; nor under such arrangements would either be answerable for the other's debts.

Taxes on land amount to about 1 per cent., in

Land worked on Shares.   329

only two counties do they reach 2 per cent. The moderate amounts thus collected suffice to meet the expenditure of the Territory, for the salaries of the Federal officers and the expenses of the courts are defrayed by the Government. The valuation, made annually, is low, seldom reaching one-half the actual value; but all improvements are taken into account so soon as they are made, and often before any benefit has accrued from them. Private bankers and money lenders make advances on landed property, usually restricting the advance to one-half the value, at 10 to 12 per cent. Such mortgages usually secure in advance interest for one year, extend generally for five years, and if registered take precedence of all other debts. Here, as at home, there is often a disposition to begin on too large a scale, take up more land than can be paid for, and buy implements and other things on a costly credit system. For implements and furniture purchased and not paid for a chattel mortgage is often taken, and if registered, the purchaser failing to complete payment, is readily compelled to give up possession of the unpaid article.

For 25 miles round Sioux Falls the land is taken up, and $6 to $12 would have to be paid for any fairly good land. Extending westward up the Dakota or James river the soil is also easily worked and productive. The farms are smaller than in the more northerly parts of the Territory, not averaging more than 160 acres. Although most farms are the property of the cultivators, a few are worked upon shares. When the landlord finds land and house, hands over a considerable proportion of the farm broken up and in fair cultivation, and also pays for the seed, he usually claims two-thirds of the grain harvested. Under this share system, where about three-fourths of the farm is in crop, landlord and tenant usually each take one-half of the grain crops, the tenant, however, having all the profits accruing from the breeding and feeding of cattle, sheep, or hogs.

The frost is usually sufficiently out of the ground to begin wheat planting during the first week in March; 15 bushels is the average crop. Harvest commences from the 15th to the 20th of July; $9 to $10 cover the total acreable cost of wheat cultivation. Indian corn is more grown than in the northerly Red River districts. Planting commences about May 15. There is always the 70° of summer heat requisite to mature this crop, while frosts, checking growth, do not occur before the middle of September. Although the corn is never so luxuriant as in the lower parts of the Missouri valley, 200 miles south, abundance of fodder and 30 to 40 bushels of shelled corn are often secured. Oats, sown in April and reaped in the middle of July, cast 30 to 60 bushels, averaging 35lb. per bushel. Potatoes and other vegetables, as well as fruit trees, grow well; but during the busy struggle for absolute necessaries, which occupy the first few years of the settler's life, the garden and orchard seldom receive adequate attention. Wheat, the poor man's crop, readily yielding rapid returns, is chiefly cultivated. But the highest authority declares 'man shall not live by bread alone,' and settlers by-and-by wisely diversify their production. Cattle, sheep, and swine are kept in increasing numbers. Milch cows in full profit cost $20 to $30; a pair of well broken, good, four-year-old, working oxen sell for $80; sheep make $3 to $3·50; horses and mules, recently advancing in value, bring $100 to $120.

Labourers are tolerably abundant. Good men are engaged at $15 to $18 per month with board; occasional help costs $1 per day. The smaller farmers are very glad to engage themselves and their teams, charging about $1·25 to $1·50 for ploughing an acre, and managing to turn over three acres daily. Farmers sometimes have to transport their produce thirty and even forty miles along the dry prairie tracks to market. I conversed with several who had thus brought their wheat these distances to Sioux Falls, had started before dawn, travelling with loads of 20 cwt. to 30 cwt. behind two or three horses, mules, or oxen, usually overtaking with horses or mules three miles an hour. They were usually in good spirits, having made nearly $1 per bushel for their wheat. Most were looking out for return loads, which generally consist of lumber, and for the transit of which 12c. to 15c. per ton per mile is earned. Although this is only very reasonable remuneration for the haulier, the hirer contrasts it unfavourably with the 5c. or 6c. per ton per mile which he pays for railway transport, and wishes 'God speed' to the railways which contemplate pushing their lines north-west from Sioux Falls, and as a Dakota poet sings—

> 'Opening this land of prairies grand
> Under skies for ever blue.'

CHAPTER XXI.

LAND AND PROSPECTS IN IOWA.

Iowa lies between the 40 and 43 parallels of north latitude: it occupies 55,046 square miles and represents an area of nearly one-half the British Islands. Seven-eighths of the State is prairie, generally more undulating than that of Southern Minnesota. Towards the western boundary, running from Spirit Lake south, is the watershed of this part of the continent, some of it 1,250 feet above the sea level, giving rise to numerous streams diverging east to the Mississippi and west to the Missouri. The rivers and lakes are well stocked with fish and most are frequented by wild fowl. Along their margin trees and scrub are generally found, but their wider extension has been prevented by annually recurring fires which overspread the prairie, but which will now be limited by the closer settlement of the country. Groves and belts of plantation, useful for fuel, for fencing, and for building purposes, are increasing and must improve the climate and aspect of the prairie. The trees chiefly planted, either from seeds or cuttings, are the rapidly growing cotton wood, white maple luxuriating in the moist lower lands, with oak and black walnut of slower development, but greater value. Fruit trees are also successfully cultivated.

So important is the sheltering growth of timber that the State of Iowa allows handsome deductions from the rateable value of the farm for every acre of well-planted timber. Some farms are thus temporarily freed of taxes, which generally amount to 4*d*. per acre. The total taxes in Iowa average about one per cent. per annum on real and personal property. County bridges and education are the most costly objects of expenditure.

The surface soil of Iowa, as of other States of the Great Mississippi basin, in the earlier periods of the world's history, has been brought down from northern mountain regions by flood and glacier and deposited on older rocks—on the calcareous formations in the north, on the coal measures in the more southerly portions of the State. As population and manufactures spread, these coal beds must prove of great value. The upper seams are unproductive, the middle and lower are described as valuable by Dr. Charles A. White in his monograph on the subject, and are stated to occupy the southern fourth of Iowa. They extend for 200 miles in a north-easterly and south-westerly direction, going from the Desmoines to the Missouri rivers, are profitably worked at Fort Dodge, and are believed to be equally accessible at many points for a hundred miles south.

Of more immediate importance to the agricultural settler are the superficial deposits which furnish anchorage and food for his crops. The older formations are thickly invested with drifts of incoherent mud, gravel, and clay, brought, as stated, from higher regions, sometimes, as in Union County, 200 feet in depth, sometimes containing boulders of granite, quartzite, and occasionally of limestone with veins of impure coal of peat and semi-petrified coniferous wood. In the northen counties the drift is more gravelly. Towards the Missouri the more recent drift, receiving the special designation of Bluff, contains more calcareous matters, represented usually by 10 per cent. of carbonate of lime. On the lower lands skirting the Missouri are rich alluvial tracts, well adapted for Indian corn and stock-rearing. Those drift bluff and alluvial deposits contain vast varied stores of plant food. For ages the prairie grasses in almost tropical luxuriance have flourished, died down, or been burnt, and thus have accumulated organic remains most valuable for the growth of plants. These deep good soils in many places have self-contained elements of fertility which, with good cultivation, will produce a long succession of profitable crops.

Clearing and breaking for a crop, which in a timber country takes several years to effect thoroughly, and entails a cost of 3*l.* or 4*l.* an acre, in Iowa, as in other prairie regions, is done by burning the grass or scrub, and bursting up the sod, which can be effected for 10*s.* an acre. Land thus turned up $2\frac{1}{2}$ to 3 inches deep in May will produce 12 or 15 bushels of flax, which, sold as it generally is, at 4*s.* per bushel, within four months brings in usefully ready money to pay for cultivation and other expenses, and admirably prepares the soil for the wheat sown in the subsequent spring. The wheat crops of Iowa in 1880 reached 45,600,000 bushels.

The cost of production is about 40s. an acre, including rent and taxes; the average yield is nearly 20 bushels; blights which several years ago were common are becoming less serious. Indian corn now reaches 225,000,000 bushels, averages nearly 40 bushels an acre, and can be grown at less than 1s. per bushel. In the northern counties fine barleys are raised, and the cultivation of oats extends. Potatoes and other roots prove profitable.

The natural prairie grasses sustain increasing herds and flocks, and blue joint grass, so famous on the limestone soils of Kentucky, with Timothy and clovers are now sown on the cultivated land for pasturage and hay, and are available two or three weeks earlier than the natural grasses. Many good herds have been introduced and are paying their way handsomely. The abundance of water favours dairying. It is estimated that there are in Iowa 250 creameries and cheese factories turning out annually 50,000,000lbs. of butter, and 1,000,000lbs. of cheese. At Philadelphia, New York, and St. Louis agricultural exhibitions Iowa dairy produce has repeatedly gained the highest awards.

The climate of Iowa is one of its important attractions. It is not liable to the extremes of Manitoba or to the malaria of many parts of Missouri or Virginia. The U. S. A. census returns show that the mortality in Iowa is one to 93, for the States generally it is one to 74, for Great Britain it is one to 46 of the total population. At Iowa City, where meteorological observations are carefully recorded, the highest temperature is reached in July and August, ranges from 75° to 90° in the shade; the lowest occurs in December, January and February, and falls sometimes to −30°. The rainfall on an average of twenty years at Iowa City is about 40 inches; rain falls in 75 days, snow on 20 days. The heaviest fall is in the winter months, notably in December, of which the average is 9 inches. The rainfall of the more northern parts of the State is 30 inches. The prevailing winds are westerly.

With varied resources in grain and live-stock, with a steady fine healthy climate, with rapidly extending settlement, with a spreading railway system now covering about 4,500 miles, the State of Iowa presents special attractions to settlers. Tracts of superior land taken up by private speculators, by the railway companies, by Messrs. Close brothers, by the Scottish American, and various English companies, are being readily sold and let to British and other emigrants. Aliens may acquire, hold or transmit land and other property. The settlers are generally industrious and thrifty. Agricultural land according to situation and quality ranges from $6 to $20 dollars an acre. Higher figures have been reached in the eastern portion of the State, and the equally good bluff lands in the west are steadily advancing in value. Many purchases made during 1879, within two years have nearly doubled in value; but there are still opportunities for profitable investment. Useful farms of 160 acres can yet be bought for 240*l.*; comfortable planked houses with double walls and adequate shedding can be put up for about 150*l.*; a span of horses or mules, three or four cows, a few young cattle and hogs, with ploughs and other necessary implements and tools sufficient to put in the first crops and make a fair start with, cost about 200*l*. With 600*l*. an industrious, prudent man can thus make a fair start as owner and occupier of 160 acres, and with diligence and care earn 30 per cent. per annum upon his enterprise. This is in favourable contrast to the 6 or 8 per cent. made from most English farms even in tolerably auspicious seasons.

The smaller settlers are always willing to hire themselves and their teams for agricultural service, and will contract to break up the prairie at 9*s*. to 10*s*. an acre, do ordinary ploughing at 6*s*., or prepare, put in, and harvest the wheat crop at 30*s*. to 32*s*. an acre. Many sections held by absentees are thus profitably farmed by contractors. This farming by deputy, I am informed by some gentlemen who have had several years' experience of it, has paid fully 20 per cent. on their investment, and their estates, besides, are steadily advancing in value. In this and adjoining States capitalists have sometimes bought land, equipped it with houses and suitable premises, and broken up portions of the prairie. The farms, thus prepared at a cost varying from 50*s*. to 60*s*. an acre, are let to industrious settlers whose limited capital is hence specially devoted to the improved cultivation of their holdings. From Canada, from the Eastern States, as well as from Europe there have always been numerous responsible applicants for these farms. Not all American settlers are determined to own the land they till. The tenancy system recommends itself to British capitalists, especially of restricted means, on account of the divided risks of bad seasons, the experience cheaply gained of a new country, and a new style of farming, and the time and opportunity obtained for deliberate purchase.

For these farms, prepared for the cultivator, the owner charges occasionally a money rent of 7*s.* to 10*s.* an acre, or more frequently is paid on the share system; receiving usually one-third of the grain grown, binding his tenant after the first year to have two-thirds or three-fourths of the holding under grain and to deliver his payment in kind at the nearest elevator. British agriculturists whose capital unfortunately has shrunk to 300*l.* or 400*l.*, under this share system in Northern Iowa have admirable opportunity of profitable investment. In addition to their proportion of the grain crops, the profits derived from any live stock grown or fed are reserved by the tenant. Taking wheat as the basis of calculation, the production costs 35*s.* an acre; 15 bushels at a very moderate estimate should be reaped and sold at 3*s.* 6*d.* per bushel. On a farm of 320 acres under this system 240 acres would be in wheat or other equally remunerative crop; this would give a total return of 3,600 bushels, which, at 3*s.* 6*d.*, yields 630*l.* The tenant's proportion of three-fourths would be 472*l.* 10*s.*, and, as stated, he would further retain any profits derived from the other fourth of the farm and from his live stock. The landlord would have his fourth—157*l.* 10*s.* Having paid 50*s.* to 60*s.* per acre for his outlay in purchasing, equipping, and breaking up the land, his annual return would be about 20 per cent. on his expenditure. Land fairly bought and under cultivation is, moreover, steadily advancing in value. Judiciously worked, this share system thus affords satisfactory returns both to capitalists and tenants.

Travelling through the north-western portions of Iowa, a great deal of well-watered, good land, adapted alike for grain and live stock, is met with. The sections deeded direct from the State are generally occupied; those held by the railway companies are being taken up. Between Sheldon and Sioux City many farms are laid out: karrals are built on the hill sides into which the cattle herded on the prairie by day are turned at night. Farmers are making better provision of hay and corn for wintering their stock, and hence are making better returns from them.

Sioux City on the Missouri, a few miles below its junction with the Big Sioux, lies amidst rich alluvial but malarial lands. The muddy Missouri, from the soft drift through which it courses, brings down large amounts of solid matters in suspension and solution. Professor Emery has found that even when the water is low it contains 52 grains per gallon of solid matters, and in flood eight times that amount is reached (White's 'Geology of Iowa'). These fertilising deposits are spread freely for several miles over the wider bed of the greater river of prehistoric times. Throughout its course of 500 miles between Iowa and Nebraska, past Omaha and Council Bluffs and on to Kansas City and St. Louis, considerable portions of this rich valley have been occupied for upwards of twenty years. Settlement in the upper Iowa portions has increased since the railroad fourteen years ago was made from Omaha north to Sioux City. The better class of settlers have wisely located on the bluffs and terraces upwards of 100ft. above the river level, where, diversifying their grain-growing with stock-keeping, they have generally done well. A Scotchman fifty miles south of Sioux City came out eleven years ago, his worldly wealth then consisting of a wife, five children, and a span of horses: he homesteaded 160 acres, now owns 640 acres besides some grazing land, has built a good house, and markets annually 100 cattle and 400 sheep. From the Western States he and his neighbours buy two-year-old cattle, keep them during the summer on grass, often up to their backs, sheltered amongst sunflowers and other semitropical vegetation 10ft. high, and finish them off on cheap Indian corn in winter.

An important feature of the Missouri valley are the terraces and bluffs rising from the alluvial flats of the river bottom. These bluffs consist of cretaceous agglomerate, contain pebbles, gravel, and lumps of marl, but no marine remains or fresh-water or mollusk shells. They apparently do not run together, crumble, or crack so much as English marls, and, although standing weather, are easily cut by pick and shovel. These bluffs rise tolerably abruptly one or two hundred feet high; they stand like grey buttressed ramparts with rounded summits; about Council Bluffs and Omaha they have crescentic fronts; frequently they are broken by ravines, the beds of streams, many of which are now dried up; their sides are often clothed or skirted with timber; their terraces and summits are well adapted for wheat and other crops.

Omaha on the western bank of the Missouri in Nebraska, 100 miles south of Sioux City, is one of the great railway *entrepôts* of Central America. Nine railways converge here. The Union Pacific thence starts west over the Rocky Mountains, nearly 2,000 miles to San Francisco. The town boasts of 20,000 inhabitants; it is laid out with wide streets, but with the usual American disregard for sound horse roads. The footpaths, mostly of wood, are, however, wide and well laid. There are good, substantially built stone churches and other public buildings, extensive iron smelting works, a flourishing distillery getting the Indian corn at low rates, and the Union Pacific work-shops occupying 35 acres. The hotel accommodation, diminished by the recent burning of one of the largest houses, is none of the best. Travellers getting in by trains after the supper room is closed at the early hour of 9 P.M. are told that the *chef* in this free country has gone to take his liberty or rest. No more food, not even a cup of tea, is obtainable on the premises; but the porter can point out a good restaurant whither the hungry travellers are constrained to proceed in anything but a quiescent frame of mind. The restaurant supper of fish, chops, grilled chickens, and fruit, is not, however, to be complained of, and is probably quite as good as that missed at the hotel, but which has nevertheless to be paid for in the five dollars daily tariff. Travellers may be spared the risk of thus being sent out for supper, may save time, trouble, and worry about their baggage, which for some inscrutable reason is detained at Council Bluffs on the Iowa side of the Missouri, and only forwarded next morning, and, besides, secure more comfortable quarters undisturbed by irritating visitors, if, instead of going over to Omaha, they remain at the new and comfortable railway hotel at Council Bluffs.

Here, in the centre of the American continent, it is curious to reflect on the ceaseless ebb and flow of traffic passing backward and forward on the wonderful 3,300 miles of iron road which connects the Atlantic and Pacific. Interest always attaches to the weather-beaten, jaded travellers in the through trains which have undertaken the seven days' journey from New York to San Francisco. Shortly steams in from the West a train specially chartered with tea from China, and silks from India and Japan, and still more numerous are the cattle trains of 16 to 20 cars destined for Chicago, St. Louis, and other eastern cities.

The stockyards at Council Bluffs were opened in the summer of 1878, accommodate 7,000 animals, and already it is in contemplation to enlarge them. The bulk of the business is done between July 1 and December 1. During this period of 1879 a hundred thousand cattle were yarded; and during 1880 the numbers continued to increase. The charge is 25 cents per head. Eastern buyers attend to make purchases; but a large proportion of the consignments are on through transit to Chicago, and are stayed here for the important purpose of resting and feeding the cattle. These resting stations on all the important western routes occur at intervals of 300 to 400 miles. Hay and corn, at market price, are provided for the stock. The allowance of hay, at each feeding for 20 cattle, varies from 150 lbs. to 250 lbs.; good managers give as much as can be promptly cleared up, and rather increase the supplies as the journey nears its close, so as to bring the animals forward in good trim for market. A few smart horses are kept at the stockyards, to pursue and bring back any bold bullock that breaks away from his companions, and makes, as happens sometimes, running across country.

From a thousand miles south, and a still greater distance west, Council Bluffs stockyards draw their supplies. The grass in the great plains and parks in most seasons begins to fail towards the beginning of September, although during the last two seasons it continued good for a month later. Owners generally round up their cattle in August, and make their selections for sale. The animals are travelled steadily on foot, often for several weeks, seldom driven more than ten miles a day, and without fatigue or damage reach the *depôt*. The various lots are often unequal in appearance and quality. Those from Texas and the sweltering south, where even robust Kentucky bulls pine and die in two years, sadly want grading up; they do not pay for winter feeding, and go direct to the slaughter-houses. More shapely and better beasts come from Oregon, Wyoming, and

Montana. Most are three years old and upwards, although occasionally amongst the lots from Oregon are seven- or eight-year-old bullocks.

The comfort of the cattle in transit, and notably their condition when they reach market after their long journey by road and rail, depends much upon the men in charge. Some of them are careful, smart fellows; are occasionally owners of a quarter section of land, situated somewhere along the line, and left in summer and autumn under the management of the wife and boys. They receive when on duty three to five dollars a day. Four or five of these men are in charge of a train-load of 400 or 500 cattle. At a glance they know the best trucks to seize for their own droves; they are usually zealous in their masters' interests; and are generally sensible and clever in loading and unloading, tending and feeding their charges. A refractory beast, demurring to enter the truck, has a rope thrown round his horns, carried round the stout frame-post of the car, and attached to the engine, which, moving gently forward, the recreant is speedily dragged into his place. When markets are brisk, the cattle trains are pushed along; a *douceur* to the engine driver secures a speed of about thirty miles an hour; delays and shunting are avoided; the twenty-four hours usually allowed for rest are shortened to one-half. When, however, markets are glutted or flat, of which intelligence is flashed down from Chicago or St. Louis, the cattle trains are slowed, and extra rest is given at the feeding stations. Very few animals are crippled or injured in transit. A careful man will handle 10,000 without a "crip." Chief amongst the accidents are broken limbs and an occasional displacement of the great yellow elastic ligament of the neck, strains from slipping, and bruising from unruly fellow-passengers. Most of the casualties depend upon the animals slipping in wet weather as they ascend or descend the wooden gangways to and from the cars. The large proportion of the cattle which come to Council Bluffs go to Chicago, either for immediate slaughter, or in the later autumn for distribution through the Indian corn regions, whence they are marketed fat during winter and spring.

On the occasion of my visit to the stockyard, October 11, 1879, upwards of 5,000 bullocks were in the yard. Useful animals, for going on, weighing 1,100 lbs., were worth 3 cents to 3·25 cents; choice lots 3·40 to 3·50 cents per lb., live weight. From Cheyenne, where thousands of cattle are now forwarded by rail, the charge for the 516 miles to Council Bluffs for the car containing 18 to 22 beasts is $85. The charge for the car-load, 500 miles to Chicago, is $50 to $60. The ordinary freight charges for 100 lbs. of goods from Omaha to Chicago is stated to be 36 cents; to New York, 60 to 70 cents. Besides the cattle in the Council Bluffs stockyards were 60 horses and as many mules resting in transit from St. Louis to California. The through railway freight from St. Louis to San Francisco is $250 per car-load, which, with feeding and expenses, puts $15 on the value of each animal. There is still a very large transport to

California both of horses and of mules, notwithstanding the central territories and Pacific States have for some years been rearing this description of stock.

With their splendid railway facilities, both Omaha and Council Bluffs are destined to develop and extend. They draw supplies of useful coal from the wide carboniferous belt which runs north and south towards the eastern slopes of the Rocky Mountains. Some of the best comes from the Bitter Creek mines 800 miles west. A carbonaceous shale, used locally for fuel, is found in the drift, and considerable quantities were collected from many of the cuttings along the Union Pacific 500 miles west of Omaha. The same impure coal appears in the drift at various points as far north as the Yellowstone and over the Canadian frontier. The same region is stated to furnish rock oil. Both these kindred products of the profuse vegetation of a long bygone era of the world's history are, I am told, still occasionally worked by any one, and without title from State or territory. Some of the earlier settlers about Omaha were Mormons driven out from Illinois. But they appear to have fallen away from their peculiar faith, or have been lost sight of amongst the numerous representatives from Eastern States, from most parts of Northern Europe, and from Canada, which here, as elsewhere throughout the States, furnishes many hardy, persevering settlers, generally making particularly good farmers.

Throughout this district, eastward into Iowa and west into Nebraska, good farming is now to be met with. Around Lincoln, 55 miles south-west of Omaha, the management appears careful and successful. Many of the earlier settlers, I am informed, had little knowledge of agriculture, and, as elsewhere, bought land, implements, and appliances on a costly credit system. There is now more disposition to keep within their means, to do their work more thoroughly, to diversify cultivation, and keep more live stock, which, like the trees, grow whilst the master is sleeping. Indian corn is the most certain and generally useful crop; it is the staple winter food of the animals of the farm. Summer heat and drought are incompatible with the successful growth of English root crops: even clover and Timothy do not thrive so well as they do farther north; but the natural grasses are luxuriant and nutritive. Haymaking is effected without the troubles and risks of a moister climate, and hay at Lincoln costs 10s. a ton. Horses and mules are worth about 20*l*.; cows, 5*l*. to 6*l*. Coal averages 20s. a ton; fencing and scantling, 4*l*. per 1,000 feet; bricks, 40s. per 1,000; lime, 5s. per bushel. Farm servants get $15 per month with board, about $23 without board; during harvest the daily wages are about $1.66 with board. Carpenters, blacksmiths, and other artisans earn about $2.50 per day, and on country jobs are usually also provided with board.

Travelling south from Council Bluffs on the Kansas City and St. Joseph Railroad, we run for 200 miles along the Missouri valley, never many miles from the great river which gives its name to the State bigger than England and Wales with the Isle of Man and the Channel Islands thrown in. A considerable proportion of Missouri is of unlevel surface; large districts are more suitable for mining than for farm-, ing; iron, lead, and copper are found in various localities, but hitherto have not been extensively worked. Along the Missouri and its tributaries are great woods of oak, elm, poplar, and walnut. Seven million acres—one-sixth of the total area—are stated to be under cultivation. One-half of the cultivated extent is devoted to Indian corn, a fourth to wheat, one-seventh to hay. Besides this, considerable tracts of plain, river bottom, and wood are grazed with cattle. Previous to the great war between North and South, Missouri was a slave-holding State. Although sixteen years have elapsed since slavery was done away with, industry and enterprise have not prospered as they have done in other Western States. Until lately there has not been much encouragement for settling. Some of the older inhabitants were not particularly courteous to new comers. Neither the black nor white labourers are remarkable for activity, diligence, or thrift. The rich alluvial lands along the river valleys are, moreover, liable to flood, and the recurring malarial fevers are trying to those unused to such dank, seething climates. Sharp frosts, although only occurring for a few weeks and over before the end of January, sometimes jeopardise the winter wheat crop, which averages about 11 bushels an acre, whilst heavy rains in July sometimes cause rust. These political and social, as well as climatic, conditions have hitherto retarded settlement in many parts of Missouri. Land in consequence in various counties is still cheaper than in several adjoining States. Promising locations along this part of the Missouri valley, ten miles back from the railway, adapted for corn, cattle, and sheep, were offered at two to three dollars per acre.

Around Nebraska Junction and Nebraska City, which is pleasantly situated on high grounds to the west, and near the next station of Hamburgh which has a population of 4,000, land is, however, worth $25 to $30 per acre. The farming is generally stated to be improving, more cattle are reared, and more are brought in from Texas and Western territories for grazing and winter feeding. Despite such extended cattle-keeping, there seems, nevertheless, an enormous extent of useful natural grass growing in wild luxuriance, uncut for hay, uneaten by stock, and plenty of good clover amongst the wheat stubbles, cut for hay the first autumn, and still, before it is pinched by frost, throwing up a splendid herbage, some of it looking like keeping a beast an acre during several weeks. This luxuriant clover crop, unused by the sparse stock, is frequently ploughed in during October, the land drilled with wheat, and, without seeding, much of the clover again comes up the following spring. This green manuring is satisfactory evidence of recuperative farming. Another evidence of progress is the fencing of the railway; whilst, to prevent cattle which happen to get on it straying widely, gates are put on at intervals of about two miles, and can be closed against such trespassers, and their range limited.

One hundred and thirty miles from Council Bluffs, a distance overtaken in six hours, St. Joseph is reached, an important thriving place of 25,000 inhabitants, many of them darkies. Good houses and public buildings, mostly of brick, are arranged in spacious streets, innocent, however, of paving or Macadam. The land about is rich, several feet deep, but subject to the overflow of the near running river. The autumn thunder-rains considerably interfere with the growth of wheat, of which the winter sorts are usually cultivated; and even of Indian corn, of which the yellow descriptions are preferred to the white. Hemp was wont to be largely grown for roping the cotton bales; but, hoop iron having taken the place of cordage, hemp here, as elsewhere, has almost gone out of cultivation. Large quantities of fine fruit are grown, and many orchards of apple and pear are being planted and carefully tended. I have further pleasant recollections of St. Joseph; for here is attached to our train, about the hungry hour of two o'clock, a comfortable dining saloon, with cooking galley and lavatory complete. Fruit and flowers decorate the tables; five well cooked courses of substantial fare are flanked with numerous vegetables and salads, followed with puddings, cakes, and ice cream; iced milk, tea and coffee, hot and cold, are offered throughout dinner; scarcely any wine or spirits are asked for; grapes, apples, and pears constitute a good dessert; and this varied and sumptuous repast is furnished for the moderate charge of a dollar.

CHAPTER XXII.

FARMING IN KANSAS.

KANSAS is situated in the centre of the United States, between the 37th and 40th parallels of north latitude, in nearly the same latitude as Portugal, Spain, and Italy. It has the form of a parallelogram 400 miles long and 200 broad; it embraces about 80,000 square miles, or is nearly double the area of New York or Pennsylvania, and as large as England and the southern half of Scotland. It is chiefly composed of wide-spreading plains and prairies, resembling those of the Red River and of Minnesota, sloping towards the setting sun with an incline ranging from two to seven feet to the mile. Its height above the sea level varies from 300 to 1,500 feet; but westward towards the Colorado frontier, amongst the foot hills of the Rocky Mountains, an altitude of 3,793 feet is reached. A ridge or watershed runs north through the centre of the State. Five great rivers flow south-east to the Missouri and Mississippi, and, with their tributaries, fertilise many districts. Kansas is free from lakes and swamps, and the climate is dry. The rainfall varies in different districts: in the eastern belt, in 1878, it reached 44 inches. In the same year in the western portions of the State the rainfall was 25, but drier seasons in dry situations have often left a chronicle of only 15 inches. The heavens are usually providentially opened when moisture is most wanted, during May, June, and July. During these months four or five inches sometimes come down in twenty-four hours, filling the shrunk rivers with a deep, turbulent flood; but the rain comes fitfully and irregularly. The moisture rapidly drains through the light, porous soil, or is dissipated by the fierce rays of the sun, which in summer often raises the thermometer in the shade 90° or 100°. The winter, however, is short, and the cold not so intense as farther north. The thermometer seldom falls much below zero. Provision for the storage of water would be advantageous in many of the drier districts. As cultivation extends, and trees, which in the midland and western parts of the State are few and far between, are planted, the rainfall will doubtless increase and become more regular. Boring 20 to 80 feet through the porous strata generally discovers water, which comes several hundred miles under the surface, from the melting snows of the Rocky Mountains, and in the tubes or wells is noticed to rise and fall with the height of the streams.

The geological maps demonstrate that the pliocene deposits, consisting mainly of sandstone, and in places rich in fossils, comprise about one-seventh of the State and are confined to the north-west. Cretaceous formations occupy three-sevenths of the south-western and central parts. The upper carboniferous beds, with their limestone, clay shale, and gypsum, take a strip of about two-sevenths running north-west, while on the south-east are the coal measures occupying the remaining seventh of the State. Lead ores, chiefly in the form of galena, have been found at Short Creek in the south-east, where in 1878 about five million pounds of lead ore were raised. Two zinc-smelting furnaces are also in operation. Besides lignite, often found very close to the surface, and in this poorly-timbered country affording cheap fuel, various seams of bituminous coal twelve to fifteen inches deep have been found in the upper carboniferous deposits. One of the best at present worked in Kansas is got at a depth of 700 feet at Leavenworth, thirty miles north-east of Kansas City, where one and a half million bushels are brought up annually. The Osage seams occupy an area running thirty miles north and south and extending fifteen miles east and west, are superficial, easily worked, and furnish useful gas coal. The Fort Scott beds, still farther south, lie irregularly, and seldom exceed two feet in thickness. Another thicker seam is the Cherokee in the south-eastern corner of the State, extending north from the Indian territory, and probably reaching for many miles. In the eastern parts of the State in connection with the coal deposits are occasional petroleum oil wells. One struck at Fort Scott, when boring for coal in 1870, gave off gas which is said to have been burning ever since. At Iola, from a cavity only twenty inches deep, 10,000 cubic feet of the petroleum gas is consumed daily for illuminating and heating. Near

Wyandotte the gas supply is so large that a gasometer holding 24,000 cubic feet is said to be filled twice in twenty-four hours, and sufficient is obtained to light a city of 30,000 inhabitants.

Kansas has a history of little more than thirty years: in 1840 there was scarcely a white man in the State; in 1860 she had a population of 100,000; now she has a million. She has twenty-one cities ranging from 2,000 to 16,000 inhabitants. Her cultivated area is nearly eight million acres; upwards of a million acres have been added since 1878. Colonisation has gone on rapidly from the Eastern States as well as from Europe. A large negro settlement has been formed in the North-West; and several hundred new comers arrive annually. Even with recent rapid settlement only one-seventh of the available territory is occupied and cultivated, and there are said to be few States in which so small a proportion of the land is unfit for corn or cattle. Probably not more than 5 per cent. represents the area unfit for cultivation. The State presents various attractions and facilities for settlers: 3,000 miles of railroad have been built; there are 2,000 to 3,000 church organisations, and 500 school houses with a school system possessing endowments amounting to twelve million dollars. There are asylums for the deaf, dumb, and blind; two asylums for the insane; a State penitentiary, and 275 newspapers. The State debt, allowing for the sinking fund, is now reduced to one million dollars; no new obligations are being contracted. The total wealth of the State is estimated at $400,000,000. This

Crops and Live Stock.

wealth is almost exclusively obtained from the soil.

Kansas stands fourth on the roll of wheat-growing States. It grows 28 million bushels. Its hot climate is, however, more suited for Indian corn, which occupies two and a half million acres, or about double that devoted to wheat. The annual produce of corn is 82 million bushels; the average yield per acre is about 34 bushels. Nearly half a million acres are devoted to oats; about one-fourth part of that area to rye; 83,200 acres are under barley; 53,400 acres grow potatoes, which yield 80 to 100 bushels per acre; whilst 850,000 acres of grass are cut for hay. The official statistics represent Kansas to have 275,000 horses of an average value of 10*l.*, 50,000 mules averaging 15*l.* 13*s.*, 321,900 milch-cows averaging 3*l.* 12*s.*, 578,300 oxen and other cattle averaging 4*l.*, 312,500 sheep averaging 9*s.* 4*d.*, and upwards of a million swine valued at 12*s.* 6*d.* Like other States and territories possessed of so great an area of unused productive soil, the growth both of corn and live stock may still be enormously developed.

The well-appointed Kansas Pacific train bound 670 miles west to Denver, the busy, flourishing capital of Colorado, carried me from Kansas City across the Missouri and for 140 miles along the banks of the Kansas river, often marked with escarpments of limestone rock, and studded with useful timber. The land here is in farms of 80 to 120 acres; the occupations are smaller than farther west; 140 acres is the average extent of the farms of Kansas. As in other parts of the State, land here a few years ago made rapid advances in value, has since retrograded, but is again improving. Near the railway useful farms of one to two hundred acres with suitable house, and the small amount of building which suffices in this country, are worth $25 to $30 per acre. The land generally is not tidily or well cultivated: sunflowers six feet high and other weeds grow in uncontrolled luxuriance. The winter wheat, which is chiefly sown, is well up by the second week of October. Farmers from the Eastern States are the chief occupiers. There are a good many hard-working Germans, Swedes, and Russians, who by careful, persevering industry have managed to pull through recent bad years, pay for their holdings, and get out of debt.

Topeka, the capital of Kansas, 67 miles west of Kansas City, was first settled in 1840, and with its suburbs now contains nearly 8,000 people. It has rolling and flour mills and a cheese factory, which annually turns out about 50,000 lbs. of cheese and 400,000 lbs. of butter. In a broad zone, running a hundred miles west of Topeka, on a rich, easily worked, sandy loam, a great deal of wheat and Indian corn are grown, and much more might be produced if it paid to grow it. There is abundance of labour on somewhat easier terms than a few years ago. Farm hands get $13 a month with board, or $20 without; carpenters, blacksmiths, and other mechanics earn about two dollars a day. As in other States, it is easy to get small farmers and contractors to take the breaking up, ploughing, sowing, and harvesting of the wheat and

The Victoria Colony. 357

maize at six to eight dollars per acre. The last few years have, however, sorely tried the patience and resources of many settlers. In 1875 and again in 1876 grasshoppers were very destructive. The wheat crop of 1877 averaged only 13·5; 1878 was better, reaching 16·3; but 1879, from the scorching spring drought, dropped to eleven bushels, while 1880 has not been much better. More than one cold, severe winter has weakened and killed many of the live stock. Stock-owners' profits, accordingly, have been diminished. There seems little local demand either for cattle or sheep, and little ready money in the hands of farmers. Useful milch-cows were selling in October, 1879, at 5l.; store sheep at 10s. to 12s.; and hogs at about 13s. per 100 lbs. live weight. Since the autumn of 1879, improved trade throughout the States has given, however, an upward turn to all agricultural produce, and most descriptions of live stock are 20 per cent. dearer than they then were.

Manhattan, 118 miles from Kansas City, at the confluence of the Big Blue and Kansas rivers, was founded in 1855, conjointly by a company from Cincinnati and another from Boston. It stands amongst limestone hills, whence are derived the admirable durable materials which build its substantial houses, churches, and Agricultural State College, from which, with its experimental farm, much useful teaching may be expected.

The Victoria colony, 280 miles west of Kansas City, is a portion of the State well known in Great Britain. In 1873 Mr. George Grant took a tract of

100,000 acres from the Kansas Pacific Railroad; allotted portions to various settlers; built comfortable houses with churches and school-houses; brought several thousand acres under wheat, maize, and millet; selected useful Texan and native cows, which he crossed with superior shorthorns and polled Angus. Some good crops were raised, and many hundreds of graded shorthorns and promising half-bred Angus. The Mexican sheep were crossed with Leicesters and Cotswolds, with great improvement to their weight of wool and mutton. But grasshoppers, drought, storms, and severe winters cut into profits. Many calves and lambs were lost from prairie wolves. The enterprise was on much too large a scale for the available capital. At Mr. Grant's death in 1879 the Victoria estates were found to be considerably involved, and realisation of the crops, stock, and land has not yet been satisfactorily concluded. The collapse of the Victoria enterprise affords another illustration of the disappointment and shipwreck which so certainly overtake the settler who goes into farming or land-buying with inadequate capital.

One of the most successful of the Victoria settlers is a young Englishman (Mr. Smithers), who has upwards of 1,000 acres of rolling prairie five miles from Hayes City. Three years ago he took his young wife from London. Both seem to enjoy their lonely home on the plains. They have a good two-storied stone house, with kitchen, cellars, and several rooms underground to avoid extremes of temperature. The house is furnished in good English style, but would be much improved if the bare brown lawn were fresh and green, and trees and shrubs flourished for shelter and ornament. Mr. Smithers's younger brother has taken up a conterminous holding. Their chief society seems to be the officers from Fort Hayes, a few miles distant. Valuable help and counsel are obtained from a Scotch lady from East Lothian, who has settled in the neighbourhood with several of her sons, but finds life and labour hard and trying, and money very difficult to make. Business on the farm or in the house overtaken, riding, driving, shooting, and fishing are enjoyed, or a trip is made on the Victoria Creek in the miniature steam-boat, whose progress along the river is at some points impeded by beaver dams.

On the easily broken land which costs less than two dollars to plough the first time, Mr. Smithers grows wheat for several years consecutively. The first and second crops are seldom so good as those which follow. In this dry climate it probably takes two or three years before the organic matter of the sod is sufficiently disintegrated to make a firm bed and yield fitting food for the wheat plant. The crop of 1879 is a sad failure, not exceeding 10 bushels an acre. That of 1880 is somewhat more encouraging. Seventy to a hundred acres of Indian corn are cultivated, and an increasing area of millet, which is used both for fodder and ripened for seed, is worth in bulk 80 cents, but is retailed in smaller quantities at $1.25. It is grown on the wheat stubbles either ploughed over, or, if the land is clean, broadcasted in April and May; half a bushel is a fair seeding. It is harvested in June and July. Cut green it produces two to four tons of hay per acre. For this purpose the Hungarian is preferred. The German variety has a strong woody stem, which renders it less valuable for fodder, but it is preferred for seed. Everywhere it grows readily, and holds its own even when rudely put in with a stocking hoe on the prairie.

Mr. Smithers, like other Kansas settlers, is devoting considerable attention to flax, of which Kansas now grows 60,000 acres. The yield is $8\frac{1}{2}$ bushels per acre. Often it is broadcasted in May on the newly upturned prairie sod, and is ready in about ninety days. Grown on a large scale, there would be difficulty in getting it pulled. The seed is worth $1 to $1.25 per bushel. Although some growers have got $5 a ton, there is hitherto a limited demand for the straw. Not one-fifth of it is utilised, and farmers do not care to undertake the tedious rotting and disagreeable scutching and hackling processes. The small mills now in operation from about 100 tons of straw make 36 tons lint and tow, worth $50 to $60 per ton. In the making of bagging, cheap jute from Calcutta very generally, however, takes the place of the stouter flax or hemp. Flax culture in suitable situations will probably extend. Disregarding the straw, the seed pays the cost of production, and flax proves a good preparation for wheat. The large importation indicates the great demand for linseed. Although handicapped with a duty of 30 cents per bushel, one and a half million bushels are, nevertheless, annually imported; the import in 1876 was two-fifths, and that of 1875 one-half more. From this imported as well as from the home-grown linseed almost all the oil is retained for home consumption; but of the residual cake 150,000 tons are annually exported.

Mr. Smithers's farm is tilled with thirty-five horses, worth on an average 20*l.* apiece, working ten to twelve hours a day, receiving when busy two quarts of oats or of Indian corn thrice daily, and about three quarts of bran worth 20*s.* a ton, all mixed together and used with chopped hay. When the draught animals are at grass or idle in the yards in winter their allowance of corn is reduced to one-half. Mr. Smithers rears a good many horses of various sorts, has several well-bred mares with fair hunting character, and a couple of bull-dogs from the Duke of Hamilton's famous strains. Hitherto he has bred few cattle or sheep, but has some capital Berkshire pigs.

Three miles south of Mr. Smithers's estate is a Russian Memnonite colony, the growth of three years, numbering about 300 souls, with holdings of 40 to 160 acres, some with tidy frame-houses of one to two stories and five to six rooms, others with hovels built of the prairie sod, which, when substantially erected, are cool in summer, warm in winter, and afford good protection against the high winds for which the Kansas plains are unpleasantly notorious. The stabling for the little, active horses which are principally of Indian breed, and for the cattle which are also of Indian origin, is likewise built of sods. Sheds accommodating six animals, are run up for about $10.

Wages, including harvest, are $12 to $15 per month, with board. In a capital school accommodating fifty pupils are maps, books, and other appliances. The lessons are given in Russian and English. The education is gratuitous. Most of these people are homesteading or pre-empting their land. Eighty acres of uncultivated soil after five years is thus acquired on payment of fees amounting to $10. The planting of ten acres of timber trees secures after seven years a patent for 40 acres, and during this period until Government gives over the land no taxes are exacted. The anxiety for territorial acquisition is strong even here. Many have taken up more land than they can pay for or find the capital to cultivate. Lots of 80 acres and upwards, broken up and often possessing some sort of house and buildings, may be bought from the earlier pioneers at $5 per acre. Water is supplied from wells sunk about 50 feet into the limestone.

The colony hitherto has not been very prosperous. The soil is a friable useful loam, 8 inches to 3 feet deep, reposing on a limestone shale, with here and there a bed of sand. In England the deep, useful soil would gladly be appropriated for gardening, and looks as if it would grow anything. Droughts are apt, however, to wither up every green thing. Corn planted on land when first broken up and even where two ploughings have been given, has not generally produced 20 bushels; whilst in moister regions it would probably have bulked 40 bushels. The wheat crops of 1879 and of 1880 have been disappointing. Very few of these industrious cultivators have had 15 bushels an acre; most not more than 10. Even potatoes and cabbage have suffered. A hundred bushels of potatoes, worth a dollar per bushel, represent an average acreable yield. Fruit trees are being planted. Few cattle and sheep are hitherto reared; but pastoral husbandry must be extended if agriculturists are to thrive in this land of drought.

North of Victoria another Memnonite colony has been settled for about four years. The experience of the settlers has not hitherto been very encouraging. The land is very good, but the crops are liable to suffer from dry springs and summers. Hayes City is one of the important centres of this district, and possesses three hostelries, not very sumptuous or ambitious in appearance, where lodging and board are provided for about $1.50 a day; and where a pair of useful horses and carriage are furnished for the day for about $4. There are good stores where all the requirements of Western life are offered. Clothing and luxuries are dear, but food is cheap; beef and mutton cost $4\frac{1}{2}d.$ per lb.; chickens 6d. to 8d. each; flour 12s. to 15s. per 100 lbs. Thirteen miles north-west is Ellis City, founded in 1873, now mustering a population of 700, many of them darkies. Fifty miles north of Ellis City is Nicodemus, a negro settlement, with a population of fully 500, recruited mostly from Missouri, poor and indifferently provided with means of cultivation, the land readily pre-empted on the usual easy terms, or purchased for cash at less than $2 per acre.

Kansas City is in the corner of Missouri State, on

the banks of the Missouri river, beyond the western banks of which extends for 400 miles the State which gives the city its name. It is a busy, enterprising place, with 55,000 inhabitants, 280 miles west of St. Louis, and nearly double that distance south-west of Chicago. Like some other rising American cities several years ago it ambitiously built, improved, speculated, and freely borrowed money. Five years of bad times frustrated, however, the immediate realisation of greatness; but now business is again booming, prosperity smiles, municipal debts are being reduced. Most of the seven lines of railways converging here for some years have been in an unsatisfactory, unprofitable condition. Now, however, they have abundance of traffic; during the two busy autumns of 1879 and 1880 they could not overtake the work entrusted to them; corn and cattle were alike delayed by the want of trucks; notwithstanding low traffic rates, dividends were being paid. Ten million bushels of wheat and fully half that amount of Indian corn are annually handled at Kansas City. Emigration westward, which for some years was tardy, is again active. Good crops and a growing, remunerative trade in cattle and hogs are bringing money to most farmers, who in their turn circulate it amongst other classes. Implement makers, unlike their brethren in Great Britain, have been 'running a very fine business;' the managers of the principal store for such goods in Kansas City tell me that they are doing double what they did three years ago, and, in further evidence of a going trade, remark that during the first nine months of 1879 they sold 1,000 wheeled carriages. Such demand would indicate considerable movement of agricultural and other produce.

Notwithstanding the depressed trade of the last few years, in spite of banking and commercial failures and the amount of money required in the working of mills, elevators, and other home enterprises, there is in this young Western city considerable accumulated wealth; and the bankers inform me that they sometimes remit large amounts to New York for investment at 6 per cent. Land and house property, which in and about Kansas City had been stationary for some years, is again mounting up. Along the limestone cliffs, above the lower older town, the river and the railway depôts, new streets and buildings are being laid out, commanding, from their elevated position, fine views of a rich, undulating, well-wooded country, with here and there peeps of the Missouri river, and of numerous lines of railroad. Throughout both the lower and upper parts of the city tram-cars, mostly drawn by mules, conveniently traverse the principal streets, which, as is too often the case in America, are not kept in good order. The side walks, raised two to three feet above the horse roads, are chiefly of wood; and Mr. William Saunders, who has written one of the most readable and instructive recent books on America, under the fanciful title of 'Through the Light Continent,' states: 'On perambulating the city after dark, my progress was somewhat impeded by the number of rats which were holding their orgies on the pavement, and seemed to have entrenched themselves in the various recesses between the timbers of which the pavement is composed.'

Want of time prevented my visiting the grain elevators, which have a storage capacity of one and a half million bushels, the flour mills, breweries, and other industries of Kansas City; but, specially interested in those great pork-packing establishments peculiar to America, where so much animal food is so cheaply handled, and forwarded in such increasing amounts to the United Kingdom, I spent an afternoon in Messrs. Plankington and Armour's hog and beef packing works. They have many points in common with the similar concerns described at Chicago. The extensive buildings, several of them four stories high, are sensibly separated to diminish the risks of fire spreading, and are conveniently encircled and intersected by railroad sidings. Extensive sheds have just been completed for the manufacture and drying of the refuse. As in many big establishments, the packing cases, boxes, and crates, and most of the meat and lard tins, are made on the premises. According to the season, from 500 to 1,000 hands are employed, a large proportion of them people of colour. The daily wages range from $1 to $2.50.

The cattle, largely drawn from Texas, are driven, grazing as they go, across the Indian territory, their journey usually occupying several months. About 300,000 are brought up every summer from Texas. They are railed from North Fork Town, Vineta, or other stations, and sent over 300 miles, to Kansas City.

Hog and Beef Packing. 367

In the yards alongside of them are dun and black beasts from New Mexico, also greatly in need of judicious selection and grading up with better bulls. Beasts of better quality are reared and forwarded from Kansas State and Colorado, and indeed from most of the great grazing regions south of the Plate River. The development of these American grazing grounds may be gathered from the fact that in 1868 the cattle brought into Kansas City numbered 4,200, the hogs reached 13,000, of sheep there were none. Now the numbers mount to 200,000 cattle, 500,000 hogs, and 40,000 sheep, and are increasing annually. On the cattle brought into the stockyards a commission of 50 cents per head is charged. They cost from $2.75 to $3.50 per 100 lbs. gross; the best weigh about 1,300 lbs.

About 12,000 are annually slaughtered by Messrs. Plankington and Armour; but, now that the canning business is brisk, it is intended to develop that trade. From a common yard the cattle are driven into small pens containing a pair of beasts. From a gangway above they are shot in the forehead. A chain round one or both hind legs, worked automatically by steam, drags the carcase into the dressing-shed, where ten or twelve minutes suffice to bleed, flay, and remove the inside. Hoisted on the gamble between the joists, they are run along to the cooling room, cut down the middle, and hung for twenty-four hours in a temperature of about 36°. Still without being handled, the firm, cool carcases are swung along, are dropped on to a big bench, and by hand-choppers and steam-driven circular saws are promptly cut into the requisite pieces. A great deal is transferred to the pickling tanks, in which it remains for thirty days; when it is transferred to barrels, and is distributed for the shipping trade, the lumberers, the sugar and cotton plantations, and for export.

During the twelve months from November to November, upwards of 3,000 hogs are packed by Messrs. Plankington and Armour. They are chiefly purchased in the city stockyards. They are of the same good type seen in other great marts—mostly black Berkshire and middle-sized Yorkshire, varying from 160 to 250 lbs. gross weight. They are not graded as at Chicago. They cost 40 to 50 cents per 100 lbs. less than at Chicago. Their value varies from $3.20 to $4.30 per 100 lbs. gross weight. During 1878 and 1879 they were lower than they have been since 1861-62. During 1880 they have averaged a dollar per cental more than in 1879. For twenty-three years the average has been $4.34 gross, or $5.24 net. The average shrinkage when the hog is killed and dressed is one-fifth; but mature well-fed hogs should not lose more than 15 per cent. They produce 18 per cent. of their net weight of lard, or, on an average, 40 lbs. per hog.

The grunters, drawn by the score into a catching pen, are strung up by a chain round one hind leg, and receive the fatal thrust. Suspended on pulleys, fixed on gently inclined iron rods screwed into the rafters, their own weight carries them along about twenty yards. By the touch of a spring a small boy unhooks them, and they plunge into a steam-heated bath; in about three minutes are raised on to a table, when five or six black fellows, usually stripped to their trousers, with steel scrapers remove the hair, but neither so promptly, thoroughly, or cheaply, as the ingenious machine scrapers do at Messrs. Armour's at Chicago. Arrangements, however, are being made to introduce scraping machinery at Kansas city. The hog is disembowelled, the viscera distributed for different uses, the leaf, from which the best lard is made, is carefully kept apart from the other fatty matters. Jets of cold water play over the carcase to ensure thorough cleansing; it is cut down the back, and suspended from the ceiling, along the labour-saving rods, is run into the cool chamber, where in a dry atmosphere cooled to 36° or 38° by some hundred tons of ice, laid in at a cost of $3.25 per ton, it looses animal heat and firms. In twenty-four to thirty-six hours the hogs are brought out, are cut into joints and pieces for different markets, and delivered down convenient shoots for drysalting, for the pickling tub, the lard vats, or the sausage machines. The bacon and pork are chiefly sent to the South and West, where the demand has been so great that to supply his customers Mr. Armour, in addition to his own large turn-out, often buys several million lbs. of sides. Here, as at Chicago, the hams are mostly sugar-cured, and a considerable porportion come to England, forwarded in crates, twenty-six, ranging from 9 to 13lbs., being packed together.

    The rendering of the lard is a most important

department in all hog-packing establishments. During 1878 and the early part of 1879, when prices of most other hog products were so low that when disposed of a new dollar was scarcely got for an old one, the lard was the redeeming feature of the business. During the winter of 1878 it was stated that at Chicago 400,000 sides of bacon were converted into lard, and a similar course was also taken at Kansas city. Most of the lard is sent to Great Britain. The price ranges from $6 to $8 per 100 lbs. Twelve tanks, heated by steam filled from above, hold each 25 to 30 tierces of 400 lbs. The purified lard is run into patent tin pails, made in Chicago, holding 3, 5, or 10 lbs., or into tins of larger capacity made in Kansas City. Vats, similar to those used for the lard, are devoted to the extraction of grease from the heads, feet, and refuse. The bristles and hair are duly taken care of, and of the latter many bales are forwarded to London and used with horsehair for stuffing furniture and railway carriage cushions. The blood, the refuse from the lard and grease tanks, and the offal, are dried by hot air, the bones and coarser parts are ground and again dried in coarse sacking between hot iron plates. A capital fertiliser is thus made, is used by market gardeners and on the cotton, sugar and tobacco plantations, is sold at the works at about $12 per ton of 2,000 lbs., and every 100 lbs. contains the following important manurial constituents :—

Nitrogen compounds equal to ammonia	8·13
Phosphoric acid equal to bone phosphate of lime	31·76

Meat Cheaply Retailed. 371

Kansas City is well situated for cheap freights. Competing railways viâ Chicago and Saint Louis give easy rates to Atlantic ports, whilst the Missouri is also used for transportation, shallow steam-tugged barges conveying down to Saint Louis 50,000 to 80,000 bushels of grain at each trip. Messrs. Plankington and Armour have shipped viâ rail to New York, a distance of 1,500 miles, at 18 cents per 100 lbs.; the rate in October, 1879, was however, 65 cents; Kansas City merchants consider 50 cents a fair charge. Wheat has sometimes been sent 500 miles to Chicago at 5 cents per bushel, but now it costs 15 cents. A barrel of flour weighing 214 lbs. is conveyed to New York for about 4s. 7d. Freights westward, where there is less competition, are higher.

Connected with the works Messrs. Plankington and Armour have a large retail meat store, turning over $600 daily, a boon to their neighbours, as well as enabling them to clear off a quantity of meat which would otherwise go into the lard vats. The best cuts of beef are sold at 12 to 13 cents. The price for various portions goes down as low as 4 cents; sides of bacon are 9 cents; spare ribs green are 2·50 to 3 cents, tender loin 4·50 to 5 cents, sugar-cured hams 9·50 cents. During 1880, however, prices have somewhat advanced, and both beef and bacon are now about one dollar per cental dearer than they were twelve months ago. Even with this advance butchers' meat is still cheap. The consumption by all classes is much larger than in Great Britain. There is more waste: cold meat and *réchauffé* are uncommon even amongst labourers and artisans in America.

Around Kansas City, farming for some years has been doing indifferently; grasshoppers, drought, short crops, low prices, and inadequate capital in turn have blighted prospects. A good many farms of all sorts and sizes were in consequence mortgaged, the amount advanced being 40 to 50 per cent. on their value. Two better seasons have, however, enabled many farmers to get out of debt and difficulty. Legal interest is 7 per cent., but needy men gladly pay more; expenses and commission are charged to the borrower. For an area of 25 miles south of the city, the pleasantly undulating well-timbered country is fairly cultivated. Many fields are fenced with the wild orange or osage, which, with reasonable care, in five years makes a stout hedge which keeps back cattle and even pigs. The running out farming practised by the earlier settlers is very generally superseded by some sort of rotation. Manure is occasionally applied; and green crops are fed upon the land. Wheat is not taken so frequently or continuously. Amongst it is sown Timothy and clover, which remain down one, two, or even three years. When this is broken up wheat is again planted, followed by maize, in its turn usually succeeded by wheat, amongst which the grasses are sown. These grasses are mown for hay or used green, often grazed by pigs, which in many Western States are hurdled over the seeds as sheep are at home.

The cost of wheat growing, including rent and

delivery to market, is about 40s. an acre. Autumn wheat is chiefly grown; the spring variety, which constitutes about one-fifth of the total produce of Kansas, is chiefly confined to the Northern parts of the State, and the yield rarely reaches one-half that of the winter sown. Even in well-cultivated districts around the city 20 bushels is a full crop. A great deal more live stock is kept than formerly, and it is of a more profitable sort. Mr. Seth Ward, on a fine grass farm near Kansas City, has a good herd of shorthorns, and uses a very superior Oxford bull. Major A. Crane, thirty miles south of Saline, has several Duchesses and other valuable Bates cattle. Following these examples other breeders are buying superior shorthorns and Herefords. Repeatedly throughout the year, sales are held at Kansas City of shorthorn and other pedigree cattle, and of well-selected Merinos, English Downs, and Leicesters, which, distributed throughout a wide district, improve both wool and mutton. Useful yearling bulls bring 15*l.* to 30*l.*, whilst bucks fetch 3*l.* to 15*l.*

Some of the southern parts of Kansas afford many attractions to settlers, and advantage is being freely taken of them. During 1878, one and a half million acres of Government school and railway lands were taken up in this southern part of the State, representing 10,000 new farms, and settlement is since proceeding with still greater rapidity. Amongst localities of good promise is Cotton Wood Valley, 140 miles south-west of Kansas City, a region fully 40 miles square, watered by many streams, pleasantly undulating, and well adapted for mixed husbandry. The natural Buffalo grass makes its spring start towards the end of March. Artificial, or, as they are termed, 'tame' grasses, such as Timothy, Kentucky blue joint, and clovers, grow kindly; lucerne is a sure crop usually standing for five or six years, and producing repeated big crops, especially where it is irrigated. Kindly nourished on the cretaceous soils, the herbage is sweet, and grows and feeds the stock well.

Still farther to the south-west the Arkansas valley extends 300 miles through the south-western part of the State, varying from 30 to 50 miles in width, pleasantly rolling, containing a great deal of good deep bottom land, porous and easily worked. A man and a pair of horses, I am told, easily work here 40 acres of Indian corn, which, when diligently cultivated, yields 30 to 40 bushels an acre. The country is generally watered by streams or with wells reaching down 30 to 60 feet into the limestone rock, pumping being sometimes effected by windmills. The Arkansas and adjacent valleys, although only settled since 1872, now produce two-fifths of the wheat grown in the State. The winter variety, generally sown, in a favourable season, yields 15 to 20 bushels. This fertile region also largely contributes to the great growth of cheaply-raised Indian corn. Running along the 38th parallel of latitude, the climate is particularly favourable for fruit growing. Peaches and grapes, as well as pears and apples, are abundantly produced. Fruit trees in six years come into profitable bearing, and orchards are already met with paying annually several hundred pounds. The produce is usually sent to the Colorado mining districts. Peaches have often been so plentiful that they sell at 20*d.* per bushel; grapes wholesale bring 1*d.* per lb. and retail at 1½*d.* to 2*d.* Land in a state of nature unprovided with buildings is to be purchased at 20*s.* to 30*s.* an acre, according to situation and nearness to water and railroad. In remote districts land may still be obtained under the Homestead Act by settlers who will reside for five years, build some sort of a house, effect improvements, and pay fees and commissions amounting to about 1*s.* an acre.

The stock-master who has well-watered ranges in the Arkansas valley, has a minimum of anxiety and expense during a short winter of two or three months. The native grasses, especially the buffalo and mosquito, are abandant: other grasses and clovers grow well. The July sun cures the grass as it stands for natural hay, which remains ready for the short days of winter. Prairie hay is machine cut, delivered, and stacked at 10*s.* per ton. With a proper provision of matured self-cured hay standing about on the runs, one ton of hay in the stack or barn is stated to be a good winter supply for 25 cattle or for 100 sheep.

There are no herds of 20,000 to 30,000, as in Colorado, Texas, or Wyoming. Shorthorn bulls are used amongst selected Texas or Colorado cows. The bullocks are sold out at three to four years old, weighing, off grass, 1,000 to 1,300 lbs.; or, when finished with corn, scaling 1,500 or 1,600 lbs. gross weight, and yielding 58 to 60 per cent. of good beef. Cattle have hitherto been more extensively and profitably reared than sheep. Mexican sheep, rough and hairy, worth about 8*s.* or 9*s.* apiece, with fleece of 2 to 2½ lbs., are being improved by crossing with Merinos, which triple their weight of fleece, and bring it up to 10*d.* or 1*s.* per lb. The sheep are not run thicker than one to the five acres. The cost of keeping is about 2*s.* per head per annum. The losses are stated not to exceed 5 per cent. Scab, occasionally introduced, is troublesome, necessitating repeated dipping in tobacco decoction at a cost of 4*d.* to 6*d.* per head. From 100 ewes 70 to 80 lambs are obtained. The wool pays all expenses The sheep at two years old average 100 to 120 lbs. gross, or fully half this when dressed. Good graded flocks, especially those which have had a cross or two of English blood, are considerably heavier, and from their gross live weight, as in this country, will dress four-sevenths of mutton. Notwithstanding the low price which for two years has ruled for hogs, Kansas State continues to breed nearly a million a year. On the natural prairie or in the grass fields they are reared at small cost, and profitably finished on the cheap maize. Good pigs, about a year old, should add to their weight 10 lbs. for every bushel of corn they consume. If 3 cents per lb. is got for the pig on the hoof, the corn is estimated to pay 1*s.* 3*d.* per bushel; which affords a better profit than disposing of it at 1*s.*, the current price in this and many other corn-growing regions.

Agriculturists in Southern Kansas are well circumstanced for markets. The Atchison, Topeka and

Santa Fe railroad, with eastern termini at Atchison and Kansas City, is in direct communication with the Atlantic markets and ports. Westward it sends various branches amongst the rapidly growing prosperous mining regions of Colorado and New Mexico; and when it is pushed westward through Arizona and California, to the Pacific, a considerable proportion of the traffic from India, Japan, China, and Australia, will travel along this route. A line from Newton is also in course of construction down the Arkansas river, towards the Mississippi, opening up, viâ New Orleans, another route to the eastern seaboard.

CHAPTER XXIII.

MISSOURI FARMING AND ST. LOUIS TRADE.

ON October 17 we were roused at 4 a.m., had a hurried cup of coffee and stepped from the hotel into the omnibus which rattles over the badly paved streets of Kansas City, picks up a few passengers from various hotels, and at 5.45 we are at the central depôt of the several railroads. In this part of America people are astir betimes, and important long distance trains start either in early morn or late in the afternoon. We are bound for St. Louis, 280 miles east. The undulating country, refreshed by recent rains, is bright and pleasant. The rail runs by the side of the Missouri amidst woods, fine straight oaks, containing 200 feet of useful timber; the black walnuts are still larger; tough hickory 3 to $3\frac{1}{2}$ feet through them six feet from the ground yield 150 to 200 feet of timber; the yellow poplar, although common in Virginia, seldom occurs west of the Mississippi. The well-wooded creeks closely covered with brushwood twenty years ago used to afford safe shelter for bushwhackers, who were wont to levy black mail and terrorise wide districts. The country, however, is now quiet and well ordered.

The Missouri Valley.

Wheat put in three weeks or a month ago is now up, looking as luxuriant as it does in England in the end of March. Much of it is sown on Indian corn stubbles amongst the shocks six or seven feet high, left untidily standing until they are required or until they are conveniently carted off during the first frost. Most of the land near the railway has been under cultivation for upwards of 20 years. The farms here are not so large as farther west: their average throughout the State of Missouri is 148 acres. Comfortable houses, good gardens and orchards are seen on most properties. The fields are divided by osage or wild orange hedges, planted at a trifling cost, and in five years making good fences and affording welcome shelter. The soil is deep and easily worked; the deepest and best, in the lower situations with good cultivation, secures 25 bushels of wheat; 50 bushels of Indian corn, and is favourable for successful fruit growing. Apples, pears, grapes, and peaches are good and plentiful, but the great peach districts lie fifty miles south. There are good evidences of prosperity and comfort; soil and climate aid the enterprise of the settler; convenient markets are obtained for all sorts of produce. Labour is tolerably plentiful, agricultural hands are generally engaged from March 1 until November at the rate of $10 to $15 per month, board and lodging inclusive. In harvest the wages are doubled. The emigration of coloured people from the bankrupt properties of Southern States keeps down the price of labour. As in England, the industry and willingness of the labourer is stated to have deteriorated during the last few years. Negro labour especially is not so effectual as it was in the slave-holding times, when good field hands were hired by the year at $200, with the proviso that they should be well fed, lodged, clothed, and doctored. The practice of paying off most of the agricultural labourers during two or three idle winter months proves demoralising. Except in a pork packing or lumbering district, they have difficulty in finding continuous winter employment. They loiter about the towns unsatisfactorily spending their summer earnings and learning idle and irregular habits.

Genial spring, towards the end of February, follows a severe but short winter, when planting of the spring crop is taken in hand. Some farmers use a particularly early spring wheat, which is cut about the end of May, yields 15 to 20 bushels per acre, and has the advantage of escaping the scorching summer heat and the attack of the chintz bug. The amount of seed in general use per acre is $1\frac{1}{2}$ bushels of wheat, 2 to $2\frac{1}{2}$ bushels of oats, and 4 pecks of Indian corn. On the useful timber land the wheat tillers, which it scarcely ever does on prairie soils. Oats, yielding 50 to 60 bushels, are cut early in July; the wheat immediately after. Indian corn costs $5.50 per acre; a man and team will cultivate thoroughly 30 acres; it stands conveniently until there is leisure to reap it; 40 bushels is an average crop, and it remains uninjured in the field until it can be conveniently carried. Its price during the past ten years has varied in this district from 20 to 50 cents per bushel.

Towards Otterville the soil is lighter; beds of gravel and flint are frequent. The land, as is generally the case along the line of railway, is all taken up; but ten miles further back farms are to be had at 30*s*. to 40*s*. per acre, and payment for any building or permanent improvements that may have been made. Approaching Jefferson City we again reach the Missouri; are in a limestone and grass country, becoming more hilly and abundantly wooded. One hundred miles from St. Louis the railroad, amongst fine timber, has its way cut along the limestone cliffs, which, in many places, rise a hundred feet on the right, with the Missouri, broad as the Thames at Richmond, flowing on the left. Owing to an unusually limited rainfall, which during 1879 only reached 25 inches, the river is so shallow that in many places it is easily forded.

Fourteen miles from St. Louis, picturesquely situated amongst hills and rocks, is Kirkwood, where many of the city merchants have pleasant villas, tastefully built of the sandstone of the district. The roads are wide and good; the comfortable farmhouses and cottages with profitable gardens show prosperity. On the deep useful sandy loams are farms, owned often by the townspeople, varying from 50 to 160 acres, some of them rented at $4 to $5 an acre. Some are run on shares, the landlord receiving one-third of the produce; some are held from year to year; others are leased for periods of five to ten years. Throughout this district the Kentucky blue grass thrives well. Many stock farmers are laying down a few acres of lucerne, which sends its tap-roots deeply into the dry soil, and hence thrives on a minimum of moisture, is frequently cut as early as the middle of April, and the cutting repeated four or five times throughout the summer and autumn. When properly manured and cleaned, lucerne, as in England, continues profitable for five or six years.

St. Louis enjoys a full share of the prosperity widely extending throughout the United States. Her population, nearly double since 1870, now numbers 355,000. Her wide streets, substantially-built stone houses, well-appointed shops, handsome public buildings, magnificent and lofty Exchange, compare favourably with those of European cities. About 2,000 buildings are annually added to the city, representing an outlay of 3 to 4 million dollars. The real estate of the city is given at $136,071,670; the personal at $27,742,250; the rate of taxation is 2·6 per cent. on the valuation. The maximum temperature of ten years is 98°, the minimum − 7·3. The mean annual rainfall is 38·9 inches, but the rainfall of 1879 was only 25·7 inches. Most rain falls in June and November. Proximity to the Mississippi, over which a magnificent bridge has been thrown, secures cool evening breezes. Changes of temperature are, however, often sudden and trying.

Eighteen railroads now centre in St. Louis, their offices conveniently included in one huge depôt. A new line has been carried south-west into Texas, opening up a great cattle and cotton district. Another, the Paola, Kansas, and Arizona, proceeds west to those rapidly developing territories. Three direct lines are open to the Missouri. With such transport facilities superadded to the older cheap river transit, business steadily expands, as is illustrated by the tonnage received and shipped by rail and river in 1875 and 1879 :—

	1875	1879
Received by rail	3,232,770	4,663,078
Received by river	663,525	688,970
Total tons	3,896,295	5,352,048
Despatched by rail	1,301,450	2,285,716
Despatched by river	639,095	677,145
Total tons	1,940,545	2,962,861

Almost every department of business has participated in this expansion since 1877. The grain trade has increased fully one-third. Wheat during 1879 has increased nearly 20 per cent. Receipts for cotton and hogs have doubled. From the annual statement of the trade and commerce of St. Louis, prepared for 1879 for the Merchants' Exchange, the following details are extracted :—

Wheat, total receipts, bushels	17,093,362
Flour manufactured, barrels	2,142,949
Flour handled, barrels	4,154,754
Indian corn handled, bushels	13,360,636
Oats handled, bushels	5,002,165
Cotton, bales	472,436
Hog products, exported, lbs.	220,891,273

Seven great elevators have a total storage capacity of 5,000,000 bushels. Besides grain in sacks, 23,000,000 bushels of loose grain passed through them in 1879; $1\frac{1}{2}$ cents per bushel is paid by the buyer for weighing and the first ten days' storage of wheat, corn, rye, and oats, ½ cent for each subsequent ten days or part thereof. Barley is charged 2 cents per bushel for the first ten days. Grain in sacks pays 4 cents per sack for ten days' storage, and 1 cent for each subsequent ten days. The wheat handled at St. Louis is mostly the winter variety. Scarcely one twenty-fifth is spring. This small import is chiefly brought from the Upper Mississippi. Nearly half this supply comes east by rail from the Missouri districts; one-fifth is forwarded north by rail or river; about one-sixth grows east of St. Louis. The great proportion is graded No. 2. The first reaped of the winter crop of wheat of 1879 was on June 18th. It sold at $1.50. The first samples of 1878 were shown on June 7, and sold at $1.25. The price for No. 2 winter during 1879 has varied from 91 cents early in January to $1.35 in the middle of October, and $1.36 in the middle of December.

Twenty-five flour mills have a capacity to turn out daily 11,370 barrels. They make five times the amount overtaken 25 years ago. The two principal are the Yeager Milling Company with a capacity of 1,500 barrels, and the Atlantic Milling Company with a capacity of 1,000. The St. Louis Mills in 1879 ground 8,996,177 bushels of wheat, producing 2,142,949 barrels of flour. Great pains have recently been taken to perfect the milling processes. More than one-third of the total production as officially inspected comes under the high class categories of 'double' and 'triple extra,' 'family,' 'choice' and 'fancy.'

The receipts of wheat at St. Louis in 1879 were 17,093,362 bushels; the shipments were 7,302,076 bushels, of which 2,715,909 bushels were exported to Europe, 4,359,081 bushels went east by rail, a large proportion of it for exportation; the balance was distributed locally. Great Britain proves St. Louis's best foreign customer. Besides receiving direct 324,912 bushels of wheat, she takes five-sixths of the flour, nearly all the cotton, canned meats and hams, lard, tallow, oil-cakes, and cotton-seed meal. England, on through bills of lading, has 353,505 barrels of flour; Scotland, 169,482; Ireland, 70,241. The flour, although estimated in barrels, is now mostly forwarded in sacks containing 140 lbs.

The public railroad rates for 100 lbs. of grain forwarded from St. Louis to New York or Montreal, distances of 1,100 to 1,200 miles, varied during 1879 from 23 to 46 cents; indeed, during May, competition was so keen that freights were 'demoralised,' and flour was taken to New York at 8 cents per barrel, and grain at $12\frac{1}{2}$ cents per 100 lbs. The terms to Philadelphia and Baltimore are usually a little lower than those to New York. The Mississippi carries down a thousand miles to New Orleans at small cost, a great amount of cargo, which, now that the mouths are opened for the admission of larger vessels, will doubtless still further increase. Several thousand tons of freight by this easy but roundabout route are carried between St. Louis and New York. Six million bushels of various sorts of grain, in large boats, were towed down the Mississippi in 1879; and but for the low state of the river in summer and autumn, the transport by water would have been greater. During the open January of 1880, 1,500,000 bushels of grain were forwarded to New Orleans, one tow taking, besides package freight, 270,000 bushels, and another 225,376 bushels. The charges to New Orleans for 1879 averaged 7 cents per bushel for corn, and ½ cent per bushel more for wheat. Thus cheaply dropped down the Mississippi stream 3,000,000 bushels of wheat and 4,500,000 bushels of corn were collected and exported from New Orleans in 1879. France still maintaining her connection with her old colony, in 1879 and 1880 had about two-thirds of the wheat and one-third of the maize.

The Mississippi and its great tributaries bring to St. Louis in rafts 131,482,871 feet of lumber, besides 40,000 logs, and quantities of roofing shingles, laths, and pickets. Nine-tenths of this timber is white pine from the Upper Mississippi, which also furnishes cottonwood. The Lower Mississippi contributes yellow pine, ash, oak, poplar, and some walnut, which also grows well along the Lower Missouri. Like so many other commodities, after several years of depression, lumber has advanced in price, and is in great demand for building, as well as for railway, purposes. Coal, coming chiefly from Ohio and Kentucky, is mostly forwarded by rail, reaches 37,000,000 bushels annually, whilst 34,000,000 bushels of coke are also received. Good coal is usually worth 15*s.* to 20*s.* per ton of 2,000 lbs.

St. Louis is the great cotton emporium of the interior. Her lines of railroad, radiating into the great growing districts, bring in twenty times the cotton imported ten years ago: 400,000 bales are now received annually. Three great companies have a compressing capacity of 6,000 bales a day, and covered storage for 200,000 bales. Three-fourths of the cotton is transported by the St. Louis Iron Mountain and Southern Railroad and brought chiefly from Arkansas, Texas, and Louisiana. Of the 104,150 bales shipped direct to Europe during twelve months to August 31, 1879, 98,598 went to Liverpool. To New York or eastern ports the freight is about 54 cents per 100 lbs. The average weight of the bales for 1878-79 was 484 lbs. The price of middling cotton has ranged from 9 to 13 cents.

Several other important industries flourish at St. Louis. Three distilleries mash and distil 614,514 bushels of grain, produce 3·62 gallons of spirits per bushel, pay a duty of 90 cents per gallon, and have yielded 2,228,088 gallons of spirits, classified as 'Bourbon,' 'alcohol,' 'gin,' 'high wines,' and 'pure neutral or Cologne spirits.' A large amount of spirit is besides rectified and compounded, and a good deal must be consumed, for the United States excise officers make a return of 10,650,084 gallons of spirits of various sorts gauged during 1879.

St. Louis has two lots of stockyards both connected with the railroad, concentrating each week 8,000 to 10,000 cattle, 3,000 to 4,000 sheep, and 25,000 to 30,000 hogs. Three-fourths of the live stock come from the west and south, chiefly forwarded by the St. Louis and San Francisco, the Missouri Pacific, the St. Louis Iron Mountain and Southern, and other lines entering Kansas and Texas. Upwards of 30,000 cattle, 66,000 sheep, and 5,023 horses and mules are yearly brought by boat, often several hundred miles down the Mississippi and Missouri. Freely using these inexpensive means of transport, comparatively few animals are now driven to market. The returns of these for 1879 comprise 11,500 cattle, 14,610 sheep, 9,511 pigs, and only 20 horses. About half the live stock pitched in St. Louis are forwarded north and east. The following are the number of animals received in the stockyards, and the numbers sent on during 1879:—

	No. Received	No. Despatched
Cattle	420,654	226,255
Sheep	182,648	88,083
Hogs	1,762,724	686,099
Horses and Mules	33,289	36,947

Numbers of mules collected by the principal breeders and brought up by road do not come into the stockyards, but are sold privately, and sent on mostly by rail, accounting for the number of horses and mules received being smaller than those despatched.

The cattle in the St. Louis, as in other stockyards, are very mixed. The Colorado and a few Oregon beasts have more compactness and quality than the Texans. A few superior three-year-old shorthorns and Hereford reaching 1,600 lbs. to 1,700 lbs. are (October 1879) worth $4\frac{1}{2}$ to $4\frac{3}{4}$ cents per lb. gross or live weight. A good many Cherokee and other native nondescript cows in poor condition weighing 700 lbs. to 800 lbs. are selling at 2½ to 3 cents. Good cows near calving are, however, generally worth 5*l.* to 8*l.* The sheep, poor light Mexicans and Merinoes, weigh 80 lbs. to 85 lbs. gross, and are worth 2 to 2½ cents per lb. Good half-breds reaching 150 lbs., and dressing nearly 20 lbs. per quarter, are worth 4½ cents per lb. live weight. Most of the pigs are useful. Although generally direct from grass or clover, or finished up with a few bushels of corn, they average 250 lbs. gross weight, and bring 3½ to 3¾ cents per lb. The winter-killed pigs are 20 to 30 lbs. heavier. From the Southern States are some big rough, flat-sided, unimproved specimens, showing a good deal of the tawny or black and brown feral colours, formidable jaws, and abundance of bristles. The packing for the year ending March 1st, 1879, made away with 629,261 hogs. The products of pork and lard were 107,821,156 lbs.

Connected with the National Stockyards are the well-arranged premises of the St. Louis Beef Canning Company, erected in 1876, occupying three acres, and costing with plant, machinery, &c., $200,000. The company employs 1,200 hands, the men receiving 4*s.* to 10*s.* per day, the women and girls 2*s.* to 3*s.* 6d. The busy period is during the summer and autumn months, while grass-fed beasts are abundant and cheap. During this period about 500 cattle are slaughtered daily, consisting chiefly of Texans, averaging 850 lbs. to 900 lbs. gross weight, costing (October

1879) 2⅝ cents per lb. live weight, producing about 55 per cent. of dressed meat, which thus costs about 5 cents or 2½d. per lb. As is generally the case throughout the continent, cold storage chambers, securing a temperature of about 36°, preserve the meat and the best of the offal. Considerable quantities of beef in a fresh state are furnished to the St. Louis butchers. Still larger amounts packed in galvanised iron drums are carried in the railway refrigerator cars to various provincial cities, and even to New York. Tons of meat, carefully boiled or stewed, are put up in the familiar square tins containing 1 lb. to 14 lbs.; 100 tons are frequently prepared and packed in a day; tongues and poultry are also put up in a similar manner. The best of the fat is used for oleomargarine, and the other waste products, economically, receive attention. Mr. Joy, the president of the company, informs me that he has no expectation of prices of cattle at St. Louis making much advance for many years: the beasts will continue to improve, he believes, as they recently have done, in quality. He anticipates no considerable increase in the cost of transport; about 1d. per lb. delivers his cases either in London or Paris; and he can afford to furnish the retail merchant with 1 lb. of good meat, free of bone and without too much fat, at 6d. Both in England and France these canned meats are in increasing demand, especially in summer, when in a small house the kitchen fire becomes a nuisance.

Mr. Whittaker's great pork packing establishment requires for its daily wants 3,000 to 5,000 hogs. They are disposed of much in the same manner as in Chicago and Kansas. With a fine connection throughout the south, Mr. Whittaker has a good demand for his bacon, but sends most of his hams and lard to Europe. From her own packing establishments and what is brought to her markets, St. Louis annually exports about 220,000,000 lbs. of various hog products, in 1879 comprising 7,500,000 lbs. of salted bacon and pork, 1,431,840 lbs. of hams, and 648,877 lbs. of lard exported direct to Europe. Of the balance, 85,051 barrels of pork, 8,473,585 lbs. hams, 114,103,781 lbs. meats, and 19,052,000 lbs. lard went south for consumption; while 4,136 barrels of pork, 12,212,094 lbs. hams, 21,581,432 lbs. of meats, and 19,048,785 lbs. lard were shipped to eastern markets.

Dairying in this part of Missouri appears tolerably prosperous. During 1879 and again in 1880 nearly 9 million lbs. of butter were sent into St. Louis, of which one-sixth part was forwarded east; 120,000 boxes of cheese, averaging 56 lbs., were marketed, of which nine-tenths were passed on. The short winter of ten weeks or three months minimises expenses. The cattle usually graze out until Christmas; a field is left rough into which in fine weather the cows are turned almost daily. I am assured by several dairymen that 200 to 300 lbs. of hay per cow is sufficient winter provision. Hay is worth from 40*s.* to 46*s.* per ton of 2,000 lbs. Besides hay and corn fodder, 4 or 5 lbs. of corn meal and 1 lb. of bran, costing 40 cents per 100 lbs., constitutes the winter dietary of cows in full milk. These Missouri dairymen tell me that the average annual cost per cow does not exceed 6 cents per day, or less than 5*l.* per annum. Many of the dairy herds include Guernseys, Jerseys, and crosses between these and the native breeds. The relative merits of deep and shallow setting are anxiously canvassed; deep setting is becoming most common. Every care is taken to keep down the temperature of the dairy. The milk is skimmed once after standing 24 or 36 hours; 17 to 19 lbs. of milk are required to make 1 lb. of butter, 6 to 8 lbs. of butter per week are yielded by good cows for 36 to 40 weeks. Some of the best comes from the rolling limestone country south of St. Louis. For town use in eight-gallon tins, increasing quantities of milk are brought night and morning, twenty to thirty miles by rail. The full can is conveyed at one cent per mile, and returned empty free of cost; 6*d.* to 7*d.* per gallon is generally got for milk delivered in St. Louis. Careful managers of repute obtain 35 to 40 cents for their butter all the year round.

St. Louis is one of the great mule markets of America. Like other descriptions of live stock, mules are bred in continually increasing numbers. The census returns have recently shown an augmentation of 100,000 a year. They now number two millions, or fully one-sixth of the number of horses. They are chiefly reared by small farmers in the States of Alabama, Tennessee, Kentucky, Illinois, and Missouri. Kentucky was wont to be the great mule-breeding State, but increasing attention having been given to horses and cattle, the mule business is proportionally restricted. They still, however, muster

120,000 in Kentucky, but in Missouri they have risen to nearly 200,000.

Mules, like horses, vary much in size and weight. Some are 17 hands high, strong and powerful as almost any horse, and when made up weigh 1,600 to 1,700 lbs. Others are as small as Shetland ponies. Between these two extremes are all varieties of size and weight. The prevailing colours are brown, bay, and grey. A few blacks and chestnuts are met with, and occasional roans and piebalds. All are hardy and long-lived; animals forty and fifty years old are frequently seen. They are very sure-footed; notwithstanding hard and trying work, broken knees are much less common than amongst horses; lamenesses are also rare; their legs and feet are very sound and strong. Many of the heavier draught mules will lift and move briskly away with a load of two tons. From properly selected parents many smart animals are reared, which carry themselves capitally, and which trot as well as most horses. At St. Louis we saw some very handsome mules well adapted for light harness work. One in a Sulky on the trotting track did her mile in 3 minutes 18 seconds, could keep up the pace for several miles, and so pleased our fellow-traveller Mr. Robert Cox of Gorgie, Edinburgh, that he bought her, and her good looks, docility, and paces are now much admired by Scotch connoisseurs. In temper and behaviour she shows more affinity to the horse than the ass. The total charges for her transport from St. Louis to Edinburgh were 15*l*.

In Great Britain mules are held in unjust contumely; they are often stated to be obstinate, treacherous, and vicious. These aspersions on their character are unfounded. A few badly broken or cruelly treated become troublesome or vicious. The great majority are, however, as docile as any horses or asses, and give no trouble either in the stable or at work. English stablemen and drivers have not, however, yet got over their prejudices against mules. Brewers and others who have tried them find their men contemptuously grumble at 'them long-eared brutes.' The London and various tram-car companies who have used them, also complain that they cannot get their servants, either on the road or in the stable, to take the pride and pleasure in the mules that they do in horses. When disabled or unsuitable for continuous quick work, mules in Great Britain find few buyers. The horse cast from tram-car or omnibus work is worth 10*l.* to 15*l.*; the mule which entered the stud at about the same price, although practically as serviceable as the cast horse, does not bring more than 5*l.*, and is even despised at the knackers', who assert that his flesh does not boil properly or make attractive cat's-meat. So long as useful horses for tramway or omnibus work are procurable as they are at present at 35*l.* to 40*l.*, the employment of mules for this work is not likely to extend in Great Britain.

Messrs. Reilly and Wolford, of St. Louis, the largest mule dealers in the world, dispose of about 15,000 a year, and also sell about 6,000 horses.

During the American war, in one year they turned over 25,000 mules; they often forward 300 a week to the West Indies, and frequently send a few to Europe. They showed me nearly 1,000 mules of different descriptions, broken and unbroken, ranging from two years old and upwards. They assure me that they are safer to go about and handle than any untried horses; and that although often yarded together in large numbers, they do not quarrel or injure each other as strange horses sometimes do. They exhibit much affection and strong gregarious habits, and always work better in pairs or several together. They are fond of horses, are often worked with them, and the strings or droves of mules, going from fair to fair, cheerfully follow a grey mare, usually decorated with a bell. They are more sensible and teachable than most horses, stand hardship better, and are more patient. Mr. Reilly corroborates the opinion of southern and many western farmers, that they are specially useful on account of their withstanding satisfactorily hot weather and the annoyance of flies. At the constant hard work of the tram-car companies, for which they are much used throughout the Mid, Southern, and Western States, they last longer than horses, some say double the time. Although they inherit the donkey's patient contentment with plain, coarse food, if they are to do good service they should get the same food as horses of the same weight and doing the same work. The farmers who use them so freely in Minnesota, Manitoba, and elsewhere, and the tram-car companies who run them in Chicago, Cincinnati, and other cities, make no difference between the feeding and stabling of their mules and horses.

The stud donkeys used in the best mule-breeding districts are tolerably carefully selected. A few are occasionally brought from Spain; but many of the home-bred appear as good as any of the imported. Where big, stout mules are desired, an ass 16 hands high is used, with bold, rather big head, good loins, and great muscular limbs. Where a stud donkey has proved his capabilities satisfactorily, he is kept in service sometimes for twenty years. The service fee varies from 20*s.* to 60*s.*—a hundred mares is a full season's work. A few 'Jinneys' are bred from the stallion horse and the ass, are rather finer about the head and ears, but are not otherwise distinguishable from the ordinary mule. The mules are dropped in April and May. They are generally suckled until July or August; but the mother the while is often employed at light work. Their rearing no ways differs from that of the horse foal. Contrary to the usual opinion, they take quite as long as a horse in coming to maturity. A big mule should not be put to work until he is five; many, however, are broken when three, and even when two years old, when they are worth 12*l.* to 15*l.* They are sent to work and to market earlier than they used to be. Useful four- and five-year-old mules, 15½ to 16 hands high, and weighing about 1,000 lbs., are worth, in Kentucky or Missouri, 20*l.* to 22*l.*; and stouter animals, adapted for heavier draught, are worth 5*l.* more.

CHAPTER XXIV.

KENTUCKY AGRICULTURAL RESOURCES.

In many parts of Kentucky the undulating surface, the old turf, the abundance of timber, the evidences of a hundred years of settlement with many comfortable farm homes and well-kept gardens, awaken recollections of various southern English counties. This is the locality to suit middle-aged fairly well-to-do British agriculturists who cling to old world habits, who pine for familiar surroundings, who demand farms already set out and under cultivation, who demur to the breaking up of prairie, the building of houses and premises, and the rough work which falls to the lot of settlers out West. There is much diversity in the 18,000,000 acres which make up the State of Kentucky; one-half of it is still estimated to be unimproved; a wide area of the lower land is in timber; in the bottoms are magnificent sycamore, oak, and walnut, often covered with luxuriant creepers. Wide breadths of the rich alluvium, exhausted by the growth of wheat and tobacco, with a few years' good management might be greatly improved. Throughout the extensive limestone regions the blue-grass flourishes, and grows and feeds admirably both cattle and sheep.

Thousands of bullocks—and they might be considerably multiplied—are fed on these rich grazings, make 400 lbs. to 500 lbs. in twelve months, reach at three years 1,500 lbs. to 1,600 lbs. live weight, are worth $4\frac{1}{4}$ cents to 5 cents per lb., and produce 60 lbs. of beef for every 100 lbs. of live weight : the winter corn-fed beasts yield a still higher per-centage of beef. The cattle are chiefly shorthorns and shorthorn grades.

Kentucky boasts of some of the most enterprising and successful American shorthorn breeders—of Mr. Abram Renick, who has moulded into their form of beauty the smart, shapely Roses of Sharon ; 'Mr. A. J. Alexander, of Woodburn, who has consistently adhered to Airdrie Duchesses, Barringtons, and other superior Bates sorts ; Messrs. Vanmeter and Hamilton, who own in this and other States upwards of 600 valuable shorthorn females ; Messrs. Thomas and Smith, who hold good Roses of Sharon and Marys ; Messrs. Bedford, who have successfully cultivated Bates families for forty years ; Colonel Sim, who keeps handsome serviceable Princesses ; Mr. Megibben of Fairview, who has Roses, Lady Bates, and other good strains ; and Mr. Warfield of Lexington, who owns a useful herd of mixed Bates and Booths. From such sources the ordinary cattle have been greatly improved, and the proportion of thriftless 'scallowags' is much smaller than in many other States. But enough home-bred stock is not reared to supply the wants of the graziers, and accordingly thousands of two- and three-year-old beasts are

Dairying and Sheep-breeding. 399

brought from the south and west to be finished either on the grass or in the yards.

On the Kentucky dairy farms, which are numerous, especially near the towns, the hard-working occupiers make a fair livelihood. They usually own, or rent at about 16*s.* to 20*s.* an acre, from 100 acres to 150 acres; ten to twelve cows are kept; their calves are mostly reared: besides bringing up the calf, each cow earns annually about 6*l.*; the milk is sold fresh at about 3*d.* per quart, or churned for butter, bringing 10*d.* to 1*s.* per lb.: not much cheese is made. Ten or twelve yearlings and the like number of two-year-olds are kept; if of good quality and well reared, the latter reach 1,000 lbs. gross weight, and realise 7*l.* to 8*l.* Milch-cows are enumerated at 260,000; oxen and other cattle, valued for assessment at 3*l.* 10*s.*, number nearly half a million.

Sheep-breeding has received a great deal of attention in Kentucky. Mr. Robert Scott, of Frankfort, and other flockmasters, by careful selection of native ewes, mated chiefly with English Leicesters, Cotswolds and Oxford Downs, have established 'the improved Kentucky'—a white-faced sheep brought to maturity in 18 to 20 months, readily reaching 22 lbs. a quarter, and with much of the appearance of the Border Leicester. Wide tracts of the upper lands in various parts of the State may still be bought at $20 to $30 an acre, and appear well adapted for sheep-breeding. With a moderate valuation of 8*s.* 6*d.* each, sheep are recorded to number one million. Hogs worth nearly 10*s.* each are enumerated at two millions.

Kentucky may be called the Yorkshire of

America; many of the larger farmers breed horses which are enumerated at 400,000, the mules, at 120,000: 9*l.* is their average value, moderately returned for assessment. Besides useful commoner horses, a large number are met with whose appearance attests crosses of superior English thorough-bred. From amongst these the agents of English dealers and jobmasters make some of their most serviceable selections, and obtain for 25*l.* to 30*l.* five- or six-year-old animals, broken but not much used, with good style and quality, flat wearing legs, well adapted for carriage purposes, with a few which make hunters. The best of these Kentucky nags are undistinguishable from Irish or English horses, excepting that they are a trifle plainer in the setting on of the head, and have scarcely so much style or delicate chiselling about the muscles of the head and face. It costs about 2*l.* to forward them to New York; the ocean freight is 9*l.*; insurance, 6 per cent. The delays and difficulties of landing at Liverpool are much complained of; and when the Milford Haven route is in full operation, it will command a large proportion of both the horse and cattle trades. With careful breaking in to the different mode of driving in England these Kentucky horses turn out well, and like those from Canada have more constitution and endurance than the animals reared in the warmer Southern States. The heavier horses bred after Clydesdale or Percheron sires are not generally so good as the lighter sorts. The American climate and soil, as well as the mode of work, appear unsuitable for the ponderous cart-horse used in most parts of Great Britain.

American waggons, vans, and lorries are much lighter than those used in England; both man and horse accomplish their work at a smarter pace. The man in charge more generally drives than leads his team; there is no anxiety, as is common at home, to curtail the quick walk into a crawl of two miles an hour; return journeys with empty vehicles are overtaken at a fair trot. On American farms stubborn clays, steep hill-sides, rough stony places, which try the patience and courage of British farmers and their horses, are not cultivated; the work is lighter and the pace smarter than in England. Hence the limited use of slow, ponderous horses weighing 17 cwt. to 20 cwt., which jar their legs and feet if urged beyond a steady walk.

As already indicated, a large area of Kentucky is in grass. The agricultural returns record that 300,000 acres are annually cut for hay. A good deal of the blue joint-grass is seeded for sale. A New York dealer informs me that in Paris, Ky., he has sometimes bought 10,000 bushels for distribution in other States, paying 50 cents, and sometimes 75 cents per bushel for extra clean lots. Indian corn is grown over two million acres, yielding an average of 25 bushels. Wheat, usually of the winter variety, and producing 10 bushels an acre, occupies a little over half a million acres; 300,000 acres are devoted to oats, which thrive fairly, and produce 26 to 30 bushels an acre.

Tobacco is one of the special features of Kentucky farming; it occupies 180,000 acres. Of the total yield of 400,000,000 lbs. which the United States produce from 543,000 acres, Kentucky grows nearly one-third ; Virginia contributes about one-fifth ; about one-twelfth is raised in Maryland and Tennessee, and one-twentieth in Pennsylvania, Ohio, and Missouri. The produce varies from 608 lbs. per acre, the average of careless cultivation in Tennessee, to 1,400 lbs. or 1,500 lbs., the result of better management in the less favourable climates of Connecticut and Massachusetts. The price per lb. varies from three to five cents in Indiana, and five cents in Kentucky and Ohio, to ten or eleven cents in Pennsylvania, Connecticut, and New York States. This great diversity in yield and price, and the better return got in the northern States, where climatic conditions are scarcely so favourable, point to the need of more careful management throughout the great tobacco producing areas. On impoverished, insufficiently manured land the gross feeding plant grows tardily. It is often inadequately attended to, it is apt to be riddled by worms, it is deteriorated by bad curing or careless packing. Hence the restricted acreable returns, the low price, the complaints that the business pays badly. It has been urged that production of late years has outstripped demand ; but, although markets are flooded with inferior qualities, there is no lack of appreciation of superior samples. The excise tax of 24 cents per lb. is complained of, but it probably does not very injuriously affect the grower who prospered previously to 1867, with tobacco worth thirteen cents per lb., and the duty reaching 33 cents per lb. Lower prices during the last four years have somewhat restricted the growth of tobacco. From a fiscal as well as a farmer's point of view it is, however, a most important crop. It contributes annually nearly 8,000,000*l*. to the U.S.A. national exchequer. Fully two-thirds of the total growth is exported, worth generally upwards of 5,000,000*l*. sterling.

From official Reports and information gathered from successful growers, I condense the following instructions regarding the successful cultivation of the manufacturing and shipping tobaccoes which constitute nine-tenths of that grown in the States. The good deep soil should be ploughed and subsoiled in autumn, and left exposed to the winter frost. In February or March a big dose of farm or town manure, amounting to 25 tons per acre, is spread on the plots and ploughed in three to four inches deep. With the bulkier farm manure, guano or other concentrated fertilisers should be applied to foster the greedy feeding plant. Probably the more economical plan is to reserve the artificials until the plants are dibbled. A subsequent ploughing is given in May to check weeds, and with drags or harrows the land is worked down to a fine tilth. A clumsy double-mould board plough is run deeply through the friable soil, throwing up lists or beds three or four feet deep. On these during June the tobacco plants, carefully reared on a seed plot, are set three to four feet apart. Frequent stirring with horse and hand hoes keeps the soil loose and free of weeds. A species of worm apt to prey on the leaves has to be sedulously guarded against by destroying the moth which produces it by surrounding the tobacco plant with lamps or bonfires, by growing Datura stramonium, of which the moth is fond, or by injecting into the flowers poisonous draughts of solution of cobalt. Any worms produced are removed by handpicking, by sprinkling affected parts with diluted oil of turpentine, or sending amongst them a flock of turkeys. Syringing the affected plants with soft soap and diluted carbolic acid, as is done with fly-infected hops, should also be effectual. To allow the succulent plants air and light, the lower leaves are trimmed off, successful growers averring that eight or nine leaves are enough for each plant. Suckers are promptly removed. The flowering bud is also topped off. Towards the middle of September cutting commences; green, unripe plants have to be left, as they spoil the sample: care must be had that the plant when cut not be scorched by too glaring a sun. Suspended over screens kept shaded, in sheds, sometimes in specially constructed flues, the dark clammy leaf is deprived of its moisture. On tier poles in larger bulk, it more gradually dries, and is ready for striking and bulking. The final operation of sorting for market requires also care and judgment to keep together only identical qualities.

Where such precautions are taken in the cultivation and selection of plants, in securing the crop and sorting it, the present poor yield at small extra cost may be doubled, and the quality so much improved, as readily to realise twice the usual price. That this is perfectly attainable is demonstrated by the figures above given as to the yield and price obtained throughout various of the New England States. With judicious and spirited management, 2,500 lbs. per acre have been procured, and such returns amply repay the care and expense necessary to secure good crops of tobacco.

Like many slave-holding States, Kentucky, for several years after the great war, was in an unsatisfactory condition; capital was withdrawn from the land; labour and improvements were paralysed; many useful farms were uncultivated. Numbers of easy-going, extravagant owners, with large retinues of idle coloured retainers, were ruined. Agriculture and other business have recently, however, improved. Farmers generally are more prosperous; they live comfortably, but, unless large holders of live stock, seldom make fortunes. Money is, however, becoming more plentiful; extending railways and better markets afford facilities for the disposal of produce. The real and personal property of the State is declared to be $318,037,875; about one-hundredth of this is owned by negroes. The State tax is 40 cents per $100 for the white population, but, somewhat unfairly, is 45 cents for the negro. The fullest amount of credit here is taken for taxes; not many settle until the last day of grace, or until the publication of such a reminder as I found posted on the Town Hall and other public places at Paris:

'*Last Call for City Taxes.*

'Having indulged the taxpayers of Paris so long as it is possible for me to do so, I will after this date proceed to levy and sell their property unless the same is paid immediately. This is fair warning to all, and I mean what I say most positively.

      (Signed) 'G. W. JUDY, *Collector.*

'PARIS, KY., *October* 16.'

 With large choice both of white and coloured people labour is more abundant than in many other States, but it is not particularly good or economical. The freed labourer is becoming, however, more reliable and provident. When first the black people became their own masters they lazily contented themselves with a very small modicum of work; they congregated in the towns, they gave themselves up to their favourite pastimes of music and dancing; unable to make proper provision for housing and clothing, which had always been provided for them, many died of cold and privation during the sharp winter. The monthly wages are about 3*l.* without board, about 2*l.* with board; carpenters, blacksmiths, and other such artisans earn 7*s.* to 8*s.* per day.

 Abram Renick, of Sharon, Clark County, Ky., has done a great deal to mould American shorthorns to their present good type, and confer on them kindly quality. He has been breeding and improving cattle since 1836, when he bought imported Illustrious of Crofton and Collings blood from the Ohio importing company. A still more valuable purchase was made in 1846 of the famous red cow Thames, and her calf Red Rose; her mother, Lady of the Lake, was from Mr. T. Bates' Rose of Sharon, by Mr.

Stephenson's Belvedere, full of Collings' Favourite strain. From this good source has grown the Rose of Sharon families, notable for their neat, well-chiselled heads, their shapely form and superior quality, deservedly extending in favour throughout America, and first introduced to English breeders by the Earl of Dunmore. Mr. Renick has generally sixty to eighty shorthorn females, kept in a very plain, unpampered way. Fourth Duke of Geneva, bred by James O. Sheldon, has rendered valuable service; Airdrie 3rd and another good level Rose of Sharon bull are now on duty. Here, as elsewhere, the bulls running out daily in paddocks are remarkably healthy and active, are kindly treated and well looked after by black boys, and are particularly quiet and docile. The practical beef-making capabilities of these pedigree cattle were satisfactorily demonstrated in the goodly appearance of forty-seven three-year-old bullocks, home-bred or bought from near neighbours, beautifully made up on grass, ranging from 1,700 lbs. to 1,800 lbs. live weight, sold at $4\frac{1}{2}$ cents per lb., and as handsome as could be found on any Leicestershire or Northamptonshire grazing. Mr. Renick believes that after charging rent, taxes, and expenses, his breeding and feeding cattle bring all round a profit of about $5 a year each. In brisk times, by the sale of a few young bulls or choice females, still better returns are obtained.

Fond of all descriptions of good live stock, Mr. Renick has 160 capital Southdown ewes and a similar number of Kentucky ewes. The mutton brings about

5 cents per lb. live weight, and the Southdown is always worth one cent more than the white-faced. Sharon further boasts of beautiful pure white goats, magnificent turkeys, black swans, and quaint-looking Indian poultry.

Mr. B. F. Vanmeter is an admirable representative of a Kentucky stockman. Besides being interested with the Messrs. Hamilton in several large shorthorn herds, he farms at Syracuse upwards of 1,000 acres of undulating grass land, abundantly sheltered with handsome timber, well watered by streams and pools, with here and there some sulphur springs bubbling forth. The fields are divided by wild orange, occasionally by zigzag post and railing, or big stone walls. The farm buildings are chiefly stone and timber, many of them thatched. Maize is the principal grain crop, the straw and corn constituting the chief winter food for the stock. Upwards of 100 acres are annually worked by contract by some of Mr. Vanmeter's smaller neighbours, who plough, plant, cultivate, and harvest the maize, for which operations they receive about $5 an acre. With his own staff he grows another 150 acres of corn. The land is clean, and free from the prevailing ragweed which in many parts of Kentucky shows itself abundantly after the summer rains. All manure is taken care of, and applied to the corn and other crops. The yield of Indian corn averages 50 bushels, and hence costs about 6*d.* per bushel.

Mr. Vanmeter has bred shorthorns for many years; he has now 200, and is increasing them annually. He has tried various strains, but prefers the Roses of Sharon, so successfully cultivated by his friend and neighbour Mr. Renick. Of this valuable sort he has nearly fifty good specimens, of wonderfully uniform type, well proportioned, near the ground, without coarseness, with shoulders well laid back, neat, rather narrow heads, and small, nicely turned horns. Length and stoutness of limb and activity, desiderated in former days, when the fatted beast had to trudge 500 or even 1,000 miles to market, have given place to more symmetry, lightness of offal, early maturity, and quality. A large proportion of these favourite animals are good reds occasionally with a shade of the Hubback yellow, often with white Duchess markings. The bulls, although not so grand and imposing as some of the more notable English shorthorn sires, leave big profitable stock. Mr. Vanmeter's yearling and two-year-old heifers compare favourably with those of the best English in size, style, shape, and uniformity; the only important character in which they were deficient was the soft, mossy, curly coat which our cooler, moister climate encourages.

Messrs. George and James C. Hamilton, of Mount Stirling, near Winchester, Ky., are amongst the most extensive shorthorn breeders in the States. They have 3,500 acres at Flat Creek, Bath County, with several tracks in Missouri and elsewhere. At Flat Creek they have now 250 shorthorn females of Rose of Sharon, Young Phyllis, Young Mary, Josephine, Kirklevington, Barrington, and other superior Bates sorts. They have used the Duchess bulls, 4th Duke of Geneva, 20th Duke of Airdrie, and have now several superior Rose of Sharon bulls.

From their Kentucky and Missouri breeding farms the Messrs. Vanmeter and Hamilton turn out annually 300 bulls, disposing of them at from eight to eighteen months old, principally at the stock sales of Chicago and Kansas City, at an average of $100 to $200. Even from their 600 cows they have been unable to supply the demand for good red and dark roan bulls. They recently had an order for 125 for the Panhandle country, whence hostile Indians are being driven out and enterprising settlers are pushing in. They forward numbers to the southern parts of Texas, to cross with the rough heavy-horned yellow Spaniards. Even amidst unfavourable scorching hot surroundings, with parching drought and summer scarcity both of food and water, which shorten their existence to two or three years, these superior shorthorns are steadily improving the narrow coarse Texans.

Excepting bulls and feeding stock, Messrs. Vanmeter and Hamilton's shorthorns are never housed. Throughout summer and winter they range the well-sheltered pastures. Calves are dropped at all seasons, but are not liked to arrive during the hot periods of June, July, and August. A few cows calving in winter are sheltered in yards; the majority lie out day and night, the calves remaining with them for eight or nine months. During winter weather, which occurs in January and February, hay or corn fodder or corn in the sheaves is provided in the pastures, and may be necessary for some of the stock during stormy weather in March, and before the grass shoots. Farming expenses are evidently considerably less than in England. Superior grazing farms in Kentucky are rented at $4 to $5 an acre. The summer grazing of adult cows or bullocks is estimated to cost $1.50 per month; for four winter months the expenses are doubled: the total cost of keeping a cow or two-year-old bullock would therefore be $24, or nearly 5*l.* per annum.

Mr. A. J. Alexander, Woodburn, near Lexington, Kentucky, is well known amongst horsemen and shorthorn breeders on both sides of the Atlantic. His property, extending to 2,000 acres, was bought towards the close of last century by his father, who emigrated from Airdrie, Scotland. The estate some twenty years ago came into possession of its present owner, who has greatly improved it. The soil is a useful, rather heavy loam on a limestone formation. Like other commodities, land in Kentucky has lately advanced in value. Some of the recent additions which Mr. Alexander has made to his estate have cost $125 an acre. Ordinary farms in the neighbourhood range, however, from $60 to $80. A compact property of 110 acres in this district, with a tolerable house, recently sold for $62 an acre. Another of 354 acres, with a particularly good house and premises, realised $78 an acre. Many useful farms, fairly equipped with house and buildings, are rented at $5 to $6 an acre, and let either by the year or on lease. Better times are advancing the value of land, both to rent and to sell.

In this part of Kentucky the valuation for taxation is taken at about two-thirds of the real value. The rate of 52 cents per dollar is charged alike on real and personal estate. The taxes on each reach a trifle over ½ per cent. per annum. For assessment, horses and mules are valued all round at $50; cattle, according to age, at $10 to $25.

Seen on a fine October day Woodburn is a charming place. It contrasts pleasantly with the bare and level prairies and plains of Western States. Houses, buildings, and surroundings have an old manorial appearance. The undulating country is beautifully timbered. The oaks, handsome as any in Worcestershire, are preserved in large numbers throughout the pastures for sheltering both live stock and grass. The fine old turf is fresh, green, and full of white clover, which thrives on the *débris* of the limestone subsoil. About 800 acres of arable land are divided as follow:—200 acres of wheat, 300 acres of maize, 150 acres of barley, and the same area of clover. The wheat is autumn sown; 1½ bushels deposited by a broad-caster suffices for seed; but little horse or hand hoeing is attempted, or, indeed, is required; the yield varies from 20 to 25 bushels; the cost of raising wheat ranges from 45*s.* to 50*s.* an acre. Indian corn follows, three to five seeds being dibbled near together in clumps, which are three to four feet from each other in every direction; opportunity is thus given for hoeing in two directions; such hoeing is repeated four or five times; 40*s.* an acre covers the cost of growing the acre of Indian corn; 50 bushels is the average yield. Barley and a few oats follow, but do not pay so well as corn or wheat. The barley casts 20 to 30 bushels. Amongst the barley, occasionally amongst the wheat, clover is sown, and is lightly grazed in autumn. Mown in early summer, a portion is generally allowed again to run up, and is saved for seed; the bulk is grazed for three months, and ploughed for wheat. The arable land is clean, and in good manurial condition. The dung from the stables and yards is taken care of and applied. The fields are generally large, ranging from 20 to 100 acres, are divided by hedges of thorn and osage, or wild orange, sometimes by posts and rails, the posts being of split locust, which last 30 or 40 years, and the rails of black walnut or oak, which last half that period. The farm is worked by 25 mules, eight horses, and four oxen. The shorthorns, thoroughbred, and trotting horses, necessitate the employment of many more hands than are usually found on American farms. Ordinary labourers with board receive about $12 a month; most are engaged for the twelve months.

A good flock of sheep is kept. On several hundred well-selected ewes of the country, Southdown rams, sometimes direct from Jonas Webb or the Duke of Richmond, are used. A few score of early lambs are generally sent to New York in May, realising about $3.50, which, although a very moderate return in the eyes of British flockmasters, pays for the ewe bought in during autumn, and leaves her and her fleece to meet expenses and profit. Two dollars (8*s.* 4*d.*) is the usual cost of the ewe kept during twelve months. This pays for pasturage, a little hay required during winter, some rock salt, and the shepherds' wages, which generally reach $16 a month.

Mr. Alexander laid the foundation of his shorthorns in 1853, with the valuable assistance of Mr. Strafford, buying from Towneley Duchess of Athol and 2nd Duke of Athol. Their descendants the Airdrie Duchesses are now the plums of the herd. But as ever will happen, mishaps affect some of the best. The splendidly bred 21st Duchess of Airdrie has twice slipped and is hopeless as a breeder, whilst 10th Duchess of Oneida, from the New York Mills, is in the same thriftless case. Gwynnes, imported from Mr. Tanqueray's, have reproduced some admirable representatives of this good old sort. There are several hardy good specimens of the J tribe. Several grand massive Barringtons have been added. Filligrees, tracing back to Mr. R. Booth's Fame, by Raspberry topped by Oxford and Duchess sires, contribute some shapely, useful cows. From Victoria, of the Cold Cream family, imported from Windsor, are some superior deeply milking Knightleys. Mazurkas are in great force, and have been introduced to the notice of English breeders by importations made by Mr. George Fox. The representatives of the Bell Bates tribe, and the Miss Wileys of Lord Spencer's and Mason's blood, are uniform, good, and shapely. Most of these imported families, bought at moderate prices, have paid well.

Ignoring the line breeding on which most

Americans insist, Mr. Alexander, on most of his stock, whether Bates, Booth, or Knightley, has used Oxford, Airdrie, or other Bates-bred bulls. The cattle have the unmistakable style and character of English Bates tribes. They have bigger frames, longer necks, large and bolder heads, and more horn than many other Kentucky shorthorns. Their numbers, from time to time, have been reduced by sales, not only of bulls, but of females. About 50, including nearly a score of bulls, were thus disposed of in July 1879, making an average of about 100 guineas. The stud bulls, in descent and appearance, thoroughly satisfy an English connoisseur. The 37th Duke of Oneida, from the New York Mills great sale, is still active, level, deep, near the ground, with good touch, Bates grandeur and good head, but rather sprawling horns, which Americans do not like. Although ten years old, judicious feeding and exercise maintain his activity. The 26th Duke of Airdrie, and several younger scions of this famous tribe, showed much size and style. The smart lengthy 2nd Duke of Barrington, by 37th Duke of Oneida, dam Baroness 12th, by 10th Duke of Thorndale, is deservedly a great favourite with Mr. Alexander; he has more than once refused 700 guineas for him, and has mated him with some of his Duchesses. Mr. Alexander for twelve months had been anxious to obtain a good Oxford bull from England, but demurred to subject any such purchase to the tedious and expensive quarantine imposed on cattle imported into the States. During the summer of 1880, he has, however, secured, from Bow Park, Toronto, a valuable young Oxford from the cow which the Hon. George Browne bought from Colonel Kingscote for 2,000 guineas. A herd thus well founded, judiciously crossed and managed, has made its mark widely, and is confidently resorted to by the many breeders who raise pedigree or superior grade bulls for the great western and southern ranches.

Besides about 70 shorthorns, Mr. Alexander has nearly 40 Jerseys and Jersey grades, and 60 to 80 superior shorthorn grades for feeding. The cattle are in the pastures for eight or nine months. Many of the younger of the grades are never housed, unless they happen to be fed off during winter, when, like the shorthorns, Jerseys, and any milkers, they are in yards or boxes from December until February; or, if the weather is boisterous or unsettled, during part of March. The cattle sheds are built of stone, some are slated, others thatched, and all are much in the style of good English premises. The loose boxes for the bulls are large and convenient. Most of them communicate with yards into which the animals are turned out for exercise for an hour or two daily.

Mr. Alexander, and his brother before him, have been very successful in breeding horses. At Woodburn there are about 120 mares; 75 to 80 of these are thoroughbreds, the remainder of superior trotting strains. Lexington, foaled in 1850, by imported Sarpedon, with a good deal of Arab blood a few generations back in his long, good pedigree, proved himself an invaluable thoroughbred. Few horses have left so many good ones. To the last the old horse was active and useful, and three years ago came to an untimely end in an unusual way. One of his molar teeth dropped out unnoticed, the socket became plugged up with foul fermenting food, which caused fatal irritation and fever. So favourably prepossessed is Mr. Alexander with the Lexington strain that he has freely used several of his sons. Phaeton, a valuable horse, full of King Tom blood, was worthily following Lexington, but died recently from mismanagement. Australian, by West Australian, was also successfully used. Glen Athole, by Blair Athole, is now in service, a smart chestnut ; dam, Greta, by Voltigeur, with Ithuriel, Bay Middleton, and Whisker standing next in the pedigree. Several of his progeny are doing remarkably well at the racing meetings which are now spreading throughout the States. From a bad cold which he caught during his voyage across the Atlantic he has lost his sight. In style and appearance, as well as in colour, he closely resembles old Blair Athole, lacks somewhat of his size and substance, and, like him, is taken in a trifle too much under the knee. Besides Glen Athole, Mr. Alexander is making tolerably free use of Tenbrook, by imported Phaeton, belonging to his neighbour, Mr. John Harper, and said to be the best thoroughbred sire in America.

Most of the thoroughbred mares come from strains which have specially distinguished themselves, either in England or America. They are remarkable for style and quality, are shapely and well put together, some of them look small, but most range from 15 to 15½ hands. They live on the sheltered beautiful pasture for nine or ten months of the year, have a shed in the field, and some hay or corn during snow or severe winter weather, or are brought up to the yards to foal. The 75 thoroughbred mares are expected to produce annually 50 foals. The yearlings sold annually in June bring 50 to 250 guineas.

Mr. Alexander is fond and proud of his trotting stud. For the stallions and horses in training he has capital healthy boxes, good exercise grounds, and a trotting track. Several of his stud horses are admirable, alike in appearance and performance. His bay Belmont, foaled in 1864, is the sire of Nutwood, Nil Desperandum, Dick Moore, and Wedgewood, all of whom have done their mile at or within 2 min. 24 sec. But aiming at the highest successes, Mr. Alexander must have several strings to his bow. In Harold, foaled in 1864, he has another horse of equal capability. By Rysdyks Hambletonian from Enchantress, by Old Abdallah, Harold has produced several horses that are already well known to fame. Chief among these is Childe Harold, bought by Mr. John Hendrie, of Glasgow, and winner of the International Handicap Stakes at Liverpool in 1878, and the still more notable Maud S., who, eclipsing all performers, has done her mile in 2 min. 11 sec. Maud S. was bought by Mr. Vanderbilt for 4,000 guineas. Mr. Alexander still has the smart grey mare Miss Russell, the dam of this trotting prodigy, and about 40 other picked specimens remarkable either for their own performances on the track, or for near consanguinity with illustrious winners. In no trotting stud are descent and performance, style and appearance, so carefully and systematically harmonised. Many of Mr. Alexander's mares have beautiful true all-round action; some have heads which indicate Arabian blood; all have strong loins and powerful quarters, sound good joints and short canon bones. In speed and smartness, many of our hacks and cobs would be great gainers if they had a cross with some of Mr. Alexander's game-trotting sorts.

The Honourable Thomas J. Megibben, of Fairview, Cynthiana, is equally well known as a successful agriculturist, a breeder of shorthorns and of horses, and a distiller of superior Bourbon whisky. He farms upwards of 2,000 acres, grows 500 acres of wheat, secures an acreable average of 20 bushels; plants 300 acres of Indian corn, of which the yield is about 40 bushels; finds oats less certain than barley or rye. Some of his barley planted in autumn is ready early in June. The general harvest in Kentucky begins between June 10th and 15th. His clover and grass he supplements with millet, which he finds useful both as green and dry forage for all animals.

His shorthorns, collected during the last ten years, number upwards of 100 and include animals of the following superior Bates strains—Rose of Sharon, Princess, Gwynne, Lady Bates, Kirklevington and Craggs. Mr. Megibben began with 14th Duke of Airdrie followed by 2nd Duke of Oneida, and has more recently been using 10th Earl of Oxford and

2nd Oxford Vinewood. His cattle are shapely, smart, and well managed, and at the public sales he has no difficulty in disposing of young bulls and surplus females. He has 50 good Southdowns, many of them imported, mated with a ram direct from Lord Walsingham, and 35 superior Cotswolds from Robert Garne and Charles Barton. Keeping these breeds distinct, Mr. Megibben is desirous to compare their relative yield of mutton and wool with that of the ordinary Kentucky sheep, which constitute the bulk of his own and his neighbours' flocks. With much taste for horses, he has 200 thoroughbreds and trotting nags, and is building up an admirable stud.

The capital requisite for these agricultural enterprises has been mostly obtained from the successful manufacture of Bourbon whisky. The materials and mode of using them differ considerably. In many distilleries about 25 per cent. of barley is used; nearly half of this is malted; five to ten per cent. of rye is sometimes added; the remainder of the mash is made up of yellow corn. The sour mash process, occupying about seventy hours, is now generally preferred to the quicker sweet mash process. By the latter 56 lbs. of grain are stated to yield 3 gallons 3 quarts of spirit 10 over proof; the same weight of grain by the sour process produces 3 gallons of spirit.

CHAPTER XXV.

AMERICAN COMPETITION IN WHEAT AND MEAT.

AMERICAN production of bread stuffs and animal food has of late years been increasing enormously. Agricultural enterprise has generally paid better in America than in Great Britain. The cheap Western lands with comparatively small labour and outlay have yielded profitable increase. The surplus produce of the New World in ever-increasing abundance has been brought to feed the more thickly peopled portions of the Old World. Whilst consumers have been greatly benefited, British farmers, and especially wheat growers, have been injuriously affected. They have had unfavourable seasons and indifferent crops coupled with somewhat low prices. British agriculturists in accommodating themselves to the altered circumstances of production markets and prices will find it to their advantage to grasp the conditions under which American competitors are working, and at the risk of reiterating some of the facts already brought forward in these pages, I shall endeavour to describe the special features connected with the growth, handling, and transport of American grain and live stock.

America produces about one-fourth of the wheat grown in the world. Her increased production has been unprecedentedly rapid, it has more than quadrupled in thirty years; it has doubled since 1868; between 1876 and 1878 it made an advance of 28 per cent. The wheat yield of the United States, and its rapid increase, are well illustrated by the following official returns:—

	Bushels of wheat
1850	100,485,944
1860	173,104,924
1870	235,884,700
1880	445,000,000

The conditions which heretofore have encouraged this extended growth still remain in operation. The wheat area, although ten times that of the British Islands, is represented by the extent of the comparatively small State of Alabama and does not yet reach one-fortieth of the cultivatable area of the States. Many years must elapse before the American limit of production is reached—before the great prairies, plains, and bluffs now uncultivated or only partially cultivated yield a fair return of golden grain. The tide of emigration and agricultural enterprise flowing steadily westward carries with it the growth of wheat. Until 1849 more than half the produce was confined to the New England and other Atlantic States; 43 per cent. was grown in the Middle States; only 5 per cent. in the trans-Mississippi States and Territories. At the rate of about nine miles a year the wheat

Extension of Recuperative Farming. 423

growth has however gone west. In the Eastern States less than 15 per cent. is now grown; in the Middle States about 40 per cent.; in the Western upwards of 45 per cent.

The lower cost of production in the Western and Pacific States discourages wheat-growing in the older Eastern States and accelerates the western movement both of wheat and Indian corn. The great extent of cheap lands, the expansion of railroads and the utilising of water traffic, enable the enterprising Western States to compete successfully in the growth of grain with the Middle and Eastern States. The New Englander, like his cousin in old England, finds it cheaper to import than to grow his wheat. Both are compelled by Western competition to readjust expenditure and modify cultivation. Farmers of the Eastern States have hitherto believed that they could not afford the outlay of 20*s.* to 30*s.* an acre requisite to manure the exhausted soils and ensure full crops. Such recuperative treatment, with yard manure, with live stock, and with concentrated fertilisers is now becoming more general. Phosphates, blood, and other manures are in increasing demand. They are generally sold with guaranteed proportions of ammonia, phosphates, and potash. The gardeners and cotton planters have hitherto been their chief purchasers; but agriculturists generally are becoming more impressed with the fact that plants, as well as animals, do not thrive without full supplies of their appropriate food.

Wheat culture in the States is generally conducted

on a cheaper rough-and-ready method than is practised in Great Britain. Instead of costing as in England 7*l.* to 8*l.* an acre, over the vast regions of the Western States where, as stated, nearly half the wheat is grown, the total expenses are covered by 40*s.* or 42*s.* an acre. In some parts of Dakota in Manitoba, and California the average cost of production is rather less.

On the level treeless prairies and plains, without timber or stones laboriously to remove, cultivation can at once be commenced. The rough grass is generally burnt, the breaking up of the friable loam costs 8*s.* to 10*s.* an acre; the sod disintegrates in two or three months, another furrow is back-set or cross ploughed for 5*s.* On all considerable farms sulky ploughs, on which the driver comfortably rides, are used, turning over a furrow 12 to 15 inches wide, and 4 to 6 inches deep, and overtaking two to three acres in a day of ten hours. When the ground is dry and hard, or an extra depth of furrow is required, three or four horses, mules, or oxen are used; most of the ploughing is however done by a pair of draught animals. Twenty miles is the usual daily journey of horses or mules at farm work. In Wisconsin, Michigan, Ohio, Kentucky, and also in California, winter wheat is planted in October and November; but in Minnesota, Iowa, and Nebraska the winter cold is great, there is seldom sufficient covering of snow to protect the plant, and spring wheat is accordingly preferred and put in as soon as the frost is out of the surface soil, which it generally is early in March. In

Minnesota and Iowa the dry hard spring wheat is much used for making the superior patent flour rich in albuminoids. One and a half bushels is a fair seeding, deposited from a broad-caster which distributes the seed from six to twenty spouts, nine or ten inches apart. No hoeing or weeding is necessary; the sharp winter and hot summer militate against weeds, and many farms, where after the first breaking up only one ploughing and several harrowings are given annually, and wheat follows regularly year after year, are cleaner than the average of land has lately been in England.

Scythes and sickles have long been superseded by reapers and now the automatic self-binder is in general use. It cuts down on an average 15 acres a day at a cost of about 7s. an acre, including wages of men, charge for horses, wire or cord for binding, and interest on the 50l.—the cost of the machine. The cord binder is taking the place of the wire binder, reducing the cost of tying, preventing injury to the thrashing drum, removing the chance of the metal wire being swallowed and injuring the cattle, and saving all trouble of untying for thrashing, the cord-bound sheaves being forked on to the machine without cutting or untying. Extra hands are generally engaged for harvest, receiving double wages or 7s. to 8s. a day, sometimes with rations.

On the great California farms a high-set reaper cuts and collects the dry ears and carries them to a thrasher in the field, where the grain is beaten out, winnowed, and sacked up for market. On some large farms the wheat is taken direct from the shock to the thrashing machine, and thence delivered to the railroad or barge. Driven by eight- or ten-horse engines, often stoked with straw instead of coal, the thrashing machine usually turns out 40 to 50 quarters a day. As at home, the cost varies considerably, but may be set down at an average of 5s. Attached to almost all thrashers besides the winnowing machine is an elevator, which saves much labour in heaping the straw which at leisure is ruthlessly burned. Summarising these expenses of American wheat-growing, the cost of an acre may be set down as follows :

	£	s.	d.
Rent or Interest on Capital employed in purchase and equipment of the farm, say 3*l.* at 10 per cent.		6	0
Taxes and rates .		1	0
Ploughing .		6	0
Seed .		6	0
Sowing and harrowing		2	0
Reaping and stacking		10	0
Thrashing .		5	0
Delivery .		2	0
Incidentals		2	0
	£2	0	0

The dry climate of the United States minimises the wheat yield, which the official averages place at less than 13 bushels an acre. The seventeen years from 1863 to 1879 inclusive present an average of 12·2; in only five years did it exceed 13; the best of the series was 1877 when the average was 13·9; locusts in 1875 and 1876 reduced it respectively to 11 and 10·4. Notwithstanding this almost accidental reduction the average wheat yield of the last eight years is the same as that of the preceding eight years. The general productiveness is fairly maintained as evidenced by the averages of the older cultivated states being kept up. During 1880 Illinois produced 18 bushels and Ohio and Missouri 20 bushels. It nevertheless generally takes two acres in America to grow the wheat which England produces on one. More careful cultivation, better selection of seed, and extended planting of moisture-attracting trees will probably, however, somewhat increase this small yield.

The average value of the wheat crop of the States for sixteen years from 1863 to 1878 inclusive is $1.20·3 or 4s. 10d. per bushel. Only in three years has it fallen below 4s. Recent abundant crops brought down the average price of 1878 to 3s. 3d. Throughout the great wheat-growing zone the average value during the past seven years is about 3s. 6d. per bushel. Even with the low average yield of 12·2 bushels per acre this gives an acreable return of 42s. 8d. Two and eightpence is a small profit on an acre of wheat, but it is better than the heavy losses which English wheat-growers have so generally sustained during the last few years. In such states and on such farms where 16 bushels an acre have been reaped a profit of 14s. 6d. has been netted, or a return sufficient in two years to purchase the land. Farmers who produce, as some do, 20 bushels an acre, and who dispose of it at 3s. 6d. per bushel, realise in one year sufficient to buy the land on which the crop grows. No wonder wheat in America is affectionately y-clept 'the poor man's friend' and constitutes the staple crop of the first settlers. But the farmer who judiciously locates in a temperate region has a varied choice of other paying crops, as Indian corn, oats, clover, and sorghum saccharatum or amber cane, the cultivation of which is extending in south-western Minnesota and other states to the south, yields a capital sugar, a useful residual cattle and hog food, and a profit of fully 20s. an acre.

Facility for the transport of the farm crops to market is an important factor in the producer's profits and an essential element in the price they are charged to the consumer. The most choice productions are of small value if they cannot be readily marketed. In the remote West wheat and maize have not unfrequently been used as fuel, and fat bacon has been the cheapest and handiest article for lighting the fires on the Mississippi steam boats. In Manitoba, throughout parts of the Red River settlements, in Dakota and elsewhere, I met teams which had laboriously brought wheat for sale fifty and even seventy miles to rail or market. Farming under such conditions must be an unsatisfactory and unprofitable business. Unless for stock farming better buy at 25s. an acre a hundred acres five miles from a good railroad than accept the gift and be compelled to till a thousand acres fifty miles from rail or market. Railroads, however, now cover 100,000 miles throughout the States, are extending at the rate of 5,000 miles annually; those in the West often costing for a single track less than 3,000*l.* a mile. River, lake, and canal transport is being utilised and improved. Competition between different railroads and between railroads and water transit keep down transport charges, which, especially for long distances, are much lower than those of the Old World. Through the great lakes and rivers in barges, ten or a dozen of which are towed by one steam tug, the grain from the West is cheaply conveyed to the eastern markets, or direct to the ocean steamer which deports it to Europe. From Saint Louis down the Mississippi a thousand miles to New Orleans one steam tug will sometimes drag 270,000 bushels of grain. The grain is almost all carried loose; the barges load 2,000 bushels and upwards; the large railroad cars hold 400 to 500 bushels; loaded east with grain and other agricultural produce, they return west with lumber and stores.

Grain is examined and graded in transit by qualified sworn inspectors. Of the several grains there are about forty grades. Spring wheat, for example, is distinguished as first, second, third, and fourth grades and rejected. Unless distinctly stipulated for in the bills of lading, consigners' lots are not kept separate; grain of the same grade is however strictly kept apart; and from the bin of 6,000 bushels of say No. 2 Spring wheat collected perhaps from many sources, at the railway elevator at Chicago or New York the consigner, who three weeks previously had his two or three thousand bushels graded No. 2 Spring at St. Paul or Omaha, draws an equivalent of quantity and quality. Separate railway cars, barges, or bins reserved for small lots would involve much extra trouble and cost.

Fixed or portable elevators cheaply and expeditiously transfer with a minimum of manual labour the loose grain from the cars or barges to the grain warehouses or to the ocean steamers. With shovels worked automatically by steam, two men empty the car of 400 bushels in twelve minutes. At the great railroad elevators 300 trucks containing 120,000 bushels are often unloaded in a day. As it passes through the elevators every parcel is weighed automatically, usually in ten ton lots, by Fairbank's scales. The elevator charges are a quarter of a cent per bushel, which includes ten days' storage and delivery into trucks or barges. For a trifle extra, at most depôts, the grain can also be winnowed in its transference to or from the great bins. These elevators connected with all the warehouses, at an infinitesimal cost, and without the tedious manual labour necessary at home, turn the grain and thus contribute to its soundness and condition. With these fixed elevators or with handy floating elevators the ocean-going vessels, provided with several convenient hatches, are readily loaded with 60,000 to 80,000 bushels in eight hours. With proper partition boards and about three layers of sacks on the top of the loose grain to keep it level when it sinks, these grain ships, *pace* Mr. Plimsol, do not shift their cargo. Unfortunately however grain, even when safely packed, cannot convert an unseaworthy ship into a safe one. The economy of the American handling of grain is notably illustrated when it is compared with the tedious expensive discharging of the grain-laden ships arrived at European ports. Every bushel is painstakingly weighed, and sacked up, often carried ashore on mens' shoulders, and the ship is detained ten or twelve days at a cost of at least 10*l.* a day. Such extra labour and cost increase the price of bread.

British agriculturists and bread consumers whose every second loaf comes from America equally desire to know what it costs to bring the cheap wheat of the Western world to British ports. Most of it grows, as already stated, in a zone 500 to 1,500 miles east of the Atlantic seaboard. The carriage of the trans-Mississippi wheat along western lines, where there is small competition, is relatively costly; but even in remoter districts a quarter of 480 lbs. is carried 200 to 300 miles for 2*s.* 6*d.* From the Heron Lake district on the St. Paul and Sioux City rail the through rates for a quarter of wheat despatched thence 650 miles to Chicago are under 5*s.* From St. Paul, the capital of Minnesota, 480 lbs. of wheat are at present carried to Chicago for 4*s.* 6*d.* Thence eastward keen competition by various lines of railroad and by water secure still cheaper freights. The railroads have carried wheat from Chicago 800 miles to New York and Baltimore at 1*s.* per quarter. During the past three years the rates have fluctuated from 2*s.* to 4*s.* By steam-tugged barges through lake and canal *viâ* Oswego to New York the rates are little more than one half those by rail. The water transit extending from June until November proves, as in other parts of America, a formidable competitor to the railways. During the last 16 years its cost has steadily diminished to the extent of 30 per cent. Cheaper working expenses, steam tugs, quick loading and unloading by elevators have reduced working charges, and dividends in consequence have not materially suffered. The adoption of new appliances, the labour-saving elevators everywhere multiplying, steel rails, enlarged traffic, and the economical management, resulting from a prolonged period of depression, will enable the American railroads profitably to continue the moderate through rates which have so largely contributed to the cheap feeding of Europe.

The ocean rates are equally moderate. Taking an average of the last five years, wheat is brought from New York to British ports at 5s. to 6s. a quarter; it has been carried as low as 8d. per cental. Barrels of flour weighing 214 lbs. are conveyed at an average charge of 3s. per steamer and 2s. 3d. per sailing vessels. From Philadelphia and Montreal rates have fluctuated from 4s. to 9s. Provisions from most of the Atlantic ports are landed in Great Britain at 30s. to 40s. a ton, whilst oil-cakes are quoted at the moderate figure of 20s. to 30s. Through rates to Europe from points remote from the seaboard are proportionately lower. Wheat and flour are transmitted from St. Paul to Liverpool at 16s. for 480 lbs. From Minneapolis, 1,200 miles west of the Atlantic, a barrel of flour is conveyed to Liverpool, Cardiff, or Glasgow for 7s. or 8s. During five years from 1876 to 1880 the freight of wheat despatched from Chicago, trans-shipped at New York, and landed at Liverpool, has averaged 12*s*. per quarter of 480 lbs. ('Agricultural Interest Commission:' Appendix). From St. Louis by direct water route flour has been forwarded at ·5*s*. per barrel. From the Pacific ports, which furnish about one-fifth of the American exports, rates are equally moderate; from San Francisco to Liverpool or London, the through freight is frequently as low as 3*s*. a quarter. These figures justify the conclusion that an average of 15*s*. will freight a quarter of wheat from the great prairies and plains of central America over 1,200 miles of land and 3,000 miles of ocean to British ports.

Here landing and other charges, amounting to 2*s*. or 2*s*. 6*d*. a quarter, are incurred. They include insurance, which averages 1 per cent., and has fluctuated from 6*s*. 8*d*. per cent. to 10 per cent., reached in a panic time after several grain-laden ships were lost. Three per cent. guaranteed for shortage more than covers any shrinking in quantity. In ships not entirely chartered for grain there is a primage of 5 per cent. Dock-dues take 8*d*. or 9*d*. per quarter; brokerage is $\frac{1}{2}$ per cent., and merchants' commission about the same. Wheat is sold in London subject to two months' discount at 5 per cent. for cash; in Liverpool three months' discount is allowed for cash; in other places only one month's discount is given.

The total cost—freight, insurance, and other charges—on a quarter of American wheat landed at British ports, may thus be summarised:

		£	s.	d.
Cost of growing one quarter of wheat, 40s. an acre being paid for cultivation with a yield of 13 bushels		1	4	8
Freight to United Kingdom ports		0	15	0
Insurance, dock, and other charges		0	2	6
		£2	2	2

At this moderate cost of 42s. per quarter American wheat can be sold in Great Britain with profit to growers, railway carriers, shippers, and all concerned. The cost of production is not likely to increase; indeed, improved cultivation, by augmenting the small yield, will cheapen production. Nor with increasing competition are transport charges likely to be enhanced. British householders may hence confidently look forward to moderate prices for bread, and British farmers must prepare to make the best of increasing food imports, and grow produce which, unlike wheat, cannot be so cheaply forwarded from afar. They cannot compete with the cheap lands of America in producing an article so readily grown and transported. They cannot afford to grow wheat at 42s. or even at 45s. a quarter, unless on the better class of soils where four quarters can be counted on, or where the straw can be sold at 4l. or 5l. an acre.

There is still another important phase of this American bread question which demands consideration. Can the United States continue to maintain her large wheat exports of recent years? Some high authorities have declared that her best lands are already 'played out,' and that expensive restorative farming is necessary to maintain wheat cultivation in

Surplus Wheat for Export. 435

its present dimensions. Such forebodings, as we have endeavoured to show, are not supported by fact or probability. In the Red River Valley, in Minnesota, in Iowa, throughout California, Oregon, and in some other states and territories are great uncultivated or very partially cultivated tracts of easily worked fertile land where, if needful, wheat could be grown in plenty to supply the shortcoming of all Europe. The able statistician of the Agricultural Department at Washington, in his official report for 1879, declares that 'the eastern, north middle, and southern groups of states do not supply their home demand; the south middle states have a small surplus; the Ohio valley has a surplus of nearly half their crop, and the more western groups produce more than a threefold supply of the home demand.' In 1867 and 1868 the United States exported respectively 12 and 13 per cent. of her total wheat crop; the exports have since steadily increased; in 1877 she was able to spare one-fourth; whilst her more recent bountiful and extending crops, besides feeding her own population of forty-four millions, leaves for export more than one-third, or nearly 20 million quarters. Of these handsome surpluses the United Kingdom has recently taken nearly one-half. In 1880 America contributed $9\frac{1}{2}$ million quarters towards the total 14 million quarters required to meet the British wheat deficit of the year. The capacity of the United States to fill the vacuum of the Old World's wants becomes very apparent when the matter is viewed in another way: $5\frac{1}{2}$ bushels of wheat is regarded as a fair annual allowance for each individual in the United Kingdom. Americans, who use freely vegetables, fruit, and other grains, grow nearly 9 bushels *per capita*, and hence have about one-third more than they need. No other country so liberally provides for her own wants, and has so much to spare for her less fortunate friends.

During recent years a great expansion has occurred in the exports of American wheat flour. Alike throughout Canada and the States, advantage has been taken of the valuable widely spread water power. New mills have been erected and filled with the most modern and effective machinery. Four million barrels of flour containing 198 lbs. were exported from the States in 1878, and the exports of 1879 were nearly a half more. In barrels and bags the United Kingdom received from the States 6,863,172 cwts. of wheat meal and flour in 1879, and 6,908,352 cwts. in 1880, or nearly double the supply of 1878, and four times that of 1877. American millers say that they can grind and forward their flour to Europe at cheaper rates than it can be made here. They have the advantage of freights as moderate as those charged for the wheat. With superior machinery and systematic management, doing a large turn over, and hence satisfied with smaller profits, the larger milling concerns, whether in Great Britain or America, are driving out the smaller millers, especially where they are unfavourably circumstanced as to water or railroad facilities. But British millers well situated for transport or markets, unlike the British wheat-growers, do not seriously suffer from the keen American competition. They have the wheat of the world on terms quite as favourable as the American miller, they use very similar machinery, are adopting modern labour-saving contrivances, and manage besides to make four times the price for their bran and offal.

American competition does not seriously interfere with the growth in Great Britain of any other grain than wheat. Barley does not much extend its area; it occupies about 1,800,000 acres, it bulks fully five million quarters; one-third is produced in California, where the yield averages 23 bushels, and the weight per bushel reaches 50 lbs. The barley generally met with elsewhere in the States is thin, steely, and not so well coloured as that usually grown at home; 800,000 quarters are generally imported to the United Kingdom. Unless in the cooler regions of Canada oats are light; they are mostly consumed at home; not 15,000 quarters are exported to Great Britain. With their American confrères, British stock-owners participate in the benefits of the cheap growth of Indian corn, which now bulks annually 180,000,000 quarters, has more than tripled since 1863, yields on an average 27 bushels an acre, and is raised in the Western and Southern trans-Mississippi States at considerably less than 1*s.* per bushel. It is mainly converted into beef, bacon, and whisky. Its export, although steadily growing, does not yet exceed 7 per cent. of the total growth.

The cheap American lands which furnish diversified grain supplies also produce increasing numbers of cattle, sheep, hogs, and horses. The numbers produced exceed the home necessities. American stockmen have hitherto earned handsome returns: they are generally prosecuting their business with much skill and energy. Without difficulty and in a comparatively short period, they can largely increase their great herds and flocks.

In the Eastern and Middle States, under a system of mixed husbandry, cattle, sheep, hogs, and horses are reared in much the same manner as they are in Great Britain; but even in these older settlements production has not reached its limits. There is still a good deal of waste land and much more imperfectly cultivated. The great dairy State of New York totals one million and a half of milch-cows, the same numbers as are enumerated for Ireland and nearly as many as are returned for all England, and supplies milk, butter, and cheese for the neighbouring industrial population and for export; 828,400 cows are similarly employed in Pennsylvania. Ohio, Illinois, and Iowa return upwards of 700,000 cows each, or together nearly as many as are enumerated in Great Britain. The official returns of the United States give a total of twelve million milch-cows. Of these, probably two millions are in Texas, Nebraska, Nevada, Colorado, and the other Territories where the exact numbers are at present unattainable. Twelve million cows in the favourable surroundings which obtain generally throughout America should soon multiply largely. At present the census further gives 22 million oxen and other cattle; it exhibits an annual increase of one million; it shows most growth throughout the vast cattle-breeding States and Territories along the banks and west of the Missouri, twenty years ago in undisturbed possession of bison, wapiti deer, and antelope. According to the official returns the average value of the cattle of the United States is only 3*l*. 5*s*.

The great cattle- and sheep-raising regions begin 150 miles west of Omaha, the starting-point of the Union Pacific Railroad, 1,400 miles west of the Atlantic. They extend west through Nebraska and Wyoming over the fertile Laramie plains to the Rocky Mountains, and a thousand miles on towards the Pacific, through Utah, Oregon, and Washington Territories, where there is ample room for more than five times the live stock now raised. Starting from the warm shores of the Gulf of Mexico, the great American grazing grounds run 1,500 miles north, over the international boundary line into Canada. They include large portions of Texas, which musters $5\frac{1}{2}$ million of cattle; Colorado, with 30 million acres adapted for the growth of grain, cattle, or sheep; Wyoming, estimated to contain 55,000 square miles of grazing; Montana, larger than the British Islands, and half of it understood to consist of fertile valleys and grass-covered plains, much of it unsurveyed and unoccupied. Throughout the well-watered river valleys and green plains of this enormous area cattle and sheep have extended irregularly and sparsely during the last twenty years, gradually displacing the wild herbivora. Since 1860 it is stated that 15 million bison have been killed, and a proportionate number of deer and antelope.

Over such a wide area the management is somewhat diversified; the herds vary from less than 1,000 to more than 50,000 head. They occupy the higher grounds in summer, the lower and more sheltered in winter. Everywhere they are reared and fed at a *minimum* of expense and trouble. The cattle are offshoots from another herd, or bought often as yearlings or two-year olds from Texas or Oregon, and are driven to any unoccupied valleys or plains, of which plenty still remain. On the principle that possession is nine points of the law, by threats, or occasionally by small payments, cattle masters already in possession of desirable ranges warn off new comers. But the State or Territorial authorities are not consulted regarding the grazing of their lands. A promising locality is chosen, well watered, with some sheltered spots for winter, at a respectful distance from previous settlers. Huts, a few sheds, and corrals are run up. Each herdsman or shepherd receives $28 to $32 per month, with lodgings and rations, and takes charge of about 1,000 animals. The ordinary work consists in riding through plains, parks, and valleys, to see that food and water are sufficient, hunting up stragglers, and on some runs providing salt.

The arduous work connected with the cattle ranche recurs twice a year, when masters and men, well mounted, 'round up' for miles all the cattle they find, drive them into convenient natural gorges or corrals, brand the young ones and all that are unmarked, separate and forward strays from neighbouring ranches which are marked, and select animals for killing or sale. For the best managed runs, numbers of well-descended, usually pure-bred shorthorn or Hereford, bulls are purchased from Kentucky, the Middle or Eastern States, at prices varying from $80 to $200. By selection of good sires and dams, by weeding out the narrow, thriftless scallowags, great improvement has of late years been made even among the Texan cattle.

The natural grasses vary somewhat in different regions. In Texas, scorched with an almost tropical sun, they are bunched, dry, and often coarse; in Northeastern Colorado a great deal of blue joint grass is met with; in the cooler regions of Wyoming and Montana, whence some of the best cattle are now brought, there occurs a more uniform, English-like carpeting of mixed grasses, which start in April and soon attain a height of 12 or 18 inches. The animals are never housed; the winter is seldom severe; even in many parts of Montana the cold season is tempered by the warm Japan current which comes over the Rocky Mountains; snow does not fall so heavily or lie so deeply as it does nearer the Atlantic. Excepting in northerly localities or at high altitudes, little provision is made for winter feeding; the luxuriant grass, uncropped, dries where it stands and leaves a natural, well-preserved, nutritive hay, from which the cattle scrape the light covering of snow.

During spring and summer, from Texas, through

the Indian reservation, thousands of cattle are driven northwards; the yearlings are sold at $7 or $8; the two- and three-year-olds at $12 to $16; the cows reach as high as $20. From Oregon increasing numbers of compact and shapely beasts, many of them still three and four years old, and a better stamp than the Texans, are driven eastward over the Rocky Mountains and grazed for a year in Wyoming, N.E. Colorado, and Nebraska.

The profits of a well-managed station are large, sometimes reaching 20 per cent. on the invested capital. Of rent and taxes there are none except the head-tax, which in various territories is 5 cents each for two-year-olds and 7 cents for three-year-olds and other cattle. Yearlings are untaxed. There is understood to be considerable latitude in making these returns, and there are no surveyors of taxes to institute impertinent inquiries. The money thus collected is chiefly employed in building and maintaining law courts and carrying out the administration of justice. The expenses of small herds of 1,000 head average $1.50 annually for each beast, but for larger herds, numbering 10,000 and upwards, they do not exceed $1. The losses from deaths, straying, and plundering by the Indians and unscrupulous neighbours, which in many localities is the chief cause of loss, are stated to range from 2 to 4 per cent. In exceptionally severe winters such as that of 1880-81, when in many districts the snow lay thickly on park and plain for upwards of three months, the losses were greatly more serious. On many larger ranches the principal stockmen are allowed a percentage on profits. Eastern capitalists are often shareholders in these western ranches. To men of known steadiness and judgment desirous of extending their business the banks often grant advances, frequently at the rate of 2 per cent. per month, and enterprises, even when thus weighted, earn, I am assured, good profits.

During summer and autumn, from their western pastures, two-, three-, and even four-year-old cattle, generally in good condition, some of them fat, are steadily driven, grazing by the way, to some depôt on the great trunk lines which pass eastward. At various stations along the Union and Northern Pacific Railroads 1,000 cattle are now loaded between June and the end of October. About 20 fill one of the covered cars. One or two stations make up a train which travels express, usually stopping every 12 or 15 hours for feeding and watering the animals, and allowing them 10 or 12 hours' rest. They are chiefly consigned to Chicago, Kansas City, St. Louis, or to Atlantic ports. On the ranches or at the Western Railway stations, the best are purchased at $1\frac{1}{2}d.$ to $2d.$ per lb. live weight. As is general throughout America, cattle, sheep, and hogs, whether fat or stores, are bought by weight, usually alive, or on the hoof, as it is termed. At every farm, every market, and every loading depôt are Fairbank's scales, on which one, twenty, or even forty animals can be weighed. The seller usually endeavours to have the weighing effected immediately after his animals have been fed and watered; the buyer manœuvres to scale them when just unloaded, hungry, and thirsty.

Thousands of the best two- and three-year-old cattle from the western grazings are every autumn distributed over the great Indian-corn regions of Illinois, Wisconsin, Iowa, Minnesota, and Missouri, where in large yards, containing 60 to 100 beasts—on corn costing about 1*s.* per bushel, on oats about the same value, with bran at 20*s.* and hay at 10*s.* per ton—they are cheaply fed. Big bullocks, fairly started, eat half a bushel of grain daily. They are bought at 1,100 lbs. to 1,200 lbs. at about 1½*d.* per lb. live weight; pigs are economically run in the yards along with the cattle, which go out fat in the later winter and spring months weighing 1,400 lbs. to 1,600 lbs., and bringing 2*d.* to 2½*d.* per lb. gross. Frequently the smaller farmers take in a yardful of cattle, feeding them on corn and hay, furnishing also some bran and salt, and receiving about 1*d.* for every lb. of increased weight when in spring the stock are scaled out. Consigned to the eastern markets, these corn-fed cattle yield 56 lbs. to 60 lbs. of beef for every 100 lbs. of live weight. Such carcasses, usually weighing 700 lbs. to 800 lbs., to the number of about 6,000 are now forwarded every week to British markets.

From June until November an important and rapidly-growing department of the cattle trade—the salting and canning business—is in active operation. From Texas, Colorado, and other States, thousands of three- and four-year-olds are forwarded to Chicago, Kansas City, St. Louis, Philadelphia, and New York. They cost 1½*d.* to 2*d.* per lb. live weight, which reaches 800 lbs. to 1,200 lbs. They are sound and healthy although sometimes rough and not over-encumbered with fat. In some of the larger establishments upwards of 1,000 cattle are slaughtered daily, and carefully and systematically disposed of.

The clean and careful manner in which the wholesome meat is handled and put up, justifies the belief that the prejudice with which American tinned meats are still sometimes regarded must speedily disappear. Careful, systematic arrangements are adopted to make the best of the so-called waste products, and the large scale on which slaughtering is conducted, and the concentration of the *abattoirs*, enable this to be more economically and effectually done than in England. Cheap rail, lake, and ocean transit secures the transmission of these valuable concentrated meats from the American manufactory to Great Britain at a cost of less than $\frac{1}{2}d.$ per lb. Through agents in Europe the goods are placed very directly, and without repeated commissions, in the hands of the consumers. So great is now the demand for this concentrated nourishing food that during one week in the spring of 1880 in London alone 150,000 cases, each containing 84 lb. of beef, were disposed of at 37s. 6d. per case. When the Texas and coarser, commoner cattle of America are graded up, which, however, will obviously take some time to accomplish, it has been urged that the advanced prices obtained for superior cattle will interfere with the packing trade. Improved stock are, however, scarcely more costly than the commoner sorts to breed, and are certainly more cheaply and quickly reared and fed, and for many years large supplies of beef must continue to be available at much the same prices as are now current.

The transit of the cattle from the great breeding and feeding regions to the Eastern markets or to Europe is very moderate. For example, from Cheyenne, in Western Nebraska, now a great centre, whence cattle are brought for several hundred miles, the railroad rate per head, 1,000 miles to Chicago, is 28*s*. From Chicago, 900 miles to New York, the rate is 16*s*. Feeding and superintendence in transit including 2*s*. per head for commissions for selling in any of the large stockyards, is defrayed by 8*s*. Transporting these western beeves to Great Britain, their passage to Liverpool during 1879 cost 4*l*. The best companies during 1880 slightly raised their freights; 25*s*. is besides expended for food and attendance during the voyage, insurance averages 6 per cent., and, with incidentals, brings up the cost to 30*s*. a head.

Endeavouring to reduce these transport and other charges, some shippers have recourse to cheaper and less trustworthy vessels, and hence arise frequently recurring mishaps and losses. Some trust to inefficient attendants, or sail with insufficient food supplies for their hungry cargo. The total charges of transport of a beast, say from North-eastern Colorado, Wyoming, or Montana, over 2,000 miles of land and 3,000 of ocean, and landing him in Great Britain, thus amount to 8*l*. or 10*l*. Presuming that he weighs 1,200 lbs., this will be about 2*d*. per lb. on his gross weight, or 4*d*. on his carcass of beef.

Rates to London are a little higher than to Liverpool; during the last eighteen months, they have been 4*l*. 10*s*. Ocean steamers unfortunately have not water to land their cargoes either at Deptford or Thames Haven. Accordingly, lying off Gravesend their freight is trans-shipped into steamers specially constructed for the trade, and at a cost of 3*s*. per head the United States animals are transferred to the lairs at Deptford, where on landing they undergo veterinary inspection. They must be slaughtered within fourteen days of arrival. Their lairage during this or any less period is 5*s*. for each beast, 2*s*. for each calf, 1*s*. for each pig, 9*d*. for each sheep. The charges for feeding per day are 1*s*. 6*d*. for each beast, 1*s*. for each calf, 6*d*. for each pig, 3*d*. for each sheep. The slaughtering charges are moderate; including the use of hot water and appliances, they are, 2*s*. for beasts, 1*s*. for calves, 6*d*. for pigs, 4*d*. for sheep. Meat slaughtered at Deptford is thence carted to the Metropolitan Market at a cost of 10*s*. to 12*s*. 6*d*. per ton. Here as well as in connection with the slaughterhouses for home-grown stock, at the Metropolitan and other large markets cold storage chambers, which are so universal in America, would secure better preservation of the meat.

Canadian live stock, amongst which contagious disease has never been discovered when consigned to London, are sometimes carried in the ocean steamers direct to the Victoria Docks. More frequently, at Gravesend they are trans-shipped into the river steamers and landed at Thames Haven, inspected, and may be forwarded alive to the Metropolitan or provincial markets. Imported Canadian store cattle and sheep have occasionally been purchased by British farmers, but even when well kept have seldom thriven or paid satisfactorily.

This is not very encouraging to those who propose, when the States show a clean bill of health, to import American store cattle to be finished off in England. The business has obvious drawbacks; it would be irregular, the demand probably uncertain; the cattle can only be brought over safely in the best of vessels and under careful, experienced supervision; even if well selected, all would not take kindly to their altered dietary and management. The transit charges on lean stock would not be much less than those on fat stock; they would obviously bear a greater proportion to the value of the low-priced store than to the higher-priced fat beast. The food to prepare the animal for the butcher costs besides more than double the price in England which it does in America. The transit of the living beast is moreover double that of the meat in carcass. Such considerations must limit the importation of American lean stock, which certainly would not be required if British and Irish cattle-breeders generally devoted themselves, as they must do, to the rearing of larger numbers of profitable young stock. Nor should there be much difficulty in developing British agricultural capabilities in this direction, inasmuch as breeding has for years admittedly paid better than feeding.

American flocks have not generally received so

much attention as the herds. Sheep require for their successful management more care and skill than cattle. Until recently they have been cultivated more for wool than for mutton. The $40\frac{1}{2}$ million sheep of the States are now not only increasing at the rate of a million annually, but are steadily improving in weight and quality both of wool and mutton. Hitherto they have not averaged much more than half the weight of British sheep: they have not clipped much more than two-thirds of the wool. The little, narrow, coarse-woolled Mexican sheep, not weighing alive, even when three years old, more than 70 lbs. or 80 lbs., and clipping 3 lbs. to 4 lbs. of rough wool, until the beginning of the century were the indigenous and only sheep of America. Beef and pork being the animal food hitherto preferred throughout the States, the mutton-producing capabilities of the flocks have been almost entirely ignored, and the lean, poor scrubs usually killed and cooked certainly have not encouraged the taste for mutton. The first substantial improvement was the introduction, early in the century, of Spanish and French Merinoes, which speedily raised the weight and value of the wool, which gradually became finer and softer, adapted for superior clothing fabrics, and for combing purposes. More recently, as in England, the demand for worsted wools has favoured the crossing alike of Mexican and Merino grades with Leicesters, long-wools, and Downs. To use the American phrase, this has more rapidly 'muttonised' the flocks. Such crossing is widely adopted in the Eastern and Middle States, where mixed husbandry prevails, and where, moreover, there is greater demand for good mutton. Hitherto instead of being dearer, mutton in America has been 25 per cent. cheaper than beef; legs and loins have ranked with the fore-quarters and second-rate parts of the ox. Like other enterprises, crossing the indigenous thriftless native sheep with superior imported rams is proceeding west. In Minnesota and Western Kansas I saw capital Leicesters, Oxfords, and other Downs. In the pastoral districts of North-western Colorado Shrops and Oxfords are largely introduced. Weight, quality, and surplus supplies of mutton are thus created and increased.

In Great Britain, notwithstanding recent losses, there are still forty sheep on every 100 acres, or three sheep on every four acres of cultivated land, excluding heath and mountain. In the United States there is but one sheep on 34 acres. An enormous area is nevertheless adapted for sheep husbandry. In many regions where it has been tried it has answered admirably. Proving profitable it promises to extend, furnishing still more food for the American people, sparing still larger supplies for exportation, growing the wool wanted in the many manufactories extending in most States and in some of the Territories.

American sheep management is of many different types. In New York, New Jersey, and Eastern Pennsylvania, flying flocks are often kept, bought in during autumn, and fed out during winter and spring. Merino grade ewes from Ohio and farther west are sometimes purchased during autumn at 13s. to 25s., for

Flocks of the Middle States. 451

raising early lambs. Frequently they are placed with Down or Cotswold rams. Mated with Merinoes, they produce a slower-growing lamb, which does not bring so much money. They are well kept on hay and Indian corn, not many roots are grown or can be spared. A few lambs are dropped in February, but in this keen, cold climate they require housing, with a good deal of care, and even at 1*s*. to 1*s*. 3*d*. per lb. they scarcely pay. Most of the lambs fall in March and April. Mother and offspring, besides hay and corn, have a few oats and bran. The lambs looking as big as their dams, averaging 90 lbs. to 110 lbs. live weight, are turned off in May and June at 20*s*. to 35*s*. The ewes, leaving a fleece of 5 lbs., worth 1*s*. per lb., shortly follow, usually making 50 per cent. more than the price at which they were bought in. With cheap provender, and allowing nothing for the manure left, 20*s*. to 30*s*. is earned for ten months' keep. Several farmers engaged in this trade assure me that they make 200 per cent. gross return on the original cost of the ewes, and that half this is clear profit.

In the Northern and Middle States many more sheep might be profitably reared and fed, paying fully as well as dairying or cattle-feeding, and raising moreover, the fertility of the soil, exhausted by years of continuous corn-growing, without any restitution of plant food. Flockmasters constantly volunteer the statement that their crops have doubled in weight since they kept sheep; but the system of recuperative sheep-farming, perhaps from insufficient capital and want of labour to provide suitable attendance and fodder crops, is not yet fully carried out on these arable farms. At no season are sheep penned in hurdles over the land as they are in many corn-growing districts in England. Ohio has about one-tenth of the sheep of the United States, or about one sheep for every six acres; but even in Ohio the flocks generally might be improved; better provision of successive crops upon the arable land might secure more continuous thriving, and a better yield might be obtained both of mutton and wool. The undulating, well-watered limestone soils of Kentucky are as well adapted for sheep as for cattle. They grow and feed mutton as good as is to be obtained in England. At New York and Boston, Kentucky sheep realise 1*d.* per lb. more than the poorer sorts reared under less favourable circumstances. A special breed of wide, shapely, useful-coated sheep, at twenty months readily weighing 130 lbs. to 150 lbs. gross, and possessed of considerable fixity of type, has been raised in Kentucky by crossing native ewes with Merinoes, and subsequently with English Leicesters, Downs, and Cotswolds. By such judicious selection of the ewes of the locality, and by careful crossing, the profitableness of the sheep stock generally might be much improved.

Between the Mississippi and the Missouri throughout many parts of Minnesota and Iowa are capital sheep grazings on the natural prairie, in open parks, amongst the woodlands, and on the readily grown artificial grasses and clovers. The climate is dry; there is no necessity for yarding the flocks for more than a few weeks during snow, or specially severe weather, nor is there much cost for providing winter food. Prairie hay costs 10s. per ton ; bran, 25s. a ton ; and Indian corn 1s. a bushel.

Between the Missouri and the Pacific, from Mexico to the British Dominions, and beyond, is an area of a million and a half square miles, not including Alaska, many parts of which are eminently suitable for sheep husbandry. On the Laramie plains of the Rocky Mountains, at an elevation of 6,000 to 7,000 feet, are fresh and abundant pastures, often well watered. Wyoming and Northern Colorado are specially well adapted for sheep-raising. In some of the higher elevations, where the better cattle do not care to range, there is fair herbage for sheep. With the native Mexican and grade Merino ewes American Merino or English-bred bucks are run. The latter are preferred where the sheep are to be disposed of for mutton. Hay is provided for occasional deep snow, or continued hard frost, which may be expected during two or three months. In some districts yards are prepared for protection against sudden storms. Sheep walks can be rented at two or three cents an acre, bought at 50 cents, and sometimes grazed without any charge whatever. The taxes of the state or territory range from three to five cents per head on the number of sheep returned over one year old. Twenty to thirty cents per sheep is estimated to provide for all expenses. A shepherd receiving 30 dollars, or 6*l.* per month, with rations, and the use of a couple of horses, aided by his dogs, attends to 1,000, and occasionally 2,500 sheep. The other expenses of the station consist mainly of hay-cutting, salt, and shearing, much of which is done by travelling hands, paid 14*s.* to 16*s.* per hundred. Washing now generally precedes shearing, 5 lbs. to 6 lbs. of wool is got, and is expected to pay for the twelve months' expenses, leaving as profit the increase of the flock and sales. Smaller flocks well looked after have generally paid better than large ones. One hundred ewes produce 80 to 90 lambs; the three-year-old sheep weighing 100 lbs. to 120 lbs. gross are worth three dollars to five dollars. Mr. Post, of Cheyenne, informs me that the yearly cost of keeping sheep on the Plate River ranges from 30 cents to 50 cents. So satisfied is he with recent results that on his own behalf and that of his firm he is steadily increasing his stock.

The sixteen Southern States embraced in the wide area between Delaware and Missouri, between Ohio and the Gulf of Mexico, including about one-fourth of the national domain, have large areas thoroughly adapted for sheep-raising. In the South, sheep have seldom, however, received the attention they deserve. Over these four hundred million acres the flocks amount only to ten millions; they are usually divided into small lots, are generally unimproved natives, receive little or no care, are often greatly injured by drought, storms, starvation in winter, and attacks of dogs. The moderate estimate of official reports collected for the senate, indicate that over this Southern area 150,000,000 sheep might be carried in spring and summer, and more than one-third of these numbers during the mild short winter. Even in the dead time of year this fertile region, it is believed, would keep twice the total number of sheep enumerated in the United States. The main cost is attendance for marking and shearing, salt, and a little hay, to which some good managers add a small allowance of cotton seed. The annual cost per head is variously estimated at 15 to 25 cents. The profits are said to range from 30 to 40 per cent. on the capital invested. The waste of unpastured grass in these regions is very great. Agricultural enterprise is not so great as farther north or west, and wide areas of good grazing lie unused. The grass frequently is burnt by accident or design. Sheep might with good profit be greatly multiplied. The cost of growing 1 lb. of wool in Georgia is stated to be six cents, whilst cotton costing four times the amount of labour cannot be produced for less than 7d. per lb. Throughout these Southern States, about one thousand establishments are engaged in making woollen goods, and using up annually ten million pounds of wool, for which the demand is steadily growing. In the States bordering the Mexican Gulf, the climate appears to be less adapted for English crossed sheep, and the best authorities prefer to run with the native Mexican ewes, bucks one-half to one-fourth Merino.

Although his grazings are cheaply stocked and his flock cheaply kept, the American sheep-breeder labours under certain disadvantages, and has expenses and losses from which his English rival is exempt. In most Northern States the sheep require to be housed and fed, and of course demand extra attention. In the Southern States housing is unnecessary, plantations, unused sheds, or tobacco houses afford the occasional shelter needed. During two or three months fitful feeding with cheap hay is needful. Winter and summer, in the yards and on the plains and prairies, it is important to supply all sheep with salt. Although the herbage is fresh and succulent, and during spring and early summer the sheep have abundance of capital food, in some regions and in some seasons drought proves most disastrous. Sheep do with somewhat less water than cattle: owing, however, to continued scarcity of water a wide expanse of such plains as those in North-west Texas prove uncertain and of low value for sheep-walks. During the summer of 1880 in Texas, Western Kansas, and other Territories, losses both of sheep and cattle from want of water have been serious. The percentage of lambs on which the American flockmaster can count is smaller than with us. The British shepherd is culpable, or the season untoward, in which a lamb is not secured for every ewe, whilst amongst Down flocks greater returns are obtained. Merinos in the North and Eastern States seldom produce their first lamb until they are three years old.

Storms, winter snows, thefts, and disease also cause heavy losses amongst ewes and, indeed, amongst all sheep. From disowning, exposure, and attacks of dogs and wolves many lambs are lost. From these preventible causes the Texan sheep-master estimates his losses at 15 per cent. Even in an old State like Delaware they reach 19 per cent., and in Kentucky, Alabama, and Missouri they exceed 21 per cent. About one-half this serious loss is ascribed to prowling dogs, which in Georgia, Mississippi, and other States are numerous, starved, and untaxed, causing a loss of 9 per cent. in Kentucky and Texas, and 8 per cent. in the Carolinas and Georgia. American farmers must be even more long-suffering than those at home to stand such preventible wholesale slaughter. Expanding settlement, the destruction of prairie wolves and roaming dogs, and closer attention to the flock will greatly lessen these losses. Provision of winter food, besides being of benefit in this way, is also enhancing the value of the mutton and wool. Judicious crossing is further greatly improving the flocks and increasing both the weight and quality of the mutton, while washing is adding to the value of the wool, which for many years will all be required in the growing manufactures of the States, which now use up nearly three times the quantity which they produce.

The hogs of the United States muster 35,000,000, or nine times the number enumerated in the United Kingdom. The abundance of the Indian corn crops of the past few years has stimulated their production at the rate of one million and a half per annum. They quickly convert the corn and oats, worth about 1*s.* per bushel, and grass, clover, and other cheap, bulky, unsaleable vegetable food, into the saleable animal which readily runs to market. The state of Illinois makes a muster of 3,330,000 pigs; Iowa and

Missouri each have nearly 3,000,000; Indiana and Kentucky each contribute 2,000,000. Berkshire and Fisher Hobbs, Essex, large and middle-sized whites, and a useful China hog are reared. All are well-grown and profitable. I did not see a thriftless pig while in America. Abundance of room and exercise, with varied food while growing, develop size and more lean meat than is exhibited among our more artificially managed, closely confined grunters. As at home, the contagious fatal hog cholera occasionally occurs, spreading from the great markets to the premises of breeders and feeders, and sometimes causing great losses. The average value of the American hogs set forth in the agricultural statistics is only 16s.; but in Colorado and other Territories they reach 30s., and in Massachusetts amount to 45s. 9d. Although of small individual value, the American farmers' capital in hogs represents a total aggregate of 22,000,000l.! In summer on grass and clover, finished off with corn in winter among the cattle in the yards, these hogs are cheaply reared and fed. They are sold at ages varying from 6 to 18 months, at weights ranging from 100 lbs. to 300 lbs. The heaviest are brought out in winter; the cheaper summer-fed sometimes fall as low as $1\frac{1}{2}d.$ per lb. gross weight. But so small is the outlay in their upbringing that even at this low figure some profit is earned.

A few hogs are slaughtered and salted by the farmers, but the great bulk pass to the packers. This is one of the special and prosperous industries of the States, commenced with small beginnings some 25 years ago, and rapidly growing with the greatly increasing demands for exportation, which now absorbs 60 per cent. of the American hog products. Until within recent years, much of the bacon and pork was salted and packed in barrels, but now it is chiefly distributed throughout the States in bulk and in boxes; throughout Europe entirely in boxes. Formerly hog slaughtering was conducted only during the winter months. Now, with abundant supplies of cheap ice, about 5,000,000 hogs are slaughtered, or nearly half the packing is overtaken, during the summer season from March 1 to November 1, when vegetable food is abundant and the pigs can be quickly and cheaply fatted. Excepting in price, American bacon cannot compare with the best Irish, Wiltshire, or Yorkshire, but it is steadily improving. Were the hogs finished off as they might be with a daily meal of barley, instead of all corn, the bacon would doubtless be firmer and less liable to shrink when cooked. It is not so fat as good English or Irish bacon; it is better boiled than grilled; when grilled it is apt to waste, and some of it also emits a peculiar flavour.

The subjoined table from the Reports of the Commissioner of Agriculture exhibits the number of hogs packed in the three great divisions of the United States during each of the three years 1876 to 1879, ending with March 1 each year :—

	1877	1878	1879
The West	7,409,174	9,048,566	10,858,692
The East	2,551,239	2,703,670	3,222,011
The Pacific Slope	305,000	310,000	400,000
	10,265,413	12,062,236	14,480,703

Canada packs about 200,000 hogs. The total annual hog products turned out by packers throughout the States now exceed 25,000,000 cwts., and are increasing yearly at the rate of about 17 per cent. The average weight of the pigs killed in 1878–79 was 217·14 lbs.; their average cost, net weight, per cental $3.56, or 50 cents less than the average price for the previous year, and only a little over half the price of 1876–77. Tempted by such low prices, packers have everywhere enlarged their business. At many convenient points throughout the West new establishments have been opened. Stocks of bacon and pork during the earlier parts of 1879 accumulated to the extent, it was estimated, of 100,000,000*l*. It seemed as if the supply had outrun the demand. The good harvest in the West increased, however, the home demand for hog products, as for so many other things; the export demand also increased; prices advanced; and surplus stocks have been cleared off, the United Kingdom paying for her year's supplies upwards of 10,000,000*l*.

These great herds and flocks are year by year multiplying largely, and outgrowing the home demand, but the British public willingly receive the surplus. The cattle, sheep, and swine are exported dead and alive. The following figures from the annual report of the Veterinary Department testify how the export of live stock, both from the United States and from Canada, have increased since its commencement in 1876.

United States Exports of Live Stock.

	Cattle	Sheep	Swine
1876	392	—	—
1877	11,538	13,120	226
1878	68,450	43,940	16,321
1879	76,117	119,350	15,180
1880	154,814	66,722	12,549

Canada Exports of Live Stock.

	Cattle	Sheep	Swine
1876	2,557	1,862	—
1877	7,649	10,275	584
1878	17,989	40,132	1,614
1879	25,185	73,913	3,663
1880	48,103	78,074	671

The proportion which these live-stock imports from the States and from Canada bear to the total from all sources, may be gathered from the following table compiled from the Board of Trade returns, showing the total cattle, sheep, and swine imported into the United Kingdom in 1880. To discover the amount of butcher's meat which they contribute, I take the figures carefully prepared by Mr. Clare S. Read and Mr. James Howard, M.P., namely, 46 imperial stones (14 lbs.) as the weight of each imported ox, 40 stones as the weight of each cow, 4 stones as the average of each sheep and lamb, and 7 stones as that of each calf and pig.

	Number	Imperial stones	Imperial stones
Oxen and bulls	317,505	46	14,605,230
Cows	33,445	40	1,337,800
Calves	38,999	7	272,993
Sheep and lambs	940,991	4	3,763,964
Swine	51,030	7	357,210
			20,337,197

Excluding cows and calves, in which America does not compete, the States and Canada together now furnish upwards of 60 per cent. of the live-cattle imports of Great Britain. The American cattle imports of 1880 are double those of 1879. The sheep imports amount to one-fifth of the European contingent. The swine which, owing to two years' low range of prices in the States, have not been so largely bred or fed, during 1880 were only two-thirds of the imports of 1879, but nevertheless constitute one-third of the European consignments. These increased American supplies more than compensate for the falling off which, owing to the prevalence of contagious disorders, has occurred of late years in the live-stock importations from Belgium, the Netherlands, France, and other parts of Europe.

The destination of these American live-stock imports is set forth in the annual reports of the Veterinary Department. London and Liverpool each take about three-sevenths of the cattle and sheep, but Liverpool attracts five-sixths of the pigs; 9,182 cattle and 12,836 sheep, in 1880, were sent to Bristol; 1,591 cattle to Southampton, but only 173 sheep; 3,107 cattle went round to Hull; 9,000 cattle from the States and 14,672 from Canada were landed at Glasgow.

These valuable importations have steadily grown in spite, not only of enhanced transport charges, but in the face of compulsory slaughter at the ports within fourteen days of landing. These restrictions have been applied to cattle since March 3, 1879; to sheep, since November 23, 1879; to swine, since May 16, 1879. They do not, as was prognosticated, arrest exportation. The surplusage must be got rid of, and it finds its way to the best market. The official reports of the Veterinary Department to the Privy Council abundantly demonstrate the necessity for these restrictions. Of 720 cargoes of live animals imported from the United States in 1880, exactly one in seven contained cases of contagious disorders. The '110 cargoes, consisting of 26,464 cattle, 12,931 sheep, and 5,013 swine, contained 229 cattle affected with pleuro-pneumonia, 21 cattle and 63 sheep affected with foot-and-mouth disease, 124 sheep affected with sheep scab, and 403 swine affected with swine fever.' It has been urged by American shippers that the cattle we get come from the West, where there is no contagious lung complaint, and that although the imported beasts may have colds or other ailments, this serious lung plague cannot be sent amongst their exports. Get it where they may, these American cattle seized at the several ports are undoubtedly affected by the too familiar contagious pleuro-pneumonia, which since 1844 has decimated our herds; and if the animals were transported alive, as some authorities propose, into the markets of our inland towns, there would be serious risk of transferring the disease to home herds. It is hence the interest of British consumers, as well as of producers of beef, that American cattle, until they can show a clean bill of health, should still be slaughtered at the ports of debarkation.

Although the provisions for the accommodation of animals on board ships are improving, in some of the vessels employed in the American trade the fittings, ventilation, and cubic space are still defective. Animals carried on deck in winter are subject to great suffering from cold and storms. Those between decks frequently suffer and sometimes are stifled from want of pure air. The attendants in charge are occasionally incompetent and careless. The food is sometimes of indifferent quality and inadequate in amount. That there is still much room for improvement in the arrangements for the transport of live stock across the Atlantic is palpable from the fact that in 1880, '13,619 animals were thrown overboard, 540 were landed dead, and 389 were so much injured or exhausted that they were killed at the place of landing, making a total number of 14,543 animals which were either lost on the passage or so much injured that it was necessary to slaughter them immediately on landing.' Upwards of one American animal in every hundred is thus sacrificed to weather and faulty shipping arrangements.

The American live cattle, sheep, and swine imported into the United Kingdom in 1880 are valued at upwards of 4,000,000*l*. But this is only part of the American animal food. The fresh and preserved meats together present a similar value. With improved means of refrigeration applied to the American *abattoirs* and storage chambers, the railroad cars, and the ocean steamers, the supplies of carcass-meat are increasing. The risks of spoiling or injury diminish. The consignments have more than doubled within four years; 5,000 carcasses of beef weighing 700 lbs. to 800 lbs. frequently come to hand in a week. The United States forwarded, during 1880, 715,547 cwts. of fresh meat, nearly the same quantity of tinned or preserved meats, and about half that amount of salted beef. At New York and other shipping ports the cattle cost about 3d. per lb. on the hoof, or about 5½d. per lb. when hung up. The chief shippers are Messrs. Sherman and Gillett, of New Jersey City; Mr. Eastman, of New York; Mr. S. W. Allerton, of Chicago, and Messrs. Martin and Fuller, of Philadelphia. After hanging for a few hours, the carcasses for exportation are transferred to a chamber, cooled in summer with ice and salt to the temperature of 34° or 35°, where they remain for one to three days, when they are cut in quarters, rolled in calico, and transferred to the ocean steamer, which usually conveys from 800 to 3,000 quarters. The refrigerating process is now very perfect and trustworthy. The meat, in chambers, surrounded with pipes containing brine chilled with ice and salt, is kept at a uniform temperature of 34° to 38°, and is landed in good condition. Sheep and pigs are usually hung in the spaces among the quarters of beef. Freight from New York to Liverpool, Cardiff, or Glasgow is 32s. per ton; bulk freight to London is 37s. 6d. The most skilful packing cannot, however, hang half a ton of meat in the 40 cubic feet of space allowed for the ton. The freight on each ton of beef accordingly averages about 80s.; 2s. 6d. per ton is charged for dock dues at Liverpool; at London they reach 6s. 2d. Commission is covered by $\frac{1}{8}d$. Meat railed from Liverpool to London costs about $\frac{1}{4}d.$ per lb.

For less than $1d.$ per lb. fresh meat in the carcass is thus conveyed from America to British ports, where it can be sold with a profit at about $6\frac{1}{2}d$. Now that the risks of spoiling in transit are minimised, the American meat supplies are only kept in their present moderate proportions by the sensitiveness of the British markets, which, if glutted by a few extra hundred carcasses, are run down $1d.$ or even $2d.$ per lb. Indeed, repeatedly, in spite of heavier consignments being pushed on to the Lancashire and Yorkshire towns, superior American beef has been sold in Liverpool at $4\frac{1}{2}d.$, and the same thing occurs with the metropolitan markets. The ready glutting of the British meat market, and consequent serious depreciation of value, is the British farmer's best protection. But with American meat available in quantities greatly in excess of the present supply, and imported profitably at about $6\frac{1}{2}d.$ per lb., the British farmer must adapt his arrangements to produce meat at $7\frac{1}{2}d.$ The superior quality of the best home meat, the nearness of markets, the convenience of killing cattle and sheep when needed, will probably always secure for home-grown meat fully $1d.$ per lb. more than can be got for American meat. With the enlarging production of cheap American meat and the certainty and cheapness of its safe transport over the Atlantic, there is, however, small prospect of any enhanced price for British meat. But farmers twenty years ago were able economically to produce both beef and mutton at 7d. per lb. They must endeavour to do so again.

What proportion, it may be inquired, do these expanding supplies of foreign meat now bear to the home production? Owing to the prevalence of contagious and other diseases on British farms, and the general depression of British agriculture, the live stock of the United Kingdom has not increased since 1876. In the Journal of the Royal Agricultural Society of England for 1878, Mr. John Algernon Clarke, analysing the statistical returns of 1876, estimated that the home herds and flocks produced annually 1,147,663 cwts. of meat, or 78½ of the total consumption. While the home growth has remained stationary the foreign has, however, steadily advanced, and the table on page 468 represents the weight and relative proportions of home-grown and of various descriptions of imported meat consumed in Great Britain in 1876 and 1880.

These figures testify to the rapid expansion of foreign competition in beef and bacon. The United Kingdom, so recently as 1876, consumed only 21 per cent. of these foreign supplies; now the consumption has mounted to 30 per cent. Detrimental although such competition has been to the agricultural interests, it has certainly secured the better feeding of the British people, and prevented famine prices of the necessaries of life. Each unit of the population enjoyed in 1876 about 98 lbs. of meat, these enlarged foreign imports in four years have raised this average allowance to 108 lbs.

Weight and relative percentage of home-grown and imported meat used in the United Kingdom in 1876 *and* 1880.

	Meat in cwts. 1876	Meat in cwts. 1880	Per cent. 1876	Per cent. 1880
Cattle, sheep, and swine home grown furnish	22,941,260	22,941,260	78·750	69·490
Cattle sheep and swine imported alive	1,862,760	2,542,150	6·400	7·700
Meat imported fresh	266,111	867,455	·913	2·627
Beef imported salted	243,342	289,422	·835	·877
Preserved Meats imported chiefly in tins	280,859	655,600	·964	1·986
Bacon imported, cwts. 2,809,990 Hams, ditto 349,455 Pork salted, ditto 350,151 Pork fresh, ditto 26,539	3,536,135	5,717,898	12·138	17·320
	29,130,467	33,013,784	100·000	100·000

America has been the bountiful source of a large proportion of these increased supplies. She has more than made up for the restricted exports of various European countries. Since 1876 she has multiplied her live-stock exports seventy-fold; she has tripled her exports of fresh meat; she has more than doubled her consignments of tinned meats; she has added one-third to the bacon, and nearly tripled the exports of hams. The annual exports of lard are valued at 5,500,000*l.*, of butter at 1,000,000*l.*, of cheese at 2,500,000*l.*

Abundant evidence has been adduced in the foregoing pages to show that these surplus supplies of American animal food can be maintained and increased. Beef, mutton, and bacon are being manufactured faster than they can be used by the rapidly multiplying American population. Great areas available for herds and flocks are still unused or used only irregularly or partially. In many regions the annually recurring prairie fires still consume more grass than is eaten by the cattle. On cheap lands in suitable situations meat can be economically raised, and the carcass profitably sold at less than 4*d*. per lb. Extending transport facilities narrow the distance that intervenes between British consumers and Western cattle ranches or Indian corn regions where grain at less than 1*s*. per bushel is grown to feed increasing numbers of bullocks and hogs. The Atlantic connects instead of separating Europe and America. The roll of agricultural producers is continuously and largely augmented by emigration, increased as it recently has been by dull trade and agricultural depression prevailing throughout the Old World, and destined in 1881 to reach nearly half a million of people. With extending and more careful cultivation of grain, and continued multiplication of improving herds and flocks, America demonstrates year by year more distinctly the truth of her proud boast, that her mission is to feed the civilised world.

INDEX.

AGRICULTURAL Colleges, 97, 130, 357
— population, 9, 38
— resources, 9, 11, 18, 234, 434, 437, 454, 464
— Shows, 119, 130, 145, 315
Alexander, A. J., Woodburn, Ky., 411
Alleghany oil regions, 125
Altoona, Pennsylvania, 123
Amber cane sugar, 12, 288, 290
America destined to feed the world, 469
American adaptiveness, 51, 83, 113, 421, 435
— competition, 8, 66, 77, 255
— grain surplus, 266, 435
— hospitality, 279, 324
— lumbering, 269
— prison life, 274
Animals of the farm, 18, 437
Apples, 7, 75, 81, 96, 147
Archbishop Tache, of St. Boniface, 231
Arkansas Valley, 375
Armour & Co., Chicago, 182
— hams, 192
— preserved meats, 195
Artisans' wages, 46, 100, 281, 356, 406
Assessment of land and personalty, 33, 37
Assiniboine River, 223

Avoca, Minn., 313
Ayrshire cattle, 91

BACON, 190, 370, 459
Barden Barden, Minn., 295
Barley, 13, 287, 436
Barnes & Shedding, 88, 250, 361
Beef exportations, 66, 444
— packing, 69, 181, 367, 389
Beer Tax, 287
Benefit Clubs, 281
Bishop Ireland's settlements, 313
Bluffs, 334, 340
Booming the logs, 271
Boston, 87
— fruit supplies, 104
— retail price of meat, 103
— stockyards, 101
Bran, 263, 270
Brawn, or collared head, 194
Bread stuffs, cheap, 26, 170, 210, 234, 265, 433
Breaking up prairie, 204, 334, 337, 359, 424
Buckwheat, 15, 302
Butter, 21, 109, 247, 392

CABBAGES, 80
Canadian exports, 460
— Government attractions, 233
— land, 26, 126

CAN

Canadian Pacific Railroad, 226
Canned meats, 67, 180, 389, 445
Capital, interest on, 28, 43, 50, 87, 118, 251, 337, 365, 372
— used in farming, 41, 337
Cattle, 66, 89, 99, 121, 136, 152, 172, 439
— branding, 173
— canning trade, 67, 180, 389, 444
— markets, 62, 171, 342, 366, 387
— slaughtering, 23, 67, 102, 177, 367
— sold by weight, 63, 174
— stores for export, 448
— transport charges, 64, 173, 343, 371, 445
— winter feeding, 92, 121, 135, 443
Cheese, 21, 99, 468
Chicago, 160
— cattle trade, 172
— grain business, 164
— hog packing, 182
— stockyards, 176
— water supply, 161
Climate, 5, 241, 335, 352
Coal, 3, 234, 347, 353
Cold storage chambers, 61, 176, 179, 189, 390
Coloured population, 363, 405
Competition, American, 8, 66, 265, 421, 435, 437
Cord binders, 303, 318, 425
Corner successful in pork, 196
Cottage accommodation, 46
Cotton, 12, 387
Council Bluffs, 340
— stockyards, 342
Cranberries, 83
Creameries, 8, 335
Crookston, Dakota, 218
Currants, 81

DAIRYING, 8, 50, 88, 99, 109, 136, 247, 391, 399

FAR

Dakota, 199, 322
— Civil Code, 326
— hospitality, 324
— milling enterprises, 325
— wages, 331
Dalrymple, Mr. O., Casselton, Dakota, 199
— cost of wheat growing, 209
— telephonic communication, 200
Deering, Mr. S., Bluffdale, St. Paul, 252
Delaware fruit culture, 81
Detroit agricultural fair, 145
Devon cattle, 117
Donkeys' stud, 396
Drake, Mr. James U., St. Paul, 207, 279
Drought, 47, 363

EASTMAN, I. C., first exporter of meat to Great Britain, 65
Elevators, 55, 167
— Chicago, 167
— New York Central, 56
Entail, laws of, 31
Exports, American, of wheat, 170, 267, 385, 435
— live stock, 66, 460
— meat, 66, 115, 390, 464

FAIRBANKS scales, 58, 63, 186, 443
Fairbault, Minn., 291
Fairmont, Minn., 290
Fargo, Dakota, 213
Farmers, 39, 45, 51
— American and English compared, 51
Farming profits, 23, 114, 118, 133, 138, 254, 307, 337, 338, 427, 442, 450
Farms let on shares, 40, 131, 283, 308, 338, 381
— on lease, 41, 307, 381
— rented, 40, 132, 213, 337

Index. 473

FAR

Farms, size of, 49, 131, 379
— worked by contract, 215, 337, 356
Fences, 100, 131, 204, 379
Fertilisers, 69, 101, 370
Fishing, 269
Flax cultivation, 287, 302, 360
Flour, cost of production, 202, 436
— Hungarian or patent, 259
— Minneapolis mills, 256
— trade, 257, 270, 286, 436
Fort Garry, Manitoba, 224
Fruit canning, 76
— cultivation, 7, 74
— export, 77
— transport, 75

GAME laws, Minnesota, 249
— Ohio, 129
Grain, cheap movement of, 52
— elevators, 55, 167
— grading of, 53
— transport, 53, 55, 210, 428
— weighed automatically, 58
Grapes, 83, 147

HAMILTON, MESSRS., Mount Stirling, Ky., 409
Hams, preparation of, 192, 369
Harrisburg, Pennsylvania, 122
Harvesters, 207, 303, 318, 425
Hay, 14, 90, 242
Hayes City, Kansas, 358
Herd law, 42, 130
Herds, enumeration of, 19, 438
Herefords, 155, 172, 289, 373
Heron Lake Junction, 310
Hessian fly, 48
Hickory, J. M., Washington Co., Penn., 115
Hog packing, 139, 186, 438, 459
— — at Chicago, 182
— — Kansas City, 368
— — St. Louis, 390
Hogs, 22, 93, 139, 180, 389, 457
Homestead acts, 32, 326, 362
Homesteaders, 33, 300, 326

LAM

Hops unprofitable, 96
Horses, 18, 100, 150, 400
— transport of, 400
Hudson's Bay Company, 224

ILLINOIS wheat-growing, 170
Indian corn, 12, 134, 242, 318, 437
Indians, 223, 248
Interest, rate of, 43, 133, 329, 365, 372
Investments, promising, 43, 311
Iowa, climate, 335
— dairying, 335
— labour abounds, 337
— prairies, 334
— share farming, 338

JASPER at Sioux Falls, 325
Jersey cattle, 91

KANSAS, 351
— climate, 352
— cost of living, 371
— farming, 355
— railroads, 364
Kansas City, 363
— stockyards, 366
Kentucky, 397
— blue grass, 401
— horses, 400, 416
— shorthorns, 398, 409, 415
— sheep, 399, 413, 451
— taxes, 405
— whisky, 420
Kildonan, near Winnipeg, 227
Kingsley, J. E., Philadelphia, 111

LABOUR-SAVING machinery, 60, 188, 277
Labourers' wages, 45, 143, 202, 229, 316, 331, 379, 413
Labourers well fed, 46, 201, 317
Lambs, 142, 156, 450

LAN

Land, acquisition of, 25, 31, 326
— cost of, 31, 42, 87, 200, 246, 209, 311, 329, 336
— enhanced value, 28, 112, 157, 213, 230, 250, 311, 320, 336
— exhaustion of, 44
— laws, 25, 326
— offices, 29
— owners, 38, 337
— pre-emption of, 31, 327, 362
— railroad, 29, 373
— school, 29, 373
— unoccupied, 9, 25, 27, 39, 312
— worked by hire, 215, 331, 337
— worked on shares, 308, 329, 338
Landlords in America, 27, 29
— — England, 27
Lard, manufacture of, 194, 370
Largest wheat farm in America, 199
Libby, McNeil, and Libby, Chicago, 178
Licenses, 36
Lincoln, Nebraska, 347
Linseed cultivation, 287, 302, 360
Live stock exports, 66, 461
Locusts, 48
Lumbering, 270
Lunatic asylum, St. Peter, 283
Luverne farm, Minn., 315

MAINE, 97
— dairying, 99
— fences, 100
— portable manures, 101
— wages, 100
Maize, 12, 134, 242, 318, 437
Manitoba, 222
— cheap land, 232
— needs transport facilities, 233
Mankato, brewery, 287
— flour mills, 285
— Minn., 284
Manures, portable, 67, 101, 320, 370

NEW

Market gardening, 51, 78, 95, 109, 246
Massachusetts, 89
— live stock, 92
— vegetable and fruit growing, 94
Meat exports, 66, 115, 464
— prices, 66, 71, 106, 115, 371
— proportion of home grown and foreign in United Kingdom, 467
— transport charges, 115, 390, 465
Megibben, Hon. T. J., Fairview, Ky., 419
Mennonite Settlements, 228, 361
Michigan Agricultural Show, 145
— fruit growing, 147
Milk, 90, 109, 392
— cows, 20, 90, 98, 137, 247
Millet, 91, 359
Milling enterprises, 257, 270, 285, 325, 436
— cost of American, 262, 286
Mineral wealth, 3, 123
Minneapolis, 239
— mills, 255
Minnesota, 236
— cattle rearing, 243
— climate, 241
— crops, 242
— railways, 245
— settlement, 245
— State university, 237
— value of land, 246, 282
Missouri dairying, 391
— mules, 392
— Valley, 340, 347, 378
Money lending, 329
Mortgages, 328, 329
Mountain chains, 2
Mules, 392
— preferred to horses, 205, 317
Mutton, 69, 450

NEW England States, 85
— Jersey fruit growing, 79
— vegetables, 80, 107

NEW

New York cold storage chambers, 68
— grain trade, 56
— meat supplies, 61
— oleomargarine, 72
— retail markets, 71
— stockyards, 64
— vegetables, 78

OATS, 13, 437
 Offal, preservation of, 68, 178, 188
Ohio State, 127
— cattle, 136
— draining, 130
— farming, 133
— hogs, 139
— sheep, 140
— statistics, 128
Oleomargarine, 71, 178
— butter, 73
Omaha, Nebraska, 341
Oranges from Florida, 74
Oregon cattle, 172, 441

PEACHES, 75, 81
 Pears, 75, 81, 147
Penitentiary at Stillwater, 274
Pennsylvania Central Railroad, 105
— dairying, 110, 120
— farming, 108
— land, free from taxes, 113
Petroleum oil, 125
Philadelphia Exhibition, 119
— market gardening
— stockyards, 114
Physical Geography, 1
Pigs, 22, 93, 139, 180, 457
Pillsbury's, Messrs., mill, Minneapolis, 257
Pipestone quarries, Dakota, 310
Pittsburgh, Pennsylvania, 125
Plankington & Armour, Kansas City, 366
Ploughing, cost of, 299, 305
Ploughs, 149, 303, 316
Potatoes, 13, 79

SHE

Prairie, 197, 204, 216, 240, 332
— breaking up, 204, 334, 337, 359
— fires, 240
Pre-emption of land, 327, 362
Prison industries, 276
Profits from farming, 50, 111, 118, 139, 306, 442

QUEEN Bee Mill, Sioux Falls, 325

RAILROADS, 54, 105, 245, 312, 377
Rainfall, 5, 6, 198, 241, 336
Ranches in the West, 439
Real estate, valuation of, 33
Red River Valley, 197, 220
Refrigeration, 68, 75, 103, 464
Reilly & Wolford, mule dealers, St. Louis, 394
Renick, Abram, Sharon, Ky., 406
Rice, production of, 11
Roads, 42
Rye, cultivation of, 13

SASKATCHEWAN Rivers 222
 Sausage-making, 193
Schools, 113, 144, 218, 237, 285, 301, 362
Selkirk, near Winnipeg, 228
Seymour, Sabine & Co., Stillwater, 272
Shakopee, Minn., 281
Share system of farming, 308, 330, 338
Sheep, 21, 69, 93, 102, 142, 155, 244, 376, 389, 399, 413, 448, 450
— losses of, 100, 456
— profits on, 93, 117, 376
— slaughtered, 21, 92, 114, 140, 155
Sherman & Gillett, meat exporters, 70

SHI

Shingles, roofing, 274
Shorthorns, 90, 119, 153, 297, 373
Sibley, General, of St. Paul, 248
Sioux City, 333
— Falls, 323
— River, 322
Smith, Mr., The Meadows, St. Paul, 250
Smithers, Mr., Victoria, Kansas, 358
Sorghum saccharatum—amber cane, 12, 288
St. Boniface, Manitoba, 224
St. Joseph, Missouri, 350
St. Louis, 382
— beef canning, 389
— merchants' exchange, 383
— railroads, 382
— stockyards, 387
St. Paul, Minnesota, 236
— extending industries, 237
St. Paul and Sioux City Railroad, 279
— Courtesy of Directors, 279
St. Peter, Minn., 281
St. Vincent, Manitoba, 223
Statistics of American farming, 11
Stillwater, Minn., 268
— penitentiary, 274
Stockyards, Chicago, 176
— Council Bluffs, 342
— Kansas City, 366
— New York, 64
— St. Louis, 387
Strawberries, 82, 96
Sugar, amber cane, 12, 288, 290
— cane, 11
Swine, 22, 93, 139, 157, 186, 389, 457

TAXATION, 34, 405
— local, 36
Taxes, 34, 128, 328, 405
Temperature, 6
Tenants, ejectment of, 41
Texan cattle, 19, 173

WHE

Thompson, the late Horace, St. Paul, 279, 302
Thrashing machines, 277, 304
— cost of, 299, 304, 425
Timber acts, 32, 327, 362
— clearing, 272
— value of, 271, 378
Tinned or canned meats, 180, 389, 445
Tobacco, 12, 402
Topeka, Kansas, 356
Transport charges, 8, 181, 210, 264, 267, 371, 385, 431, 464
Trotting horses, 100, 151, 418
Trucking, or market gardening, 78

UNITED STATES statistics, 15, 17, 460
— — exports, 435, 461
University at Minneapolis, 237

VALUATION of crops, 16, 94, 296, 427
Vanmeter, B. F., Syracuse, Ky., 408
Vegetables, extensive use of, 7, 80
— cultivation of, 78, 94, 109
Vermont butter, 92
— strawberries, 96
Victoria, Kansas, 357

WAGES, 45, 100, 143, 202, 229, 300, 306, 331
Warehouses, grain, 56
Warren, Manitoba, 219
Washburn, ex-Governor, Minneapolis, 261
Western living, cost of, 285, 350, 363
Westward Ho, 120
Wheat, 12, 422
— continuous growth of, 211, 434

WHE

Wheat, cost of growing, 305, 426, 433
— exports, 170, 267, 385, 435
— Illinois, 170
— in Dakota, 330
— Iowa, 335
— Kansas, 373
— Kentucky, 412
— Manitoba, 227
— Minnesota, 296, 305
— Missouri, 348
— Ohio, 133
— profits of, 216, 338, 427
— Red River, 209
— transport charges, 54, 210, 267, 306, 431
Willow Lake, Windom, 309

YIE

Wilson's beef canning, Chicago, 181
Windom, Minn., 294
Wine, 74
Winnebago, Minn., 289
Winnipeg, 225
— extending resources, 227
Women's rights, 328
— work, 45
Wool, 23, 454
Work done by contract, 204, 215,
Worthington Agricultural Show, Minn., 315

YIELD of crops, 17

LONDON: PRINTED BY
SPOTTISWOODE AND CO., NEW-STREET SQUARE
AND PARLIAMENT STREET

By the same Author.

LANDLORDS and TENANTS in IRELAND;
being a Series of Letters communicated to the *Times* in 1881.
Crown 8vo. price 6s.

'Many of our readers have doubtless in the last few months perused the letters which have appeared in the *Times* from the special commissioner of that paper relative to land tenure in Ireland, estate management, and the condition of tenants and labourers. Mr. FINLAY DUN was the *Times* special commissioner, and this volume is a compilation or selection from, rather than a reprint of, his letters. Mr. DUN went to Ireland, with no political bias to one party or another, in order to get information upon the present agricultural condition of Ireland. He is well known to be a business man, and his observations therefore are fresh and practical, and in these respects offer a pleasing contrast to much that has been recently written and spoken on the Irish land question. Mr. DUN visited personally all the principal properties in each of the four provinces, and also investigated the condition of the cottiers and smaller occupiers in the West, and in every case he was afforded exceptional facilities for obtaining accurate information. *His report therefore may be taken to be one of the most authoritative upon the subject of Ireland that has yet been published.*' The FIELD.

London, LONGMANS & CO.

JUNE 1881.

GENERAL LISTS OF NEW WORKS

PUBLISHED BY

Messrs. LONGMANS, GREEN & CO.

PATERNOSTER ROW, LONDON.

HISTORY, POLITICS, HISTORICAL MEMOIRS &c.

Armitage's Childhood of the English Nation. Fcp. 8vo. 2s. 6d.
Arnold's Lectures on Modern History. 8vo. 7s. 6d.
Bagehot's Literary Studies, edited by Hutton. 2 vols. 8vo. 28s.
Browning's Modern France, 1814–1879. Fcp. 8vo. 1s.
Buckle's History of Civilisation. 3 vols. crown 8vo. 24s.
Chesney's Waterloo Lectures. 8vo. 10s. 6d.
Dun's Landlord and Tenant in Ireland. Crown 8vo. 6s.

Epochs of Ancient History:—
    Beesly's Gracchi, Marius, and Sulla, 2s. 6d.
    Capes's Age of the Antonines, 2s. 6d.
    — Early Roman Empire, 2s. 6d.
    Cox's Athenian Empire, 2s. 6d.
    — Greeks and Persians, 2s. 6d.
    Curteis's Rise of the Macedonian Empire, 2s. 6d.
    Ihne's Rome to its Capture by the Gauls, 2s. 6d.
    Merivale's Roman Triumvirates, 2s. 6d.
    Sankey's Spartan and Theban Supremacies, 2s. 6d.
    Smith's Rome and Carthage, the Punic Wars, 2s. 6d.

Epochs of English History, complete in One Volume. Fcp. 8vo. 5s.
    Creighton's Shilling History of England (Introductory Volume). Fcp. 8vo. 1s.
    Browning's Modern England, 1820–1875, 9d.
    Cordery's Struggle against Absolute Monarchy, 1603–1688, 9d.
    Creighton's (Mrs.) England a Continental Power, 1066–1216, 9d.
    Creighton's (Rev. M.) Tudors and the Reformation, 1485–1603, 9d.
    Rowley's Rise of the People, 1215–1485, 9d.
    Rowley's Settlement of the Constitution, 1688–1778, 9d.
    Tancock's England during the American & European Wars, 1778–1820, 9d.
    York-Powell's Early England to the Conquest, 1s.

Epochs of Modern History:—
    Church's Beginning of the Middle Ages, 2s. 6d.
    Cox's Crusades, 2s. 6d.
    Creighton's Age of Elizabeth, 2s. 6d.
    Gairdner's Houses of Lancaster and York, 2s. 6d.
    Gardiner's Puritan Revolution, 2s. 6d.
    — Thirty Years' War, 2s. 6d.
    Hale's Fall of the Stuarts, 2s. 6d.

London, LONGMANS & CO.

General Lists of New Works.

Epochs of Modern History—*continued.*
- Johnson's Normans in Europe, 2s. 6d.
- Longman's Frederick the Great and the Seven Years' War, 2s. 6d.
- Ludlow's War of American Independence, 2s. 6d.
- Morris's Age of Queen Anne, 2s. 6d.
- Seebohm's Protestant Revolution, 2s. 6d.
- Stubbs's Early Plantagenets, 2s. 6d.
- Warburton's Edward III., 2s. 6d.

Froude's English in Ireland in the 18th Century. 3 vols. crown 8vo. 18s.
— History of England. 12 vols. 8vo. £8. 18s. 12 vols. crown 8vo. 42s.
— Julius Cæsar, a Sketch. 8vo. 16s.
Gardiner's England under Buckingham and Charles I., 1624–1628. 2 vols. 8vo. 24s.
— Personal Government of Charles I., 1628–1637. 2 vols. 8vo. 24s.
Greville's Journal of the Reigns of George IV. & William IV. 3 vols. 8vo. 36s.
Hayward's Selected Essays. 2 vols. crown 8vo. 12s.
Ihne's History of Rome. 3 vols. 8vo. 45s.
Lecky's History of England. Vols. I. & II. 1700–1760. 8vo. 36s.
— — — European Morals. 2 vols. crown 8vo. 16s.
— — — Rationalism in Europe. 2 vols. crown 8vo. 16s.
Lewes's History of Philosophy. 2 vols. 8vo. 32s.
Longman's Lectures on the History of England. 8vo. 15s.
— Life and Times of Edward III. 2 vols. 8vo. 28s.
Macaulay's Complete Works. Library Edition. 8 vols. 8vo. £5. 5s.
— — Cabinet Edition. 16 vols. crown 8vo. £4. 16s.
— History of England :—
  Student's Edition. 2 vols. cr. 8vo. 12s. | Cabinet Edition. 8 vols. post 8vo. 48s.
  People's Edition. 4 vols. cr. 8vo. 16s. | Library Edition. 5 vols. 8vo. £4.
Macaulay's Critical and Historical Essays. Cheap Edition. Crown 8vo. 3s. 6d.
  Student's Edition. 1 vol. cr. 8vo. 6s. | Cabinet Edition. 4 vols. post 8vo. 24s.
  People's Edition. 2 vols. cr. 8vo. 8s. | Library Edition. 3 vols. 8vo. 36s.
May's Constitutional History of England, 1760–1870. 3 vols. crown 8vo. 18s.
— Democracy in Europe. 2 vols. 8vo. 32s.
Merivale's Fall of the Roman Republic. 12mo. 7s. 6d.
— General History of Rome, B.C. 753—A.D. 476. Crown 8vo. 7s. 6d.
— History of the Romans under the Empire. 8 vols. post 8vo. 48s.
Minto (Lord) in India from 1807 to 1814. Post 8vo. 12s.
Rawlinson's Ancient Egypt. 2 vols. 8vo. 63s.
— — Seventh Great Oriental Monarchy—The Sassanians. 8vo. 28s.
Russia Before and After the War, translated by E. F. Taylor. 8vo. 14s.
Russia and England from 1876 to 1880. By O. K. 8vo. 14s.
Seebohm's Oxford Reformers—Colet, Erasmus, & More. 8vo. 14s.
Sewell's Popular History of France to the Death of Louis XIV. Crown 8vo. 7s. 6d.
Short's History of the Church of England. Crown 8vo. 7s. 6d.
Smith's Carthage and the Carthaginians. Crown 8vo. 10s. 6d.
Taylor's Manual of the History of India. Crown 8vo. 7s. 6d.
Todd's Parliamentary Government in England. 2 vols. 8vo. 37s.
— — — the British Colonies. 8vo. 21s.
Trench's Realities of Irish Life. Crown 8vo. 2s. 6d.
Trevelyan's Early History of Charles James Fox. Crown 8vo. 6s.
Walpole's History of England, 1815–1841. Vols. I. & II. 8vo. 36s. Vol. III. 18s.
Webb's Civil War in Herefordshire. 2 vols. 8vo. Illustrations, 42s.

London LONGMANS & CO.

BIOGRAPHICAL WORKS.

Bagehot's Biographical Studies. 1 vol. 8vo. 12s.
Burke's Vicissitudes of Families. 2 vols. crown 8vo. 21s.
Cates's Dictionary of General Biography. Medium 8vo. 28s.
Gleig's Life of the Duke of Wellington. Crown 8vo. 6s.
Jerrold's Life of Napoleon III. Vols. I. to III. 8vo. price 18s. each.
Lecky's Leaders of Public Opinion in Ireland. Crown 8vo. 7s. 6d.
Life (The) and Letters of Lord Macaulay. By his Nephew, G. Otto Trevelyan, M.P. Cabinet Edition, 2 vols. post 8vo. 12s. Library Edition, 2 vols. 8vo. 36s.
Marshman's Memoirs of Havelock. Crown 8vo. 3s. 6d.
Memoirs of Anna Jameson, by Gerardine Macpherson. 8vo. 12s. 6d.
Mendelssohn's Letters. Translated by Lady Wallace. 2 vols. cr. 8vo. 5s. each.
Mill's (John Stuart) Autobiography. 8vo. 7s. 6d.
Missionary Secretariat of Henry Venn, B.D. 8ve. Portrait. 18s.
Newman's Apologia pro Vitâ Suâ. Crown 8vo. 6s.
Nohl's Life of Mozart. Translated by Lady Wallace. 2 vols. crown 8vo. 21s.
Overton's Life &c. of William Law. 8vo. 15s.
Spedding's Letters and Life of Francis Bacon. 7 vols. 8vo. £4. 4s.
Stephen's Essays in Ecclesiastical Biography. Crown 8vo. 7s. 6d.

MENTAL AND POLITICAL PHILOSOPHY.

Amos's View of the Science of Jurisprudence. 8vo. 18s.
— Fifty Years of the English Constitution, 1830-1880. Crown 8vo. 10s. 6d.
— Primer of the English Constitution. Crown 8vo. 6s.
Bacon's Essays, with Annotations by Whately. 8vo. 10s. 6d.
— Works, edited by Spedding. 7 vols. 8vo. 73s. 6d.
Bagehot's Economic Studies, edited by Hutton. 8vo. 10s. 6d.
Bain's Logic, Deductive and Inductive. Crown 8vo. 10s. 6d.
PART I. Deduction, 4s. | PART II. Induction, 6s. 6d.
Bolland & Lang's Aristotle's Politics. Crown 8vo. 7s. 6d.
Brassey's Foreign Work and English Wages. 8vo. 10s. 6d.
Comte's System of Positive Polity, or Treatise upon Sociology. 4 vols. 8vo. £4.
Congreve's Politics of Aristotle; Greek Text, English Notes. 8vo. 18s.
Grant's Ethics of Aristotle; Greek Text, English Notes. 2 vols. 8vo. 32s.
Griffith's A B C of Philosophy. Crown 8vo. 5s.
Hillebrand's Lectures on German Thought. Crown 8vo. 7s. 6d.
Hodgson's Philosophy of Reflection. 2 vols. 8vo. 21s.
Kalisch's Path and Goal. 8vo. 12s. 8d.
Lewis on Authority in Matters of Opinion. 8vo. 14s.
Leslie's Essays in Political and Moral Philosophy. 8vo. 10s. 6d.
Macaulay's Speeches corrected by Himself. Crown 8vo. 3s. 6d.
Macleod's Economical Philosophy. Vol. I. 8vo. 15s. Vol. II. Part I. 12s.
Mill on Representative Government. Crown 8vo. 2s.
— — Liberty. Post 8vo. 7s. 6d. Crown 8vo. 1s. 4d.
Mill's Analysis of the Phenomena of the Human Mind. 2 vols. 8vo. 28s.
— Dissertations and Discussions. 4 vols. 8vo. 47s.
— Essays on Unsettled Questions of Political Economy. 8vo. 6s. 6d.
— Examination of Hamilton's Philosophy. 8vo. 16s.

London, LONGMANS & CO.

Mill's Logic, Ratiocinative and Inductive. 2 vols. 8vo. 25s.
— Principles of Political Economy. 2 vols. 8vo. 30s. 1 vol. crown 8vo. 5s.
— Subjection of Women. Crown 8vo. 6s.
— Utilitarianism. 8vo. 5s.
Müller's (Max) Chips from a German Workshop. 4 vols. 8vo. 36s.
— — Hibbert Lectures on Origin and Growth of Religion. 8vo. 10s. 6d.
— — Selected Essays on Language, Mythology, and Religion. 2 vols. crown 8vo. 16s.
Sandars's Institutes of Justinian, with English Notes. 8vo. 18s.
Swinburne's Picture Logic. Post 8vo. 5s.
Thomson's Outline of Necessary Laws of Thought. Crown 8vo. 6s.
Tocqueville's Democracy in America, translated by Reeve. 2 vols. crown 8vo. 16s.
Twiss's Law of Nations, 8vo. in Time of Peace, 12s. in Time of War, 21s.
Whately's Elements of Logic. 8vo. 10s. 6d. Crown 8vo. 4s. 6d.
— — — Rhetoric. 8vo. 10s. 6d. Crown 8vo. 4s. 6d.
— English Synonymes. Fcp. 8vo. 3s.
Williams's Nicomachean Ethics of Aristotle translated. Crown 8vo. 7s. 6d.
Zeller's Socrates and the Socratic Schools. Crown 8vo. 10s. 6d.
— Stoics, Epicureans, and Sceptics. Crown 8vo. 15s.
— Plato and the Older Academy. Crown 8vo. 18s.
— Pre-Socratic Schools. 2 vols. crown 8vo. 30s.

MISCELLANEOUS AND CRITICAL WORKS.

Arnold's (Dr. Thomas) Miscellaneous Works. 8vo. 7s. 6d.
— (T.) Manual of English Literature. Crown 8vo. 7s. 6d.
— English Authors, Poetry and Prose Specimens.
Bain's Emotions and the Will. 8vo. 15s.
— Mental and Moral Science. Crown 8vo. 10s. 6d.
— Senses and the Intellect. 8vo. 15s.
Becker's *Charicles* and *Gallus*, by Metcalfe. Post 8vo. 7s. 6d. each.
Blackley's German and English Dictionary. Post 8vo. 7s. 6d.
Conington's Miscellaneous Writings. 2 vols. 8vo. 28s.
Contanseau's Practical French & English Dictionary. Post 8vo. 7s. 6d.
— Pocket French and English Dictionary. Square 18mo. 3s. 6d.
Davison's Thousand Thoughts from Various Authors. Crown 8vo. 7s. 6d.
Farrar's Language and Languages. Crown 8vo. 6s.
Froude's Short Studies on Great Subjects. 3 vols. crown 8vo. 18s.
German Home Life, reprinted from *Fraser's Magazine*. Crown 8vo. 8s.
Gibson's Cavalier's Note-Book. Small 4to. 14s.
Greville's (Lady Violet) Faiths and Fashions. Crown 8vo. 7s. 6d.
Hodgson's Outcast Essays and Verse Translations. Crown 8vo. 8s. 6d.
Hume's Essays, edited by Green & Grose. 2 vols. 8vo. 28s.
— Treatise on Human Nature, edited by Green & Grose. 2 vols. 8vo. 28s.
Latham's Handbook of the English Language. Crown 8vo. 6s.
— English Dictionary. 1 vol. medium 8vo. 14s. 4 vols. 4to. £7.
Liddell & Scott's Greek-English Lexicon. Crown 4to. 36s.
— — — Abridged Greek-English Lexicon. Square 12mo. 7s. 6d.
Longman's Pocket German and English Dictionary. 18mo. 5s.
Macaulay's Miscellaneous Writings. 2 vols. 8vo. 21s. 1 vol. crown 8vo. 4s.

London, LONGMANS & CO.

Macaulay's Miscellaneous Writings and Speeches. Crown 8vo. 6s.
Macaulay's Miscellaneous Writings, Speeches, Lays of Ancient Rome, &c. Cabinet Edition. 4 vols. crown 8vo. 24s.
Mahaffy's Classical Greek Literature. Crown 8vo. Vol. I. the Poets, 7s. 6d. Vol. II. the Prose Writers, 7s. 6d.
Müller's (Max) Lectures on the Science of Language. 2 vols. crown 8vo. 16s.
Owen's Evenings with the Skeptics. 2 vols. 8vo. 32s.
Rich's Dictionary of Roman and Greek Antiquities. Crown 8vo. 7s. 6d.
Rogers's Eclipse of Faith. Fcp. 8vo. 5s.
— Defence of the Eclipse of Faith Fcp. 8vo. 3s. 6d.
Roget's Thesaurus of English Words and Phrases. Crown 8vo. 10s. 6d.
Savile's Apparitions, a Narrative of Facts. Crown 8vo. 5s.
Selections from the Writings of Lord Macaulay. Crown 8vo. 6s.
The Essays and Contributions of A. K. H. B. Crown 8vo.
  Autumn Holidays of a Country Parson. 3s. 6d.
  Changed Aspects of Unchanged Truths. 3s. 6d.
  Common-place Philosopher in Town and Country. 3s. 6d.
  Counsel and Comfort spoken from a City Pulpit. 3s. 6d.
  Critical Essays of a Country Parson. 3s. 6d.
  Graver Thoughts of a Country Parson. Three Series, 3s. 6d. each.
  Landscapes, Churches, and Moralities. 3s. 6d.
  Leisure Hours in Town. 3s. 6d. Lessons of Middle Age. 3s. 6d.
  Present-day Thoughts. 3s. 6d.
  Recreations of a Country Parson. Three Series, 3s. 6d. each.
  Seaside Musings on Sundays and Week-Days. 3s. 6d.
  Sunday Afternoons in the Parish Church of a University City. 3s. 6d.
White & Riddle's Large Latin-English Dictionary. 4to. 21s.
White's College Latin-English Dictionary. Royal 8vo. 12s.
— Junior Student's Lat.-Eng. and Eng.-Lat. Dictionary. Square 12mo. 12s.
  Separately { The English-Latin Dictionary, 5s. 6d.
       The Latin-English Dictionary, 7s. 6d.
Wit and Wisdom of the Rev. Sydney Smith, 16mo. 3s. 6d.
Yonge's English-Greek Lexicon. Square 12mo. 8s. 6d. 4to. 21s.

ASTRONOMY, METEOROLOGY, GEOGRAPHY &C.

Freeman's Historical Geography of Europe. 2 vols. 8vo. 31s. 6d.
Herschel's Outlines of Astronomy. Square crown 8vo. 12s.
Keith Johnston's Dictionary of Geography, or General Gazetteer. 8vo. 42s.
Nelson's Work on the Moon. Medium 8vo. 31s. 6d.
Proctor's Essays on Astronomy. 8vo. 12s. Proctor's Moon. Crown 8vo. 10s. 6d.
 — Larger Star Atlas. Folio, 15s. or Maps only, 12s. 6d.
 — New Star Atlas. Crown 8vo. 5s. Orbs Around Us. Crown 8vo. 7s. 6d.
 — Other Worlds than Ours. Crown 8vo. 10s. 6d.
 — Saturn and its System. 8vo. 14s. Proctor's Sun. Crown 8vo. 14s.
 — Universe of Stars. 8vo. 10s. 6d.
Smith's Air and Rain. 8vo. 24s.
The Public Schools Atlas of Ancient Geography. Imperial 8vo. 7s. 6d.
— — Atlas of Modern Geography. Imperial 8vo. 5s.

NATURAL HISTORY & POPULAR SCIENCE.

Arnott's Elements of Physics or Natural Philosophy. Crown 8vo. 12s. 6d.
Brande's Dictionary of Science, Literature, and Art. 3 vols. medium 8vo. 63s.

London, LONGMANS & CO.

Buckton's Town and Window Gardening. Crown 8vo. 2*s*.
Decaisne and Le Maout's General System of Botany. Imperial 8vo. 81*s*. 8*d*.
Dixon's Rural Bird Life. Crown 8vo. Illustrations, 7*s*. 6*d*.
Evans's Bronze Implements &c. of Great Britain. 8vo. 25*s*.
Ganot's Elementary Treatise on Physics, by Atkinson. Large crown 8vo. 15*s*.
— Natural Philosophy, by Atkinson. Crown 8vo. 7*s*. 6*d*.
Goodeve's Elements of Mechanism. Crown 8vo. 6*s*.
Grove's Correlation of Physical Forces. 8vo. 15*s*.
Hartwig's Aerial World. 8vo. 10*s*. 6*d*. Polar World. 8vo. 10*s*. 6*d*.
— Sea and its Living Wonders. 8vo. 10*s*. 6*d*.
— Subterranean World. 8vo. 10*s*. 6*d*. Tropical World. 8vo. 10*s*. 6*d*.
Haughton's Six Lectures on Physical Geography. 8vo. 15*s*.
Heer's Primæval World of Switzerland. 2 vols. 8vo. 12*s*.
Helmholtz's Lectures on Scientific Subjects. 2 vols. cr. 8vo. 7*s*. 6*d*. each.
Helmholtz on the Sensations of Tone, by Ellis. 8vo. 36*s*.
Hullah's Lectures on the History of Modern Music. 8vo. 8*s*. 6*d*.
— Transition Period of Musical History. 8vo. 10*s*. 6*d*.
Keller's Lake Dwellings of Switzerland, by Lee. 2 vols. royal 8vo. 42*s*.
Lee's Note Book of an Amateur Geologist. 8vo. 21*s*.
Lloyd's Treatise on Magnetism. 8vo. 10*s*. 6*d*.
— — on the Wave-Theory of Light. 8vo. 10*s*. 6*d*.
Loudon's Encyclopædia of Plants. 8vo. 42*s*.
Lubbock on the Origin of Civilisation & Primitive Condition of Man. 8vo. 18*s*.
Macalister's Zoology and Morphology of Vertebrate Animals. 8vo. 10*s*. 6*d*.
Nicols' Puzzle of Life. Crown 8vo. 3*s*. 6*d*.
Owen's Comparative Anatomy and Physiology of the Vertebrate Animals. 8 vols. 8vo. 73*s*. 6*d*.
Proctor's Light Science for Leisure Hours. 2 vols. crown 8vo. 7*s*. 6*d*. each.
Rivers's Orchard House. Sixteenth Edition. Crown 8vo. 5*s*.
— Rose Amateur's Guide. Fcp. 8vo. 4*s*. 6*d*.
Stanley's Familiar History of British Birds. Crown 8vo. 6*s*.
Text-Books of Science, Mechanical and Physical.
    Abney's Photography, 3*s*. 6*d*.
    Anderson's (Sir John) Strength of Materials, 3*s*. 6*d*.
    Armstrong's Organic Chemistry, 3*s*. 6*d*.
    Ball's Astronomy, 6*s*.
    Barry's Railway Appliances, 3*s*. 6*d*. Bloxam's Metals, 3*s*. 6*d*.
    Bauerman's Systematic Mineralogy, 6*s*.
    Goodeve's Principles of Mechanics, 3*s*. 6*d*.
    Gore's Electro-Metallurgy, 6*s*.
    Griffin's Algebra and Trigonometry, 3*s*. 6*d*.
    Jenkin's Electricity and Magnetism, 3*s*. 6*d*.
    Maxwell's Theory of Heat, 3*s*. 6*d*.
    Merrifield's Technical Arithmetic and Mensuration, 3*s*. 6*d*.
    Miller's Inorganic Chemistry, 3*s*. 6*d*.
    Preece & Sivewright's Telegraphy, 3*s*. 6*d*.
    Rutley's Study of Rocks, 4*s*. 6*d*.
    Shelley's Workshop Appliances, 3*s*. 6*d*.
    Thomé's Structural and Physiological Botany, 6*s*.
    Thorpe's Quantitative Chemical Analysis, 4*s*. 6*d*.
    Thorpe & Muir's Qualitative Analysis, 3*s*. 6*d*.
    Tilden's Chemical Philosophy, 3*s*. 6*d*.

London, LONGMANS & CO.

General Lists of New Works. 7

Text-Books of Science, Mechanical and Physical—*continued.*
    Unwin's Machine Design, 3s. 6d.
    Watson's Plane and Solid Geometry, 8s. 6d.
Tyndall on Sound. New Edition in the press.
Tyndall's Contributions to Molecular Physics. 8vo. 16s.
   — Fragments of Science. 2 vols. post 8vo. 16s.
   — Heat a Mode of Motion. Crown 8vo. 12s.
   — Notes on Electrical Phenomena. Crown 8vo. 1s. sewed, 1s. 6d. cloth.
   — Notes of Lectures on Light. Crown 8vo. 1s. sewed, 1s. 6d. cloth.
   — Lectures on Light delivered in America. Crown 8vo. 7s. 6d.
   — Lessons in Electricity. Crown 8vo. 2s. 6d.
Von Cotta on Rocks, by Lawrence. Post 8vo. 14s.
Woodward's Geology of England and Wales. Crown 8vo. 14s.
Wood's Bible Animals. With 112 Vignettes. 8vo. 14s.
   — Homes Without Hands. 8vo. 14s. Insects Abroad. 8vo. 14s.
   — Insects at Home. With 700 Illustrations. 8vo. 14s.
   — Out of Doors. Crown 8vo. 7s. 6d. Strange Dwellings. Crown 8vo. 7s. 6d.

CHEMISTRY & PHYSIOLOGY.

Buckton's Health in the House, Lectures on Elementary Physiology. Cr. 8vo. 2s.
Crookes's Select Methods in Chemical Analysis. Crown 8vo. 12s. 6d.
Kingzett's Animal Chemistry. 8vo. 18s.
   — History, Products and Processes of the Alkali Trade. 8vo. 12s.
Miller's Elements of Chemistry, Theoretical and Practical. 3 vols. 8vo. Part I. Chemical Physics, 16s. Part II. Inorganic Chemistry, 24s. Part III. Organic Chemistry, Section I. price 31s. 6d.
Reynolds's Experimental Chemistry, Part I. Fcp. 8vo. 1s. 6d.
Thudichum's Annals of Chemical Medicine. Vol. I. 8vo. 14s.
Tilden's Practical Chemistry. Fcp. 8vo. 1s. 6d.
Watts's Dictionary of Chemistry. 7 vols. medium 8vo. £10. 16s. 6d.
   — Third Supplementary Volume, in Two Parts. PART I. 36s.

THE FINE ARTS & ILLUSTRATED EDITIONS.

Doyle's Fairyland; Pictures from the Elf-World. Folio, 15s.
Dresser's Arts and Art Industries of Japan.;   [*In preparation.*
Jameson's Sacred and Legendary Art. 6 vols. square crown 8vo.
    Legends of the Madonna. 1 vol. 21s.
    — — — Monastic Orders. 1 vol. 21s.
    — — — Saints and Martyrs. 2 vols. 31s. 6d.
    — — — Saviour. Completed by Lady Eastlake. 2 vols. 42s.
Longman's Three Cathedrals Dedicated to St. Paul. Square crown 8vo. 21s.
Macaulay's Lays of Ancient Rome, illustrated by Scharf. Fcp. 4to. 21s. imp. 16mo. 10s. 6d.
   — — — illustrated by Weguelin. Crown 8vo. 6s.
Macfarren's Lectures on Harmony. 8vo. 12s.
Moore's Irish Melodies. With 161 Plates by D. Maclise, R.A. Super-royal 8vo. 21s.
   — Lalla Rookh, illustrated by Tenniel. Square crown 8vo. 10s. 6d.
Perry on Greek and Roman Sculpture. 8vo.   [*In preparation.*

THE USEFUL ARTS, MANUFACTURES &c.

Bourne's Catechism of the Steam Engine. Fcp. 8vo. 6s.
   — Examples of Steam, Air, and Gas Engines. 4to. 70s.

London, LONGMANS & CO.

Bourne's Handbook of the Steam Engine. Fcp. 8vo. 9s.
— Recent Improvements in the Steam Engine. Fcp. 8vo. 6s.
— Treatise on the Steam Engine. 4to. 42s.
Brassey's English and Foreign Ships of War. 2 vols. 8vo. Plates.
Cresy's Encyclopædia of Civil Engineering. 8vo. 25s.
Culley's Handbook of Practical Telegraphy. 8vo. 16s.
Eastlake's Household Taste in Furniture, &c. Square crown 8vo. 14s.
Fairbairn's Useful Information for Engineers. 3 vols. crown 8vo. 31s. 6d.
— Applications of Cast and Wrought Iron. 8vo. 16s.
— Mills and Millwork. 1 vol. 8vo. 25s.
Gwilt's Encyclopædia of Architecture. 8vo. 52s. 6d.
Hobson's Amateur Mechanic's Practical Handbook. Crown 8vo. 2s. 6d.
Hoskold's Engineer's Valuing Assistant. 8vo. 31s. 6d.
Kerl's Metallurgy, adapted by Crookes and Röhrig. 3 vols. 8vo. £4. 19s.
London's Encyclopædia of Agriculture. 8vo. 21s.
— — — Gardening. 8vo. 21s.
Mitchell's Manual of Practical Assaying. 8vo. 31s. 6d.
Northcott's Lathes and Turning. 8vo. 18s.
Payen's Industrial Chemistry Edited by B. H. Paul, Ph.D. 8vo. 42s.
Piesse's Art of Perfumery. Fourth Edition. Square crown 8vo. 21s.
Stoney's Theory of Strains in Girders. Royal 8vo. 36s.
Ure's Dictionary of Arts, Manufactures, & Mines. 4 vols. medium 8vo. £7. 7s.
Ville on Artificial Manures. By Crookes. 8vo. 21s.

RELIGIOUS & MORAL WORKS.

Abbey & Overton's English Church in the Eighteenth Century. 2 vols. 8vo. 36s.
Arnold's (Rev. Dr. Thomas) Sermons. 6 vols. crown 8vo. 5s. each.
Bishop Jeremy Taylor's Entire Works. With Life by Bishop Heber. Edited by the Rev. C. P. Eden. 10 vols. 8vo. £5. 5s.
Boultbee's Commentary on the 39 Articles. Crown 8vo. 6s.
— History of the Church of England, Pre-Reformation Period. 8vo. 15s.
Browne's (Bishop) Exposition of the 39 Articles. 8vo. 16s.
Bunsen's Angel-Messiah of Buddhists, &c. 8vo. 10s. 6d.
Colenso's Lectures on the Pentateuch and the Moabite Stone. 8vo. 12s.
Colenso on the Pentateuch and Book of Joshua. Crown 8vo. 6s.
— — Part VII. completion of the larger Work. 8vo. 24s.
Conder's Handbook of the Bible. Post 8vo. 7s. 6d.
Conybeare & Howson's Life and Letters of St. Paul :—
   Library Edition, with all the Original Illustrations, Maps, Landscapes on Steel, Woodcuts, &c. 2 vols. 4to. 42s.
   Intermediate Edition, with a Selection of Maps, Plates, and Woodcuts. 2 vols. square crown 8vo. 21s.
   Student's Edition, revised and condensed, with 46 Illustrations and Maps. 1 vol. crown 8vo. 7s. 6d.
Ellicott's (Bishop) Commentary on St. Paul's Epistles. 8vo. Galatians, 8s. 6d. Ephesians, 8s. 6d. Pastoral Epistles, 10s. 6d. Philippians, Colossians, and Philemon, 10s. 6d. Thessalonians, 7s. 6d.
Ellicott's Lectures on the Life of our Lord. 8vo. 12s.
Ewald's History of Israel, translated by Carpenter. 5 vols. 8vo. 63s.

London, LONGMANS & CO.

General Lists of New Works.

Ewald's Antiquities of Israel, translated by Solly. 8vo. 12s. 6d.
Gospel (The) for the Nineteenth Century. 4th Edition. 8vo. 10s. 6d.
Hopkins's Christ the Consoler. Fcp. 8vo. 2s. 6d.
Jukes's Types of Genesis. Crown 8vo. 7s. 6d.
— Second Death and the Restitution of all Things. Crown 8vo. 3s. 6d.
Kalisch's Bible Studies. PART I. the Prophecies of Balaam. 8vo. 10s. 6d.
— — — PART II. the Book of Jonah. 8vo. 10s. 6d.
— Historical and Critical Commentary on the Old Testament; with a New Translation. Vol. I. *Genesis*, 8vo. 18s. or adapted for the General Reader, 12s. Vol. II. *Exodus*, 15s. or adapted for the General Reader, 12s. Vol. III. *Leviticus*, Part I. 15s. or adapted for the General Reader, 8s. Vol. IV. *Leviticus*, Part II. 15s. or adapted for the General Reader, 8s.
Lyra Germanica: Hymns translated by Miss Winkworth. Fcp. 8vo. 5s.
Martineau's Endeavours after the Christian Life. Crown 8vo. 7s. 6d.
— Hymns of Praise and Prayer. Crown 8vo. 4s. 6d. 32mo. 1s. 6d.
— Sermons, Hours of Thought on Sacred Things. 2 vols. 7s. 6d. each.
Mill's Three Essays on Religion. 8vo. 10s. 6d.
Missionary Secretariat of Henry Venn, B.D. 8vo. Portrait. 18s.
Monsell's Spiritual Songs for Sundays and Holidays. Fcp. 8vo. 5s. 18mo. 2s.
Müller's (Max) Lectures on the Science of Religion. Crown 8vo. 10s. 6d.
Newman's Apologia pro Vitâ Suâ. Crown 8vo. 6s.
Passing Thoughts on Religion. By Miss Sewell. Fcp. 8vo. 3s. 6d.
Sewell's (Miss) Preparation for the Holy Communion. 32mo. 8s.
— — Private Devotions for Young Persons. 18mo. 2s.
Smith's Voyage and Shipwreck of St. Paul. Crown 8vo. 7s. 6d.
Supernatural Religion. Complete Edition. 3 vols. 8vo. 36s.
Thoughts for the Age. By Miss Sewell. Fcp. 8vo. 3s. 6d.
Whately's Lessons on the Christian Evidences. 18mo. 6d.
White's Four Gospels in Greek, with Greek-English Lexicon. 32mo. 5s.

TRAVELS, VOYAGES, &c.

Baker's Rifle and Hound in Ceylon. Crown 8vo. 7s. 6d.
— Eight Years in Ceylon. Crown 8vo. 7s. 6d.
Ball's Alpine Guide. 3 vols. post 8vo. with Maps and Illustrations:—I. Western Alps, 6s. 6d. II. Central Alps, 7s. 6d. III. Eastern Alps, 10s. 6d.
Ball on Alpine Travelling, and on the Geology of the Alps, 1s.
Brassey's Sunshine and Storm in the East. 8vo. 21s.
— Voyage in the Yacht 'Sunbeam.' Cr. 8vo. 7s. 6d. School Edition, 2s.
Edwards's (A. B.) Thousand Miles up the Nile. Imperial 8vo. 42s.
Hassall's San Remo and the Western Riviera. Crown 8vo. 10s. 6d.
Macnamara's Medical Geography of India. 8vo. 21s.
Miller's Wintering in the Riviera. Post 8vo. Illustrations, 7s. 6d.
Packe's Guide to the Pyrenees, for Mountaineers. Crown 8vo. 7s. 6d.
Rigby's Letters from France, &c. in 1789. Crown 8vo. 10s. 6d.
Shore's Flight of the 'Lapwing', Sketches in China and Japan. 8vo. 15s.
The Alpine Club Map of Switzerland. In Four Sheets. 42s.
Tozer's Turkish Armenia and Eastern Asia Minor. 8vo. 16s.
Weld's Sacred Palmlands. Crown 8vo. 10s. 6d.

London, LONGMANS & CO.

WORKS OF FICTION.

Blues and Buffs. By Arthur Mills. Crown 8vo. 6s.
Buried Alive, Ten Years of Penal Servitude in Siberia. Crown 8vo. 6s.
Crookit Meg (The). By Shirley. Crown 8vo. 6s.
Hawthorne's (J.) Yellow-Cap and other Fairy Stories. Crown 8vo. 6s.

Cabinet Edition of Stories and Tales by Miss Sewell:—

- Amy Herbert, 2s. 6d.
- Cleve Hall, 2s. 6d.
- The Earl's Daughter, 2s. 6d.
- Experience of Life, 2s. 6d.
- Gertrude, 2s. 6d.
- Ivors, 2s. 6d.
- Katharine Ashton, 2s. 6d.
- Laneton Parsonage, 3s. 6d.
- Margaret Percival, 8s. 6d.
- Ursula, 8s. 6d.

Novels and Tales by the Right Hon. the Earl of Beaconsfield, K.G. Cabinet Edition, Eleven Volumes, crown 8vo. price £3. 6s.

Endymion, 6s.

- Lothair, 6s.
- Coningsby, 6s.
- Sybil, 6s.
- Tancred, 6s.
- Venetia, 6s.
- Henrietta Temple, 6s.
- Contarini Fleming, 6s.
- Alroy, Ixion, &c. 6s.
- The Young Duke, &c. 6s.
- Vivian Grey, 6s.

The Modern Novelist's Library. Each Work in crown 8vo. A Single Volume, complete in itself, price 2s. boards, or 2s. 6d. cloth:—

By the Earl of Beaconsfield, K.G.
- Lothair.
- Coningsby.
- Sybil.
- Tancred.
- Venetia.
- Henrietta Temple.
- Contarini Fleming.
- Alroy, Ixion, &c.
- The Young Duke, &c.
- Vivian Grey.

By Anthony Trollope.
- Barchester Towers.
- The Warden.

By the Author of 'the Rose Garden.'
- Unawares.

By Major Whyte-Melville.
- Digby Grand.
- General Bounce.
- Kate Coventry.
- The Gladiators.
- Good for Nothing.
- Holmby House.
- The Interpreter.
- The Queen's Maries.

By the Author of 'the Atelier du Lys.'
- Mademoiselle Mori.
- The Atelier du Lys.

By Various Writers.
- Atherstone Priory.
- The Burgomaster's Family.
- Elsa and her Vulture.
- The Six Sisters of the Valleys.

Lord Beaconsfield's Novels and Tales. 10 vols. cloth extra, gilt edges, 30s.

Whispers from Fairy Land. By the Right Hon. Lord Brabourne. With Nine Illustrations. Crown 8vo. 3s. 6d.

Higgledy-Piggledy; or, Stories for Everybody and Everybody's Children. By the Right Hon. Lord Brabourne. With Nine Illustrations from Designs by R. Doyle. Crown 8vo. 3s. 6d.

POETRY & THE DRAMA.

Bailey's Festus, a Poem. Crown 8vo. 12s. 6d.
Bowdler's Family Shakspeare. Medium 8vo. 14s. 6 vols. fcp. 8vo. 21s.
Cayley's Iliad of Homer, Homometrically translated. 8vo. 12s. 6d.
Conington's Æneid of Virgil, translated into English Verse. Crown 8vo. 9s.

London, LONGMANS & CO.

General Lists of New Works.

Goethe's Faust, translated by Birds. Large crown 8vo. 12s. 6d.
— — translated by Webb. 8vo. 12s. 6d.
— — edited by Selss. Crown 8vo. 5s.
Ingelow's Poems. New Edition. 2 vols. fcp. 8vo. 12s.
Macaulay's Lays of Ancient Rome, with Ivry and the Armada. 16mo. 3s. 6d.
Ormsby's Poem of the Cid. Translated. Post 8vo. 5s.
Southey's Poetical Works. Medium 8vo. 14s.

RURAL SPORTS, HORSE & CATTLE MANAGEMENT &c.

Blaine's Encyclopædia of Rural Sports. 8vo. 21s.
Francis's Treatise on Fishing in all its Branches. Post 8vo. 15s.
Horses and Roads. By Free-Lance. Crown 8vo. 6s.
Miles's Horse's Foot, and How to Keep it Sound. Imperial 8vo. 12s. 6d.
— Plain Treatise on Horse-Shoeing. Post 8vo. 2s. 6d.
— Stables and Stable-Fittings. Imperial 8vo. 15s.
— Remarks on Horses' Teeth. Post 8vo. 1s. 8d.
Nevile's Horses and Riding. Crown 8vo. 6s.
Ronalds's Fly-Fisher's Entomology. 8vo. 14s.
Steel's Diseases of the Ox, being a Manual of Bovine Pathology. 8vo. 15s.
Stonehenge's Dog in Health and Disease. Square crown 8vo. 7s. 6d.
— Greyhound. Square crown 8vo. 15s.
Youatt's Work on the Dog. 8vo. 6s.
— — — — Horse. 8vo. 7s. 6d.
Wilcocks's Sea-Fisherman. Post 8vo. 12s. 6d.

WORKS OF UTILITY & GENERAL INFORMATION.

Acton's Modern Cookery for Private Families. Fcp. 8vo. 6s.
Black's Practical Treatise on Brewing. 8vo. 10s. 6d.
Buckton's Food and Home Cookery. Crown 8vo. 2s.
Bull on the Maternal Management of Children. Fcp. 8vo. 2s. 6d.
Bull's Hints to Mothers on the Management of their Health during the Period of Pregnancy and in the Lying-in Room. Fcp. 8vo. 2s. 6d.
Campbell-Walker's Correct Card, or How to Play at Whist. Fcp. 8vo. 2s. 6d.
Edwards on the Ventilation of Dwelling-Houses. Royal 8vo. 10s. 6d.
Johnson's (W. & J. H.) Patentee's Manual. Fourth Edition. 8vo. 10s. 6d.
Longman's Chess Openings. Fcp. 8vo. 2s. 6d.
Macleod's Economics for Beginners. Small crown 8vo. 2s. 6d.
— Elements of Economics. 2 vols. small crown 8vo. VOL. I. 7s. 6d.
— Theory and Practice of Banking. 2 vols. 8vo. 26s.
— Elements of Banking. Fourth Edition. Crown 8vo. 5s.
M'Culloch's Dictionary of Commerce and Commercial Navigation. 8vo. 63s.

London, LONGMANS & CO.

Maunder's Biographical Treasury. Fcp. 8vo. 6s.
— Historical Treasury. Fcp. 8vo. 6s.
— Scientific and Literary Treasury. Fcp. 8vo. 6s.
— Treasury of Bible Knowledge, edited by Ayre. Fcp. 8vo. 6s.
— Treasury of Botany, edited by Lindley & Moore. Two Parts, 12s.
— Treasury of Geography. Fcp. 8vo. 6s.
— Treasury of Knowledge and Library of Reference. Fcp. 8vo. 6s.
— Treasury of Natural History. Fcp. 8vo. 6s.
Pereira's Materia Medica, by Bentley and Redwood. 8vo. 25s.
Pewtner's Comprehensive Specifier; Building-Artificers' Work. Crown 8vo. 6s.
Pole's Theory of the Modern Scientific Game of Whist. Fcp. 8vo. 2s. 6d.
Reader's Time Tables. Third Edition. Crown 8vo. 7s. 6d.
Scott's Farm Valuer. Crown 8vo. 5s.
— Rents and Purchases. Crown 8vo. 6s.
Smith's Handbook for Midwives. Crown 8vo. 5s.
The Cabinet Lawyer, a Popular Digest of the Laws of England. Fcp. 8vo. 9s.
West on the Diseases of Infancy and Childhood. 8vo. 18s.
Wilson on Banking Reform. 8vo. 7s. 6d.
— on the Resources of Modern Countries 2 vols. 8vo. 24s.

MUSICAL WORKS BY JOHN HULLAH, LL.D.

Hullah's Method of Teaching Singing. Crown 8vo. 2s. 6d.
Exercises and Figures in the same. Crown 8vo. 1s. or 2 Parts, 6d. each.
Large Sheets, containing the 'Exercises and Figures in Hullah's Method,' in Parcels of Eight, price 6s. each.
Chromatic Scale, with the Inflected Syllables, on Large Sheet. 1s. 6d.
Card of Chromatic Scale. 1d.
Exercises for the Cultivation of the Voice. For Soprano or Tenor, 2s. 6d.
Grammar of Musical Harmony. Royal 8vo. 2 Parts, each 1s. 6d.
Exercises to Grammar of Musical Harmony. 1s.
Grammar of Counterpoint. Part I. super-royal 8vo. 2s. 6d.
Wilhem's Manual of Singing. Parts I. & II. 2s. 6d.; or together, 5s.
Exercises and Figures contained in Parts I. and II. of Wilhem's Manual. Books I. & II. each 8d.
Large Sheets, Nos. 1 to 8, containing the Figures in Part I. of Wilhem's Manual, in a Parcel, 6s.
Large Sheets, Nos. 9 to 40, containing the Exercises in Part I. of Wilhem's Manual, in Four Parcels of Eight Nos. each, per Parcel, 6s.
Large Sheets, Nos. 41 to 52, containing the Figures in Part II. in a Parcel, 9s.
Hymns for the Young, set to Music. Royal 8vo. 8d.
Infant School Songs. 6d.
Notation, the Musical Alphabet. Crown 8vo. 6d.
Old English Songs for Schools, Harmonised. 6d.
Rudiments of Musical Grammar. Royal 8vo. 3s.
School Songs for 2 and 3 Voices. 2 Books, 8vo. each 6d.

London, LONGMANS & CO.

www.ingramcontent.com/pod-product-compliance
Lightning Source LLC
Chambersburg PA
CBHW021414300426
44114CB00010B/493